The Software Project
Manager's Handbook

T0180667

The Software Project Manager's Handbook

Principles that Work at Work

Second Edition

Dwayne Phillips

A JOHN WILEY & SONS, INC., PUBLICATION

Published by John Wiley & Sons, Inc., Hoboken, New Jersey.
Published simultaneously in Canada.

For general information on our other products and services please contact our Customer Care Department within the U.S. at 877-762-2974, outside the U.S. at 317-572-3993 or fax 317-572-4002.

Wiley also publishes its books in a variety of electronic formats. Some content that appears in print, however, may not be available in electronic format.

Library of Congress Cataloging-in-Publication Data is available.
ISBN: 978-0-471-674207
ISBN: 0471674206

10 9 8 7 6 5 4 3 2

Contents

Part 3

Preface

I still like to write software. The material in this book and the relative success of the first edition have caused my own senior managers to pull me away from writing software and push me more into managing software and systems projects. Although I miss writing software, I do like to manage projects.

The first edition of this book sold well, at least that is what the fine people at the IEEE Computer Society have told me. It has been most gratifying to hear from people who have read the first edition. Some people have told me that they generally "like the book," whereas others have pointed to specific pages and related how something that has worked for me also worked for them. Recently, a project manager told me how her team had never liked the concept of earned value, but something clicked when they saw the figures in the first edition. Since then, they bother her until she updates the earned value charts and posts them publicly so everyone can see how they are progressing.

Although gratified at hearing this, I also winced a bit because I felt that I had erred in some of my descriptions of earned value. There were several other things in the first edition that I wished I had described differently. That is the main reason for the second edition of *The Software Project Manager's Handbook*.

Another reason for the second edition is that I have learned a few things in the past five years that I have seen work at work. I wanted to update the book so that I could remember and use them better.

Several events have occurred in my life since the first edition that have had a significant impact on the second edition. First, I was able to meet Jerry Weinberg and attend several of his seminars. The ideas I had read in his books came to life. I am most grateful to Jerry and to some of the fine people I met at his seminars. Notable among these are Johanna Rothman, Dale

Emery, Steve Smith, Elizabeth Hendrickson, Don Gray, Esther Derby, Naomi Karten, and Jerry's wife Dani. I had the great pleasure of attending one of Jerry's writers workshops. That wonderful week led me to write another book on project management with Roy O'Bryan—*It Sounded Good When We Started*—also published by the IEEE Computer Society and Wiley.

A second event that occurred since the first edition of this book was that I attended a seminar on requirements led by James Robertson. This was significant for two reasons. First, the second day of the seminar was that terrible day of September 11, 2001. James was sensitive to our needs as people as well as students. Second, I learned much about the requirements techniques that James and his wife Suzanne wrote about in their book.

The third significant event has been the agile methods movement. This has influenced much in the field of software. Agile methods have emphasized the idea of thinking about who is doing what on a project (the people and the product) and choosing a process that best fits that situation. For many projects undertaken today, the agile methods are the best processes. There is room for many other types of projects, so the other processes I describe herein still have their place.

Given these events in my life and our field, I have updated this book. There is about 20% more material in each chapter. I have changed the wording of many passages in the book to help reach the reader. In all, people who have read the first edition have the opportunity to learn a few things by reading this second edition.

I thank the IEEE Computer Society for allowing me to update the book. I thank my wife Karen for loving me for five more years and supporting my writing. My three sons are five years older, and the eldest, Seth, is a college student studying computer engineering (no, he has not bothered to read a page of this). My second son Nathan is a senior in high school and undecided on his next step, but is showing me the joy and creativity of the skateboard and guitar. My youngest son Adam is in ninth grade and impressing me everyday with the effort he puts into things that do not come naturally and the ease with which he influences people.

Thanks are due to the many people in our field who have written and spoken about the things that have helped them at work. Their names are referenced in many places throughout this book. It has been my privilege to use their ideas in my work and my pleasure to pass them along in this book.

Dwayne Phillips

Reston, Virginia
March 2004

PART 1

ELEMENTS OF EFFECTIVE SOFTWARE MANAGEMENT

Effective software management requires a good manager, a good project management approach, and disciplined, directed management applied daily. Chapter 1 describes what it takes to be a good software manager. It can help you decide if you have or want the required qualities. Chapter 2 introduces the four ingredients of a successful software project, which are the main themes of this book: (1) the right balance of people, process, and product; (2) the diligent application of visibility techniques; (3) the correct use of configuration management; and (4) a reliance on standards. Chapter 3 looks at what happens when project managers violate these four principles. Chapter 4 illustrates how a project can succeed a day at a time—a concept that seems obvious but is often not realized in practice.

Chapter 1

What Makes a Good Software Manager?

Developing and maintaining software has become one of the most challenging and rewarding tasks a person can do. I've been privileged to attempt it in various settings for the last 15 years, and I've seen good software managers and bad ones. I've also *been* both at one time or another. This rather humbling experience has taught me what to value in a project manager. It has taught me that many managers approach software somewhat like the model in Figure 1.1. The project starts, everyone works hard, and software comes out some time later. If someone asks about progress, the project is always "almost finished." (If the project is headed by a more experienced project manager, it is always "93.7% finished.")

After much thought and observation, I believe this cloudy view of project management stems from a lack of three key perspectives. Of course, just having these perspectives does not guarantee a successful project, but it will go a long way toward making success possible.

1.1 PEOPLE PERSPECTIVE

Before I was a manager, I was a programmer, happily banging out solutions on the keyboard. I did well working alone. But software project management is not a loner's world. Loners who want to become software project managers must ask themselves hard questions: Do I like working closely with people? Do I want to understand what they mean when they talk to me? Do I basically *like* people? If the answer to these questions is a resounding "no," then you must ask another set of questions: Am I willing to change? Am I willing to

The Software Project Manager's Handbook. By Dwayne Phillips.
ISBN 0-471-67420-6 © 2004 IEEE Computer Society

Start ⇨   ⇨ Finish

Figure 1.1   Typical software project management

study, take courses, read books, apply myself to people as diligently as I have ever applied myself to anything? If the answer is still "no," stop reading right now, and give this book to a friend. Stay in coding and have a challenging, rewarding life.

If you are still reading, you must have answered "yes" to at least one set of questions. Now take a hard look at how you feel about yourself. Gerald Weinberg (Weinberg, 1994), an excellent source of advice on people, has pointed out that we need a good sense of self-worth, self-esteem, self-confidence, and self-examination to work closely with people. If we don't have these, we will be hurt and hurt others often and deeply.

I have seen the truth of this on more than one occasion when a manager would attempt to change the way people do their jobs. Improvement, a goal for all, requires change and most people don't like to change. If I as a manager walk into a gathering of programmers and announce that the group would be better off changing the way they do things, I can almost always expect unanimous rejection. If I do not have confidence and self-esteem, I will drag my bruised ego out of the room and never implement the needed improvement. If, however, I do like myself and believe in my knowledge and abilities, I am more likely to realize that the group's negative reaction is a normal response to potential change, not a personal attack. A self-confident manager works through the fear of change person by person over time and implements the improvement.

I was able to move a group of programmers from coding cowboys to SEI CMM level 2. (Chapter 6 describes the Software Engineering Institute's Capability Maturity Model in more detail.) It was neither easy nor quick, but it happened. Patience, knowledge, and self-esteem are required, and most people with a little determination can do the same.

Unfortunately, most of us are operating with a distinct handicap. We weren't taught people or management skills. When we were in school, the instructor described the problem, and students individually coded a solution. Problems at work, however, require interaction with people, which can be fraught with difficulties. As Weinberg says, "the three causes of [software project] failure are people, people, and people." (Weinberg, 1994) The lack of a people perspective has helped litter the software industry with failed projects. Rob Thomsett (Thomsett, 1995) states that "most projects fail because of people and project management concerns rather than technical issues." I agree. I've seen new managers tell a group of talented programmers exactly how to solve a problem. The resulting revolt is quick, decisive, and puzzling. As a new manager, I asked myself countless times, "How could these people not embrace my carefully thought-through technical solution and management plan?" Besides, wasn't I the manager (translation, "the boss")? Weren't they supposed to do what I said? And wasn't I appointed manager because I was the smartest person in the group? If they didn't agree with me soon, we would all fail.

As long as attitudes like these continue, people skills will be in demand. Over the years, through much trial and error, I have identified some core people skills and personal qualities anyone who attempts to manage will need. The list below is by no means inclusive.

- *Be flexible.* Let your people perform. The same people will react differently to a new project with a new product. Managers cannot manage each project just like the last one. The basic repeatable principles remain the same; only the particulars change (Constantine, 1995).

- *Have compassion.* You must also learn how to deal compassionately with difficult people. In Chapter 4 on managing a project day to day, I call for removing toxic people from projects. Some people habitually hurt others; some lie and steal. However, removing them does not always mean firing them. Some of the people who act this way can be helped. An organization should never condone theft, dishonesty, or hatred, but it should also strive to act with kindness, patience, and compassion in helping to correct such actions. Try to help reform problem employees and help good employees when they need help. Be careful, however, about attempting to perform miracles. Rescuing can become a destructive addiction. Do what you can, recognize your limitations, and call in professional help when needed.

- *Know when to lead and when to manage.* Lead people; manage the process and product. Leading means that others are following, so set an example. If you act honestly and courteously all the time, people are apt to do the same. Examples also extend to behavior with other groups. You can be sure that your people will be watching as you talk to upper management, so tell the truth.

- *Accept the role of meetings.* You will perpetually be in meetings (Maguire, 1994; Gause and Weinberg, 1989). They will be held in halls, offices, parking lots, and even in rooms. These meetings are not just bureaucracy; they are communication. If they are bureaucracy, it is your fault and you should empower yourself to correct it. Chapter 5 gives you some techniques for doing this.

Perhaps the best advice comes from the sports and recreation world (Hawkins, 1994). Choose the best people, keep the team small, minimize distractions, train them, meet together as a team regularly, know them, and set an example. This is common sense, but all too uncommon in practice. As managers, we know what we should do and we have the means to do it. The last step is to get in the habit of doing it regularly.

1.2 BUSINESS PERSPECTIVE

The software industry is plagued with problems. Projects fall behind schedule, have cost overruns, or fail outright. And the failures are sometimes spectacular (who can forget the Denver International Airport baggage handling system or the Federal Aviation Administration's traffic control system?).

I'm convinced that a good part of the reason for these failures is a lack of business perspective. Most of us were introduced to software through programming. The problems were easy enough and we were smart enough to sit down and code the solutions without much thought. The problems we face now are more difficult, and we can't solve them alone. This requires different techniques and delving into what seems like mindless bureaucracy. Tasks like writing requirements, selecting a design alternative, and having others review our work are some techniques that can make us smart enough to solve these larger, more complex problems.

But these tasks encompass more than an immediate perspective. They require some idea of the big picture. They mean that we must look hard at management problems in the context of business requirements.

A well-known study by the Standish Group (Glass, 2002) paints an embarrassing picture. In the survey, 23% of the projects were canceled before completion (projects couldn't be saved); 49% of the projects were finished, but were over budget, late, and did not have the required functionality. Only 28% were on budget with all the desired functions. These numbers were improved from 1995 (Johnson, 1995), but still have much room for improvement.

I suspect that projects fail to deliver as frequently as they do because practitioners don't see the needs of the business enterprise. Building software at work is done for the benefit of the business. This means asking questions like "Who will use the software? Who wants it and who doesn't? What will the software do for the user and our business? Where will people use it? When do the users need (not want) it? Why do the users want it? Why does our business need it? Why are we developing it? What can we do differently that will bring greater benefit to our business and consequently to us as employees?

I agree with Howard Rubin (Rubin, 1996), who said "a world-class (software) organization's primary distinguishing aspect is a common understanding of how its technical performance is transferred into *value for the enterprise.*"

One of the best pieces of advice a software project manager can heed is to build only the software people want (Szmyt, 1994). This seems obvious, but it is ignored all too frequently. Programmers build software; they don't look for reasons not to. When programmers learn a new technique, they quickly create a new solution (whether or not anyone else wants it) and invent a problem for it.

Unfortunately, if people don't want the software, they won't use it. All the money spent building it and trying to have people use it is wasted. Companies that waste money go out of business, and people lose paying jobs. Build interesting new software at home; at work, build software that people want and the business needs.

The key is to add value to the customer's endeavors. I close with a comment from Jerry Weinberg's SHAPE forum (Weinberg, 1997). "We all think we add value, but it's not value if the customer doesn't see it that way. If what you value is not what the customer values, it doesn't mean either one of you is "bad." It just means there is not a very good fit." One simple way to determine if I am adding value to the customers is to ask them. In my experience, they answer honestly. I place these comments here because they span the concepts of the people and business perspectives. Business, as most things, comes down to people. If the people aren't satisfied, the business isn't either.

1.3   PROCESS PERSPECTIVE

Software project managers must do the right things in software projects. This is known as using the right process or applying best practices. Table 1.1 takes a look at current level of practice and what is recommended for a successful project. The left column shows that the build phase or coding always occurs (McConnell, 1993). If there is no code, there is no software. The second column shows the tasks some projects may complete, although often unintentionally. Software managers should state the problem clearly (define requirements), decide among alternative solutions (design), bring together the elements of software into a product, and test the result systematically. The third column (when combined with the first two) shows what should be done. If you are a software manager who does not do each one of these on every project, this book is for you.

Table 1.1   Always, maybe, and should do on a software project

Always do this	May do this (without knowing it)	Should do this
Build	Requirements	Risk management
	Design	Configuration management
	Integration	Inspections and reviews
	Test	Quality assurance
		Project management
		Process improvement

1.3.1 *Successful Process Techniques*

A major influence in the process movement has been the Capability Maturity Model of the Software Engineering Institute (Humphrey, 1989; CMU/SEI, 1995). The CMM is a progression of levels, each of which contains key processes. An organization starts at the Initial level (see Chapter 6) and step by step adopts processes that lead to a greater ability to produce software. The SEI produced several more capability maturity models (e.g., one for software acquisition, one for people management, one for system engineering, etc.). They consolidated and replaced these with the Capability Maturity Model Integrated (CMMI). The CMMI contains proven engineering and management basics. Some people have maligned these CMMs as being too bureaucratic (government and defense oriented) and instead pushed best practices and, more recently, agile methods. If you look closely at the two, however, most best practices lists contain the same items as the CMMI.

I believe the CMMI works, and I've seen it work. I prefer not to debate whether it can be improved. A couple dozen experts in the United States are qualified to argue the finer points of the CMMI; the rest of us would be much better off if we simply followed it.

Humphrey created a CMM for the individual called the Personal Software Process (PSP) (Humphrey, 1995). The PSP (see Chapter 6) guides an individual programmer through a similar progression of processes. I worked through Humphrey's method and found that it also works at work. The exercise proved, much to my annoyance, that I was not smart enough to sit down and code off the top of my head. The PSP makes you write out a design, review it, write code, print the code, and review the code before compiling it the first time. My own metrics proved that with this mindful bureaucracy, I could produce more error-free software in less time.

These techniques (the CMMI, PSP, and others like them) apply basic engineering and management principles to software. Over the years, we software practitioners convinced ourselves that software was different. The basics did not apply to us; we needed to break the mold. We were wrong. Software is different in some ways, but it has more in common with other fields than we want to admit. We must use what others have proven works at work.

Some people feel they cannot do the right thing in their current job. I've heard it all: "Our management won't let us write requirements and hold a requirements inspection." "Our programmers would revolt if we asked them to let others inspect their code."

To these objections, I respond with two statements, which are easier said than done, but are not impossible to either say or do. You can probably fill in the blanks better than I can.

- Life is too short to _____ ("work for indecisive management," "chase out-of-control projects," "argue about proven practices," "fix errors late instead of early").

- We have never done _____ here ("code inspections," "configuration management," "planning," "quality assurance," "metrics").

On my 35th birthday, I woke up and realized I was halfway to my biblical three score and ten years. Being on my second half, I decided that I would no longer run out-of-control projects. I would do the things I knew would work. If other people did not like that, I decided life is too short to put up with people who will not do the things proven to work at work.

1.3.2 Best Practices

The idea behind best practices (Glass, 1995) is to examine organizations that succeed consistently to discover what they do. If enough of these best-performing organizations practice similar tasks, these become a best practice for the industry. This is similar to, but not the same as, the emphasis on process. The best practices also include elements of people and product.

Below is a best practices list compiled from the best practices lists of many well-known authors: (Bach, 1995; Comaford, 1995; Jones, 1996a; Jones, 1996b; Johnson, 1995; Parnas, 1996; Racko, 1995; Reid, 1995; Sharp, 1995; Wirth, 1995). Note that the newest of these sources dates from 1996. Although I have read several dozen papers and texts since then that discuss best practices, none of them offer anything beyond this list. All the latest best practices come from one form or another of those listed here. I will repeat this list and discuss it again in Chapter 6.

- Risk management
- User manuals (as system specifications)
- Reviews, inspections, and walkthroughs
- Metrics (measurement data)
- Quality gates (binary quality decision gates)
- Milestones (requirements, specifications, design, code, test, manuals)
- Visibility of plans and progress
- Defect tracking
- Clear management accountability
- Technical performance related to value for the business
- Testing early and often
- Fewer, better people (project managers and technical people)
- Use of specialists
- Opposition of featuritis and creeping requirements
- Documentation for everything
- Design before implementing

- Planning (and use of planning tools)
- Cost estimation (using tools, realistic versus optimistic)
- Quality control
- Change management
- Reusable items
- Project tracking
- Users—understand them
- Buy-in and ownership of the project by all participants
- Executive sponsor
- Requirements

1.3.3   Management "Secrets"

There is no one big secret to developing software. If there were, more people would succeed at it. Fortunately, there are several little secrets, which can make a big difference to a project.

Avoid having team members work in isolation. Users, designers, programmers, testers, and managers, should be able to talk face to face in a matter of minutes. These days, that does not necessarily mean they are in the same building. It does mean, however, that you avoid saving up issues for the monthly flight to the coast. People who interact daily come to know one another, and the group of individuals more easily becomes a team. If possible, physically colocate everyone; if not possible, virtually colocate them. Inexpensive video conferencing provides a means for quick, easy discussion and is the closest thing to a physical meeting. Daily e-mail is a step down, but still permits inexpensive information transfer. With ftp sites and the like, people can work on the same virtual computer as if they were sitting down the hall. Think and use these technologies to provide fast, frequent contact at work.

Stay with your project team. Most of us started in front of the computer, programming solutions. We feel comfortable there, but the computer will not complete the project; the people will. Spend most of your time with the people working on your project. Most people drift to what is comfortable when under stress. For most of us, this means we go back to the computer terminal. Watch out for that tendency and spend your time with your people.

Concentrate on tasks, not tools. Learn how to perform a task first, and perform it until it becomes second nature. The tasks must become an established part of your culture. It takes time and money to learn how to use a tool. That learning cannot occur at the same time you learn how to perform a task. For example, learn how to plan projects using cards, sticky notes, and other common objects. Once you have mastered that task, learn how to use Microsoft Project or another schedule tracking tool. Don't try to learn both at the same time.

Do your homework. An informed manager is more likely to succeed. People and organizations worldwide are documenting their successes. Ideas are published in books, taught in seminars, and appear on Web sites. Our industry is often guilty of "ignorant originality" (Parnas, 1996), inventing techniques that have been proven to fail and creating techniques that someone else described years ago. Anything more than five years old is dismissed as irrelevant. Read books and magazines, attend seminars, and search the Internet. Keep a folder containing notes on everything you learn (Buzan, 1991).

1.4 KEY THOUGHTS IN THIS CHAPTER

Successful project managers acknowledge a project from three main perspectives: people, business, and process.

The lack of a people perspective has helped litter the software industry with failed projects. You need a good sense of self-worth, self-esteem, self-confidence, and self-examination to work closely with people. If you don't have them, you will be hurt and hurt others often and deeply. Be flexible, have compassion, and know when to lead and when to manage. Choose the best people, keep the team small, minimize distractions, train them, meet together as a team regularly, know them, and set an example.

Project tasks like writing requirements, selecting a design alternative, and having others review our work mean looking hard at management problems in the context of business requirements. Build only the software people want and the business needs.

Use processes that are proven to work at work. The process should include stating the problem clearly (define requirements), deciding among alternative solutions (design), bringing together the elements of software into a product, and testing the result systematically. Follow models like the Capability Maturity Model and Personal Software Process, which apply sound engineering and management principles to software. Best practices also reflect proven processes.

There is no one secret to successful project management. It is a mix of common sense, people skills, planning, and awareness. Don't let people become isolated; be a presence; focus on tasks, not tools; and keep informed.

REFERENCES

J. Bach, "The Challenge of Good Enough Software," *American Programmer*, October 1995, pp. 2–11.

T. Buzan, *Use Both Sides of Your Brain*, 3rd ed., Penguin Books, New York, 1991.

The Capability Maturity Model: Guidelines for Improving the Software Process, Carnegie Mellon University/Software Engineering Institute, Addison-Wesley, Reading, MA, 1995.

C. Comaford, "What's Wrong with Software Development?" *Software Development*, November 1995, pp. 27–28.

L. Constantine, "Software by Teamwork: Working Smarter," *Software Development*, July 1995, pp. 36–45.

D. Gause and G. M. Weinberg, *Exploring Requirements: Quality Before Design*, Dorset House, New York, 1989.

R. Glass, "In Search of Self-Belief: The 'BOP' Phenomenon," *Computer*, January 1995, pp. 55–57.

R. Glass, "Failure is Looking More Like Success These Days," *IEEE Software*, January February 2002, p. 102.

"Coach Your Team to Success," *Software Development*, July 1994, pp. 36-43.

W. Humphrey, *Managing the Software Process*, Addison-Wesley, Reading, MA, 1989.

W. Humphrey, *A Discipline for Software Engineering*, Addison-Wesley, Reading, MA, 1995.

J. Johnson, "Creating Chaos," *American Programmer*, July 1995, pp. 3-7.

C. Jones, "Our Worst Current Development Practices," *IEEE Software*, March 1996a, pp. 102–104.

C. Jones, *Patterns of Software Systems Failure and Success*, International Thomson Computer Press, Boston, 1996b.

S. Maguire, *Debugging the Development Process*, Microsoft Press, Redmond, WA, 1994.

S. McConnell, *Code Complete*, Microsoft Press, Redmond, Washington, 1993.

D. Parnas, "Why Software Jewels Are Rare,"' *Computer*, February 1996, pp. 57–60.

R. Racko, "Hedging Your Bets: Part 2," *Software Development*, August 1995, pp. 73–76.

W. Reid, "You Call That A System? Part 2," *American Programmer*, August 1995, pp. 25–33.

H. Rubin, "World-Class Information Technology Organizations," *IT Metrics Strategies*, January 1996, pp. 1–2.

O. Sharp, "How to Build Reliable Code," *Byte*, December 1995, pp. 50–51.

P. Szmyt, "User Centered Development," *Software Development*, November 1994, pp. 49–59.

R. Thomsett, "Project Pathology: A Study of Project Failures," *American Programmer*, July 1995, pp. 8–16.

G. M. Weinberg, *Quality Software Management: Vol. 3, Congruent Action*, Dorset House, New York, 1994.

G. M. Weinberg, The SHAPE Forum, *www.geraldmweinberg.com*, September 1997.

N. Wirth, "A Plea for Lean Software," *Computer*, February 1995, pp. 64–68.

Four Basics That Work

Time and toil have taught me that although it is difficult, you can develop and maintain software successfully by applying basic principles with discipline and perseverance. Over the years, I have been able to characterize these principles as (1) balance people, process, and product; (2) promote visibility; (3) organize by using configuration management tools properly; and (4) use standards judiciously. These techniques amplify the qualities of a good software manager described in the previous chapter.

2.1 PEOPLE, PROCESS, AND PRODUCT

All undertakings include the 3Ps: people, process, and product. Successful undertakings require keeping these three in harmony. *People* in this context are all those who influence project. People are inherently complex; each person has a different mixture of experience, attitudes, comfort zones, and so on. The *process* consists of the steps taken to write the software. At one end of the process spectrum is the waterfall model, a straightforward process of defining requirements, designing a solution, writing code, testing code, and finishing. At the other end are prototyping, experimenting, delivering products in phases, building on experience, and delivering a "final" product (although this last step sometimes never happens). There are many paths to the same goal. The best path depends on who is traveling it and their intended destination.

The *product* is the project's final outcome. Products include software, documentation, and training and maintenance services. The variety of products is immense. The wonderful thing about software is that, given a computer and a compiler, nearly anyone can build any product.

Balancing the 3Ps means looking at who is trying to build what. For example, suppose your task as project manager is to build a word processor. If your project team's background is in something else, you will need a different process than if they had built many such products. If your company mandates the use of, say, the waterfall process, you will need different kinds of people than if you were using a simpler process. In other words, you must think about the 3Ps at the project's start. As project manager, you will generally know at least one of the three, and sometimes two. With this information, you can extrapolate to get characteristics of the remaining parts.

Balancing the 3Ps as you continue through the development life cycle is also a challenge, as I describe later. All this is common sense, but has escaped a good many software project managers (including me) for too long.

2.1.1 People

People are critical to software development and maintenance. Your best asset on a software project is people who know what they are doing, have the self-discipline to do it, and possess the courage to tell the truth to those who often want to hear otherwise.

To most of us, people are far more important than product. Software is people intensive. It involves creating ideas where there were none and detailing ideas until you have source code. Software organizations that do well tend to have bright people and provide an environment that lets them do their best. The software industry has a history of wide variance among organizations (DeMarco and Lister, 1987), which can be explained to some degree by how large a part individuals have in creating and maintaining the software (Jones, 1995). The ability and performance of individuals play a key role in this. Software work is a mental and creative activity, so people differ greatly in their abilities. And because everyone has good and bad days, performance can vary widely from day to day.

There is no shortage of material on people issues. The classic work is *Peopleware* (DeMarco and Lister, 1987), and I recommend reading just about anything Gerald Weinberg ever wrote (Weinberg, 1992, 1993, 1994, 1997).

2.1.2 Process

Process has become the most discussed aspect of the 3Ps in recent years. The Capability Maturity Model, the ISO 9000 series, best practices, and agile methods are well-known parts of the process movement.

Process is important because it lets people build products. Iteration in a project shows the nature of a product and its users. Process gives management a channel of influence on software development and maintenance. When managers require formal inspections and monthly project reviews, they are telling everyone on the project that quality and teamwork are important.

Unlike the other Ps, process is repeatable (you rarely have the same combination of people on two projects and you are not likely to build the same product twice), but the same process does not fit all projects, even those with similar goals. For example, suppose the task is to manage a project to develop an accounting program, and the staff assigned have done nothing but write accounting software for the last five years. The straight waterfall process (no design until all requirements are known, no coding until design is done, no testing until all code is written, and so on) will be the most efficient for this product and these people. Evolving the product through iterations would simply bore the people and waste other resources.

Now suppose the task is to develop an accounting program with a slick Windows user interface. The people have experience in accounting, but only with text mode terminals. No one has ever written Windows interface accounting software (or even used it). These people need a project that permits learning to develop this product. An evolutionary delivery process is a good choice. The first evolution would be text mode only, with all the accounting functions. The next evolution would have a text mode interface in the Windows environment. Each successive evolution would have a better Windows interface. This process allows the programmers to learn how to write a Windows interface. The project is "finished" when the user interface is good enough for its intended users. The waterfall process would be dangerous here. It is unlikely that people could meet the challenge of a new user interface on top of difficult accounting software on the first try.

As another example, consider a traditional defense contractor whose expertise is weapons systems but who now needs to move into commercial work by writing an accounting system with a Windows user interface. The product is completely unknown to the people. The best course of action in a situation with such a bad fit of people and product is to find a firm with experience in this area and pay them to write it. In this example, however, the company needs this project to move into new business areas. This project has high risks, so a spiral process is necessary. This permits frequent risk assessment, planning for short iterations, project reviews, and many occasions for learning. It is also helpful to bring in experts in accounting and Windows as consultants at key risk assessment and planning points. The waterfall process in this project would almost ensure disaster. The people at all levels in the organization are unfamiliar with the product. The probability of producing a successful product on the first try is zero.

2.1.3 Product

The objective of software development is to create a product; the objective of a maintenance project is to maintain a product. Therefore, the object of every project is a product of some sort. The product must satisfy the customers and have them coming back for more. Without a product, there is no customer, no income, and no software-producing organization. You could say that, of the 3Ps, product is the most important because without it there would be no need for a project team (people) or process.

There are far too many product types and details to discuss in any one place. The best approach is to study books on the product type you are building. There is, however, one measurable characteristic that all products have in common: software quality.

Figure 2.1 is a version of the diagram commonly used to discuss software quality (Blum, 1992). As the figure shows, software quality has two views— external and internal. External quality (the upper right corner) sums up the user's feelings about the product. It includes words such as efficiency, human engineering, usability, integrity, correctness, and reliability. Questions pertinent to external quality are: Does it do everything desired? Does it do it well? Does it make sense? Does it increase the user's ability to do his job?

The key step in producing software with high external quality is requirements gathering. This is the time to understand the users and what they need. Most of the new techniques in software development were created in this area: rapid prototyping, JAD sessions, use-case scenarios, customer collaboration, and so on. (Chapter 5 describes requirements in more detail.)

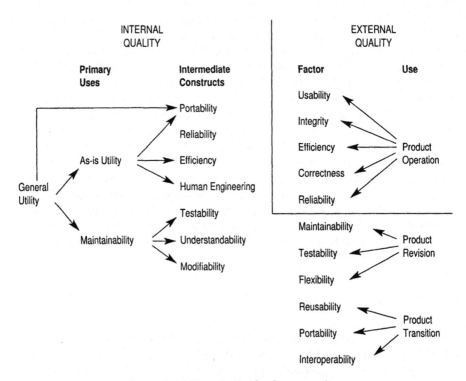

Figure 2.1   Two views of software quality.

Internal quality (left part and lower right corner of Figure 2.1) is the developer's view of the software. This includes factors such as portability, testability, understandability, modifiability, flexibility, and interoperability. These factors influence how the designer, programmer, tester, and project manager perform their tasks. Internal quality looks at software in the long term, directing us to build software that has the lowest possible cost over time (Strassman, 1996).

Internal quality results in software that follows the Phillips law of software half life: *software outlives hardware.* Think about it. Hardware has moved through six generations, and basically the same software has gone along with it. Descendants of several PC word processors written in the early 1980s for the Z80 8-bit processor and the CP/M operating system are still being used. Unfortunately, the originators of software that is 20 or 30 years old never intended or anticipated its longevity.

The lesson in this is to aim for long-life software with high internal quality. When building a product, always ask how the software will look to someone five years and then 10 years from now (see the discussion of software maintenance in Chapter 10). The key steps in producing this kind of software are design and coding. Concentrate on the internal qualities listed in Figure 2.1. Step back and ask if these factors are present and if someone else will be able to see them in 10 years. Bring in outsiders to examine the design and code. Ask them if the structure is clear and understandable, and if it isn't, ask them what is confusing and what you could change to make things clearer. This is especially important in design tasks. Do not rush through design in an effort to begin coding. We often feel anxious if we are not coding, but that is a fallback to school days when we started coding as soon as the professor said go. (Chapter 8 discusses design concerns in more detail.)

It may seem that the extra time and care needed in requirements and design to achieve high external and internal quality is too expensive, but the time pays for itself in the long term. Steve McConnell stated in his general principle of software quality (McConnell, 1993) that "Improving quality reduces development costs." I have seen this principle in action in real-world projects. Low-quality software has a high number of errors. People don't ship such software; they keep working on it until the errors are at an acceptable level, which costs time and money. If the requirements match what the users want (high external quality), fewer of these costly changes are needed. If the design of the software is clean and understandable (high internal quality), moving the software to a new platform (generally inevitable these days) is less expensive, so quick requirements and design do not save anyone anything.

2.1.4 *Balancing the 3Ps*

Figure 2.2 shows how people, process, and product fit together. The axes represent the capabilities of people and process. The distance from the origin of the graph represents how difficult the product is to build. Each band rippling

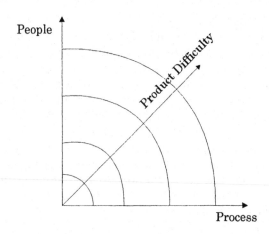

Figure 2.2   Considering people, process, and product together.

out from the origin represents a more difficult product to build; all points within a band represent equal difficulty.

How difficult the product is to build depends on who is building it. A text editor is an easy product to build for someone who has written several of them and difficult for someone who has done nothing but write image processing software. The people and process axes show that the increased challenge of more difficult products requires more capability from people, process, or both.

You cannot build a more difficult product without increasing capability. Increased capability comes through people, process, or both. Attempting a new type of product without changing the people or the process invites disaster. Moving to a more difficult product through people would mean hiring those experienced in and knowledgable about a product, training the current people, or bringing in consultants at key points in the project. Moving to a more difficult product through process would mean increasing the capability of the process by using a pilot (throwaway) project, prototyping, and evolving the product. These changes to the process permit the people to learn (increase their capabilities) while building. You could also move to a more difficult product by increasing the capabilities of both the people and the process. This could mean having four days of training before the project starts and evolving the product through four or five releases.

These approaches may seem simple, but they are extremely powerful and not common practice.

2.2   VISIBILITY

Software is largely invisible. Relative to hardware, it is mostly intellectual. We can touch a computer, a car, or a house. We can hold a printout of software or a disk or CD containing magnetic images of software, but the real software is in the minds of its developers. Software is also qualitative, whereas hardware is quantitative. A car is easy to quantify both in existence (weight, length, height) and performance (miles per gallon, 0-to-60-mph in seconds), but after 50 years, we still have trouble measuring software. We can easily determine its storage requirements, but that does not relate to its value in the same way that, say, a car's miles per gallon relates to its value. The number of lines of code indicate the cost of producing software, but it is a valid measure only under constrained conditions. That is, different styles of programming lead to different versions of the same program that differ in lines of code count by 20% or 30%. Function points are another software measure, but different people define function points in different ways.

Software projects also tend to be invisible. They have a clear start time, and we typically know when they are finished, but the body of the project is largely hidden. No one is sure where it is or what its condition is. People on the project are afraid to uncover it, and people outside the project are afraid to ask about it.

If allowed to be, software will remain invisible. People will form their own ideas about the software, and their ideas will differ, sometimes drastically. Changing software from this individual vision to a shared vision is the goal of visibility techniques. People can then focus on the same item and bring their collective brain power to the problem.

Visibility techniques represent the software, and when a thought becomes visible, other people can consider it, test it, and improve it. The minds of many can now work together on problems. The greatest time waster in software construction is finding and fixing errors. Visibility makes it easier for people to examine ideas and catch errors and ambiguities early on, when corrections are easy and quick.

Many types of software diagrams are available to represent ideas, including context, dataflow, SADT, Warnier-Orr, and state transition diagrams, as well as structure charts and CRC cards. (Chapters 5 and 8 describe these diagrams in detail.) Which one of these classic diagrams you use depends largely on the situation. Techniques for sharing and improving ideas include inspections and JAD sessions. Code inspections give a high return on investment. JAD sessions bring people together for a couple of days to review what they told a facilitator individually. The group works through ideas that are displayed in a visible manner. The result is a better shared vision of the problem and improved ideas.

Lesser known visibility tools include mindmaps, storyboards, cards on the walls, and quantitative charts. Walls (not an esoteric technology, just those things that hold up a room) are inexpensive and I haven't seen a workplace yet that doesn't have them. Walls let you display ideas so that people can see the big picture and grasp the context of the project and their role in it.

The classic and most dreaded visibility tool is the document. The document captures and records ideas in a convenient format so that people can study, critique, and improve the ideas put forth. Unfortunately, documents are largely disdained, perhaps because they are associated with bureaucracy and unneeded paperwork. Programmers like sitting in front of a computer banging out solutions, not reading. The challenge is to create a document that captures detailed information and is not boring. A related challenge is to convince management of the difficulty and importance of creating good documents and paying those who do it well on a par with their importance.

Regardless of what visibility technique you choose, always remember one thing: *No activity of software development can afford to be invisible.* Groups of people, not individuals, build software at work. A basic property of successful development is that each person can see what every other person is doing. The process you choose makes little difference. In all cases, *requirements* activities seek to reach a common understanding of what the user needs. A typical invisible situation is when one person has the requirements in his head. This is an individual versus a common understanding. If the individual has it right, then all is well, but the odds of that are less than slim. *Design* activities show the solution at a high level. A visible design lets programmers build small parts of the solution in parallel and combine the small parts into the whole solution. If the design is invisible or fuzzy, the parts will never combine. Visibility in *programming* is when programmers see each other's code in process. They understand what other programmers are trying to do and help ensure that it is done well.

There are many benefits to visible software. First, groups of people can work together and review the product in light of established standards. Software that meets the standards is accepted, whereas software that does not is typically rejected and corrected. This is common sense.

Second, visible software enables communication. When each person holds a different view of the software, misunderstandings are commonplace. People think they are talking about the same thing, but they are really only confusing themselves and one another. When people can see the software as a unit, they have a common basis and can stop wasting time trying to win others over to their individual view.

Finally, visible software permits quality assurance and control. Quality practices have many connotations, but they all have the same prerequisite—visibility.

Visibility in a software project makes it easier to manage. Some people fear and loathe interference from management; programmers are artists who cannot be managed like assembly line workers (at least that's what we keep telling ourselves). Proper management, however, keeps projects on track and helps companies stay in business. When companies stay in business, people keep their jobs and can feed their families.

2.2.1   Basic Visibility Techniques

The basic concept of visible software is communicating ideas to a group. This communication is a fundamental ingredient of team success, and when team members work together successfully, their product is typically of high quality. Richard Zahniser (Zahniser, 1994) defined three factors for team success:

1. *Shared vision.* Each member knows where the team is going.
2. *Member commitment.* All members contribute to creating the shared vision. Mission statements decreed from on high almost always fail.
3. *Group memory.* This is the visible representation of ideas—documents, papers, on-line information, diagrams, and the like. It permits more than one person to simultaneously focus on the collective idea.

I offer only a sampling of visibility techniques in this book, many of which involve displays. Edward Tufte has written three excellent books on this topic (Tufte, 1983, 1990, 1997) that you should add to your working library to improve the content of all your displays.

Walls. Walls are a key factor in visibility and group memory. Walls hold information in a way that permits groups of people to focus on the same issues at the same time. The entire team can simultaneously observe a project's group memory on, say, three walls. Because everyone is looking at the same tangible thing, they can discuss what they see, write on it, change it, and improve it. People can "walk the wall"—walk along the wall looking at the visible ideas. While walking, they can think and express their thoughts. This is the purpose of visibility. Walls covered with displays push people into discussing ideas and solving problems. They are concentrating on the ideas, not on who's who or politics, but on ideas.

Walls are big and can hold big pictures, something the project team needs to see often. Figure 2.3 shows an early *mindmap* (more about mindmaps in Chapter 5) of this book. This single, big picture showed me the entire book at once, which enabled me to more accurately place topics and details.

Computer screens cannot (yet) replace walls in this way. I acknowledge the love affair many have with their monitors; however, screens are too small to show sufficient information legibly. Television networks and entertainment studios cover walls with screens to show large amounts of information to groups, but at this time such devices are too expensive for widespread use.

Writing. People don't always read well-written documents, but they will *never* read poorly written ones. Some argue that the written word should not be a part of software development; after all, "software is created by programmers, not writers." But a well-written document is an efficient, effective visibility item. It lets different people see a description of the software in different places at different times (sometimes years apart). For some organizations with limited funds, documents are the only means they have to make their projects visible. This section is for these organizations. If you hate documents, read this section anyway. It may help you in other forms of written communication.

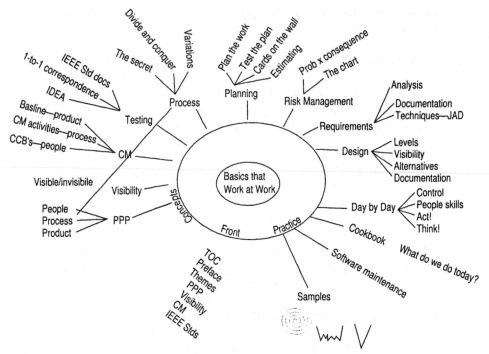

Figure 2.3 An early mindmap of this book.

Writing for the software industry is a skill, not an art. The purpose is to present information, not impress people with your prose. "Keep it simple" is still the best overall rule. Use short sentences, the active voice, and clear construction. These are the most common problems in software writing. If you can correct these, you will at least have people reading the document. An example I've seen many times in official documents (regrettably) is a good illustration: "The contractor shall be responsible for implementing all activities that may be needed to facilitate the design of the software." Translation: "The contractor shall design the software."

It is also important to write clearly and concisely. The rule of thumb is that the more complex the material, the simpler and more consistent the explanation. Robert Pressman (Pressman, 1997) and Daniel Freedman and Gerald Weinberg (Freedman & Weinberg, 1990) have published excellent examples of how to write good software documentation. Some of their rules follow the same basic rules of clear writing offered by general texts, such as *Elements of Style* (Strunk & White, 1972):

- *Avoid ambiguity.* Avoid vague phrases like "sometimes needs input from the customer" or "achieves good performance." Instead state exactly what you mean: when exactly is input needed? What is "good" performance? Concepts from software such as subroutines, definitions, and structures, can help you organize your document.

- *Make your description consistent.* If the text describes the same concept in two places, use the same terminology in both. This would make a boring novel, but it helps a technical reader understand by iterating an idea and creating a common set of terms for representing it. Remember, you have been immersed in these concepts for months, but the reader is looking at it for the first time. You aren't writing a Russian novel; there's no need to have five names for the same thing.

It helps to use a process to develop documents, just as you do to create the software (Mancuso, 1990). Writing instructions that are easy to follow is not easy. Edmund Weiss has provided some excellent techniques (Weiss, 1985). There are many other good books on how to present material (Brusaw et al., 1996; Tufte, 1983, 1990, 1997).

Easing the Pain of Document Writing. The following is a technique that I use to help ease the pain of writing documents. It has three parts. Start with a document standard such as MIL-STD-498 or the IEEE's 12207 standard. Both standards contain expanded outlines for documents called Data Item Descriptions (DIDs). The document standard serves two purposes: it acts as a checklist to remind people what should be in the document, and it organizes the document by showing where to put what information.

Next, cut up the outline of the document and stick the pieces on a wall (or several walls). This permits the developers to see the layout of the entire document. Now, gather the developers—as a group, not individually. Each person scribbles information on sticky notes and sticks the information on the wall. Grammar and spelling don't count. They also don't have to stick the information in the right section at first, as the sticky notes are easy to move around. What is important is to let the information pour out onto the wall.

The final piece is the recorder, who sits in the back of the group with a PC and enters the information poured out by the developers. When the developers are finished, the recorder touches up the finished document.

This simple technique works well for several reasons. First, everyone can see the entire document. This helps them think and contribute. Second, this method creates synergy. I know you have heard that word used and abused, but it does exist, and it does occur. When several people are thinking about the same problem together, they create better solutions than when working individually. Finally, the people who write software are not writing documents. They are scribbling and throwing information onto a wall. Someone else does the organizing, typing, and writing.

PASE. PASE (Post-Its™ Assisted Software Engineering) (Wood & Silver, 1995). Post-Its make information mobile. (Post-Its is a registered trademark of the

3M corporation. The generic term for such products is sticky notes). They are wonderful tools for creative processes. Suppose four people are trying to lay out a tree of subroutine calls. Each person has a sticky notes pad and a dark marker. The group discusses the structure of the program. Whenever someone decides they need a subroutine, he (I use "he" and "him" throughout this book to refer to a single person, male or female; I do not mean to insult the many outstanding women in the software field) writes the name of the routine on a sticky note and sticks it on the wall. A white board works well, too, because you can then draw lines to connect the notes. Anyone can create a subroutine at anytime, so subroutines appear on the wall in rapid fashion. The group can discuss the structure, move subroutines around, throw them away, or create new ones.

By putting sticky notes on a wall, a group can quickly create a structure. When they are finished, someone can type the structure into a computer. The group created the structure and owns it (this is our design, not Joe's, so we can all tolerate it).

A computer-assisted engineering (CASE) tool cannot enable the same type of team effort. The computer screen is too small, and there is only one keyboard. This prevents everyone from seeing the structure and contributing to it. One day, it may be possible to have simultaneous access to a CASE screen from multiple workstations, but it will be a long time before such a tool will be cheaper than a wall and a few sticky notes pads.

Sticky notes on a wall are not restricted to PASE. They can help with all aspects of a project, from constructing a schedule to outlining a document. The mindmap in Figure 2.3 began as sticky notes on a wall. As ideas came into my head (over weeks), I scribbled them on sticky notes and slapped them on the wall. (My wife is very understanding.) I moved them around, revised them, threw some away, and so on.

2.2.2 Using the Techniques

Many of the techniques I just described become even more powerful when combined. Always use walls. I predict that after practicing these techniques in groups, you will want more, large, blank walls in your workplace. Placing items on a wall can help you focus on the problem; PASE provides an easy way to juggle information.

Warm-up exercises can help get the group accustomed to these new techniques. They act as kick-starts for project brainstorming and get the group acting as a team. I describe warm-up techniques in more detail when I describe more advanced visibility techniques in Chapter 6.

Remember that visibility is not just pictures. It can be text or a growing number of folders in a cardboard box. The team should select a room for displaying all visible items for a project. I describe this concept in more detail in the next section on configuration management.

2.3 CONFIGURATION MANAGEMENT

Configuration management (CM) is coordination and communication that frees the project manager from drowning in details and lets him concentrate on the people and technical details. It comprises the processes people use to preserve the product's integrity. Listing the benefits of CM may seem out of line with its reputation. Indeed, it is probably the single most misunderstood topic in software (Phillips, 1996a, 1996b, 2002a). It is often considered the epitome of bureaucracy, needless meetings, and paperwork; to many, it means "just say no" to great new ideas.

The reason for this mismatch is that people have used CM to slow down and abuse others. Such misuse usually takes the following form:

Person A: "You cannot change that without my approval."
Person B: "If you say so."

What we don't hear is what Person B is *thinking*, which is "You can't tell me what to do. What do you know? I'll change it anyway and hide the change so well that you'll never find it." It is no wonder that programmers view CM as either an opportunity for creative workarounds or a good reason to quit and move on.

In reality, CM has many benefits. Properly used, it helps people hold the project together and improve both the quality and timeliness of the product. CM helps organize people into efficient and effective groups. These groups work only on their part of the project and contain only the necessary people, no one else.

Software projects comprise countless details and often slow to a crawl as key people chase details instead of doing their intended jobs. CM bundles details into manageable packages that let people do *only* their intended jobs. The most benefit goes to the project manager. Good use of CM and a good CM staff free the project manager from chasing details and let him concentrate on what is important—talking with people and working on technical challenges.

The foundation for using CM is the *CM plan*. CM itself comprises *baselines, activities,* and *people,* including the CM staff, the Configuration Control Boards, and the project manager. Appendix B contains a CM tutorial that also covers these topics.

2.3.1 The CM Plan

The greatest barrier to proper use of CM is ignorance. People, including myself, are not taught CM in college or in the workplace. (I had three degrees and 15 years on the job before I learned what CM was and how it helps.) This ignorance means that everyone has their own opinion of what CM is and what it does (or does not) do. IEEE Std 1042-1987 (see References) defines CM in a way that will set the record straight for everyone involved.

The CM plan documents how you plan to apply CM in a project. I highly recommend writing it according to IEEE Std 1042-1987. Every project needs its own CM plan. Many parts of the plan can be shared among projects, but a project's CM plan should reflect its unique mix of people, process, and product. Do not try to have a one-plan-fits-all approach. Cutting and pasting can eliminate rewriting the parts of the plan you can share. Your CM staff (discussed later) will help you avoid reinventing the wheel. There are many ways to use your resources efficiently, but having a single CM plan for everything is not one of them.

A good CM plan must

- *Have the executive sponsor's support.* The executive sponsor is a person high up in the organization, above everyone working on the project, who takes a personal, visible interest in the project's success. He often initiates projects and then assigns them to a project manager. The executive sponsor must endorse and enforce the CM plan. These actions tell everyone that the CM plan is not just part of a mandatory checklist. It will be a fundamental day-in, day-out resource for the project.

- *Be in place on day one of the project.* CM affects many items in a project—from who has authority over the software requirements to whether page numbers are at the top or bottom of documents (those little details that would be bothering key people if you didn't use CM). If the CM plan comes later in a project, most of what has been done will need to be redone. Writing a CM plan before the project begins doesn't mean you must know which algorithms the team will use to solve technical problems or how the user interface will appear. It simply means that you know how to organize the people and provide the means for them to decide technical questions.

2.3.2   Basic Baselines

Baselines are formal definitions of the work accomplished to date and form the foundation for future work. For example, the requirements baseline is a problem description. The right people in the project agree on this description and capture it. They create, build, and test a solution from this problem description. If the description changes, the ensuing workflow will change accordingly.

Figure 2.4 shows the basic baselines used in CM. Different projects may have a different set of baselines. These generic baselines resemble the classic (and much maligned) waterfall model of software development, but they can exist in projects that use any process model.

The *functional* baseline contains the system's requirements, usually as a document or database. The requirements are the foundation for the remain-

Functional
Allocated
Design
Development
Product
Operational

Figure 2.4   Basic baselines.

der of the baselines and the project. The software being developed must satisfy the requirements. (Chapter 5 discusses requirements, their creation, and documentation in detail.)

The *allocated* baseline is a high-level design that will satisfy the requirements, usually a document or set of documents. It shows how the requirements will be allocated to or satisfied by large subsystems. The high-level design typically states generic systems and does not mention particular vendors. For example, the data entry subsystem will use desktop computers (not specifying Windows systems, Macintoshes, or Unix workstations).

The *design* baseline is a detailed design, usually a set of documents. It gives specifics not mentioned in the allocated baseline. The design baseline goes into the low levels of software design. The depth and degree of detail depends on the situation. Because this baseline is nearing the programming level, automated tools may be used to create and display it. (Chapter 8 describes design and design documentation in detail.)

The *development* baseline is what the programmers are working on or developing. It exists as source code. This baseline is the most fluid and difficult to understand. It is neither a design nor tested and approved software. It is something in between. Because of its nature, this baseline is hard to control. You may want to use control tools such as RCS (revision control system) or one of its many commercial counterparts.

The *product* baseline is represented as tested and approved components and systems. It exists as executable programs and associated documentation. When a programmer is writing a set of subroutines, he is in the development baseline. When those subroutines have been tested and approved by someone, they become part of the product baseline. Depending on the process model used, the first product baseline may contain only the system's core. This baseline grows as functions are written, tested, and added to the core system. The product baseline is not the product the end user gets; only the developers use it.

The *operational* baseline is the product the customers are using.

Progress in a project can be summarized as the creation, maturation, completion, and change to baselines. The baselines are the work completed in a project. When seen in this correct manner, it is easy to understand how CM and baselines are an integral part of a well-organized project.

2.3.3 Activities

The four primary CM activities are identification, control, auditing, and status accounting—performed in that order. Most people think change control is the only CM activity. People cannot, however, control changes to something they have not yet identified. People cannot be sure the intended changes were made without auditing, and they cannot know the status of everything without an accounting.

Identification. Identification takes an idea or concept, separates it from everything else, and gives it a name. That idea becomes a concrete, specific, visible item with its own importance in a baseline and its own fit in the project. You can trace its background to previous baselines and analyze the impact it will have on future baselines. If it doesn't fit in this backward and forward analysis, you should get rid of it.

People identify baselines by gathering information and placing it in a visible form (document, poster, display, and so on). Identification also involves naming documents, disk directories, files, and even subroutines and variables in source code. There should be no confusion about what is in a baseline and how to refer to each item.

For example, if a person picks up a paper labeled "FB V07 CI27 of 1-2-95," he should know it is configuration item 27 of the seventh version of the functional baseline approved on January 2, 1995. This may seem like red tape and bureaucracy, but consider the alternative: people roaming the halls trying to decide high-level things like whether they should convert grams to kilograms or ounces.

Identification schemes and instructions in the CM plan, given to everyone on day one of the project, save time and energy. People don't have to invent individual schemes and work with others to blend them into a single scheme six weeks later. CM removes these organizational details so that people can use their creative energy to develop software.

Control. Control is the most often recognized CM activity. When a baseline exists, people must manage it, take care of it, and control it. The first aspect of control is safeguarding. Misplacing a baseline is catastrophic, but it happens. The CM staff and the project manager must ensure that copies of each version of each baseline are stored securely. Consider keeping extra copies of baselines in another city. This may seem extreme and costly, but fires, floods, tornadoes, and earthquakes happen. Building insurance will not pay for you to start a project over to rebuild your baselines.

The major work involves controlling the changes inevitable in any software project. Initial baselines change as the project team begins to better understand the problem and suggest more effective solutions.

Many people discard CM because they incorrectly believe it will prevent change. *Change control is not change prevention.* It is thinking about suggested changes, bringing together the right people to discuss the right issues and make informed decisions, and coordinating and communicating the change.

A change begins when someone requests it formally according to the procedures set forth in the CM plan. If the change is contained in one baseline, the Configuration Control Board for that baseline meets to consider the change (more on CCBs later). If the change affects more than one baseline, several CCBs will meet.

Change requests trigger tracing and impact analysis. *Tracing* looks back at previous baselines for possible effects. Suppose someone wants to replace inches in the software being coded with centimeters. Tracing finds that the design baselines called for inches because the functional baseline specified it. The users want inches. The users, who are paying the bills, would immediately protest when they first see the software. If there is an excellent reason for this change, the requesters should meet with the people who control the functional and design baselines to describe why they requested the change. Given sufficient reason, those people (who may be accountable to the users as the project progresses) may agree to change the baselines to accommodate the request.

Impact analysis looks forward to succeeding baselines. Suppose that late in the project (while coding is in progress), a user requests changing inches to centimeters. This request first appears at the functional baseline. Impact analysis looks forward to the design and development baselines. The inches requirement shows up in those baselines, but in relatively well-confined areas. Changing the functional baseline will require reworking the other baselines. Once again, the requesters should meet with the people controlling the design and development baselines to describe why they requested the change. If everyone agrees, the change can be made.

The project manager and the CM staff perform the tracing and impact analysis. They determine what the changes will affect and present this information to the different groups of people.

With tracing and impact analysis, people make informed decisions openly and visibly. They don't make them while chatting with friends in the hall or on Sunday afternoon when no one else is around. I have seen both these practices and the disasters that follow.

This kind of control is hard work. People sit face to face in substantive meetings and hammer out decisions that determine the course of the project. People must move away from their workstations and work through issues with others. Another thing to remember is that tracing, impact analysis, substantive meetings, and informed decisions do not happen without clearly identified baselines.

Auditing. Audits compare what *is* with what *should be*. The CM staff checks all incoming products to ensure they are what they should be. Have you ever had programmers waste time debugging their routines when the problem was that the delivered library contained the wrong version of functions? What about having a PC with a different BIOS than expected, or a compiler version that had different calls to graphics than those presumed? An audit examines a delivered product to see if it does what it should do and is what it should be. The "does" portion is a *functional* audit. The "is" portion is a *physical* audit.

Functional audits determine if the required functions are in a product. The functional audit may either test the functions or determine if the functions are present. The second case is done more often because usually a group of testers will run detailed test cases to verify that the functions are correct. For example, the auditors will ensure that the software calculates the interest on a 30-year mortgage; a test group will verify that the interest calculation is correct.

Physical audits document the product's state. For example, when a new PC arrives, the auditors will compare the contents with the order form. Does the PC have the right amount of RAM? The right disk drive? The right BIOS version? The right processor speed? Does it have the purchased software packages?

Physical audits are crucial in software development. This may be hard to believe, but I have spent weeks trying to find an error in development code only to discover that the problem was an outdated version of a compiler library. Physical audits check the dates and versions of software delivered to your development team. Physical audits are needed now more than ever because compiler versions arrive every three months on CD-ROMs or every week over the Internet.

Do not make assumptions about the tools your programmers are using. Audit those tools when they arrive. Most people on the project will not like audits. Audits take time and delay the delivery of tools to the development team. Programmers are anxious to program (it's great to work in an industry where people are anxious to start work). When a tool arrives at the door, they want it now, not after the audit.

However, audits actually save time. The CM staff performs the audits and reports the results to the project manager as specified in the CM plan, which saves time for the project manager. Programmers and others also benefit because they need not check the versions of products that come to them. Instead, when a tool arrives they can start using it.

The project team may resist audits even knowing these benefits. Encourage patience. One approach is to set up an office in another building for receiving and auditing products. The programmers may hear that a product has arrived, but they are removed from the temptation of "just taking a look." When the product arrives at their building, they know they can start using it.

Status Accounting. A project has many baselines, many people, and many tasks in progress. Status accounting tells everyone on the project where they are at a given time. The CM staff inspects project items at regular intervals and reports their findings. This tells the project manager if routines have been written yet, if modules have moved into the test area, or if documents are out for review. If the CM staff did not perform these status accountings, the project manager would be run ragged trying to gather all the particulars. In projects without status accounting, project managers typically drown in details and have neither the time nor the energy to think and talk with people.

Status accounting typically looks at the work areas. For example, source code development takes place in known disk areas. Checking the disks weekly tells what routines are under development, are being tested, or have been accepted—without pressuring those developing and testing the code. Again, the workers are doing their intended jobs, not other tasks like writing weekly reports. Similar accounting reveals the status of baselines, documents, revisions, and so on.

You must take care to do status accounting properly. This is not big brother spying on people to see if they are working. This is visibility, communication, and coordination. A programmer's progress becomes visible and is communicated to the project. Everyone, including upper management, knows how the code is advancing without interrupting the programmers every 10 minutes to ask. If a programmer is not making progress and problems arise as a result, people know about it and can help before the programmer asks. Chapter 4 discusses how to use status accounting to help people and the project rather than destroy them.

2.3.4   CM People

CM people are key people on the project, not grumpy old men far removed from the project who delight in saying no to new ideas. CM people are part of the project team, typically those with the greatest interest in and knowledge of the baselines. CM people consist of the Configuration Control Board, the CM staff, and the project manager.

Configuration Control Board. The CCB's task is to control the baselines by deciding on all change proposals. Each CCB is responsible for a baseline. The CM plan states who in general will be on each CCB. It also states specifically who will appoint the members of each CCB and how they will appoint them.

This separation of concerns is key to the performance of CM activities. Only necessary people attend meetings and meetings are held only when necessary. The requirements CCB focuses on requirements; people concerned with writing code are not wasting time in requirements CCB meetings. People concerned with requirements are not wasting time in development CCB meetings.

Each CCB

- Meets only when their baseline is involved in a change request, and the meeting involves only the people necessary to discuss the relevant issues. The meetings are substantive and efficient, and people make decisions that shape the project.

- Works with the project manager to create the baseline according to the CM plan. The CM staff helps with the physical baseline, but the CCB creates the content.
- Considers requests for changes to its baseline. If the requested change is internal to a single baseline, the CCB decides on the request by itself and reports the result to the CM staff. If the request will change the external interface of the baseline, several CCBs are involved.

CCBs help make great teams. The people are empowered to control their own baseline. CCBs and baselines are not heaven on earth, but they are much more desirable than the alternative.

The membership of each CCB reflects its characteristics and tasks. Groups or representatives of groups (if the groups are large) directly involved in each baseline are on the corresponding CCBs. The functional baseline CCB comprises customers, users, or marketing—the people who know best what they need in the software. The allocated baseline is a system or high-level design, so the members of its CCB should be the senior or best designers. Senior programmers will make up the design baseline (detailed design) CCB. The development baseline CCB comprises the programmers. Programmers and testers will be on the product baseline CCB, and the users will be on the operational baseline CCB.

CM Staff. The CM staff holds CM and the project together. As I described earlier, CM staff take care of the CM details so that the project manager, designers, programmers, testers, and others can concentrate on their jobs. This gives the project the benefits of CM without turning it into a hated bureaucracy for everyone.

The CM staff is involved in all CM activities. They write the CM plan, capture the baselines, keep safe copies of baselines, perform baseline tracing and impact analysis, report the results of that analysis, audit products, report results of audits, perform status accounting, and submit status reports. They attend meetings daily. This does not mean they are bureaucrats. It simply means they work face to face with people. They listen, talk, understand, record, and report what people need. They make the people's thoughts visible.

The size of the CM staff depends on the size of the project. If the project has a project manager and four other people, the project manager will be the CM staff. If 100 people are on the project, four or five should be devoted to the CM staff. Choose those people carefully because the quality of their work greatly affects everyone else's. The CM staff needs to be disciplined and meticulous. They must take their job but not themselves seriously. They must also work behind the scenes. This means they play a critical but supporting role on the project team. This requires a certain degree of maturity and humility. They must cater to the egos of others without developing a poor self-image. As project manager, you will need to regularly nurture your CM staff.

Project Manager. If you are the project manager, you are the person responsible for the project. The most important CM task for you is establishing CM. This means having the project's executive sponsor endorse and enforce CM and the CM plan. If this is not done, your job is much more difficult. No one will pay attention to baselines. Requirements and everything else will creep (grow), and you will spend your time chasing details.

Once CM is established, you can ride the wave. The structure and organization created by CM smoothes, but does not eliminate, the project's potholes. The CCBs will take care of their parts of the project (their baselines), and the CM staff will record the details. You can spend time and energy on the important tasks: working with people and solving technical problems.

As project manager, you coordinate the CCBs when a change affects more than one baseline. You present the results of tracing and impact analysis and lead the ensuing discussion. You close the discussion with a well-documented and well-understood decision.

You must also care for the CM staff. A project manager is ultimately responsible for everything about the project—even things he cannot know. The more you know, the more confidently you can assume responsibility. The CM staff toils in the background, serving everyone on the project. They receive little or no credit because they do not design anything or write any code. You are the only one who can give them due credit and recognize their contribution publicly. Reward them in a way they can appreciate. Sometimes, this means moving them off the CM staff on the next project.

2.3.5 CM Sketch

A complete written CM plan may not be possible for every organization. Cultural change, no matter how beneficial, requires time. When in the middle of a hectic project, writing a first CM plan is out of the question. The customers and management will not stop work for a couple of weeks while the project team learns how to write a CM plan.

A CM sketch is a good alternative. It shows who is who in a project and their areas of responsibility. It brings much of the organization and benefit of a CM plan but in less time.

Figure 2.5 shows a CM sketch for a fictitious software project. The project involves a fictitious company with departments of information resources, sales and service, engineering, and manufacturing. Each department has a vice president. The sales and service department needs a new information system. This will involve new hardware, networks, and custom software. The project manager is in the information services department. He will use some of that department's employees as well as hardware, network, and software consultants. The consultants will help the company come up to speed on the unfamiliar technologies.

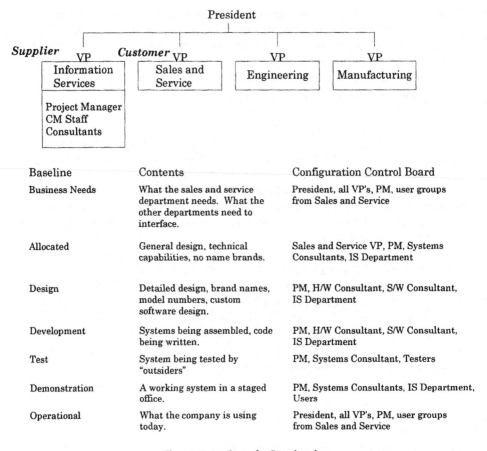

Figure 2.5   Sample CM sketch.

The project team will evolve the system through requirements (business needs), a general design (allocated), and a detailed design (design). They will then assemble the hardware and network components with off-the-shelf and custom software (development). After internal testing, they will put the system into a staged office so that the sales and service department can use it in a safe environment (test). This staging will no doubt produce changes to the requirements. These will work their way through the process. The entire process will repeat two to four times.

At the top of Figure 2.5 is the organization chart (who is who) for the fictitious company. Below the organization chart is a table showing what is what and who is responsible for what. It establishes the baselines, describes their contents, and states who is on the corresponding CCB.

As project manager, you can make a preliminary CM sketch on a large piece of paper. Take it around to the project participants and discuss it with them. Show how each group of people will control that part of the project they know best. Show the lines of communication. Illustrate how you will help coordinate the different groups so that the people who know the issues best can discuss and solve substantive problems.

Put the CM sketch in a public place. Whenever people ask a question they could answer by looking at the CM sketch, don't give the answer directly. Go to the CM sketch and discuss the question in that context. Use the CM sketch as a first step to formal CM. Let people gradually experience the benefits that come from the organization provided by CM. Maybe the next project will then be ready for a full CM plan.

2.4 STANDARDS

Standards have paid off repeatedly, yet many people still feel that standards belong on bookshelves and in the offices of bureaucrats. I believe this view is short-sighted. Standards can be dry and hard to understand, but using them wisely can greatly help your software project.

Experts wrote the standards. Why not listen to them? Suppose you had to write a document describing requirements. Where do you start? What should it contain? Where can you find a sample? You could do your best on this document, learn from the experience, and write a better one the on the next project (and a better one on the next, and on the next, and so on), but you would basically be reinventing the wheel. IEEE Std. 830-1993 tells you just how to write a requirements document see References for IEEE Standards. IEEE Std 1042-1987 tells you how to write a CM plan in detail. Your documents need not be exactly to the standards. Using them as guides, however, will save you time and money. Invest in the IEEE's collection of standards for software engineering (IEEE, 1997).

Standards are frameworks that let creative people solve their problems. Without a framework to guide and channel your efforts, "creativity becomes meaningless chaos" (Fairly, 1985).

Military and commercial software standards specify everything to do on a project (MIL-STD-498, IEEE/EIA 12207.0, IEEE/EIA 12207.1, IEEE/EIA 12207.2). They are less detailed than the individual IEEE standards, but everything is in one short package. They are good guides for a complete project.

Of course, like most tools, standards are not going to help you if you don't see them in light of the big picture and if each person on the project doesn't understand the part he plays. As Weinberg says,

> For standards to be effective, everyone from managers on down needs to understand: (a) how their job contributes to the goals of the organization (mission), (b) how their software product contributes to the mission, (c) how the standards contribute to the quality of the product, and (d) how the standards contribute to the success of the mission. (Weinberg, 1993)

This text focuses on IEEE standards. Although the IEEE does not hold a monopoly on useful standards, it does have a complete set of software standards and is accepted worldwide as a standard-setting organization. The U.S. military standards are also quite helpful. In my experience, military standards are not well accepted in commercial organizations and government organizations that are not in the U.S. Department of Defense. Inserting an IEEE standard is easier than using a military standard, especially for organizations that formerly produced hardware and used IEEE hardware standards.

2.5   KEY THOUGHTS IN THIS CHAPTER

Four basic principles work well if used consistently and accurately: (1) balance people, process, and product; (2) promote visibility; (3) organize by using configuration management tools properly; and (4) use standards judiciously.

All undertakings include people, process, and product. The challenge of the project manager is to keep the three in harmony; how you build something depends on who is building what.

Visible projects unite people and provide more opportunities for improving the product. Techniques like using sticky notes on walls can provide the team with a unified vision of the project goals and allow them to easily manipulate the product's structure.

Properly used, configuration management lets you control the project and keep key people focused on the tasks they do best, not on administrative details. You are free to concentrate on talking to people and dealing with technical challenges. The details of CM for a project are documented in the CM plan. The main parts of CM are baselines, activities, and the Configuration Control Board.

Standards keep you from reinventing the wheel, which will save you time and money.

REFERENCES

B. Blum, *Software Engineering, A Holistic View*, Oxford University Press, New York, 1992.

C. Brusaw, G. Alred, and W. Oliu, *The Concise Handbook for Technical Writing*, St. Martin's Press, New York, 1996.

T. DeMarco and T. Lister, *Peopleware*, Dorset House, New York, 1987.

R. Fairley, *Software Engineering Principles*, McGraw-Hill, New York, 1985.

D. Freedman and G. Weinberg, *Handbook of Walkthroughs, Evaluations, and Technical Reviews*, Dorset House, New York, 1990.

IEEE Standard, ANSI/IEEE Std 830-1993, *IEEE Recommended Practice for Software Requirements Specifications*, IEEE Press, Piscataway, NJ, 1993.

IEEE Standard, ANSI/IEEE Std 1042-1987, *IEEE Guide to Software Configuration Management,* (reaffirmed 1993) IEEE Press, Piscataway, NJ, 1993.

IEEE Standards Collection, Software Engineering, IEEE Press, Piscataway, NJ, 1997.

Industry Implementation of ISO/IEC 12207:1995—Standard for Information Technology—Software Life Cycle Processes.

Industry Implementation of ISO/IEC 12207:1995—Standard for Information Technology—Software Life Cycle Processes—Life Cycle Data.

Industry Implementation of International Standard ISO/IEC 12207: 1995; Standard for Information Technology—Software Life Cycle Processes—Implementation Considerations.

C. Jones, "Function Point Focus," *IT Metrics Strategies,* Cutter Information Corp., p. 8, December 1995.

J. Mancuso, *Mastering Technical Writing,* Addison-Wesley, Reading, MA, 1990.

Military Standard, *Software Development and Documentation,* U.S. Department of Defense, Washington, DC, Dec. 1994, http://www.itsi.disa.mil.

S. McConnell, *Code Complete,* Microsoft Press, Redmond, WA, 1993.

D. Phillips, "Project Management: Filling in the Gaps," *IEEE Software,* July 1996a, pp. 17–18.

D. Phillips, "Configuration Management: Understanding the Big Picture," *Software Development,* December 1996b, pp. 47–53.

D. Phillips, "Go Configure! Understanding the principles and promises of configuration management," *STQE,* May-June 2002a, pp. 54.

R. Pressman, *Software Engineering, A Practitioner's Approach,* 4th ed., McGraw-Hill, New York, 1997.

P. Strassman, "Strategic Planning and the Three Little Pigs," *American Programmer,* March 1996, pp. 2–8.

W. Strunk and E. B. White, *The Elements of Style,* 2nd edition, Macmillan, New York, 1972.

E. Tufte, *The Visual Display of Quantitative Information,* Graphics Press, Chesire CT, 1983.

E. Tufte, *Envisioning Information,* Graphics Press, Chesire, CT, 1990.

E. Tufte, *Visual Explanations,* Graphics Press, Chesire, CT., 1997.

G. Weinberg, *Quality Software Management: Vol. 1, Systems Thinking,* Dorset House Publishing, New York, 1992.

G. Weinberg, *Quality Software Management: Vol. 2, First Order Measurement,* Dorset House Publishing, New York, 1993.

G. Weinberg, *Quality Software Management: Vol. 3, Congruent Action,* Dorset House, New York, 1994.

G. Weinberg, *Quality Software Management: Vol. 4, Anticipating Change;* Dorset House Publishing, New York, 1997.

E. Weiss, *How to Write A Usable User Manual,* ISI Press, Philadelphia, 1985.

J. Wood and D. Silver, *Joint Application Development,* 2nd ed., Wiley, New York, 1995.

R. Zahniser, "Low Tech Groupware for Team Success," *Software Development Conference,* Miller-Freeman, San Francisco, 1994.

Chapter 3

What Doesn't Work and Why

In the last chapter, I outlined four basics that work if used properly. This chapter is for those who are still skeptical. It contains anecdotes of disasters with names changed out of courtesy to the organizations, who have already suffered enough. Each of these disasters can be traced to an omission of one of the four basic principles: (1) balance people, process, and product concerns; (2) promote visibility; (3) use configuration management wisely; and (4) apply standards judiciously.

3.1 WHEN THE 3Ps ARE OUT OF BALANCE

I once was associated with a failed project ($20 million spent, nothing produced) (Phillips, 1995). The goal was to build a digital signal processing (DSP) system that pushed the state of the art. The system was to use custom-made processors attached to a VAX. Software was needed to control and coordinate these processors to move data through a series of complex DSP algorithms.

$20 million later, nothing worked. The algorithms were correct, but the processors were not coordinated, and the data did not flow.

The project had the best DSP people available, the best project managers, and good programmers. Everyone used a proven process that included inspections, risk management, configuration management, planning, requirements, and so on. On the surface, this project had everything going for it. The only problem was that the people, process, and product did not fit.

The failed project used a straight waterfall process. All the requirements were written and reviewed before design began. The design was finished and reviewed before any coding. All the code modules were finished before any integration. At integration, nothing worked.

An evolutionary process would have helped this case. The difficult part of the software was not the DSP algorithms. It was coordinating parallel processors, and the programmers did not have any experience in this. The project needed a process that let people learn while building the product. If concurrent processing experts were used on this project, the waterfall process would have been best.

Another recent project I observed met all its objectives, but was inefficient. An organization was to perform a major software modification on an existing system. Half the new software would be copied from the old, a quarter would be modified from the old, and another quarter would be new code.

The project proceeded with an evolutionary delivery approach. Each month, they delivered 5–10% more functionality. Each monthly delivery included a formal meeting in which the requirements, design, and code for that delivery were presented. The same topics were covered for the deliveries of the next three months. The project went smoothly and delivered the final software. The only problem was that it took three years to get a product. The evolutionary approach was chosen because the participants had read articles praising it as the modern way to deliver software.

In reality, the project could have been completed in half that time. The people knew the product, so a simple process would have been sufficient. The evolutionary process caused the project staff to spend far too much time managing the project. They stopped working on software and spent the fourth week of each month preparing for a formal meeting. The first week of the next month was spent hosting the meeting and then planning the work for that month. As a result, only two to two-and-a-half weeks per month were spent developing software.

A straight waterfall process would have been more efficient. The waterfall process would have required three or four formal reviews instead of 36. The programmers had the knowledge and experience to complete the project in large pieces.

3.2   WHEN THERE'S NOT ENOUGH VISIBILITY

Lack of visibility has hurt too many software projects to mention. At one extreme, a major American business was purchasing software from an outside vendor. The software was not needed for any existing product lines, but would add a major new product line. The software was due in nine months. The day before the software was due, the company called the vendor to see how it was doing. The vendor asked for nine more months. Nine months later, the company called the vendor for the second time to see how it was doing. The vendor again needed more time. Two phone calls in 18 months must be some sort of record for lack of visibility. The vendor eventually delivered the software and it was a success. Most organizations, however, do not have the reserves to absorb such late deliveries.

Similar lack of attention occurs on all levels. I was managing a software shop of a dozen programmers, and we had half a dozen projects in progress at all times. One project was a "small, simple" database application. A quiet programmer was working the database for an equally quiet customer. Every three months I would pass by and ask the programmer and customer how it was going. The project was always going well with just a few small issues to work through. After a year, there was no product in hand or in sight. I had been lulled to sleep by the two quiet, trusting parties. I did not pull a plan from them. I did not pull a requirements or design sheet from them. I did not pull anything visible on paper from them. Those items existed in my mind, and I assumed they existed on paper. I was wrong. The programmer wasted a year and the customer never received the needed application.

A frequent lack of visibility results when projects reduce paper documents to save money. A recent contractor project saved money by not delivering us a software design document. The contractor would, of course, create a design, but would not spend the time and money to place it in a formal document. The project progressed through the requirements, design, and coding phases. When the test and integration stage arrived, dozens of errors appeared. The contractor needed to find and correct the errors quickly. That did not happen because common operations were spread throughout the system instead of being in one location. When a code fix was found, it had to be inserted in many different places. This continued for months, and cost us a half million dollars.

Eliminating the software design document costs much more in time and money. We relax our standards when we don't put software information in a formal document. The resulting design, requirements, or test procedure are not as good because we carry information in our minds instead of recording it on paper. Information in a person's mind is invisible. It is rarely the same information that is in everyone else's mind. The result of reduced visibility is always the same. Organizations waste time and money because no one actually understands what everyone thought everybody understood.

3.3 WHEN CONFIGURATION MANAGEMENT IS MISSING OR ABUSED

This project, which I will call DSP-SW, involved the use, maintenance, and evolution of digital signal processing software. Figure 3.1 summarizes the project's situation.

Scattered around the United States were six government-sponsored signal processing labs, each using the DSP-SW. DSP-SW comprised several hundred Fortran programs, or micros. The labs used Unix computers and the users called up the micros using text commands. The users would then create Unix scripts that put together the micros to form macros. The ability to have macros greatly increased the software's flexibility and power.

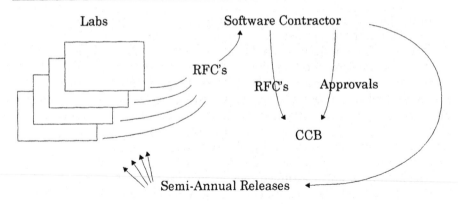

Figure 3.1   The DSP-SW project.

A separate software contractor performed software changes and fixes. Each lab sent requests for changes (RFCs) to the software contractor. The labs generated most of the RFCs in response to errors they found in the micros.

Representatives of the labs met once a month in a CCB to discuss and approve the RFCs. On rare occasions, they disapproved an RFC. Twice a year, the CCB directed the software contractor to send a new release of DSP-SW to each lab. The labs replaced their current software with the new release and continued their work.

At first glance, it would appear that the DSP-SW project was using CM effectively. It had a CCB, a CM plan, RFCs, and controlled releases. However, Figure 3.2 paints quite a different picture. Baselines were either missing or they were not quite there (those in gray in the figure) in the true sense of having a baseline. The functional baseline did not exist. There was no precise requirement or definition for each micro. Everyone had their own idea of what each micro should do. The design baseline did not exist. No one formally designed the micros; they just wrote them. Many of the micros were similar, and there could have been a consistent design style for them. The absence of consistent design meant that each micro had a style of its own. This made them difficult to read, understand, and maintain. The development baseline in the figure is gray because, in practice, a development baseline should contain the code being written or revised. Because large parts of the DSP-SW were always being revised, no one was sure what was and was not under revision.

Development
Product
Operational

Figure 3.2   DSP-SW baselines.

The product baseline almost existed, but not quite. It should have contained the micros under test, but repeatable test scripts did not exist. How could there be a test script for a program that did not have a precise definition? The programmers doing the revising tested their work as they saw fit. The operation baseline did exist, but it was weak. Each lab received the complete DSP-SW source code as part of the semiannual release. The users in the lab quickly modified the code to fit their needs. The operational baseline existed for one day.

Thus, the people on the DSP-SW project (and I was one of them) attempted to have a project with one CCB and one baseline. The resulting problems were predictable to anyone with a proper understanding of CM, which I did not have at that time. Without multiple, controlled baselines, there was no tracing or impact analysis.

The monthly CCB met and discussed the RFCs. The people who talked about the requested changes were intelligent and reasonable, but they did not have visible baselines to trace because everything was in their heads. The software contractor made the requested and approved changes to the micros. Many of these changes broke macros. No one could analyze the possible impact of the changes. No one could remember how all the micros were used in all the macros.

People in the labs would partially reverse the changes made to the micros so that their macros would still work. These reversals put back errors that triggered an RFC in the first place. The labs would then try to fix that, and the cycle would continue. The absence of CM hurt visibility and limited coordination and communication. Without a functional baseline, everyone had their own idea of DSP-SW. People wrote RFCs because they thought a micro was broken while others thought the micro was fine. This left many people and their efforts completely uncoordinated. Communication suffered because people were never sure what they were discussing. There were many informal conversations at the monthly CCB, but most of this was wasted time.

We could have done many things differently. The first step would have been to write and enforce a CM plan with functional, design, development, product, and operational baselines and CCBs for each one:

- *Functional baseline CCB.* The project would need a transition period to go to the new situation. Over 12 to 18 months, the functional baseline CCB would write a formal definition for each micro, one by one. This CCB would include representatives of each lab and the software contractor (just like the previously described CCB).

- *Design baseline CCB.* The design baseline CCB (the software contractor) would take each definition of a micro, and the existing source code for that micro, and write a design for it. These designs would recommend changes to the source code to improve the consistency of the micros.

- *Development baseline CCB.* The development baseline CCB (the software contractor) would alter the code as required by the design baseline. They would also work on RFCs as before.
- *Product baseline CCB.* The product baseline CCB (the software contractor) would test the changed micros. The difference would be that they would now have a set of definitions for the micros. They could write and use repeatable test scripts.
- *Operational baseline CCB.* The operational baseline CCB would comprise representatives of each lab and the software contractor. Their role would not change much from the previous situation.

The plan would also call for a CM staff. These people would come from the software contractor, but would not be programmers or testers. Status accountings and audits would show how the baselines would grow through the transition period. The CM staff's biggest contribution would be tracing and impact analysis for RFCs. This would enable the CCBs to make informed decisions.

3.4   WHEN STANDARDS ARE DISMISSED

When standards are dismissed, trouble usually follows. Often, products are incomplete, everything becomes subjective, everything is reinvented every time, and communication breaks down. Several projects I supervised involved people who did not want to write documents according to standards. They worked with best intentions, but the documents were incomplete. The items lacking in the documents caused errors in the software, and these cost time and money to correct. The missing items were small, yet significant ("specify interfaces between modules," "include a data dictionary before design"). If a standard had been consulted, these things would have not been forgotten.

Standards provide an objective reference. Without such an impersonal reference, personalities and politics grind the project down every day. I worked on a project whose members ignored a process standard early on that called for a concept of operations document to be written first. The eventual users of the system would contribute to this document. This document was skipped. Every meeting during the project always degenerated into an argument over the system operation. Different factions called for different forms of a concept of operations document. No one could agree. The differences of opinion were small, but they were based on personality and politics, so no one could give in. What was right did not matter; who was right was everything.

Other arguments occur when people ignore standards on a single document. "The interfaces should be described in the first section, not the third." "The data dictionary belongs in its own document." People have their favorite ways of doing things. Agreeing to use a standard satisfies no one completely, but satisfies everyone enough for the project to succeed.

The absence of standards also causes projects to reinvent the wheel, which almost always causes errors because the reinvented wheel is missing something. It results in losses in time and money, because no one knows where to start. Once a coworker struggled an entire day to start writing a software development plan. At the end of the day nothing was on paper, and the coworker was looking for someone else to write the plan. I sat with the coworker the next day with a standard in front of us. The outline of the plan was finished in an hour, and all but a few details were written by the end of the day.

Lack of standards frequently causes communication problems. Standards for diagrams define the equivalent of languages. Using the standard diagrams lets different groups communicate. No standard diagrams are perfect, and communication difficulties always exist, but a standard can reduce the cost of such communication difficulties.

In a recent project, I was in a group on one coast interacting with a group on the other coast. Both groups assumed the other was using the same types of diagrams. When we received documents from the other group, we were disappointed in the number of errors they had in their diagrams. We spent days working through these errors until their designs made sense. As we were discussing our anger at the other group, the other group was going through the same exercise of correcting our many errors. After several months, our two groups met to discuss progress. The first meetings were heated, as we both expressed disappointment in the errors introduced by the other. It took several meetings before we realized we were speaking different languages. We were fortunate to catch our mutual misunderstanding before we started writing code.

3.5   KEY THOUGHTS IN THIS CHAPTER

Projects usually fail when people neglect to (1) balance people, process, and product; (2) promote visibility; (3) organize their use of configuration management; and (4) use standards.

When the project manager does not balance people, process, and product, people are presented with problems they cannot solve, or projects "succeed" inefficiently. In either case, developing software takes too long and cost too much.

People make assumptions when visibility is lacking. These assumptions are often wrong, and projects suffer. On several projects, I used assumptions rather than pulling needed information into the light. The absence of visibility hurt on every occasion.

Misuse of configuration management breeds confusion. Absence of baselines prevents people from knowing the subject of their work. They work hard, but different groups of people work toward different ends. Hopefully, they will all come together in the end, but often this does not happen.

When standards are dismissed, products are incomplete, everything becomes subjective, everything is reinvented every time, and communication breaks down. Standards are written from experience, and following them gives projects a complete and objective reference point. Dismissing standards invites errors and arguments.

REFERENCE

D. Phillips, "People, Process, and Product," *American Programmer*, January 1995, pp. 15–20.

Chapter 4

Managing a Project Day by Day

The project is underway and you, the project manager, find yourself sitting at your desk wondering what you will be doing from one day to the next. People are gathering requirements, designing, writing code, testing modules, reporting on status, writing documents, and so on. What should *you* be doing to manage the project day by day?

Many authors have attempted to answer this question. Some concentrate on metrics, others on politics, budgets, customers, or psychology. The most recent books focus on people aspects (Maguire, 1994; McCarthy, 1995). [The classic *Peopleware* (DeMarco, 1987) is still as valid today as it was a decade ago.] Many management books approach the subject from the process or best-practices perspective (Humphrey, 1989).

As the previous chapters describe, experience has taught me to think in terms of four principles: balancing people, process, and product; keeping everything visible; staying organized via configuration management; and using standards when appropriate.

Your business enterprise has made commitments and is trusting that you will strive to keep them. There are many famous examples of project managers who did not do this—not because they were unintelligent, but because they let the project wander out of control: the FAA traffic control system, the C-17 cargo plane, and the baggage handling system at the Denver International airport are some of the more noteworthy. By the way, out-of-control projects are not unique to government organizations. It only seems that way. Government projects spend public money, so their failures are public. Private companies also have colossal failures, but only the insiders hear about them.

In controlling the project, you avoid controlling people's lives. This requires establishing an environment in which you can lead people and manage the process and the product.

In this chapter I first show how you can create and maintain a good work environment and then how to apply a simple equation for controlling a project day to day (without controlling the people). As in other chapters, I follow the four themes introduced in Chapter 2.

4.1   BALANCING THE 3Ps TO CREATE A GOOD ENVIRONMENT

The best thing the project manager can do for the people on a project is to create and sustain a good environment for them to work in. People are intelligent and want to do a good job, but they cannot work in a crowded, noisy, distrustful, uncomfortable, and hateful place.

Gerald Weinberg likens this to gardening (Weinberg, 1986). A gardener cannot force plants to grow. The gardener prepares the soil, plants the seeds, nourishes them with water and minerals, and protects them from hostile plants, animals, and weather. If the environment is good, the plants will grow. Likewise, you cannot force people to work well. If they don't like the environment, they can and usually do find a job elsewhere. Create an environment that is physically, mentally, and emotionally healthy. Pull weeds if necessary. It is unfortunate, but some people find pleasure in making life miserable for others. Remove them.

Once you've created the environment, be religious about maintaining it. A gardener cannot water a garden on the first day and let it go for the next six months. Take care that the details of the project do not cloud your vision. The people do the work. Neglecting their environment will prevent them from succeeding.

Everyone has a top-five list of what makes a good work environment. Some want a big quiet office; others prefer a messy, active one. The environment elements I give here are based heavily on my experience. I'm sure you can think of many more.

4.1.1   Emotional Safety

The project manager must hold himself to a high and consistent standard. Your people will watch you. They will see how you behave when the project is going well and when it is not. If you act hypocritically, so will they. If you lie to superiors, so will they (hint: you are their superior, so they will lie to you). A software project needs people who tell the truth because (among many reasons) much of the software exists only in people's minds. You cannot check what is there; they must tell you. If the workplace is frightening, people will hide things. Most software people are intelligent and creative. If they see that hiding the truth is in their best interest, they will hide it so that no one will find it. Remove people who deride, blame, and otherwise hurt and scare others. Everyone becomes frustrated and blows off steam every now and then. Those who do this daily or weekly should leave.

This also means being honest and open with your values. Don't gradually leak them out to select people in private discussions and force the team to piece them together like clues in a mystery novel. Strive instead for open lines of communication among all the people on the project. Lead by example. If you are completely open about what you expect from everyone, they are much more likely to be open with their expectations of you and the project. In this safe environment, everyone benefits and you are likely to get a product that is much closer to what you envisioned.

4.1.2   Emphasis on Team Empowerment

Empowerment is one of the foundations of total quality management. It has been tossed about so much and in so many ways, that many have become cynical about it. This is unfortunate. Stress to a group of people that they are a team responsible for producing something (McCarthy, 1994). If their processes and practices are not working, they can look only to themselves. They cannot blame the system, the company, or some outside monster. They have the authority to make decisions. If they can show you that the organization's policies are detrimental to the current project, you should let them change the policy for the project. This means being flexible and trusting the team's judgment. It also means the team must do their homework and present their case professionally.

4.1.3   High Degree of Personal Interaction

Talk to people in their offices. The "my door is always open" philosophy does not foster open communication. People do not talk well sitting in the boss's office. They are far more comfortable and open in their own surroundings. Walk around and talk to people where they are comfortable, and talk to them about the weather as well as the project. If you talk to someone only when a problem occurs, you become associated with problems—you are not a resource; you are just trouble. Talk about good news as well as bad, family and home as well as business. When you walk into a room people should expect to hear "congratulations" as well as "we have a problem."

4.1.4   Good Balance of Work and Rest

Make sure people go home at the end of the day. Scott Adams of *Dilbert* fame stresses this in his "out at five" model of a good organization (Adams, 1996).

Kent Beck of eXtreme Programming fame agrees (Beck, 1999). They are not alone in this sentiment. Work smart for eight hours and go home. Read the comics, play with the kids, make ceramics, eat well, sleep eight hours, and come back to work ready to produce. I have seen people work 16-hour days and come in an hour early the next morning to get a jump on the day. They are so tired they make mistakes, and everyone else has to work all week to correct them. Developing and creating software are mental and creative tasks that require mental rest and well being.

4.15   Structure that Promotes Success

There are several ways to plan for success.

Let people succeed frequently. Success breeds success, so you should structure the project in a way that lets people succeed every week. People will go home on Friday feeling better, have a better weekend, a happier home, and come back on Monday eager to repeat their success. Create goals and tasks that can be finished successfully by Friday afternoon. As people grow in their abilities, set bigger goals.

I managed a project in which four programmers and I were porting programs. The project was to take one year. I decided that succeeding once a year was not enough, so I set a goal of completely porting two programs each week, which was enough to finish in one year. Every Friday afternoon I submitted a one-page progress report to our management. The progress report told everyone, especially us, that we succeeded every week. We all went home happy, and it was one of the most pleasant and productive projects in my career.

Recognize and deal with the causes of failure. To ensure success, you must prevent failure. Weinberg (Weinberg, 1993) has identified eight Fs—characteristics of people that cause failures: frailty, folly, fatuousness, fun, fraud, fanaticism, failure, and fate.

The first three deal with mistakes. *Frailty* simply means that people, especially project managers, make mistakes. Motivation and arm-twisting will not change this. If you are wise, you will accept this inevitability and prepare for it. Use inspections, reviews, or any visibility technique available so that people can catch each other's mistakes before they become expensive to fix. *Folly* means someone did what they intended, but the intention was wrong. This usually occurs when someone designs and builds a product well, but the requirements were wrong so the product was not what the customer wanted. *Fatuousness* is making the same mistake repeatedly without learning from it. Process improvement is the answer for this. It begins with measuring everything (as I describe later).

The next three Fs are about people trying to get attention. *Fun* is a person's attempt to joke around. This seems harmless, but, unfortunately, no one can predict what another person considers as "just having some fun." Talk to people. Give them the attention they deserve so that they will not feel the need to make jokes. *Fraud* is illegally extracting personal gain from a project. Some people steal, and that is a tragedy. A good work environment helps prevent fraud, and if it does occur, audits from the configuration management staff help catch it. *Fanaticism* is destroying something for revenge. It is a deliberate attempt to hurt someone. Again, create a good work environment and pay attention to people.

The last two Fs concern making excuses. *Failure* is when programmers blame the hardware for software errors. Hardware does fail and can fool people into thinking there are software errors, but this is about as rare as a total eclipse of the sun. If programmers suspect hardware problems, investigate with great care and professionalism. Software should check for hardware failures and deal with them. *Fate* is "bad luck." Whenever someone says bad luck, replace "luck" with "management." Unexpected events occur, which is why disciplined people practice risk management.

Reinforce healthy work principles. One tool I use to create and sustain a good work environment is the annual pizza lunch. I host a lunch (pizza is convenient, but anything will suffice) for those who work under me on the project. Superiors, with all due respect, are not invited.

I supply the food, but the attendees have to listen to me talk. After they've eaten most of the food, I present the principles for the workplace listed in Figure 4.1. These may change with time, but I have used the same list for several years.

The first principle emphasizes that *pleasant and productive* go hand in hand: we must produce *and* we must be pleasant. Trust means that I trust people to always tell me the truth. I will not doubt their word. If, however, I learn that someone has been less than completely honest, there will be problems. In *reading and writing,* my goal is to have people read professional software journals, books, and online discussion groups so that they can grow in ability and generate new ideas. Writing is a fundamental visibility technique. The *draw me a picture* principle emphasizes that the people working under me know more about what they are doing than I do. I need them to explain it to me

- Pleasant and productive
- Trust
- Reading and writing
- Draw me a picture
- I make mistakes

Figure 4.1 Principles for the workplace.

quickly and clearly, using whatever visibility technique is required. When I get to *I make mistakes*, I have everyone in the room stand and repeat the phrase. I say it with them as it applies to me as much to anyone. It may seem silly, but once that is said, everything else is much easier.

Systematically creating and maintaining a good workplace may seem like overkill to some. After all, people should know how to act at work and they should know what is expected of them. Unfortunately, that wasn't true even in the 1950s, let alone today. All of us are complex, and we each have our own values. The best way to cope with this unpredictability and complexity is to create an environment that fosters professionalism and open communication.

4.2   VISIBILITY: PROJECT CONTROL IN A SIMPLE EQUATION

Once you establish a plan for creating a good working environment, you should begin to look at ways to control individual projects. I learned a simple equation for project control:

$$control = plan + status + corrective\ action$$

A project must have a plan. Without it, chaos rules. I have seen intelligent, conscientious people attempt to manage a project without a plan. There is high stress, lots of waste, low productivity, and people get hurt mentally, emotionally, and financially.

In the late 1990s, people began pushing what became known as the agile development methods. Some even contrasted agile methods with plan-driven methods. Some people mistakenly perceived that having a plan was a bad thing to do. Planning is a cornerstone of agile methods. The plans do not cover as long a period of time, but they are still plans. People know what they are to do and can know what their colleagues are doing.

A project manager must be aware of the project's status. The plan tells where the project should be. Status tells where it actually is. Status comes from visibility—taking measurements and talking to people.

With a plan and current status, the project manager together with the project team can take one of three corrective actions: continue on the current course, change the plan and project, or cancel the project. The third choice is not pleasant, but it should be used more often than it is.

4.2.1   Collecting Status

Day by day during a project, you must observe and collect status. Sometimes, you will collect the information personally; other times, you will rely on others to report it. The goal is to collect status that indicates how the project is following the plan. To be usable, the status and observations must have three qualities (Weinberg, 1993):

1. *It must be available.* The people on the project must allow someone to see what they are doing.
2. *It must be visible.* The status collected must be presented in a format that lets people think about it.
3. *It must be undistorted.* The key status is not hidden among useless data.

The following sections describe how to collect status in light of these three qualities so that you can take action to keep the project on course. You must also be able to analyze what you have collected.

4.2.2   Collection Guidelines

Collecting status is a large, important, daily task that several groups share. The project manager collects soft status about the health of the people and the project. The CM staff collects official status on progress. The individual engineers and programmers report detailed status on process and tasks.

As project manager, you play a large role in collecting status. Talk to everyone. As discussed earlier, talk to people about various topics and talk to them in their office. Be sure to talk to the "hard to talk to" people. The larger the project and the more people on it, the more time you should spend with people. You should spend most of your day encouraging people. This is management by walking around. It tells people that they and what they are doing is important.

I gather information by asking each person three questions. Before discussing the questions, let's discuss a meta-question or what I call the "valid question." It is, "In order for this question to be valid, what must also be valid?" The answer to the valid question provides much more information than the answers to the direct questions. This might sound strange, but let's apply it to the three questions as we ask them.

The first question to ask is, "What are you doing today?" Now let's apply the valid question. For this question to be valid, the team member must (1) be doing something today and (2) be able to observe that he is doing something today. I have often found these two answers to the valid question to be false. For the first validity condition, there are days when people aren't doing anything. They may have completed their tasks and are waiting for further instructions from someone (like me). Maybe they are waiting for a product from someone else before they start their task, and that other person is out sick. These are important pieces of information. As for the second condition, many people do things that are valuable to a project, but don't realize it. This is because no one (like me) has explained the importance.

The second question to ask is, "What does the plan say you are supposed to be doing today?" For this question to be valid, (1) the project must have a plan and (2) the person must know how he fits in the plan. As above, these conditions are not always true. If the project does not have a plan, I need to gather the team and create one. If we have a plan but the person doesn't know how he fits into it, I haven't helped him observe it and I need to do that right now.

The third question to ask is, "If the answers to the first two questions don't match, why not?" This third question is the crucial one as it shows me the "difference that makes a difference." For this question to be valid, the person must be able to (1) observe differences and (2) reason about the differences. Once again, I do not always find these conditions to be true.

As for the first condition, as surprising as it may seem, people don't always realize that they are doing something that differs from the plan. On one project I monitored, the project manager was absent for one week for jury duty. When he returned, he learned that his team had done almost nothing per the plan. They had all worked hard during his absence and knew mentally that what they were doing was not in the plan. Nevertheless, it wasn't until the project manager return that they realized they had wasted a week.

As for the second condition, it requires an extra step for a person to understand why they are not working per the plan. Most people I know have plenty to do and don't spend time pondering "why" questions like this one. It is important, however, that they can answer this question in plain terms. Sometimes, the answer is obvious—the project is two months behind schedule and no one is doing what the plan says. At other times, the answer is not obvious but quite enlightening. For example, "I'm not working on my task because Dave is struggling and I am helping him," or, "I'm not working on my task because the configuration management system went down two days ago."

After I have spoken with everyone, I should know (1) what everyone is doing, (2) what everyone should be doing, and (3) if they are not working per the plan, why they aren't.

To gather information in this manner, you must call on your self-esteem. People will not always be anxious to talk to you. You will need confidence to accept occasional rejection. Do not grow weary and neglect the walking around and talking. The information and feelings collected during this time are crucial to the project's success. Do not excuse anyone from being available to view. Different authors use different expressions for this (going dark, disguising the smell). Most projects have someone whose work is critical to the project, but whose personality is such that people leave them alone. They are sensitive to scrutiny, like to be left alone, or work strange hours so no one sees them. They usually do excellent work, but do not let people see how they are doing until they are finished. Trouble occurs when no one checks on them for a month only to learn that they are a month behind schedule. Talk to everyone. Keep everything and everyone involved in the project visible.

A crucial task is to have people volunteer status on problems. No one likes to admit he's having trouble, but you must bring problems to the surface so that the project team can fix them. You are responsible for knowing about and applying resources to problems. This goes back to the environment of no fear that you created earlier. Everyone can admit to mistakes. You should tell people about your past mistakes and ask them to help you see your current ones. Such honest admissions relax people and reduce fear.

The CM staff collects the official status for the project. In Chapter 2, I described their role in collecting information for status accounting and audits. Their reports tell you how the project is progressing by focusing on the configuration items in the baselines. You will know that eight of the ten subsystems are finished because they are in the product areas of the disk system. You will know that half the delivered computers were sent back to the supplier because they failed their physical audits.

The individual engineers and programmers report status on process and tasks. They measure and record how many lines of code are in each subroutine and the time required to design, code, test, and fix each one. Each person reports this status through the person responsible for the subroutine. This may be a team leader, supervisor, technical lead, or the project manager himself. Omit the names of people when reporting metrics (more on metrics etiquette later).

Reviews, walkthroughs, and inspections. A must in software development is to look at a person's work before passing it along to another in the project. Whether you call them reviews, walkthroughs, or inspections, they are on everyone's best practices list. People who study these techniques carefully, debate the differences among these three practices. For convenience, I refer to all such practices as "inspections."

Finding and correcting mistakes are the most costly and time-consuming tasks in software. The sooner we find a mistake, the cheaper and faster it is to correct. Software is a people-intensive endeavor, and we all make mistakes. A different set of eyes picks up those mistakes more quickly. Inspections are the most cost-effective practice in software projects.

Some of the best work done with inspections comes from Tom Gilb and Dorothy Graham (Gilb & Graham, 1993). Figure 4.2 shows Gilb and Graham's general process, which begins when a *producer* has a *product* to review. This product can be a document, design, source code, and so on. The inspection leader performs the *entry* task. This is a quick inspection of the product to ensure that it passes basic tests. If it does not, it is sent back to the producer to avoid wasting the time of several inspectors.

Once the product enters the process, the inspection leader *plans* the inspection. Each step of the inspection process can be performed in several ways. The leader tailors the process for the situation.

The inspection leader gathers the participants and materials for the first time at the *kickoff* meeting. He assigns roles, states the schedules, and ensures that everyone knows what is expected of them. Nothing is assumed; everything is stated specifically.

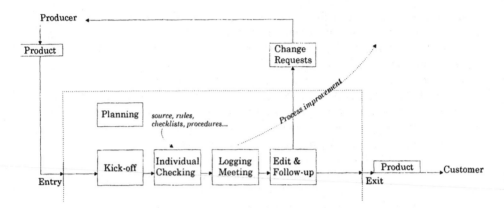

Figure 4.2   An inspection process.

The *individual checking* box in the figure is where the inspectors pore over the product in minute detail using rules, checklists, and procedures as guidance. This guiding material is essential. Consult books on programming (documentation, design, and so on) to glean the appropriate checklists. Inspectors cannot say "I don't like the way you did this." They must say "This construct violates programming guideline 23." If it is a bad construct not mentioned in the programming guideline, change the guideline.

Critical to Gilb and Graham's method is the review speed. They recommend starting at one page per hour. Let me repeat: *one* page per hour. That sounds incredibly slow, and may even be too slow, but pay attention to the review rate. Record the rates, how many errors are found, and how many errors slip through the inspection to later stages. Adjust the rate according to the measured data. Do not leave this to chance.

The *logging meeting* gathers everyone together again. It records all the issues found during individual checking. The issues are not errors yet. The group inevitably finds new issues while individuals read off the issues they found. The group also discusses the product in light of the process and guidelines used to inspect it. They record suggestions for improvement and pass them to the inspection leader for future use.

An editor—usually the person who produced the product in the first place—examines the issues produced by the logging meeting in the *edit and follow-up* step. Often, the issues are misunderstandings. The editor can clarify these issues immediately. If the issue is an error, the editor sends a change request to the producer. The inspection leader performs the follow-up step. He checks the editor's work to ensure that all issues have either been clarified or sent back as change requests.

If the inspection process produces *change requests*, the producer must work these. After the rework, the process begins again. If no change requests come out of the edit and follow-up step, the inspection leader performs the *exit* step. He ensures the inspection process was complete and correct. The product, even though not perfect, will have acceptable quality. The inspection process will produce all the required forms, data, inspection rates, and so on.

Gilb and Graham's inspection process may seem too bureaucratic and time-consuming, but it works. Your organization may not be able to jump into such an inspection process. Change takes time, so start slowly and build up, but start. Inspections save time in the long run.

A side benefit, and possibly the best benefit, of inspections is that the participants learn (Weinberg, 2003). Weinberg once did an experiment in a class regarding the number of errors students made in programming assignments. He found that students who came from organizations where inspections were a common practice made far fewer mistakes than other students. He felt that one year of working in an environment with inspections was worth three years experience otherwise.

What to collect? The key question in collecting status is "what should you collect?" This haunts everyone involved in software metrics. What are the one or two things we should focus our attention on? The current best answer is that it is not possible to focus on one or two things. In the guidelines I offer here, there are closer to a dozen items to collect. The basic rule is to collect status that indicates how well the project is following the plan. The plan lays out a network of tasks that build and combine products to yield a final product that satisfies the customer. Determine if the project is healthy (on plan). The I/O subsystem was supposed to finish coding last week and move into testing this week. Did it? Is it ahead of schedule? Is it above cost? Have tasks taken longer than planned? Will the final product be a month late? Will it cost more or less than budgeted? Will you need to ask your management for more people?

Figure 4.3 lists the most frequent sources of risk (described in more detail in Chapter 7 on risk management). These can kill a project. Look for anything that will indicate that a risk on this list is about to become a problem. The risk analysis produced the indicators. Watch for them.

- Personnel shortfalls
- Unrealistic schedules and budgets
- Developing the wrong software functions
- Developing the wrong user interface
- Gold plating (paying too much attention to what the customer wants changed)
- Continuing stream of requirements changes
- Shortfalls in externally furnished components
- Real-time performance shortfalls
- Straining computer science capabilities

Figure 4.3 Most frequent sources of risk.

Collect status that indicates real progress on the final product. I once attended a meeting in which a group of experienced project managers was advising a younger colleague. The younger project manager was attempting to monitor an outside software contractor. One elder adviser recommended asking the contractor every day for the number of debugged lines of code. Why did he advise that? Surely he knew about GUI builders, object-orientation, milestones, and everything else. The answer is simple. That piece of status was a direct indication of progress on the final product. What the more experienced manager was advising is to cut through all the useless management status available and get to the point—the product. The point in your project may not be debugged lines of code, but find out whatever it is and concentrate on it.

Another guideline is to collect and measure everything—well, almost everything. When someone who has never measured anything starts collecting status, it seems as if they are measuring everything. Watts Humphrey's Personal Software Process (PSP) (Humphrey, 1995) gives an excellent example. Recall the words of Capers Jones (Jones, 1996): "The number one root cause of cancellations, schedule slippages, and cost overruns is the chronic failure of the software industry to collect accurate historic data for ongoing and completed projects."

Collect status on who did what and when. "Who" is the person who did something. Collect the title of the person and their cost to the organization (total compensation), *but not their name.* Among Robert Grady's collection of metrics etiquette (Grady, 1992) is the fundamental policy of keeping individuals out of metrics. The purpose of status and metrics is to help the project, not to review individual performance. If people believe that metrics and status are collected to measure their individual performance (salary review, demotion, firing), they will alter the data or not participate.

"What" is the product. A product has a name, size, and function in the project. Measure the size consistently. Humphrey advocates counting lines of code. Others advocate function points or GUI screens, HTML pages, or other common items in a software product. Use what works for your organization. Write standards to guide measurement and apply them consistently across projects.

"When" is time and timing. How much time did the person use to make the product? In what phase of the project did this occur? What was the total time required to design, inspect, code, inspect again, test, fix, and integrate a subroutine?

Pay special attention to errors. I agree with the statement by Capers Jones: "Finding and fixing bugs is the most expensive and time-consuming aspect of software development, especially for large systems" (Jones, 1996). Record how many errors occurred, when they were made, what type of person made them, when they were found, how much time was needed to find them, and how much time was needed to fix them. The purpose is to discover how and when errors occur and how to catch them earlier or prevent them. Focusing on errors is the root of substantial process improvement.

All these measurements will give you the cost per product and point to how you can reduce that cost. Work and time are not free; they cost the business enterprise money. How much does one line of code, one GUI screen, or one page of documentation cost? Why does it cost so much? How can we make better products at a lower cost?

Use the goal, question, metric (GQM) paradigm (Basili & Weiss, 1984) to help in collecting status:

- *Start with a set of goals* for the project (reduce cost, improve quality).
- *Create a set of questions* that indicate if the project is reaching those goals (How much did functions cost on this project? How much did they cost on the last project? How many errors were released on the last project? On this project?)
- *Measure the items* that will answer those questions (who did what when). Do not ask your people to collect and report status without explaining why the project and the organization need it.

Figure 4.4 summarizes the status to collect day by day during a project. The *task status* relates to the tasks you and the team created during the planning stage of the product development cycle (more on this later) The task name, group (not individual) responsible for performing it, and the planned dates, hours, and cost for it are from the plan. Collect status on the actual dates, hours, and cost to complete the task. *Product status* for is about the products or results of the tasks from the plan. The product name, task name to produce it, and planned size and cost are from the plan. Collect status on the product's actual size and cost. *People status* for is a log completed by each individual (no

Task Status

Task Name	Responsible Group	Start-Stop Dates Planned/Actual	Man Hours Planned/Actual	Cost Planned/Actual

Product Status

Product Name	Task Name	Product Size Planned/Actual	Product Cost Planned/Actual

People Status

Date	Salary Class	Time	Task Name

Error Status

Committed in Task	Discovered in Task	Time to Fix	Cost to Fix	Description

Figure 4.4 Status types to collect.

names) each day of the project. The individual fills in the date, their salary class (used to calculate cost), and the amount of time (minutes) they worked on a task. The *error status* focuses on costly errors. Collect the task in which each error was committed and found, the time and cost to fix it, and a description of the error.

These measures are one way of collecting information on the four basics espoused by Putnam and Myers in their book (Putnam & Myers, 1992) and other places. These basics are (1) size, (2) effort, (3) quality, and (4) schedule. The "size" is the size of the product in lines of code, function points, or whatever makes sense. The "effort" is the man-hours needed to build the product. The "quality" is a measure of defects or customer satisfaction, and the "schedule" is the calendar time needed to build the product.

I find these four measures are adequate for tracking a software project. My experience with metrics puzzles me. When I try to introduce metrics to a project, most people shy away because they think the metrics will take too much time and effort. I try to introduce simple methods to collect information in the four areas listed above. Once people see these, they try to inject a dozen more pieces of information they want to collect.

I encourage people to collect metrics in a simple manner (Phillips, 1999). Tack a large spreadsheet to a wall in the management information center (see later—a place where the people on the project gather frequently). Figure 4.5 shows a sample spreadsheet. As the project manager, enter the names of the tasks and the estimated values. Have the people on the project pencil in the other values as the events occur. It takes about five minutes for someone to enter information for the project.

The above spreadsheet method is simple and works well, but is not perfect. It is an uncomfortable and difficult task for people to collect metrics. Dave Smith (Smith, xxxx) describes an interesting experiment he did with metrics. Smith collected metrics on himself and noted how he felt and acted while doing so. (I have done a similar experiment with myself and I encourage readers to do the same). He noticed that the data he collected were not complete. He also started to notice how the data could be used against him if attacking him personally was someone's goal. The pure numbers did not always tell the entire story. He kept notes along with the numbers to explain what was happening and why he thought the numbers appeared as they did. There was a great temptation to "fix" the numbers.

Such "fixing" of numbers is also known as cheating. People may try to cheat with their metrics. Such cheating is a loud message to you and your upper management that there is something terribly wrong in your organization. A metrics program, when used properly, is a tool for discovering the current situation and helping to improve it. These processes serve the business and the people who work for the business. Everyone should understand this, and the best way for that to happen is for managers to state clearly what we are to measure and why. If people see a metric as a potential problem, they must stand up and say so.

Task	Size of Product		Man-Hours		Errors		Start		End	
	Estimated	Actual	Estimated	Actual	Found	Corrected	Estimated Date	Actual Date	Estimated Date	Actual Date

Figure 4.5 A metrics-collecting spreadsheet.

4.2.3 Making Status Visible and Undistorted

Halfway between collecting status and analyzing the situation is making the status visible by plotting it. Plots are crucial for analysis because they transform numbers into information. They fulfill the second and third qualities of observations I gave earlier because the status can be visualized and is undistorted. Plots help the project manager and everyone else see the status better and think about it more clearly.

Many of the plots I describe below show the plan and the status (actual condition) together. The current status is necessary but not sufficient. It must be shown in light of the plan. The two together show the difference, and the difference is what permits corrective action. Some of the plots also project the actual into the future. This is the best guess of how the project will finish without corrective action.

The *management information center* is a room designated for displaying all the plots and charts that make the project status visible. Make and keep all the status public—no secrets. The purpose is not to embarrass those who are behind, but rather to bring available resources to those who need them. Again, your working environment is crucial: Everyone makes mistakes, admits this publicly, accepts help today, and lends help tomorrow.

Update the top-risks list. If a risk has passed, delete it. Risks can change. The project team learns as the project progresses. Tasks that seemed difficult can become easier and those that seemed easy can become more difficult. The probability of a risk becoming a problem can change. Update the probabilities and consequences of the risks on the list. Think about the risk aversion strategies and change them if necessary.

Management information center. Figure 4.6 shows a management information center (MIC) (and yes, people will add "KEY MOUSE" at the end of the

Figure 4.6   A typical management information center.

acronym). The MIC, reminiscent of a control center or war room in old movies, displays the charts and diagrams produced in the project. The project manager and the CM staff should do this. If the project is large enough, there will be a MIC staff and they can do the updating.

The size and number of charts and diagrams are limited only by the size of the walls. Mistakes in different parts of the project are obvious when those parts are displayed in a MIC. There are no illusions. When someone finds a mistake, everyone sees it and works to correct it. Establish a procedure for people to flag errors on the MIC displays.

The diagrams, charts, and documents in the MIC point to detailed versions of the information stored on computers. Place a public access terminal in the MIC. When a chart in the MIC spurs a debate, the people involved should be able to find the information on-line without leaving the MIC. If the project and the MIC are large enough, it is good to have a full-time MIC librarian to assist searches.

Always put the MIC where the project personnel are and make it as comfortable as possible so that they will visit it often (at least once a day). Putting the MIC in the building where the managers are defeats the purpose. Place a coffeepot, microwave, refrigerator (full of free drinks and snacks), magazine racks, and so on in the MIC. Hold short, stand-up meetings in the MIC. Frequent the MIC and have the project personnel do the same.

Many projects today use teams of people that are dispersed physically and connected electronically. This is not a good situation, but people have learned to work with it (see Section on 4.2.9). One way to have an electronic version of a MIC is to create a project web page (McConnell, 1997). The project web page helps keep people in touch and helps ensure that everyone is reading the same versions of a project's documents.

Types of charts. The first examples of visible status are the basic management indicators in the Gantt and network of tasks charts. Figure 4.7 shows the schedule status in a Gantt chart. The task name is to the left and the time the task requires is shown in bars under the months to the right. The solid line is the original plan; the dotted line under it is the actual time required. The vertical line at the start of March shows today. The "Test Routine X" task should be finished, but because of overruns in other tasks it has yet to start. The dots extend the remaining tasks to a projected completion date. This is several weeks later than planned. The network of tasks in Figure 4.8 shows the same information but emphasizes the relationships among tasks (what task must finish before another can begin) as opposed to a strictly calendar view. Both charts are necessary because neither shows everything. These charts show everyone how the project is progressing relative to the plan. No one will be surprised on the delivery date when they are told the project will take another two weeks.

Figure 4.9 shows a size status chart, which compares each software unit's planned size to the actual size when completed. Each point plotted (X's) is

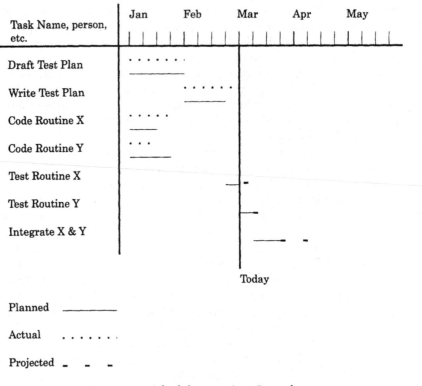

Figure 4.7   Schedule status in a Gantt chart.

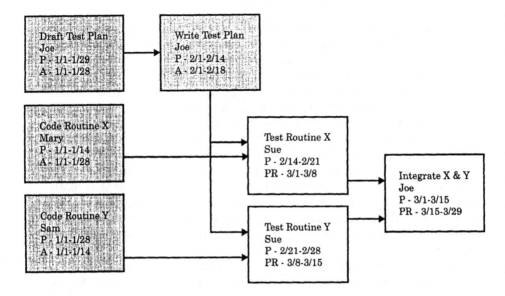

Figure 4.8   A network of tasks chart during a project.

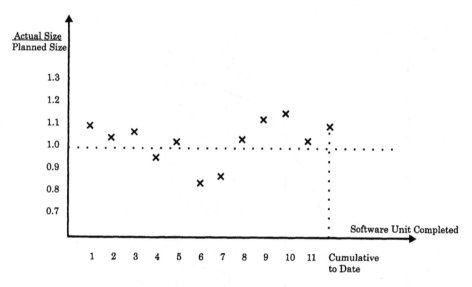

Figure 4.9   Software size status.

the ratio of actual to planned size. Values greater than one (above the dotted line) indicate units that are larger than planned. The cumulative to date value (right side) indicates the actual-to-planned ratio for all software completed. Here, it is 1.15, which means that so far the software is 15% larger than planned. You can reasonably conclude that the remaining software will also be 15% bigger and the schedule will be at least 15% longer than planned. You must now decide if this is acceptable, or if the team should act now to correct it.

Figure 4.10 shows the cumulative project cost. Here the idea is to see the trends of the two curves. The planned curve is derived from the project plan. The shape of the two curves is typical of most projects. Spending is gradual at first, increases sharply during the main coding and testing activities, and slows near product delivery. The dotted line (Actual) shows the actual spending as gathered day by day. The coarser dotted line (Projected) shows what spending is expected after the current time. In this example, actual spending is greater than that planned up to today.

People often act as if they will bring spending under control. This ignores reality, which is that the trend identified early on will probably continue. The spending trend to date indicates that insufficient funds were planned. If the funding is insufficient today, why should it be fine for the rest of the project? Trends continue on projects unless people take drastic action. Is the trend in the chart acceptable or should the team act now? Whatever the decision, everyone can see what is happening and what will happen without corrective action.

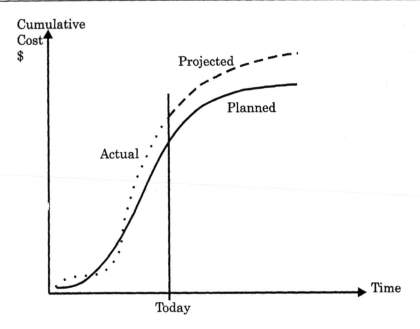

Figure 4.10   Cumulative cost of the project.

Figure 4.11 gives another perspective on the cost. It is similar to Figure 4.10 because it compares the actual cost of a completed task to the planned cost. However, Figure 4.11 provides new information because a product's actual and planned sizes can be the same whereas the task's actual cost can be twice what was planned. If the actual cost of all tasks completed to date is 15% higher than planned, the cost of the remaining tasks will probably at least 15% higher than planned.

Figures 4.12 and 4.13 show the staffing status. The Plan line is based on the staffing plan derived (described in detail in Chapter 6). The dotted line (Actual) shows the actual staffing to date; the coarser dotted line (Projected) shows it projected to the end of the project. This project will be six weeks late because of a people shortage. Figure 4.13 gives a different perspective on staffing. This Rayleigh curve (described in detail in Chapter 6) is for a larger project. The bars show the planned staffing, and the X's show the actual. The curves represent the upper and lower control limits on staffing. This staffing chart is appropriate for large projects. Upper and lower control limits are important on large projects because of the magnitude of risk. In a small project, if a seven-person, 17-week project is six weeks late, that is a problem. In a large project, if a 200-person, 100-week project is late, that is a multi-million-dollar problem. The magnitude of risk is much different. The project manager of a large project must watch staffing closely and inform upper management

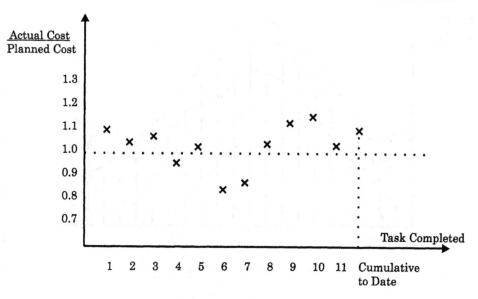

Figure 4.11 Cost status.

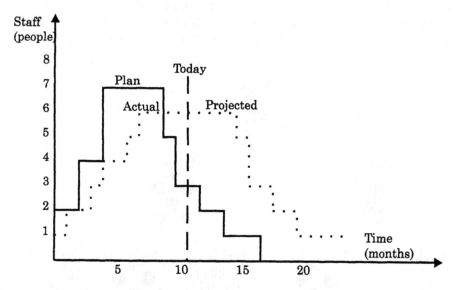

Figure 4.12 Staffing status 1.

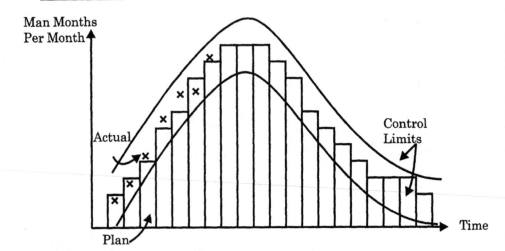

Figure 4.13   Staffing status 2.

if it falls outside the control limits. The project is in grave trouble if the actual staffing goes outside either limit.

Another method for tracking progress on the product is by showing the state of a product in a picture (Tackett & Van Doren, 1999). Figure 4.14 illustrates how this works. The figure shows eight circles that represent eight software modules in a system. Each module is filled with a different pattern that indicates its state. The four circles at the bottom of the figure show the legend

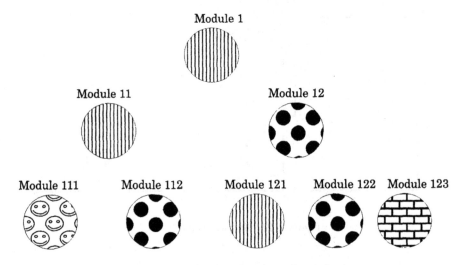

Figure 4.14   Showing the state of a product.

for the fill patterns. (I prefer using colors to indicate the states, but this book is not published in color, so we must use fill patterns.) A quick glance at the figure shows that one of the modules (Module 111 on the lower left) has completed all four states and is finished. Three of the modules have completed three of the states, three of the modules have completed two states, and one module has only completed the first state. This type of chart gives people a quick feel for how far along the product is in its development. If the chart has lots of smiley faces (or green circles), the product is nearing completion. I used such a chart for many months on a large project that had several hundred modules. The gradual change of color in the chart showed us that we were making progress.

Earned Value Tracking. Earned value tracking (EVT) is an important management tool for tracking progress and predicting the completion of a project. You can create an EVT plot from the project plan and update it with status gathered during the project. Let us first look at a simple use of EVT in which it helps predict the project's completion early on. To perform EVT, you assign a value to each task in the planned network of tasks. Suppose a project has 500 hours in its plan and Task 1 is planned to take five hours, or 1%, of that. When task 1 is finished, the project has earned 1% of its total value.

If a task is half finished, the project has earned nothing; there is no such thing as a partial credit. This forces people to complete tasks (products) instead of starting several tasks (products) and finishing none. One of the worst situations is to be half finished on all subroutines. Nothing is done, and nothing works.

EVT links completed tasks with products. A task is not finished until its product is inspected and approved. When the five-hour task is completed, the project has a product that is useful for the remainder of the project.

Creating an EVT plot starts with the project plan (see Chapter 6). You then add the time—say, days—for all tasks in the plan. Assign each task its percentage of the total time so that the sum of all tasks equals 100%. At the end of day one, determine how many tasks should be completed. Add the percentages of those tasks and plot that level. Continue through the project plan until you reach the 100% level—the end of the project.

Figure 4.15 illustrates this process with a simple 10-task project. The top part of the figure is a table of tasks showing the days required for each. The project has 50 days total, so a one-day task earns 2%. The two rightmost columns show the points to plot. The lower part of the figure is the EVT plot for this project. It shows how much value the project has earned on any day. Notice that the project is not planned to earn any additional value between days 11 and 21. This example assumes the 10 tasks are performed sequentially (a one-person project). Most projects involve more people, with tasks being performed in parallel, but the EVT plotting process is the same, as will be shown in later examples.

Task	Days Required	% Earned Value	Day Cumulative	% Cumulative
1	2	4	2	4
2	5	10	7	14
3	4	8	11	22
4	10	20	21	42
5	5	10	26	52
6	3	6	29	58
7	10	20	39	78
8	8	16	47	94
9	2	4	49	98
10	1	2	50	100

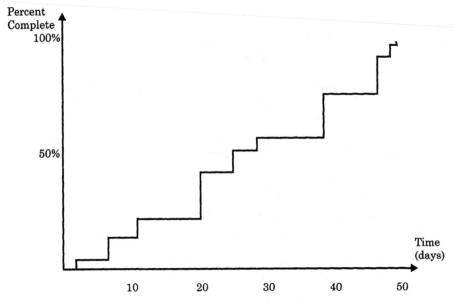

Figure 4.15 Earned value tracking example.

EVT is an excellent tool for realistically predicting project completion. If the first few tasks take 30% longer than planned, EVT assumes the remaining tasks will take at least 30% longer than planned. EVT helps curb overly optimistic project managers who hope to make up for lost time later. Their reasoning is that, although the project had a slow start, things are really moving now. More often than not, however, their optimism is unjustified. If a project is moving slower than planned, why would it suddenly pick up speed? Why would problems go away? Being behind schedule indicates something that is a strong characteristic of or influence on the group (lack of process, technology, expertise, and so on). That something will not go away in a day. It can go away slowly with much hard work, but it will keep the current project on its current pace.

Figures 4.16 and 4.17 are two examples of how to use EVT plots to predict project completion. Figure 4.16 shows the EVT levels from the project plan in solid lines. A dotted stair-step line shows the actual EVT. The project is behind schedule because the earned value for any date is less than planned. The light line curving through the actual earned value and extending out to the 100% level is the projected finish, which is much later than the planned finish. Notice how you can predict the planned finish after only two or three actual points on the plot. In contrast, Figure 4.17 shows a project ahead of schedule, where the actual earned value is higher than planned.

EVT forces the project manager to know which tasks are 100% completed and compare them to when they should be completed. With an EVT plot, everyone can see where the project completion is heading. There are no secrets. With these early indications, the project manager has a clear mandate to act early.

The preceding discussion of EVT is adequate when everyone on the project earns the same per-hour salary or when cost is not an important factor. The following discussion takes into account costs and other factors. Please refer to Fleming and Koppelman (2000) for more details.

Let us first define a few terms. The value of a task is the cost to complete it. For example, if a person works 20 hours on a task and is paid $50 per hour,

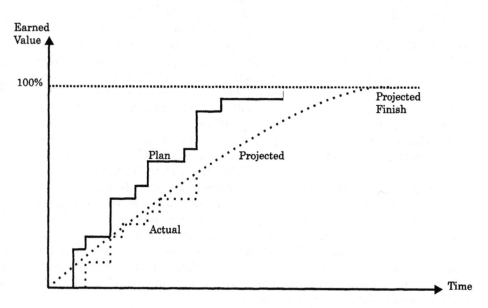

Figure 4.16   Earned value tracking to predict project completion—Plot 1: project behind schedule.

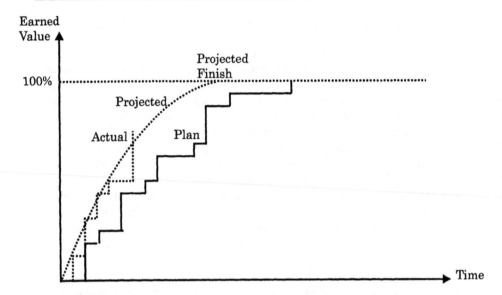

Figure 4.17 Earned value tracking to predict project completion—Plot 2: project ahead of schedule.

the value of that task is $1,000. When planning the task, we state that the planned value of that task is $1,000. When the task is finished, we have earned the value in the task, so its earned value is $1,000. If the person actually worked 30 hours to complete the task, the actual cost was $1,500 (the earned value is still $1,000). In another case, we employed a higher-paid person to do the task. For example, we might have employed a person working for $80 an hour to do the task. If that person completed the task in 20 hours, the actual cost for the task would be $1,600 (the earned value is still $1,000).

There are two ratios used in EVT to indicate the status of a project. The first is the cost performance index or CPI. The CPI indicates how well the project is doing relative to money. The CPI equals the earned value to date divided by the actual costs to date. If a task has an earned value of $1,000 and its actual cost was $1,200, its CPI is $1,000/$1,200 = 0.83. This is a bad situation, as the actual cost is more than the Earned Value. We want CPI to be 1.0 or greater.

The second ratio of EVT is the schedule performance index or SPI. The SPI indicates how well the project is doing relative to schedule. The SPI equals the earned value divided by the planned value. If at a point in the project, the total the earned value is $8,000 (we have completed eight tasks) but the planned value is $10,000 (ten sample tasks planned), the SPI is $8,000/$10,000 = 0.8. This is a bad situation, as we are behind schedule (only eight tasks finished instead of ten as planned).

The following figures illustrate these ideas with the basic EVT plots. Figure 4.18 is an EVT plot for a project that is behind schedule and over cost. The

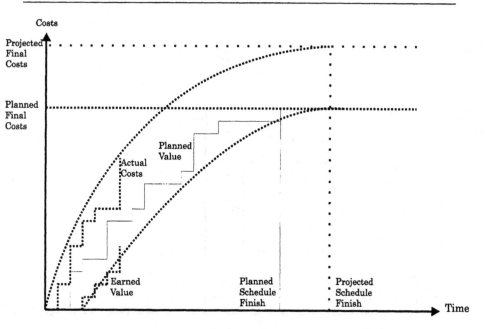

Figure 4.18 The EVT plot of a project that is behind schedule and above cost.

earned value line is below the planned value line (the SPI is less than 1.0). This shows that we are behind schedule. The actual costs line is above the earned value line (the CPI is less than 1.0), and this shows that we are above cost. Notice how the dotted line extrapolates the earned value line until it intersects with the planned final costs line. This shows the projected schedule finish—we will finish late. Now notice how the actual costs line extrapolates out to where it intersects the project schedule finish line. This shows the projected final costs of the project—far above the planned final costs.

Figures 4.19 and 4.20 show how we can use the EVT plot to calculate the cost and schedule variances in time and money. Figure 4.19 is a repeat of Figure 4.18 with these variances indicated. The cost variance is simply the delta between the actual costs and earned value lines. The schedule variance is the delta between the planned value and earned value lines. Notice how we are calculating a schedule variance in terms of money. This indicates how much money the project manager might need to add to the project to compensate for the schedule problem.

Figure 4.20 is a repeat of Figure 4.18 with the variances indicated in time. Given today's earned value point, the schedule variance in time is the difference between the earned value point and the same time number on the planned value plot. It makes sense to calculate schedule variance in time, and this shows how far behind schedule the project is. Now let us calculate cost variance in time. Given today's actual costs point, the variance is the differ-

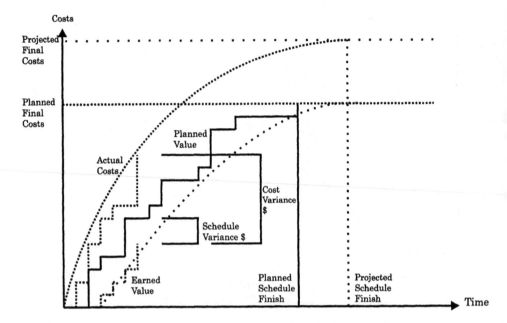

Figure 4.19 Calculating the cost and schedule variances in dollars.

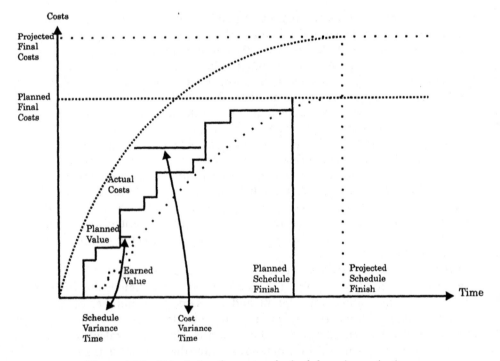

Figure 4.20 Calculating the cost and schedule variances in time.

ence between the actual costs point and the same number on the planned value plot. This shows the project manager how much time has been expended by spending more money than planned.

Figure 4.21 shows the EVT plot of a project that is the opposite case of the previous three plots. This project is ahead of schedule and running under cost. Notice how the earned value line is above the planned value line (the CPI is greater than 1.0). Also notice how the earned value line is above the actual costs line (SPI greater than 1.0). Extrapolate the earned value and actual costs lines like in Figure 4.18 to find the projected schedule finish and the projected final costs. These are less than the planned schedule finish and the planned final costs.

Requirements Tracking. The CM staff and the project manager need to track the growth of requirements. Figure 4.22 shows a simple chart for this task. In large projects, requirements usually grow at a rate of 1% per month (Jones, 1996). The requirements stability chart shows a line that starts at the initial number of requirements and grows at this rate. The X's plot the actual growth of requirements. If the X's are above the line, as in this example, you should act now to bring requirements growth back under control. The CM staff tracks the growth of requirements in the functional baseline. The functional baseline Configuration Control Board approves all changes to the baseline. (See Chapter 2 and Appendix B for a description of CCBs and baselines.) Given the CCB, the CM staff, and the baseline, no one should ever be surprised by a rampant growth in requirements.

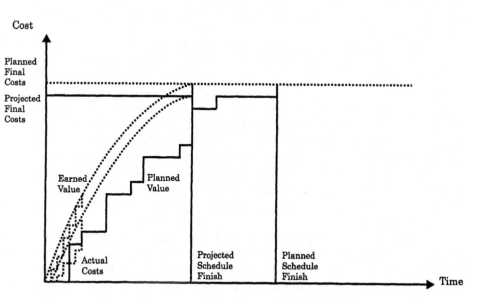

Figure 4.21 The EVT plot of a project that is ahead of schedule and under cost.

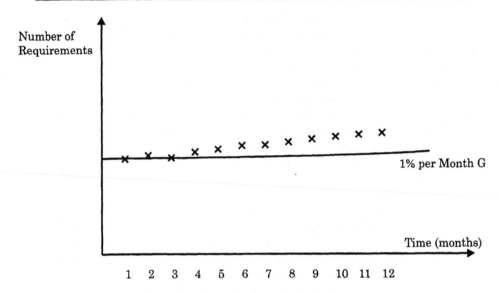

Figure 4.22   Requirements stability.

Environment. The final set of status plots indicates the project's environment. Earlier in this chapter, I emphasized the need to create and sustain a healthy environment for the people on the project. The tools for evaluating environment are slip and lead charts (Weinberg, 1993). You can create these charts from the product's announced delivery dates for almost any public company or government organization. (It is interesting to do these for political promises, too.)

A slip equals the newly announced delivery date minus the previously announced one. Slips are almost always a positive number, but can be negative if the product is shipping early. Figure 4.23 shows a slip chart based on days, but any time unit works. The horizontal axis is the date the organization makes an announcement about product delivery. The vertical axis is the delivery date announced, which here is day 200. The lighter line is the progression of slips. On day 100, the organization slipped the delivery date to day 230. On day 240, they slipped the delivery date to day 260. The product shipped on day 280.

The baseline is a set of points at which the announcement date equals the delivery date. The project finishes when the two lines intersect. The two lines should grow closer with time. If they run parallel or start to separate, the project will never finish.

Figure 4.24 shows the slip-lead data taken from Figure 4.23. The lead is the difference between the previously announced delivery date and the date the new delivery date was announced. The final two columns of the table show the slips and leads for the project in Figure 4.23. Figure 4.25 plots the slips versus the leads in a slip-lead chart.

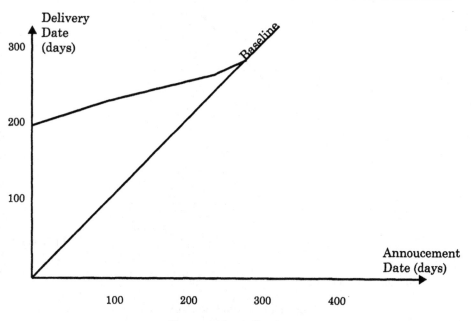

Figure 4.23 A slip chart.

In the slip-lead chart, the baseline shows where the slips equal the leads. Leads greater than slips (below the baseline) or equal to slips (on the baseline) indicate a relatively good environment. In a sick environment, the slip is much greater than the lead (points would be above the baseline). An organization that announces a 50-day slip on day 199 of a 200-day project has a lead of 1 and a slip of 50. This indicates either that no one was paying attention to status or that someone was lying about it. Either way, the work environment definitely needs fixing.

Too many points on the slip-lead chart also indicate trouble. If a project continues to slip, chances are the managers are replanning the project weekly. They are simply not thinking it through.

Announcement Date	Delivery Date	Slip	Lead
0	200	.	.
100	230	30	100
200	250	20	30
240	260	10	10
280	280	20	20

Figure 4.24 Slip-lead data from Figure 4.23.

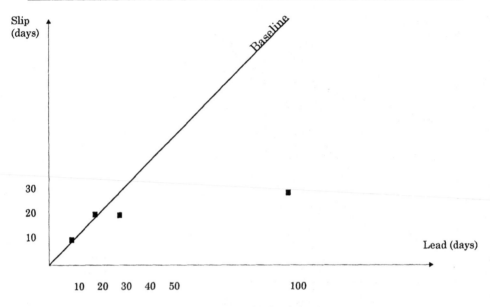

Figure 4.25   A slip-lead chart.

Figures 4.26 and 4.27 show the slip-lead data for the first version of Microsoft Word for Windows (McConnell, 1996). The project was initially declared to be a one-year effort but eventually lasted five years. Microsoft announced over a dozen delivery dates before finally marketing the product.

In Figure 4.26, note how the slope of the line approaching the baseline changes little during five years. A person could predict the actual delivery given the first three points. In Figure 4.27, the slip-lead chart, many points are above the baseline, including a negative lead point that indicates a new delivery date was announced after the previous one had passed.

Microsoft is only one example. Many organizations have projects with charts like these.

Storing what you collect. A basic visibility tool is the *unit development folder* (UDF)—a physical container that holds everything relevant to a software unit. The software unit can be a single subroutine or an entire system, depending on the project. The physical container can be a standard manila office folder, a three-ring binder, or even a shoebox. I prefer three-ring binders because they are sturdy, store well, can hold all the paper printouts, and can accommodate magnetic media with inserts. Notice that I refer to paper. People need hardware and software to view magnetic media. Paper, with all it faults, requires only that you take the time to review it. Therefore, I recommend including paper and magnetic media.

A UDF tells what the unit is, its origin, its reason for existing, how it fits in the software, how it works, and how we will know when it works correctly. If

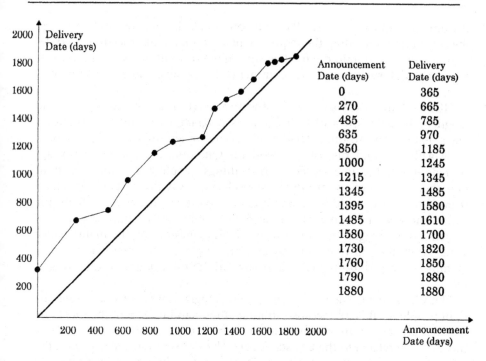

Announcement Date (days)	Delivery Date (days)
0	365
270	665
485	785
635	970
850	1185
1000	1245
1215	1345
1345	1485
1395	1580
1485	1610
1580	1700
1730	1820
1760	1850
1790	1880
1880	1880

Figure 4.26   The slip chart for Microsoft's Word for Windows 1.0.

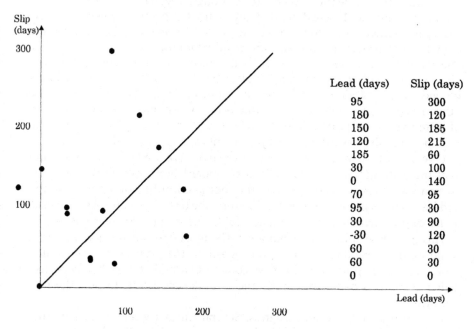

Lead (days)	Slip (days)
95	300
180	120
150	185
120	215
185	60
30	100
0	140
70	95
95	30
30	90
-30	120
60	30
60	30
0	0

Figure 4.27   The slip-lead chart for Microsoft's Word for Windows 1.0.

the unit is a subroutine, the UDF will contain all the material that preceded the subroutine, including the requirements, test plan and procedure, and design. It will also contain the final version of the subroutine itself and postcreation material, such as reviewer comments, test results, and any documentation.

UDFs enhance the visibility of software at work. The software is no longer magnetic blotches on a disk. It becomes diagrams, sketches, explanations, dates, names, and so on. A UDF gives people something to spread out on a table, gather around, discuss, and work on. Questions and speculation disappear along with the time wasted on those things. People stop mumbling about how they thought of a subroutine last week and a way to test it and how it all seemed to be a good idea at the time, but now that idea escapes them. Joe would know what they meant, but he left the company two months ago.

Perhaps the biggest benefit of using UDFs comes during the maintenance years. When the software unit's creators are long gone, the maintenance programmers can pick up the UDF and have all the information at their fingertips.

The CM staff can also help with UDFs. Programmers are not always the right people for this job because although they stand to benefit the most, the benefits are not immediately evident. Creating and maintaining UDFs is more closely related to the CM staff's role. The CM staff must also protect the UDFs from being lost or damaged. There is a fine line between protecting UDFs and preventing anyone from using them. Walk this line carefully.

I cannot emphasize the value of UDFs enough. If you cannot use any of the visibility techniques I have described, use UDFs. On my first project as project manager, I entered after the project had started. Several people were porting digital signal processing software from minicomputers to supercomputers. The software was divided into individual Fortran programs called primitives. There was no project management in place. The individual programmers were individuals acting alone. Each moved primitives from one machine to the other in whatever way he saw fit for that primitive on that day. Each had a list of primitives to be ported, and they checked them off as they ported them. Each person's list was different. As you might expect, chaos ruled.

One of my first actions was to establish UDFs. We used manila folders and kept them in alphabetical order in a cardboard box. Each folder held the Fortran source code, a description of the code and how it worked, a test script, and instructions on how to run and interpret the test. We created a single master list of primitives to port and made a folder for each primitive we ported.

This gave us visibility in several ways. The most basic visibility was that we could hold the product in our hands. Many of the primitives were similar. When we were to port a primitive, we could find a similar one already ported, gather around its paperwork, and quickly understand how to port the new primitive.

We could also gauge our progress. Several times a week we put another folder in the box when we finished porting a primitive. The box gradually filled up with folders. It was a big day when we had to get a second box. This gave us visibility with upper management. When they understood what the UDF box represented, they could answer their own "how's it going?" questions immediately. They could count the folders to see progress and read the labels to know what functions the supercomputer system had.

Make no mistake. The transition was not easy. The programmers were not enthusiastic, even in the face of these benefits. They saw UDFs only as extra paperwork they had to do when they finished their real work. We did not have a CM staff to help us, so it was up to me to help and encourage the programmers. However, just two years later, the UDFs saved us. We had to port the primitives to another supercomputer. Even with a small software group and low turnover, and only two years later, we had a completely different group of programmers on the second porting job. The UDF boxes were invaluable. The folders explained each primitive, how it was ported before, and how to test it. The second porting was much easier, quicker, and less expensive. Again, saving money at work is not just for charts on the year-end summary. Saving money saves jobs and helps people.

4.2.4 Analyzing the Situation

The project is in progress; people are working; a plan and status are available; plans, status and projections are plotted for everyone to see. It is now time to sit down and just think about the project. Mark it as meetings with yourself or someone who does not exist, but reserve those hours. Programmers think about code, designers think about designs, and nobody considers that a waste of time. It is logical that the project manager should think about the project.

Visit the MIC daily. If the MIC and the work environment are good, other people will gather there to talk. Look at all the displays and listen to what others are saying when they look at them. Think and plan ahead.

At least once a day, ask yourself "Should we kill this project?" This will help you to think about serious issues. What are the risks and benefits? Has its environment changed since you started? Should the project change course because of outside events? Look back at the goals, policies, and strategies in the planning documents (Chapters 5 and 6 describe these documents). Is the project still in line with these big ideas? Did you and the team get so busy you forgot something obvious?

Hold a retrospective (see below) during the project, not just at the end. Each milestone is a good time for this reflection. What went wrong? What went right? Why? What was wasteful? Where were errors introduced? What will prevent them in the future? Do past problems influence the top-risks list? Should the risks be reevaluated?

Thinking will generate conclusions. Weinberg recommends examining your conclusions by asking "What did you see or hear that makes you think that?" (Weinberg, 1993). An easy answer is, "I saw it in the status plots." A tougher answer is, "I'm not sure, but I just have this feeling." Dig into it. Ask more questions, gather more status, and think more. Find data to support conclusions. Try to avoid basing decisions that will affect an entire business enterprise on feelings. Objective data is usually available to support a decision if you look for it.

Retrospectives. A retrospective is like a postmortem. An excellent source of information on retrospectives is Norman Kerth's text (Kerth, 2001). The goals of the retrospective are for the team to review the project and answer the following questions:

1. What is it we did well, that we want to make sure we don't forget?
2. What did we learn?
3. What should we do differently next time?
4. What still puzzles us?

Kerth advises having a trained facilitator take the project's team through a timeline of the project. The team draws on paper on a wall or tacks pieces of paper to the wall. This timeline helps the team remember what happened during the project and also helps them see patterns and how their individual work fits into the whole. Each piece of information posted on the wall was a key event in the project. There are no "right answers" to post on the wall. Each individual participating has their own event that was important to them during the project. While posting to the wall, the facilitator asks the people to tell stories about the events. These stories are their personal retrospectives.

The next step is to create proposals for improvement. The team members probably learned things during the project and its retrospective. They should try to write these lessons in the form of proposals that they can implement on succeeding projects. At the end of the retrospective, the team returns to work and puts up posters that summarize their proposals for improvement. These posters help the team members remember the lessons and keep the improvement projects on track.

My key to Kerth's method is what he calls the prime directive. It is, "Regardless of what we discover, we understand and truly believe that everyone did the best job they could, given what they knew at the time, their skills and abilities, the resources available, and the situation at hand." I find this directive to be effective in retrospectives and in the day-to-day managing of a project. I keep a copy of it on my desk.

4.2.5   Taking Action

Implicit in the word "manager" is the taking of action of some sort. Gathering information and thinking are necessary actions, but they are not sufficient.

Beware of analyzing the project to death (literally). Act *small* and *early* (Weinberg, 1992). Act to steer the project back to its planned course. Large actions usually overcorrect the project, causing more actions that overcorrect in the other direction. Small actions do not correct enough, unless they are taken early when the difference between the planned and actual is small.

I recommend taking actions in three important areas:

1. *Act on yourself.* You are a leader by example whether you want to be or not. A good manager does not reward people who create a crisis and then work 12-hour days to manage it. Always be thinking, planning ahead, and acting (Weinberg, 1992). If you do these things, people will generally follow your lead.

2. *Act creatively.* There are no rules. You are empowered in the same way as everyone else. Upper management does not typically understand the software field in any depth. They do not typically tell the software project manager what to do because they do not know what he should do. You, therefore, have great freedom in choosing how to manage a project and great responsibility to do what you know is right. For example, instead of adding staff to a late project, which only makes it later (Brooks, 1975), increase support to key people on the project—people involved in tasks that can save the project time. Adding more programmers only slows down the current staff because they must stop work and familiarize the new people with the project. Instead of adding a programmer to the project at $50 an hour, add a baby-sitter, someone to mow the lawn, or someone to take a child to and from soccer practice (a total of $20 an hour for all three). Allow a spouse to come into the executive dining room and have a free dinner with this key person. The people who are working harder benefit from not worrying about their families. The project benefits from not getting later. Everyone may win when you act creatively.

3. *Act on the top-risks list.* The fun action is deleting a risk from the list because it has passed. However, deleting one item may mean only that another rises from the ranks. Change the probabilities and effects for the risks. Time teaches the project about risks, so use that knowledge to update the list. When a risk starts to become a problem, invoke your risk aversion strategy (see Chapter 7 for more on this). Insert the aversion plan into the project plan.

4.2.6 Making and Communicating Decisions

An important part of taking action is making and communicating decisions. Try to use some formal decision-making and documenting methods (such as those described in the next section). Quantify your decision as much as possible. Avoid the temptation to make decisions on hunches or feelings. Make your decision visible to everyone by putting it in the MIC. People on the project deserve to know what is happening and why. Your decision essentially determines the project's direction. You can continue on the current course, change the plan, or cancel the project. Choosing the first alternative means you have concluded that the project is healthy enough as it is. This is not a nondecision; it is a decision to continue. Make this decision in a firm manner and communicate it to everyone.

Choosing the second alternative means you must take corrective action. Use all the visibility and planning techniques I have described. Work on the network of tasks and change the baselines as needed. Work with the CCBs, the CM staff, the requirements analysts, the designers, and so on. If you have been paying attention, thinking, and planning ahead, you should be able to take small actions to correct the project's course. The third alternative is a hard choice, but not necessarily a bad one. Some projects try to produce software no one wants. Some projects are high risk by nature and use (or should be using) development processes that recognize high risk, like the spiral process, which has planned "do we cancel?" decision points (see Chapters 6 and 11 for more on the spiral process). Such cancellations were part of the project from the beginning. They are simply public announcements that we now know the project's potential costs outweigh its potential benefits.

Be sure to communicate problems upward. As project manager, it is your responsibility to tell the people managing the business enterprise when problems occur. The project can become a financial drain on the enterprise, something of direct concern to upper management. Be open and honest. If the MIC is well run, everyone will see the problems anyway.

4.2.7 Making a Decision Visible

Once you have chosen one of the three alternatives just listed (we are fine as is, take corrective action, cancel the project), how do you make your decision visible? The first step is to write the problem or question in a group setting on a whiteboard. You can capture it and its attendant parts later and place them online for everyone to see. Use several sentences and, if it helps, add figures. Next, describe the alternatives or answers (several sentences each), and assign one word to represent each alternative. Describe the attributes or factors influencing the decision. Again, use several sentences and assign one word to represent the attribute. Assign a relative weight to each attribute to show its importance and explain these weights (why is speed of execution three times more important than disk space required?).

Put this information in a form similar to that in Figure 4.28. In this example, the decision involves changing part of a design. The short question appears at the top of the figure. The alternatives appear on the left side of

Problem/Question Statement:
What should we do with the design of the I/O subsystem?

Alternatives	Attributes/Weights						Total Score
	Short-term cost	Long-term cost	Low risk	Short schedule	Low technology	Quality	
	x5	x6	x3	x2	x7	x8	

Figure 4.28 A decision-making table.

the table, and the attributes and their relative weights appear across the top. These weights define the decision. They state what is important for this issue at this time. Issues change with time and weights can change too. The intersection of an alternative and an attribute is a raw score (0 to 10) indicating how well that alternative solves the question in light of the attribute. The far-right column holds the sum of the products of the raw scores and attribute weights. The biggest number in this column indicates the best alternative.

Putting decisions in this kind of format moves them from the invisible to the visible. In everyday decisions, people use a question, alternatives, attributes, weights, raw scores, and total scores, but everything is in their heads. This is fine for most things, but decisions can kill projects, so you must make them visible.

Visible decisions are also crucial to maintaining the software being developed. During maintenance, decisions are often to change the software's structure. These maintenance decisions are much easier and safer to make if we know why the software is the way it is. And we can know that only if the developers made their decisions visible. For example, suppose a subsystem must change because government regulations regarding accounting practices have changed. The original subsystem was written in a complex and convoluted manner. In exploring why, you find that the decision documentation shows the following requirement: the subsystem had to execute in less than two seconds and use less than 50 Kbytes of memory. These attributes (speed and size) had high relative weights and caused the developers to use a complex and convoluted algorithm.

The situation has changed drastically. Current processors are much faster and memory is much more plentiful and inexpensive. The relative weights for speed and size are smaller, whereas those for portability and simplicity are larger. The algorithm for the new replacement subsystem will be much simpler and more portable.

4.2.8 Keeping the Environment Good

As I described earlier, status charts can indicate problems with the working environment. If, as project manager, you conclude that your working environment is in trouble, how can you act to fix it? In this case, act early and *not* small. People keep software projects going, but people are human. When the project goes through rough times, they can become tense, angry, and just plain mean. You must be able to act quickly and do whatever it takes to care for your people.

Your people come before everything else. Never let an outsider walk in and abuse them. If someone is sick or hurting, drop everything and take care of him. First, this is the right thing to do. Second, it will pay off in the long run in loyalty and motivation. Everyone else will see that you care about your people. They will work harder for you knowing that you will help them if they need it.

Take care when motivating people to gain performance. Weinberg found that people perform better as management applies motivation, but only to a point. Jim Cox, a colleague of mine and a graduate of the school of hard knocks, extended Weinberg's motivation and performance curve (Weinberg, 1992) as shown in Figure 4.29. As Weinberg's curve (solid line) shows, performance tends to drop off after a point. As Cox's extension (dotted line) shows, more and more motivation yields less and less performance. People become demoralized and cannot concentrate—and when concentration goes, everything goes. In Cox's curve, performance actually becomes a negative, which is known as sabotage, and although sabotage is wrong, it is a greater wrong to pressure people until they feel that sabotage can be their only response. As Philip Crosby states [Crosby], "People just want their rights until you try to trample them. Then they want revenge."

Sometimes, you need to say no. People will keep asking for more functions, more speed, more everything. Some people think it is wrong for a project manager to say no. They kill themselves, their people, and the project trying to please everyone all the time. Customers and everyone else can ask for too much too late. Tell them what the project can do and what it will cost. If they ask for too much for too little, tell them no. Be polite and professional, but tell them no.

Help your people learn during the project. Your project is part of their career. They need to learn, grow, and progress. If people stand still during your projects, no one will want to work with you. I recommend using three practical, inexpensive techniques to help people learn:

1. *Set goals every two months.* Yearly goal setting, such as through a performance review or goal session, is not enough. Steven Maguire (Maguire,

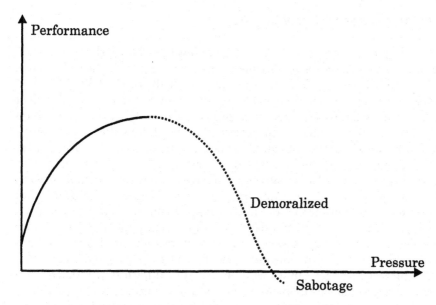

Figure 4.29 Weinberg's original motivation and performance with Cox's extension.

1994) recommends setting a goal for each person every two months. As situations arise, use them as learning experiences. Give each person a challenge to master in two months. At the end of a year, that person has mastered six major items. Your project has been a positive and productive experience. People grow, have fun, and want to work on your next project.

2. *Initiate coaching or teaching.* Experienced project managers can coach inexperienced ones; the same can be said for CM staff, requirements analysts, designers, programmers, and technical writers. Have your experienced people spend a couple hours a week with newer people. They will all learn.

3. *Form a study group.* The idea behind study groups, which have become popular recently, is to discuss a topic or a book at lunch once a week. There are degrees of formality, but the concept remains the same. Instead of discussing the weather, the group discusses a new technical topic. A common format is for everyone to read a chapter of the same book before the group meets. During the meeting, one person (different each week) will present the chapter as if they were the author. Everyone else will critique the presenter's (author's) view. They will also discuss how this can help them on the current project and future ones. Everyone participates, everyone learns, and everyone reads and absorbs the material in two or three good books each year. It is a tremendous accomplishment to have your people read three books each year.

4.2.9 Managing an External Supplier

A project needs a subcontractor in two situations (generally). The first is when the project does not have the people to do everything in the available time. The second is when the subcontractor can provide the product faster and better than the project's own people. In choosing a subcontractor, examine their track record. What percentage of their projects deliver the desired product on time? How do they manage their projects? Do they follow the Software Engineering Institute's CMM, ISO 9000, or best practices? Demand proper management practices. Demand the type of plans and status needed for EVT.

An organization and subcontractor can have a variety of contracts between them. At one end of the spectrum, the product supplied by the subcontractor is almost always commercial or shrink-wrapped software. The parties sign a contract, and the subcontractor delivers the product on the due date with no interaction. At the other extreme, the subcontractor's employees come to work at the contracting organization's facility and are managed directly.

The project manager cannot assume that subcontractors will deliver, but must attempt to manage them. Managing a subcontractor is the same as managing in-house people except that you will be gathering status less frequently and trusting more. Normally, you would gather status daily, plot the planned and actual progress, and project the plots to the end of the project. With a subcontractor, however, although the procedure is the same, you will probably gather status weekly or even monthly. The reason for this is cost. With a subcontractor, gathering status costs time and money. The subcontractors want to look their best, so they stop working on your software to prepare impressive presentations and demonstrations. Even though they can submit regular status reports electronically, they will not report it until their time cards are done, accounting does its thing, payroll does its thing, and so on.

It may be tempting to accept the subcontractor's word about the project's earned value, but subcontractors make mistakes just like everyone else. Bring testers and users with you to confirm all earned value. Outside testers and users ensure that the subcontractor is building the correct software correctly. This is independent verification and validation as discussed in Chapter 9.

You should, of course, gather status as often as you can afford to and track the earned value as you would in an internal project. Watch the EVT plots carefully. If the subcontractor falls behind (if the plot looks like Figure 4.14), act immediately. You won't have as much warning without daily indicators. When EVT shows a problem with a subcontractor, the problem is already big.

The basics of subcontracting or acquisition are known and have been published (Marciniak and Reifer, 1990; SPMN, 1996). As with in-house projects, acquisition and subcontracting projects are driven by people (Phillips, 1998). Key things to watch in the area of people include:

1. Work with people who want everyone to succeed.
2. Never assume that someone else understands what you want.

3. Keep people focused on the task at hand.

4. Obtain regular, frequent status information that shows progress on the product.

5. Use the status information to make timely, intelligent decisions.

There are potential problems for your business when everything appears to go well in a subcontracted project. The major problem could be that you lose intellectual capital (Thomsett, 1998; Mah, 1999). This means that your people may forget how to develop software. Also, other people in another company will learn the details of your business. Remember, IBM once subcontracted with a small and little-known company (Microsoft) to write the operating system for their first personal computer.

A part of business today is subcontracting with companies outside the homeland. American companies frequently hire software companies in India, Ireland, Israel, China, the Philippines, etc. This means a loss of jobs in America, and that is a growing problem. Offshore subcontracts are attractive because the programmers in these developing countries are paid one-half to one-tenth of their American counterparts. There are, however, other expenses involved in offshore subcontracts. Communication across time zones and cultures is difficult. The buying company must commit resources and energy to working in such situations. The best advice is to spend time face-to-face with the offshore developers at the start of the project and frequently during the project. Also, try to reduce the temporal distance by holding live telephone conversations daily if possible. These are better than e-mail in many respects.

4.3   CM: MANAGING BASELINES WITH MILESTONES

As I describe in Chapter 2 and Appendix B, CM is a key part of successfully managing a software project. The foundation of CM is the baselines. In a well-managed project, baselines should be tied to major milestones—big events that signal the passing of phases.

Figure 4.30 shows a possible baseline–milestone scheme in which milestones are meetings (other milestones may be more appropriate for your project). Work begins with the functional baseline (left column). When there is a meeting, the baseline materials are approved and become the official baseline product. This process occurs throughout the project for the different baselines.

Milestones give the project and its baselines high visibility. High-level managers often attend and observe the big events in a project. Although they do not participate much, their presence lends authority to the results. Everyone from top to bottom knows that the project has progressed successfully to a significant point. Projects are summarized to outsiders as "having reached TRR" or "having failed at CDR." This is the same as saying "we've made it

Baselines	**Corresponding Major Milestones**
Functional	PSR - Product Specification Review
Allocated	PDR - Preliminary Design Review
Design	CDR - Critical Design Review
Development	TRR - Test Readiness Review
Product	QAR - Qualification Acceptance Review
Operational	OAR - Operational Acceptance Review

Figure 4.30   Baselines and milestones.

through to the development baseline" or "the design baseline is not yet ready."

Milestones are also proven management tools. They work so well that people have recently advocated inch–pebble or tiny milestones in projects. This means inspecting the product of every task before accepting it as a product. In a sense, the success of milestones has also been their downfall. Milestones (big reviews) led to inspecting all products (reviews all the time), and this has reduced the need for milestones.

Consider the functional baseline in more detail. Many people are performing many tasks in parallel. People analyze the situation, talk to users, and gather information. The requirements analysts inspect, revise, and approve each small product. Each individually approved product goes into a special area on disk where the CM staff sees it during their status accountings. The CM staff reports this progress to management. The analysts and CM staff eventually gather all the individual products into one *Software Requirements Specification* (SRS; see Chapter 5 for more on SRSs). The users and their managers see the parts of the SRS that involve them the most. They know the significant content of the SRS. Finally, the milestone occurs (in this case the Product Specification Review). Everyone involved is represented and, depending on the importance of the project to the business enterprise, high-level managers also attend. The high-level managers ensure that everyone is acting responsibly and in the best interest of the business. The review accepts the SRS, it becomes the functional baseline, and the project moves forward. All this sounds like the waterfall model because it was invented using the waterfall model, but baselines and milestones work in all process models.

4.4   LOOKING TO STANDARDS FOR HELP

Standards help the project manager every day by providing emotional and creative relief—probably the last thing people expect from a boring standard. Imagine you are in the middle of a difficult project. The project has struggled to stay on schedule, technical problems abound, and some of your best people have been pulled away several times to help other projects. Everyone is mentally and emotionally drained. Management adds a couple more requirements late in the project, and you must plan to test them. What do you do? Planning and writing are difficult.

Fortunately, people have already done a lot of thinking and experimenting on how to write a test plan and procedure and documented their efforts in an IEEE standard (see Chapter 9). The standard tells you where to start, what to include, and how to tie different documents together. It can be a lifesaver for those who are emotionally and creatively drained.

Standards exist for many common situations (writing requirements, design solutions, writing test plans, and so on). If we forget that standards exist and neglect using them, we take precious hours away from the creative activities that make a software product unique. Standards also prevent embarrassment when you and the team are too tired to remember all the interrelationships within a plan or procedure.

4.5   KEY THOUGHTS IN THIS CHAPTER

The project manager is responsible for managing and controlling the project day by day. This follows the equation *control = status + plan + corrective action.* Think ahead and act early and small. Large actions can result in overcorrection, which requires new corrective action.

The project manager should create and sustain an environment in which people can work. Hold yourself to high standards, drive out fear, and let people go home at the end of an eight-hour day. Structure the project so that people succeed—success breeds success. Prevent failure and beware of the eight F's. Make time to tell everyone exactly what you expect.

The project manager must collect status and make it visible. Talk to everyone on every day, without exception. Record who did what and when. Emphasize items related to the project's plan and risks. Pay special attention to errors. (Where were they made? How much will it cost to correct them?) Diagram the project's plan, status, and projections.

Make everything public by placing the diagrams in the management information center. Avail yourself of the many charts that can reveal when the project is in trouble. Store what you have collected in unit development folders—a physical container for each software unit that contains all the information about it, both pre- and postcreation. If you are not using any visibility tools and techniques, UDFs are a simple way to start.

With the plan and status, analyze the situation and take action. Schedule time to think and ask others for their thoughts. After analyzing, make decisions, document them for everyone to see, and execute them. At all times, keep the environment good.

A project may sometimes depend on external suppliers. The management actions are the same in these cases, but reduced visibility requires more trust. Choose external suppliers with great care.

The proper use of configuration management is key to managing a project. Baselines are the foundation of CM. Tie baselines to major milestones and have the CCBs control their content.

Use standards whenever you need to write a document. People have done a lot of thinking about a certain topic so that you and your people don't have to do as much.

REFERENCES

S. Adams, *The Dilbert Principle*, HarperCollins, New York, 1996.

V. Basili and D. Weiss, "A Methodology for Collecting Valid Software Engineering Data," *IEEE Transactions on Software Engineering*, November 1984.

K. Beck, *Extreme Programming Explained: Embrace Change*, Pearson Education, Upper Saddle River, NJ, 1999.

F. Brooks, Jr., *The Mythical Man-Month*, Addison-Wesley, Reading, MA, 1975.

P. Crosby, *Quality is Free*, Mentor Books, New York, 1980.

T. DeMarco and T. Lister, *Peopleware*, Dorset House, New York, 1987.

Q. Fleming and J. Koppelman, *Earned Value Project Management*, 2nd ed., Project Management Institute, 2000.

T. Gilb and D. Graham, *Software Inspection*, Addison-Wesley, Reading, MA, 1993.

R. Grady, *Practical Software Metrics for Project Management and Process Improvement*, Prentice-Hall, Englewood Cliffs, NJ, 1992.

W. Humphrey, *Managing the Software Process*, Addison-Wesley, Reading, MA, 1989.

W. Humphrey, *A Discipline for Software Engineering*, Addison-Wesley, Reading, MA, 1995.

C. Jones, *Patterns of Software Systems Failure and Success*, International Thomson Computer Press, Boston, 1996.

N. Kerth, *Project Retrospectives, A Handbook for Team Reviews*, Dorset House Publishing, New York, 2001.

S. Maguire, *Debugging the Development Process*, Microsoft Press, Redmond, WA, 1994.

M. Mah, "Managing Outsourcing Expectations," *Cutter IT Journal*, October 1999, pp. 6-16.

J. Marciniak and D. Reifer, *Software Acquisition Management*, Wiley, New York, 1990.

J. McCarthy, *Dynamics of Software Development*, Microsoft Press, Redmond, WA, 1995.

S. McConnell, *Rapid Development*, Microsoft Press, Redmond, WA, 1996.

S. McConnell, "Tool Support for Project Tracking," *IEEE Software*, September October 1997, pp. 119-120.

D. Phillips, "How People Drive the Outsourcing Process Sometimes Off the Road)," *Cutter IT Journal*, July 1998, pp. 37-42.

D. Phillips, "Back to Basics: Metrics that Work for Software Projects," *Cutter IT Journal*, April 1999, pp. 36-42.

L. H. Putnam and W. Myers, *Measures for Excellence—Reliable Software on Time, within Budget*, Yourdon Press, Englewood Cliffs, NJ, 1992.

D. Smith, xxxx

Software Program Manager's Network, *The Program Manager's Guide to Software Acquisition Best Practices*, Arlington, VA: US Department of Defense Software Acquisition Best Practices Initiative, The Software Program Managers Network, 1996.

B. Tackett and B. Van Doren, "Process Control for Error-Free Software: A Software Success Story," *IEEE Software*, May June 1999, pp. 24–29.

R. Thomsett, "Outsourcing: The Great Debate," *Cutter IT Journal*, July 1998, pp. 11–21.

G. Weinberg, *Becoming a Technical Leader*, Dorset House, New York, 1986.

G. Weinberg, *Quality Software Management: Vol. 1, Systems Thinking*, Dorset House, New York, 1992.

G. Weinberg, *Quality Software Management: Vol. 2, First-Order Measurement*, Dorset House, New York, 1993.

G. Weinberg, "What's So Great about Technical Reviews?" *STQE*, March April 2003, pp. 16–19.

PART 2

THE DEVELOPMENT LIFE CYCLE: EARLY STAGES

In this section, I begin applying the four themes introduced in the previous section to the familiar stages of the product development life cycle. This section focuses on the early stages: requirements, planning, and risk management. This is the longest section in the book because it is here that project managers must make some of their most critical decisions.

The chapters in this section are closely linked, although some stages tend to emphasize certain topics more than others. For example, requirements emphasizes problem analysis, whereas planning focuses more on selecting a process and creating tasks. Risk management's main goal is to identify specific risks and form a risk management plan. If you were to diagram these three stages, you would have massive overlapping and many feedback arrows. How, for example, do you plan without considering the project's risks and requirements? How do you determine a project's risks if you don't fully understand the set of requirements? And, of course, when something changes in one stage, it typically affects the other two.

The V-chart below illustrates the phases in a typical project. The phases start with analyzing the user's needs to produce a set of requirements. The requirements (a description of the problem) lead to several levels of design (a solution to the problem). Design leads to building the smallest units and combining and testing them to produce a system. These tasks—requirements, design, building, and integration and testing—are the basic steps, and all process models are variations on them.

The Software Project Manager's Handbook. By Dwayne Phillips.
ISBN 0-471-67420-6 © 2004 IEEE Computer Society

User Need   User Product

    User Requirements   System Validation

       System Requirements   System Verification

         System Design   System Integration and Test

           Subsystem Design   Subsystem Integration and Test

             Unit Design   Unit Integration and Test

              Unit Build and Test

The basic project process in a V-chart.

Now let us examine how the V-chart works. As you descend the left side of the V, the project team refines the initial vague idea of user needs into many small, specific problems. At the bottom of the V, they build small units, or subroutines. As you move up the right side, the team is repeatedly combining the units into larger subsystems and then, finally, into a system that meets the user's needs.

Requirements, planning, and risk management occur during the first three steps of the V-chart shown here. During these steps, we concentrate on what the users need, the steps we will take to meet those needs, and identifying and avoiding possible problems. In the next section of the book, I will discuss meeting the user needs (the design activities).

Chapter 5

Requirements

The team has labored for months, carefully following the correct design process and testing procedure. Integration has been excellent. Unfortunately, right around the corner is the nightmare—the sickening realization that you have flawlessly built the wrong system. You look back at the time saved during the requirements stage and you remember thinking, "We'll make up for requirements oversights later during programming, since that's our strength." Too late, you recognize that designing, writing, integrating, and testing software are all in vain if the requirements are wrong.

It has taken many hard knocks, but the software community is finally recognizing the importance of proper requirements engineering. As Alan Davis puts it, requirements engineering is "the systematic use of proven principles, techniques, languages, and tools for the cost-effective analysis, documentation, and ongoing evolution of user needs and the specification of the external behavior of the system to satisfy those user needs" (Davis, xxxx). And as Robert Glass states it, "One of the two most common causes of runaway projects is unstable requirements" (Glass, 2003). It is not a few interviews, some cursory look at relevant documentation, or what Joe says the customer can live with.

Balancing the 3Ps is critical here. If the requirements are wrong, the product will be wrong, and you will likely chose the wrong process to produce it. The accuracy of the requirements depends on both the people stating the requirements (the customers) and those who will be documenting them (the developers).

Requirements is also a classic area for practicing visibility. The customers have an idea of what they want, but their ideas must be expressed in a visible form so that the developers can build a system that will satisfy the customers. The requirements are stated in the *software requirements specification*, which documents the functional baseline.

The use of CM is important in identifying and managing requirements. The customer and developers are the functional baseline Configuration Control Board. Their job is to identify, capture, and control the requirements. The CM plan will guide them in their activities. Following the CM plan makes the job easy. Disregarding the CM plan and diving in undirected makes the job hard. I have done it both ways and highly recommend the first approach.

The SRS should be patterned after IEEE Std 830-1998 (IEEE, 19xx). You can use any appropriate medium to document the needs of the user. Posters, screen images, and videotapes are good candidates for recording requirements. Regardless of the form chosen, read the standard. Intelligent, experienced practitioners have given you free expertise about gathering and documenting requirements.

5.1 BALANCING THE 3Ps: REQUIREMENTS ANALYSIS, DOCUMENTATION, AND MANAGEMENT

The major steps in requirements engineering are to analyze the requirements, document them, and manage them. These steps are not taken in phases—analysis does not end before documentation begins, which does not end before management begins. The requirements engineer (the developer working on the requirements problem) will move among the three—analyzing, documenting, managing, talking with the customer, adjusting his view, and repeating the process.

In general, requirements analysis and management tend to be more oriented toward people than documentation. For that reason, I defer talking about documentation until the next section on visibility. I will first discuss requirements analysis and then requirements management.

Requirements or problem analysis consists of requirements gathering and a thorough study of the requirements gathered. This step is largely about interacting with people. Sitting in front of a terminal will not produce a list of customer needs. Instead, you must be with people for long periods, making strangers trust you enough to tell you what it is they really need to do their jobs successfully. Trust, emotions, psychology, and other "touchy-feely" factors are critical.

The process is also critical. Gathering and analyzing requirements seems like a straightforward matter of asking people what they want and then recording it. However, in between is the massive gray area of organizing the information to record it. Customers can flood you with all manner of information. Projects may have hundreds and thousands of requirements. Some of them are critical, many are trivial, and the customer will not tell you which is which.

It almost goes without saying that requirements gathering and analysis are critical to the product. If you want to build software that people will use, you must successfully complete these activities.

In some ways, requirements gathering and analysis is just as difficult as writing software. Once you accept this, you have taken a big stride toward performing the task correctly:

- *Identify what must be learned and who has the needed information.* Think in terms of objects, functions, and states.
- *Gather the information.* Interview the identified people for the needed information. Information may be available from sources such as manuals for present systems, standard operating procedures, or employee handbooks. Look to these sources for background before talking to people. Do not, however, satisfy yourself with these other sources. You are trying to satisfy people with software; talk to people.
- *Analyze the information.* Interviews often provide information in a seemingly random manner. Identifying the "what" and "who" before interviews reduces but does not eliminate this randomness. Study what the interviews yielded. Cover a wall with notes and use the system storyboarding technique (described later) to organize everything. Also look at the information in light of original goals. Does the information answer all the questions about what must be learned? Do new questions come to mind? If so, who knows the answers?
- *Check everything.* Remember that this is just as hard as the hardest program you ever wrote. Also remember that gathering requirements is the most important step in building software that people will use. Test everything using the IDEA concept (inspection, demonstration, execution, and analysis) described in Chapter 9.

Volere. An excellent source of information regarding requirements gathering, documenting, and management is the Robertson's *Mastering the Requirements Process*, (1999). In this book, Suzanne and James Robertson describe their Volere approach (volere is Italian for "to wish" or "to want"). The Robertsons have created a complete method comprising processes and templates that flow and fit together. Throughout this chapter, I will refer to parts of Volere.

An early step in Volere is what the Robertsons call "trawling for requirements." The requirements engineer ventures out among the stakeholders to learn what they want. Key to this is "the work" of the users—the business activity of the user. The ultimate goal of system builders is to create a system that improves the work of the users.

5.1.1 Selecting the Requirements Engineer

The requirements engineer can be invaluable to a project. If he does not learn the requirements, your team will be blamed, not the customer. Therefore, you must select this individual with care.

The requirements engineer must possess several important qualities, the most important of which is being able to work with people. Users and marketing representatives can drive engineers crazy, and personality differences can be difficult to overcome. The requirements engineer must empathize with the user. This means looking, sounding, and acting like a user while gathering information. He must, however, switch back to looking, sounding, and acting like an engineer again when talking to the other developers. Otherwise, the developers will accuse him of going over to "the other side" and will ignore his information.

The requirements engineer must also be an analyst, sorting information and giving it meaning. He must be able to hear different customer perspectives and winnow out the core needs. He must be able to withstand pressure from customers who want their features in the product and never consider what the group across the hall wants. Fighting among customers happens often, and the requirements engineer is usually caught in the middle.

He must also have the tenacity to dig beneath surface statements. The customer may be wrong when first describing needs. The requirements engineer must be willing to investigate to find the real need. He must ask probing questions to draw out user *needs* as opposed to *wants*. He must also take care not to frustrate the users and risk losing information the project needs.

5.1.2 Interviewing Customers

Interviewing is a critical step foreign to most software people. There are, however, proven techniques for interviewing people effectively. Peter Schenck recommends five steps (Schenck, 1994):

1. *Prepare.* Understand the interview's goals—what the interview should produce. Create questions that lead to the goals. Do not ask about the user interface if the goal is to learn how accurate the calculations are. This may seem obvious, but I have seen people travel across the country, spend two weeks interviewing customers, and return to discover that they don't know what type of computer the customer uses. Be prepared before the interview. Look at your questions. Are they clear enough? How can they be better? Do they lead to the goals? Practice asking the questions with your team. What tone of voice should you use? What about your demeanor, posture, and dress? Gain as much information as you can about the work habits of your interviewees. How do they act and dress? Do they like to drink coffee during interviews? Do they like to interview in the morning, over lunch, or in the afternoon? Some of these questions may seem silly, but they can make the difference between a fruitful interview and a waste of time. People should be professional, show up for work, and answer questions when

directed to do so, but people are people. If they are uncomfortable with you as the interviewer, they will not give you the information you need.

2. *Introduce.* Start the interview with courteous introductions. Begin with casual talk. Jumping into requirements before saying good morning and asking how a person feels (and listening when they tell you) gives the impression that the job is more important than the person. If you as the interviewer feel that way, you should find another task or line of work (see Chapter 1).

3. *Interview.* The interview itself should be friendly. The interviewer is there to help the customers by learning what they need and providing it. Run through the questions created to meet the goals of the interview. Write down the answers the customer gives word for word. Do not put them into your own words. If possible, bring a partner to the interview so that one of you can catch points the other misses.

4. *Close.* When all the questions have been answered, summarize the interview by repeating what the customer said. Try to find your misunderstandings (they will be there). Ask several open-ended questions such as "Is there anything else you'd like to say?" "Is there anything else I should have asked you?" and "Did I miss anything?" Do not assume the interview has been successful.

5. *Follow up.* After the interview, transcribe the customer's answers and put them in a document with the questions. Create finished drawings from any sketches scribbled during the interview. Above all else, *do what you said you would do* (DWYSYWD). If you promised to check something and get back to the customer in two days, do it. If the information is not available, call the customer in two days and tell him that. Breaking promises promotes distrust. When the customer distrusts the developer, the project becomes very difficult.

Interviews can be done from several perspectives. One is what Weinberg calls *emic* interviewing, which involves analyzing behavior patterns (Weinberg, 1993). The interviewer tries to empathize with the customer and has the customer teach him how to do the customer's job. The interviewer prompts the customer with questions: Would you show me how to do that? When do you do that? Where do you go for that? Whom do you talk to next? Why do you use those words? What is your product? Learning how to do someone's job provides insight into what he needs. The discussion often helps the customers see what they are doing in a new light. They realize things they have taken for granted. Use emic interviewing, but beware of the tense situations it may cause (described later).

Another perspective on interviewing comes from Richard Zultner (Zultner, 1994). Do not assume customers know what they want or need, or that they can state it. Zultner feels that customers do not give requirements, but verbatims. The interviewer records the customers' thoughts word for word. To analyze the interview, Zultner advises sorting these verbatims by customer type (first-line manager, upper manager, secretary, engineer, clerk, and so on). Use hierarchies and other classifications. Find the requirements the customers did and did not state. Rank the customers and their needs and concentrate on the most important requirements. Do not assume the customer is all knowing, but don't act as if he's clueless, either. Always strive to be helpful and let the customer know that is your goal.

Volere provides another perspective on interviewing, in which the requirements engineer concentrates on business events. A business event is something that happens in the world outside the system. The business event is important to the user's work in that the work must respond to the business event. Business events help the requirements engineer partition the work. Suppose a business event for a bank is "customer withdraws cash." Part of the work interfaces with the customer, part of the work interfaces with the cash vault, part of the work interfaces with account records, and so on.

An extension of the business event is the use case. The use case is the work's desired response to the business event. There are several variations of use cases being employed in the software industry. Common to these various use cases is the concept of the actor (in this case, the bank customer) interacting or using the system (in this case, the bank). A use case contains a collection of requirements. For example, the use case for the business event "customer withdraws cash" would include things like,

1. System confirms customer's identity
2. System confirms bank account number
3. System confirms that the customer's account has adequate funds

These statements tell the requirements engineer some of the things that the system must do.

Whatever interview perspective you take, keep the customers' goals in the forefront (Cooper, 1996). Developers and customers can easily become immersed in all the individual tasks the customer performs. The tasks are important, but also look at what the customers are ultimately seeking. This means filtering through all the information to see the big picture.

For example, suppose you are to write diagnostic software for a car. Concentrating on the tasks alone to find a solution will produce a list of functions that indicate the state of the car's major subsystems (air quality, spark condition, compression, fluid levels, brake system, and so on). These are logical choices for helping the mechanic repair the car. However, they lose sight of the car owner's goal—to go down the road again as quickly and cheaply as possible with minimum disruption to the day's routine. A good solution in this context is a communications system between the car and the repair shop that tells the repair shop the car's location and condition. If the repair is small, the mechanic can drive to the broken car and fix it on the spot. If the trouble is bigger, the mechanic can call for a rental car to pick up the car owner, while sending a tow truck to take the disabled car to the shop.

This relates to designing while gathering requirements (discussed later). Developers and customers who are too familiar with the problem cannot see it in a different light. Outsiders can see the situation in unusual and sometimes brilliant ways. People experienced with car diagnostics and repair would see the above example as a technical and mechanical problem. A busy salesperson would see it as how to go down the road.

5.13 Conducting Group Meetings

Requirements gathering means plenty of meetings with groups of people as well as one-on-one interviews. Most people dislike meetings, but they are necessary. As project manager, you must make meetings as productive as possible. Most good meeting techniques (Maguire, 1994; Gause, 1989; Carnes, 1987) involve the following principles:

- *Ensure that the meeting's value is greater than its cost.* If a meeting will decide how to spend $1,000, do not invite 20 people who each cost $100 an hour for a one-hour meeting.
- *Have a well-defined and well-publicized reason for the meeting.* Send this reason to those you invite so that they can come prepared or not come at all if the topic does not involve them. State the reason for the meeting at its start. People sometimes misunderstand why meetings are held. Give everyone a chance to leave a meeting before it begins. Once a meeting starts, people may feel too self-conscious to leave.
- *Organize the logistics of the meeting.* Ensure that a good note taker is present. The note taker needs equipment to enter notes and print everyone a copy before they leave. Arrange an adequate room for the meeting. It should be large and comfortable enough to allow people to think and contribute. Do not assume these logistics will take care of themselves.
- *Keep the meeting focused.* If it drifts off the stated issue, bring it back gently, but bring it back. Do not embarrass people who drift off the subject, but remind them of the meeting's purpose and promise to convene another meeting to discuss their topic if necessary.
- *Organize the meeting logically.* If it involves two issues, complete one first and go to the next. When the first is finished, announce that and allow anyone not interested in the second issue to leave. Do not stretch meetings to arbitrary times. I have sat in countless meetings that were finished after 40 minutes. The meetings, however, did not end because the participants felt compelled to stay for the mandatory 60 minutes. Leaving early might have made them look lazy or uninterested.

- *Use visibility techniques.* Do not just talk and let people imagine what you are discussing. Use diagrams, figures, charts, videos, handouts, and whatever else will communicate (more on these later in this chapter). You are there to make some decision. Record the decision and print it before the participants leave. Everyone should sign the group copy and take an individual copy with them. Do not assume that everyone has the same understanding of what was discussed and decided. Make it a concrete, visible decision.

- *Return on Time Invested.* Colleagues Esther Derby (Derby, xxxx) and Steve Smith (Smith, xxxx) contributed what they call the Return on Time Invested or ROTI. At the end of a meeting, they ask the participants to rate the benefit received for their time. The scale is 0 through 4, where 0 is "Lost Principle: no benefit received for time invested," 2 is "Break Even: received benefit equal to time invested," and 4 is "High Return on Investment: received benefit greater than time invested." The benefit received will differ depending on the purpose of the meeting. Example purposes include (1) information sharing, (2) decision making, (3) problem solving, and (4) work planning. After the participants state their rating, build a histogram like the one shown in Table 4.1. This will help you as the meeting organizer to determine your effectiveness. You should investigate the ratings to learn how to improve the meetings.

5.1.4 Diffusing Tense Situations

Requirements gathering is an intense phase that can give rise to heated situations. As project manager, you can generally diffuse them if you remain professional and use common sense.

When Customers Fight. When customers compete for product features, be diplomatic. Try to arrange Configuration Control Board meetings at which the customers and the project's executive sponsor must make decisions. Stay with the decisions made in such meetings. Customers will come by later and try to win favors that were voted down during the meetings. Gently remind them that decisions reached during the meetings must guide the project.

Table 4.1   The ROTI Histogram

Meeting ROTI	
4	|
3	||
2	||||
1	|
0	|

When Customers are Frustrated. The requirements engineer spends countless hours with the customers trying to learn what they do, how they do it, how software can help, what software they need, and so on. Some customers get frustrated. They know their job, but many cannot describe it in sufficient detail. They grow weary of being asked about it in a dozen different ways. When you hear things like "When are these guys going to start producing software and stop bothering us?" immediately back away for a couple of days. The customers may be polite and respectful on the outside, but seething on the inside. Such passive–aggressive behavior is out there, and you typically learn about it after you deliver software and no one uses it. Try to uncover such behavior by talking to customers one on one casually in their offices. Connect with them first, and then ask how they feel about the project. Ask this a half dozen ways.

Show the customers something each week so that they will know the product is taking shape if only as requirements. Consider building simple prototypes or providing demonstrations. Keep the customers in the project. If they quit or lose interest, they will not use the software and the project will never get off the ground.

When the Problem Is Bad Management. The requirements engineer may discover that the customer really does not need software or new computers. What they are missing is management. Instead of training, discipline, documentation, or adherence to standards, someone in the customer's organization decided that a new software package would cure their problems.

You face two issues here. The first is how to tell a paying customer to look elsewhere for a solution. They are paying you to write software, not run their business. The second is how to tell your company that they don't need this paying customer.

Gerald Weinberg has some good advice for both problems (Weinberg, 1993). For the first problem, he tells the requirements engineer to dig into the situation: "Real quality starts (not ends) with knowing what your customers want (not think they want)." The customers want to succeed. Perhaps rather than additional software, they just need a different kind of software. Help them discover what that is.

For the second problem, Weinberg advises that "professionals excuse themselves when the customer wants something they cannot support professionally." Sometimes, walking away from a paying customer is the right action to take both ethically and financially. On the ethical side, it means you always tell the truth. Neither programmers nor customers want to work with a liar. On the business side, it makes sense because building software the customer does not need will eventually produce an ex-customer.

Managing Expectations. Requirements set the expectations for the project. The user feels that they have told the requirements engineer exactly what to build, and that is what the requirements engineer should have put into the requirements and later the product. No matter how successful the engineer thinks a project is, if it did not meet the expectations of the user, the user will consider it a failure. Often, the engineer (1) has too strong a desire to please, (2) is overenthusiastic, and (3) lives in a culture that is vastly different from the user's culture (Boehm, 2000). This creates a high probability of a mismatch in expectations.

The requirements engineer needs to manage the expectations. Key to this is to communicate well (much easier said than done). Excellent tips may be found in Karten's *Communication Gaps* (Karten, 2002). The visibility techniques in this and other chapters also offer things that help with communication. An excellent technique comes from Karten's *Managing Expectations* (Karten, 1994). This is the "That's not it" exercise. The concept is for the requirements engineer to show the user as clearly and specifically as possible what he has thinks the user wants. The requirements engineer should do this early in the process before too much work is wasted in the wrong direction. If the requirements engineer has misread the expectations of the user, the user has the opportunity to say, "That's not it!"

I have been able to use the "That's not it" exercise frequently and successfully. On one occasion I was leading an expensive team of two dozen engineers trying to create a standard for operating systems use in a 10,000 person organization. I thought I knew what everyone expected, so I stopped a meeting, took 15 minutes, and wrote in great detail what I had in mind on the whiteboard. I turned to the crowd only to see two dozen disappointed faces nodding no. "Well," I said triumphantly, "At least we know 'That's not it!'" That exercise in managing expectations saved us millions of dollars.

5.1.5 Evolving Requirements

Requirements seldom come ready made from the information process. Most tend to evolve through refinement of raw data. Gause and Weinberg (1989) provide a good discussion of how to evolve requirements by listing all functions, attributes, and constraints and then combining them.

The *functions* are the "what" of the product. They are verbs representing the actions the software will perform. Many refer to these functions as functional requirements. You find these by having the customer complete the statement, "We need software that will _____." You can prompt the customer with questions like: How would you like to use the system? What is the purpose of the system? Cost and feasibility aside for the moment, what would you like the system to do? As you find the functions, number each F_1 through F_n. so that they are easy to reference. These functions are called *functional requirements* in Volere.

The *attributes* are characteristics the customer desires. They are the adjectives and adverbs. Many refer to attributes as nonfunctional requirements because the customer wants them but they are not things the software will do.

Ask the customer to complete the statement, "We need software that will be _____." Again, as you find attributes, number each A_1 through A_n. You can attach each attribute to one or more functions. The attributes are called *nonfunctional requirements* in Volere.

Attributes expand the problem's solution space but in a different way than functional requirements. Sometimes, attributes are more important to the customer than the functional requirements. For example, the customer is attached to the idea of a friendly graphical interface and sound effects, although all he really needs are accurate loan amortization calculations. This has led to much of today's "fatware." Spending time and money on attributes is a business decision.

The *constraints* are objective statements of the attributes. They place quantitative limits or constraints on the customer's desires. If an attribute is "easy to learn," a constraint could be "a person with a high-school education must be able to use the software after a two-hour class." Know the limitations and keep the problem analysis in the real world. For example, sometimes the customer unknowingly pushes the solution in a bad direction. Suppose the attribute is "We need software that will be written in Fred's Super Basic." You can challenge that with "We could cut time and money in half if we used macros for Joe's spreadsheet instead." Time and money are probably the most common limitations. Assign a constraint to each important attribute. Number the constraints C_1 through C_n for easy reference.

As a last step, combine the functions, constraints, and attributes into English language requirements.

If your organization gathers requirements using a back-of-the-envelope approach, start the trek toward standards using this requirements-evolution method. As your group matures, add the more detailed and formal techniques given in the next section.

Part of evolving the requirements is determining which ones are implemented now and which ones are delayed until later. One method of doing this is through requirements triage (Davis, 2003). This is named after the medical practice of determining which people receive immediate medical attention in a war or catastrophe. In requirements triage, the requirements engineer divides the requirements into three categories:

1. Requirements that the next version must satisfy
2. Requirements that the next version need not satisfy
3. Requirements that could be in the next version, but the engineers must first weigh them against available resources

5.1.6 Requirements Versus Design

Many projects confuse requirements engineering and design. Requirements engineering is concerned with the "what" of the problem; design states "how" to solve the problem. Requirements are what the customer sees as important. Design, on the other hand, is left to the developer. The developer can design and build the product as he wishes as long as he meets the requirements.

Some design during the requirements phase is inevitable and probably should be done. It is impossible not to at least consider solutions while learning about a problem. People view problems using the vocabulary of solutions, which is why established organizations sometimes become mired in old solutions and newer companies often spearhead innovation. Sometimes it is appropriate to design during requirements gathering. If the customer and developer know the problem well, have years of experience with it, and know the best solution to it, they can design while gathering requirements. This situation does not occur often, but it does occur. Design during requirements is the most efficient approach under these circumstances.

Unfortunately, design during requirements tends to occur frequently and for the wrong reasons. People see a new technique and want to apply it. They have an answer in hand and try to find a problem it will solve. However, having a solution in mind while trying to understand and document the problem is like wearing blinders. It changes the perception of the problem and can prevent proper analysis. Resist this temptation. Focus on the task at hand and seek to answer "what is the problem?"

Several approaches can help you curb design during requirements. One is to bring in outsiders during requirements engineering. The outsiders are not just consultants, but may be total strangers to the project's context. Use a physicist on a banking project, or a medical doctor on a telecommunications project. They are likely to provide a completely different perspective and vocabulary of solutions. They are also better able to see when preconceived solutions are driving the problem's analysis. If using outsiders is not practical, have someone play the role of an outsider. Question everything. Ask why people keep talking in terms of one solution or another. Try to gain a different perspective by reading and studying problems and solutions from other fields.

Another approach is to save possible solutions. When solutions come to mind, record them. Also state openly that the requirements phase is not the time to be designing. Save the ideas for the design phase (never throw away an idea). Try not to let the ideas color problem analysis, however.

5.1.7 Requirements Management

The previous pages contained a discussion of analyzing information to find requirements. The following pages on visibility will show various ways to document requirements. Those activities gather a lot of information that is critical to the success of a software project. One question concerning that information is how do you manage it? How can you keep it in a place so you can use it without that place becoming a hindrance to "real work?"

Requirements management is the heart of that topic. Requirements management is simple in principle, but difficult in practice. The Software Engineering Institute's Capability Maturity Model (CMM) (Software Engineering Institute, xxxx) describes requirements management in three simple actions:

1. Establish a common understanding of the requirements with the customer.
2. Document that understanding.
3. Make changes in an organized manner.

This all sounds so simple. As with most difficult tasks, the difficulty comes with people. Engineers, people who like to work on technical problems, run software projects. Most engineers avoid or trip over other problems.

Requirements analysis and documentation are technical problems (although, as the previous pages documented, there are many people issues in analysis). Engineers gather information, draw diagrams, and analyze them to prepare for design. Engineers use all their technical skills and apply themselves wholeheartedly. In contrast, requirements management is a management problem. It involves having meetings, reaching agreements face to face, and keeping detailed records. Most engineers see requirements management as a clerical job and hate it.

Life with requirements management is distasteful to many engineers. Life without requirements management, however, can be painful. In the short term, the project without requirements management is fun. The engineers look at the requirements, grab what seems interesting, and build a system that meets most of the interesting requirements.

This isn't hard work since there isn't any target at which the engineers aim; any product will do in this situation. The problem comes at the end of the project. The product doesn't do much of what the customer wanted. Therefore, few if any people use the product, the company fails, and the engineers are all unemployed.

Sometimes, engineers strive to satisfy customers in the absence of requirements management. This can be quite stressful as people add, subtract, and modify requirements. No one is keeping track of all this, so they struggle daily to understand what they are trying to build. Most people hate the product because it doesn't do what they thought it would. Many people hate the engineers because, from their perspective, the engineers lied about what they were building.

Requirements management is distasteful but essential, so managers need to do something with it. The simple answer is to provide help. This does not mean to threaten engineers and project managers with, "Do requirements management or else!" Help means realizing that requirements management probably won't be done well and providing the project manager with resources and direction. I divide such help into four areas.

The first form of help in requirements management is to understand and use configuration management. That is one of the four themes of this book, and I discuss how it relates to requirements later in this chapter.

The second form of help is to appoint a full-time requirements manager. This is a person who understands technical issues, but likes and is good at managing things. The requirements manager performs all the face-to-face meetings and detailed record-keeping tasks. This person has the personality and temperament to keep the customer happy and the engineers out of trouble.

The third form of help is to define clear responsibilities in the area of requirements. There should be a poster in the management information center that states precisely who is responsible for what on the project. This includes who represents the customer. If it is a large project, it should state who represents the customer's user interface issues, who represents the customer's database issues, etc. This reduces the amount of changing directions to try to satisfy everyone you bump into in the hall.

The fourth form of help is in the area of review boards. Any proposed change to the requirements should be reviewed by a group of "outsiders." These outsiders—a review board—provide a needed perspective on changes. It is unfortunate, but most review boards are too slow, don't understand the project well enough, and generally become such a hindrance to the project manager that the project manager tells little white lies to avoid the review board. The review board should have only three or four members. These people should have flexible schedules so that they can meet the demands of the engineers instead of requiring the engineers to meet their demands. The review board should emphasize content over format. If the engineers bring information on 3" × 5" cards, that is fine. There is no need to transcribe everything to fancy viewgraphs and have six people work through grammatical errors before bringing the information to the review board.

5.2   VISIBILITY: MAKING REQUIREMENTS KNOWN

Visibility techniques are vital during both requirements-engineering steps. During problem analysis, they help everyone see the customers' ideas. During documentation, they provide numerous diagrams of perspectives that are available to the customer and the entire project team. The requirements engineer can show the diagrams to the customer and reconcile differences between their two views.

Many so-called new software design methods, such as role playing, acting out scenarios, and prototyping user interfaces, are in actuality visibility techniques aimed at requirements gathering and analysis. Some may disagree with me, but requirements help the customer describe the problem. If a method is aimed at understanding the problem, it should be used as a requirements-gathering tool, not a design approach.

Do not hesitate to use the visibility techniques in this text. I advise starting simply. Petitioning your company to make them part of official company policy will probably just delay everything. Use the one-on-one technique in small customer meetings. Don't announce that everyone is about to experience the such and such, just use it. After it works, people will ask about it and you can explain it in detail.

Choose the techniques wisely. Techniques are process, and process must fit with the people and product. During requirements gathering, give extra consideration to the customers. What visibility techniques do they normally use? What types of meetings do they hold (formal, stand-up, in the hall, in a room)? What are the product's visibility characteristics? Do not use a visibility technique because it worked on the last project. Use it because it fits the people and process of this particular project.

5.2.1 An Overview of Techniques

Problems are much easier to analyze when they are visible. Most requirements are customer ideas, and ideas are difficult to see. Therefore, the requirements engineer must employ every available visibility technique while gathering requirements. The following paragraphs give an overview of how different techniques and their end products (both appear in italics) fit together. The techniques themselves are described in detail after the overview.

The first major part of requirements analysis is to have everyone understand the basic problem. Draw a large, simple sketch of the problem and use a *context diagram*. Place the sketch on the front door or some other obvious place. Quiz people on the sketch on their first afternoon on the project. Remove any confusion immediately. This may seem like overkill, but people at work have much on their minds. It is easy to lose focus and start drifting into areas that are interesting but do not help in understanding and solving the problem at hand.

A *concept of operations (ConOps)*, the user's view of the final system, is useful at this stage. It is not a detailed technical specification. It can be videotapes, computer screens, or an actual document. Anyone should be able to go through the ConOps in an hour and learn the project's fundamentals.

To understand the why, what, and how of the software, conduct a *context analysis*. The context diagram and *project context document* (see Chapter 6) are products of this analysis. The analysis will tell you why the business enterprise needs the software, which will help keep everyone focused. Software needed to reduce the time a customer stands in line is different from software needed to reduce paperwork.

The *functional specification* explains what the software is to do. At this time, the details of the functions are not needed. Everyone, however, does need to understand the three most important functions. I was involved in a $10 million project in which people debated the major functions until final delivery. Needless to say, the customer was not happy with the result.

Frame the understanding of the problem in objects, functions, and states (Davis, xxxx). Whenever discussing the problem with customers or developers, always think in terms of these three concepts. The topic of discussion will be either an object, function, or state.

Objects are real-world entities (not to be confused with objects in the object-oriented analysis, design, and programming world). They are nouns relevant to the situation being analyzed. They include people, offices, organizations, data, computers, networks—persons, places, and things.

Functions are tasks performed in the real world or to be performed by the software. Think of verbs or action words. Common functions include calculate, store, move, filter, transform, interpret, and, of course, create, retrieve, update, and delete (CRUD).

States deal with condition, history, and timing. A system is off or on. It is in the backup mode or maintenance mode. The users enter the data; the system checks for input errors; it calculates customer balances, and then prints reports. These actions occur in sequence and require time. A *state-transition diagram* shows how the system moves from state to state.

An excellent requirements gathering and visibility technique is the use of *facilitated meetings*. These are more than meetings as they include one-on-one interviews, public memos, traditional documents, group working sessions, and many other visibility tools. The product is a complete statement of requirements agreed on by the customer and produced rapidly and efficiently. Facilitated meetings incorporate all the visibility ideas expressed here in one package.

CRC cards are also good for exploring a problem. They were created to help with object-oriented analysis, but their concepts are useful in all types of requirements engineering.

Group working techniques, such as brainstorming, are good for eliciting many ideas quickly. The *system storyboarding technique* is an excellent improvement on brainstorming.

Software diagrams are invaluable because they express software and system requirements in a way that is easy to understand. Most diagrams have a simple and complex form. Use the simple form when talking with customers and the complex form with developers. Customers do not want to be forced to learn diagrammatic intricacies from the software profession.

Rapid prototyping is also an excellent visibility tool in requirements gathering. *Prototypes* engage the customer at a time when their ideas of what they want are not well organized. The prototype, whether screens or flip charts, lets the customers see possibilities. Their thoughts take shape and the requirements become real. Rapid prototyping works well when the customers cannot explain what they need in software.

Another visibility exercise is to *act out the software* with the customers (Coad, 1995). This is useful when the customers use a complex series of tasks in their jobs. They do their jobs correctly, but they cannot seem to describe how they do it. The "job is too complicated" or "there are too many variations to explain."

Start with the basics of objects, functions, and states. Make props to represent the objects. A piece of paper with "Annual Report" written in big letters is sufficient. Use a cardboard box with in and out slots to represent a computer system that takes in data and sends out a report. Pretend to perform tasks to represent the functions. Walk through sequences of tasks or scenarios. The scenarios show the system's different states. Videotape the sessions or have several observers take detailed notes.

Acting out a system gives customers a different perspective of what they do and shows them how a software system can help them do it. The software becomes something they demand, not something management is forcing on them. They are anxious to help the developers build the software and they will use it when it is delivered.

5.2.2 Facilitated Meetings—JAD

An excellent method for analyzing and documenting requirements is the use of facilitated meetings. This type of meeting has been available for decades and gained popularity in the mid- to late 1990s. There are a few forms of these meetings. For years, Gary Rush has taught his FAST Session Leader's classes. Rush has collected and generalized a number of facilitation techniques. His methods enable groups of people to gather and document almost any type of information. Sam Kaner (Kaner, 1996) has also written a text on many useful techniques a facilitator can use in a meeting. Ellen Gottesdiener (Gottesdiener, 2002) has focused such techniques on the subject of requirements. Another well-known method focused on requirements is JAD or Joint Application Development (Wood & Silver, 1995). This section will focus on JAD.

The heart of JAD is a two-to-five-day workshop, or *JAD session*. Customers and developers work out the details of the requirements using many of the visibility techniques described in this chapter.

The JAD process has five main steps: define the scope, familiarize key people, prepare for the workshop, conduct the workshop, and produce the final document.

In the first step, *define the scope*, an executive sponsor—someone above the users, developers, and their managers—defines the project's scope by writing a contract with the JAD leader. This directs the leader to create the requirements or other document and gives him the authority to do it. The JAD leader should be trained in leading or facilitating JAD sessions. He could be a consultant or part of the project team.

To *familiarize key people*, the leader spends one day interviewing key users and managers about the requirements. The interviews provide the leader with background information and many of the requirements.

Prepare for the workshop is probably the most time-consuming step. It involves four major tasks:

1. *Draft the requirements document.* The draft of the requirements results from the scope contract and the information from the interviews. In non-JAD situations, the draft is used as a semifinal version. Usually, the facilitator conducts interviews, drafts a document, passes it out for comment, and uses the comments to make the final document. In JAD, the draft is the starting point for the workshop.

2. *Distribute the draft.* The facilitator gives a copy of the draft to each participant several days before the workshop, and the participants study it. If this workshop is a first for the group, they should understand that the draft needs intense work. Most people are used to sitting in a meeting where a document is presented and the group approves it. This is not what happens in a JAD workshop. The participants must be familiar with the draft document for the workshop to succeed.

3. *Organize needed assistance.* Assistants help the facilitator ensure a successful workshop. They are not active participants, but strive to keep the workshop rolling by doing whatever needs to be done. One assistant needs to take detailed notes. Another assistant needs to transcribe the sketches, flip-charts, or scribbled sticky notes into a word processor, drawing package, or CASE tool. The JAD workshop is an extremely focused exchange of information, and many ideas vital to progress are exchanged in a short time. The transcription is best done when the group is not in the room (this means working late during the workshop). The facilitator also needs a runner (executive assistant) to get an extra pot of coffee, a handful of pencils, a reference book, a sketch forgotten in the adjacent building, and so on. Keeping the flow of ideas going is essential. You don't want to stop the workshop while the facilitator and participants scatter to fetch these odds and ends. The runner is essential.

4. *Obtain a suitable room.* This task may not seem as important as the others, but it is not a "no-brainer." The room must be large enough; be accessible but not too accessible (to avoid interruptions); have proper heating, ventilation, and air conditioning; and have access to rest rooms, chairs, and tables. Each individual and group will need supplies (sticky notes, markers, flip-chart pads, overhead projector, and so on), as well as drinks and snacks. The facilitator cannot let the room take care of itself while he handles the important items. Uncomfortable people will not be at their best, and the quality of the entire workshop may suffer.

In *conduct the workshop*, the requirements become visible. The facilitator guides the group through a detailed reworking of the draft document. The facilitator will use many of the visibility techniques given here to elicit requirements. The group works the document as a unit and thus owns the final product. Their requirements, not the facilitator's requirements, are what they can tolerate. The result of the workshop is all the information, diagrams, screens, and thoughts for a complete requirements document.

In the last step, *produce the final document,* the facilitator and assistants take the information and write a (nearly) final requirements document. The document must be written quickly. The JAD workshop is expensive; a dozen people have devoted several full days to it and poured out their emotions and energy. Everyone needs to see results. I don't like to talk about tools like word processors because people usually devote too much time to gadgets and not enough time to substance. This is one place, however, where you must know how to use the full power of word processors, CAD packages, scanners, and desktop publishers to put the workshop results into a first-class document in two or three days. I don't usually recommend working weekends, but if a JAD workshop ends on Thursday and the participants receive a (nearly) final document on Monday, the project will probably succeed. (Be sure to give yourself and others who have worked to produce the document the rest of the week off.)

The group will meet once again to review the (nearly) final document. This review ensures that what was stated in the workshop is in the document. It is not a time for new ideas or debates.

JAD has several benefits. It accelerates the process of creating a requirements document. The usual requirements document needs weeks of interviewing people one at a time when their schedules permit. A draft is written and distributed and comments dribble in for several more weeks. The revised document goes out and the weeks-long commenting process repeats several times.

It brings together key people for several intense days. The individuals in the group feed on one another to produce ideas. Ideas are captured and documented in a few days.

It improves the quality and accuracy of the requirements document. The people in the JAD workshop are sitting face to face thinking, talking, and scribbling; they are communicating. Misunderstandings ("when the document said this, I thought it meant that") are eliminated. Because the people in the workshop feed on each other's ideas, the document contains more of the necessary requirements.

I recommend buying copies of three books (Wood & Silver, 1995; Kaner, 1996; Gottesdiener, 2002) for your company. They contain detailed descriptions of the process, outlines for the memos and documents, and tips on facilitated meetings. Excellent training is available from Rush Systems (www.mgrush.com).

5.2.3　Design by Walking Around

Design by walking around (DBWA) is a group visibility technique developed by Richard Zahniser (Zahniser, 1993a). The background for this technique is the 90/10 rule of work, shown in Figure 5.1. The rule states that the first 90%

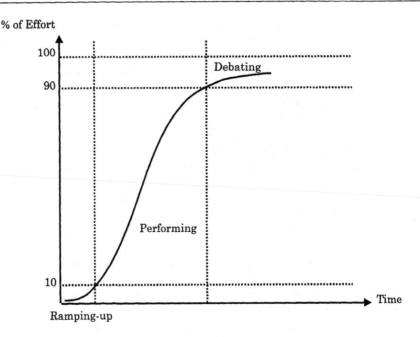

Figure 5.1   The 90/10 rule of work.

of the work requires 90% of the time and the last 10% of the work requires the other 10% of the time. The lower-left corner shows that the first 10% of the effort moves slowly as the group or individual launches into the problem (ramping up). The area of the graph from 10% to 90% of the effort is the performing region. This is where work gets done. People's minds are working; they see the problem, and they produce.

Progress slows to a crawl in the final region from 90% to 100% (the debating region). In a group setting, two people debate minutiae while everyone else stares at the ceiling. In an individual setting, a person struggles endlessly trying to find that one last sentence or final touch to a design.

In DBWA, the group (or individual) works on one view of the problem until hitting the debating region (the 90% mark). Instead of continuing here diligently but inefficiently, work stops and moves on to another view of the problem. This process of working on one view until hitting the wall and moving on to another continues until all the views have received one good attempt. At this time, the group returns to the first view, which is 90% complete. Their understanding of the problem is much better now because they have looked at it from several views. The last 10% of the effort can progress at the same rate as in the performing region of the graph. The group continues and completes the last 10% of the effort for each view.

Figure 5.2 shows the views Zahniser suggests completing in a "design" session. The first view is always the context diagram (described later). The order

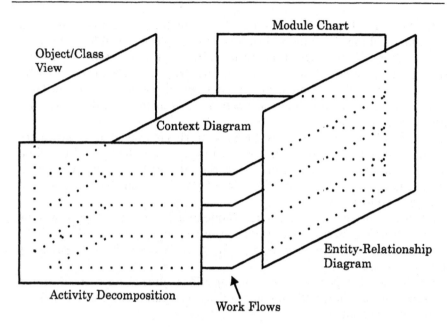

Figure 5.2   Views for the design by the walking around approach.

of the other views depends on the situation, as long as each view is attempted once before returning to the context diagram. This figure illustrates that the design problem is multidimensional. We see the entire design by walking around it and examining it from the different views.

Design by walking around is an efficient and effective technique. Zahniser describes it in specific terms, but it is useful as a general technique for many situations. For example, in creating a document, a technical writer will make an outline, sketch figures, write a draft, and make revisions. The four views are the outline, figures, draft, and revisions. It is not written in stone that the writer must complete 100% of one view before starting another. The writer can outline some, sketch several figures, draft some of the document, revise some, and return to the outline. Walking around the document will reduce the amount of writer's block or dead time.

5.2.4 System Storyboarding Technique

The system storyboarding technique (SST) is another practice developed by Zahniser (Zahniser, 1993b) to help people work together creatively. In an SST session, people sit at tables facing a facilitator, who is at a wall. Each person has a sticky notes pad and a felt-tip marker that allows the writing to be read from a distance.

The facilitator begins the session by describing the problem (structure of a program, database elements, and so on). The people at the table start throwing out ideas. When a person has an idea, he says it aloud, scribbles it on a sticky note (usually one word will do), and gives it to the facilitator, who places it on the wall. The interaction is a free-for-all; anyone can give the facilitator a sticky note at any time. Each person hears the ideas of the others and sees them on the wall.

After a while, the flow of ideas slows down. This is a signal to the facilitator that the first 90% of the problem has consumed 90% of the time. The facilitator stops the action and works on the ideas on the wall. He sorts them, eliminates redundancies, and, with the help of the people at the table, tries to arrange them logically.

SST is an efficient and effective technique to use at work. Zahniser calls the free-for-all of ideas *concurrent creation*. The people at the table do not take turns as in the classic brainstorming technique. The result is that more ideas come out in less time.

SST is also inexpensive. Most organizations already have sticky notes, markers, tables, chairs, and, of course, walls. You can use SST as formally or informally as you like.

5.2.5 Concept of Operations

The ConOps is the user's view of the system—the user being the person who will ultimately use the software; not the user's manager, the company president, or a consultant. The ConOps is created early in the project before any other documents. Sometimes, the customers create it themselves; sometimes, they have the developer do it; sometimes, they hire a consultant to do it.

The ConOps presents the user's world to everyone else; it bounds the problem and keeps everyone on track. It can take many forms. The traditional document works as long as it contains ample figures and narratives. Videotapes that show a user doing his job using the proposed software are an excellent way to create a ConOps. A sequence of computer screen images also makes a good ConOps.

Show the ConOps to people on their first day on the project to give them an immediate perspective. For example, suppose the project is to build the Road ID System, a software system that will connect police cars to a central computer to aid officers in identifying suspects. A good ConOps is a five-minute video showing an officer stopping a speeding car and escorting the driver to the police car. The officer holds the suspect's hand to a plate of glass (scanner), presses a couple of buttons, and the system shows the officer all known information related to the suspect. This software, if it could be built, would involve state-of-the art technology in several fields (communications, image processing, artificial intelligence, etc.). Every law-enforcement official in the country, however, would understand the ConOps video. Every developer would understand what the users wanted.

Using a ConOps is particularly important if the desired software interacts with the outside world in a complicated manner.

5.2.6 Mind Maps

Mind maps, created by Tony Buzan (Buzan, 1991), represent what is in a person's mind concerning a particular topic. In Figure 2.3 in Chapter 2, I presented a mind map of an earlier version of this book. Figure 5.3 shows a mind map of the Road ID System just described. A mind map contains key words, symbols, and figures connected by lines. The shape, color, and content of the mind map should be easy to remember and recreate.

The Road ID System mind map is, of course, my particular view of the software. The roadside stop portion shows that I foresee several ways to identify a suspect. The officer simply pushes a button to send this information through a communications system to a storage facility. The mind map indicates several options for the communications system and desired characteristics of the storage facility. I could go on discussing this mindmap for several more pages. That illustrates its imaging power.

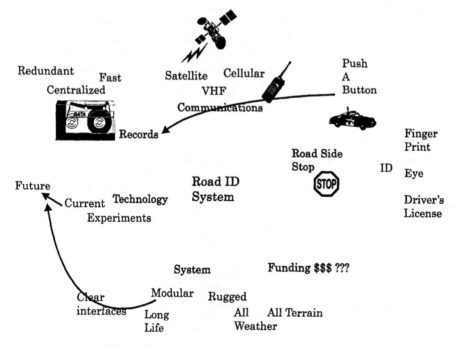

Figure 5.3 A mind map of the Road ID System.

I typically draw a mind map before doing anything else on a new project, regardless of the project's size. The mind map crystallizes my perceptions and lets me share them with coworkers. I walk through the mind map with the first few people joining me on the project. We change the mind map until it becomes our view instead of my view. This is a quick, efficient, and effective way for the core group of a project team to reach a common understanding of a project.

Mind maps are powerful and useful for putting a person's thoughts on paper—exactly what we want to do to make software visible. Looking at Buzan's material as one page in this book cannot do it justice. I urge you to get a book on mind maps, either Buzan's or some other, and practice this technique by making several dozen mind maps of familiar topics. Making a mind map is an excellent way to start a project or approach any new problem.

5.2.7 *Gilb Charts*

Software is largely qualitative. Everyone wants "user friendly" software, but one person's interpretation of that term can differ radically from another's. There must be some way to transform such loose, qualitative interpretations into concrete, measurable, quantitative items. Tom Gilb (Gilb, 1988, 1996) has argued this point well and provided techniques to accomplish it.

Figure 5.4 shows a Gilb chart. The chart concerns a *function* (top) such as "easy to use." The goal is to change this function into a quantifiable *attribute*. *Scale* is the unit of measure for the attribute (in this case, minutes, but it could be bytes, staff hours and so on). *Test* describes how to test the attribute (ask a user to perform a function and time him from start to finish). It helps to have this column refer to a complete description of the test in the test plan (see

We want the system to be "easy to use"

Function: Time required for a user to learn to use the system given a tutorial manual.

Attribute	Scale	Test	Worst	Plan	Best
Enter a patient record	Time (mins)	Give a user the manual and ask them to perform the attribute operation.	10	5	2
Create weekly report	Time (mins)	Give a user the manual and ask them to perform the attribute operation.	30	15	10
Perform system backup	Time (mins)	Give a user the manual and ask them to perform the attribute operation.	20	10	5

Figure 5.4 A Gilb chart to quantify "easy to use."

Chapter 9). *Worst* gives the worst acceptable result of the test (for the user to take 10 minutes to enter a patient record is unacceptable). *Plan* gives the expected result or goal of the test (we want the user to take five minutes). *Best* gives an upper threshold of performance (an entry time of two minutes would be outstanding). *Now* states the outcome of the test performed on the current system (the user now needs 60 minutes to enter a record). This column is empty when the software lets users do something they currently cannot do.

Thus, the software attribute "easy to use" is made quantitative and visible. If a user can perform a system backup in 10 minutes with only a tutorial document, that part of the system is easy to use.

Most developers do not bother trying to change qualitative statements into quantitative ones. They take the easy way out by saying "This is touch and feel and we cannot measure it." This need not be the case. The vast majority of software features will transform into a measurable test if you exercise a little creativity and persistence. It may be difficult to be precise, but it is necessary.

5.2.8 Diagram of Effects

An excellent method of making a situation visible is through a diagram of effects (Weinberg, 1992). This helps illustrate a system that can contain computers, software, hardware, and other things including, most importantly, people. Figure 5.5 shows two diagrams of effects.

Each cloud in the diagram represents a quantity that we can measure. The cloud symbol is used because we may not be measuring the quantity for various reasons, but we know it is there and seem to understand when it varies. A line from one cloud to another with an arrow indicates that as one quantity varies it has an effect on the other quantity, so it also varies. A plain line (like the ones in the upper diagram) means the two quantities change in the same direction. For example, in the upper diagram as the ease of use of a product increases the amount of use also increases. A plain line with a circle on it means that two quantities change in opposite directions. For example, in the lower diagram, as the ease of use of a product increases, the desire for a new product decreases.

The two diagrams in Figure 5.5 are simple, but they illustrate a complex situation. In the upper figure, we have a system in which, as the ease of use of a product increases, the amount of use increases. This is a positive feedback loop, because as the amount of use increases, the ease of use increases as the users become more familiar with the system, which causes the amount of use to increase, which causes the ease of use to increase, and so on. This positive feedback also works in the opposite direction. If we change the system so that the ease of use decreases, the amount of use will also decrease as users become disgusted with the system. As the amount of use decreases, so will the ease of use as users become less familiar with the system,

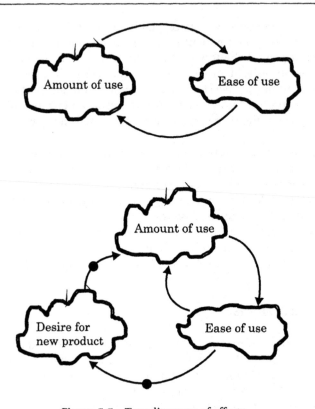

Figure 5.5 Two diagrams of effects.

which means the amount of use decreases, which means the ease of use decreases, and so on.

The diagram in the lower part of Figure 5.5 inserts another quantity into the system. If people are happy with the current product, the ease of use increases (more familiarity). As the ease of use increases, the desire for a new product decreases. As that desire decreases, the amount of use of the current product increases. The opposite can also be true here. If we change the product and the ease of use decreases, the desire for a new product increases.

This diagram tells us that if we wanted the users to desire a new product, we could sabotage the current one. Its ease of use would decrease and the desire for a new product would increase. We could also interrupt the users' day so that the amount of use would decrease. As it decreases, the ease of use would decrease and the desire for a new product would increase. We could add the quantity "interruptions" to the diagram of effects. Some thought will bring to mind several other quantities that we could add.

The diagram of effects can help us understand the culture of an organization. That will help us to understand their work, their systems, and the requirements for any new systems.

5.2.9   Rapid Prototyping

Rapid prototyping is an excellent technique for gathering nonfunctional requirements. The developers build something (a prototype) that the users can
see—a visual representation of their ideas. The users explain the difference between what is on the screen and what is in their minds. After several iterations, the users and developers have the same ideas, and the developers can
build what the users want.

Rapid prototyping tools help build "something to see" quickly and cheaply. Such tools are plentiful and inexpensive in today's visual programming environments. A programmer skilled with such tools can generate several
screens with buttons, menus, scroll bars, and so on, in a day. You can also
draw screens on a flip chart and flip through typical work scenarios. Use
sticky notes as buttons and menus; change the content of the sticky notes and
move them around on the flip chart pages. Working with users and such tools
can capture a user interface in a few hours.

Rapid prototyping is a requirements gathering technique, so its results are
part of the functional baseline. If you use rapid prototyping, put the agreed-on
prototype screens in the functional baseline. Videotape them or store them on
disk and attach this to the requirements document and functional baseline.

5.2.10   Software Diagrams

Figures 5.6 through 5.15 show classic diagrams used in software engineering.
Each has its own place in making software visible. They are tools to know and

Symbols
    = is composed of
    + and
    () optional, may be present or absent
    {} iteration
    {} select one of several alternatives
    ** comments
    @ identifier (key field) for a store
    | separates alternatives in the [] construct

Examples
    name = title + given-name + (second-name) + family-name
    title = [Mr. | Miss | Ms. | Dr.]
    Given-name = {character}
    second-name = {character}
    family-name = {character}
    character = [A-Z | a-z]

Figure 5.6   The data dictionary.

use because they work at work. Data dictionaries define the nouns or the object of the actions in software. Context diagrams, dataflow diagrams, structure charts, and SADT diagrams move among the actions or processes. HIPO and Warnier–Orr diagrams weave the objects and actions together in single diagrams. CRC cards let people act out the objects and actions to see if the software will work before writing it.

Data Dictionary. As Figure 5.7 shows, a data dictionary defines the important data elements for a piece of software. The top part of the figure gives a notation scheme. The scheme used is not important if everyone is consistent and persistent. The bottom part of the figure shows the definition of a name data element. The data dictionary is a simple and effective way to show people what their software will be working on. Too often, people assume everyone knows the definition of the data. They don't record it, and this costs money later during maintenance. The data dictionary is essential in all software methods.

Context Diagram. Figure 5.6 is a context diagram, which shows how people and things interact with a system. The system is in an oval at the center; groups of people are shown as boxes around the system. Items of information flow between the people and system. The context diagram is useful early in a project because it shows the people, system, and information in a broad context. The context diagram is a special case of a dataflow diagram.

Dataflow Diagram. Figure 5.8 is a dataflow diagram, which partitions a system into distinct processes and defines the interfaces between them. In this

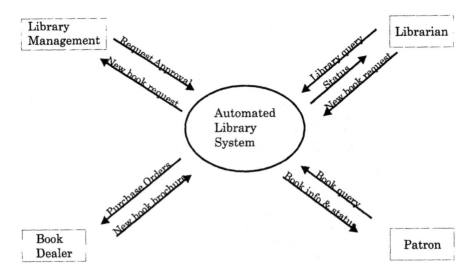

Figure 5.7   A context diagram.

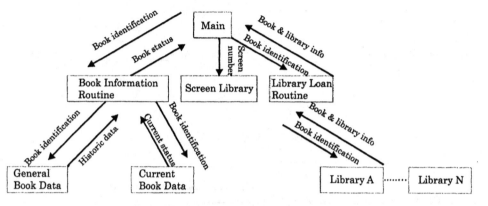

Figure 5.8 A dataflow diagram.

diagram, data is flowing among routines and files in a program, but items can be people or systems—anything appropriate.

Structure Chart. Figure 5.9 is a structure chart that shows the calling hierarchy or tree for a program. Structure charts show how a change in one part of the program may affect the remainder. This indicates the magnitude of a proposed change and helps you decide if a change is worth the work. Most commercial development environments (Microsoft, Borland, and Symantec, among others) can create calling hierarchies in one form or another.

SADT Diagrams. Figure 5.10 is a SADT (Structured Analysis and Design Technique) diagram (SADT is a trademark of Softech Inc.), which represents

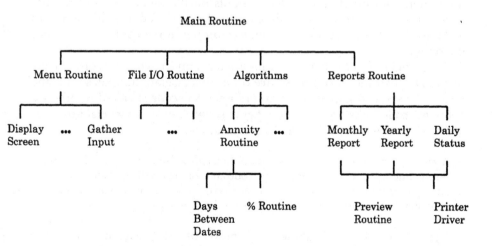

Figure 5.9 A structure chart.

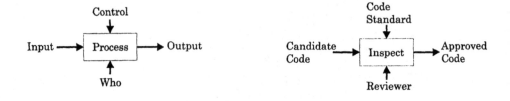

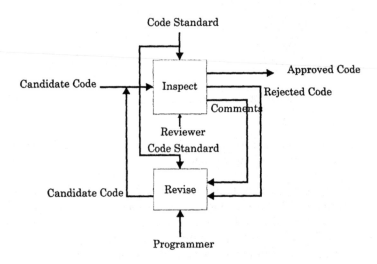

Figure 5.10   A SADT diagram.

a process flow. At top left are the chart's basic components. The process is in the center, with inputs on the left, outputs on the right, a control mechanism on the top, and people (who) on the bottom. The diagram translates to "who does the process to the input according to the control to produce the output."

To the right of this generic diagram is a diagram showing the components of a SADT chart for inspecting source code. This diagram translates into "the reviewer inspects candidate code according to the code standard to produce approved code." The bottom of the figure shows how to tie several boxes together and use multiple outputs. This translates to

> A reviewer inspects candidate code according to the code standard. This pro-
> duces either approved code or rejected code and comments. If the code is reject-
> ed, a programmer revises the rejected code according to the comments and the
> code standard to produce candidate code for the reviewer.

Figure 5.10 shows only some of the power of SADT diagrams. The situation under study is limited only by the size of the paper or wall. Use a wall and a stack of sticky notes to create a complete SADT diagram of the system or situation.

Processes can also be represented using a hierarchy of diagrams. The first would show the basic process, then detailed diagrams would explode the process boxes of the first diagram. A good SADT diagram can communicate a hundred pages of text with far fewer misinterpretations.

HIPO Diagrams. Figures 5.11 and 5.12 illustrate hierarchy–input–process–output, or the more familiar HIPO, diagrams. These are related to structure charts because they illustrate how routines call one another and what the individual routines do. They are excellent for documenting existing programs or designing new programs.

Figure 5.11 shows a HIPO visual table of contents. This is the first diagram in a HIPO set and gives a directory to the other diagrams. It is a structure chart because each number or block represents one subroutine whose name is listed in the table of contents to the left. If the subroutines cannot fit on one

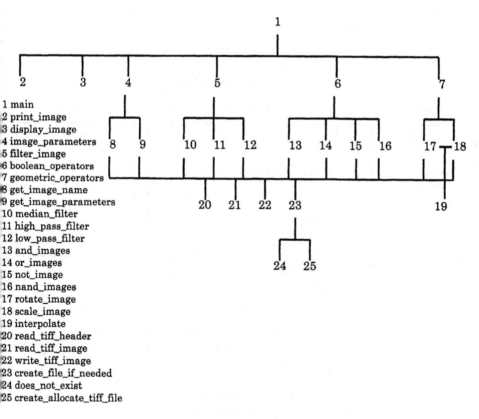

1 main
2 print_image
3 display_image
4 image_parameters
5 filter_image
6 boolean_operators
7 geometric_operators
8 get_image_name
9 get_image_parameters
10 median_filter
11 high_pass_filter
12 low_pass_filter
13 and_images
14 or_images
15 not_image
16 nand_images
17 rotate_image
18 scale_image
19 interpolate
20 read_tiff_header
21 read_tiff_image
22 write_tiff_image
23 create_file_if_needed
24 does_not_exist
25 create_allocate_tiff_file

Figure 5.11 A HIPO visual table of contents.

page, each block or page number can point to an overview chart. An overview chart is an intermediate diagram that represents the calling structure of several related subroutines.

Figure 5.12 shows a HIPO detail diagram for one subroutine: and_images. The top portion lists the subroutine(s) that call and_images (in this case only Boolean_operators), and the bottom portion lists the subroutines called by and_images. The left side contains the parameters passed to the subroutine, whereas the right lists those returned by it. The process block in the center contains the high-level algorithm or pseudocode for the subroutine.

Use a wall and a stack of sticky notes to design and fully document a program using HIPO diagrams.

Warnier–Orr Diagrams. Figure 5.13 illustrates two Warnier–Orr diagrams, which use curly brackets to group data and actions. The first represents a data structure. A library book record has a description and a status. The *description*

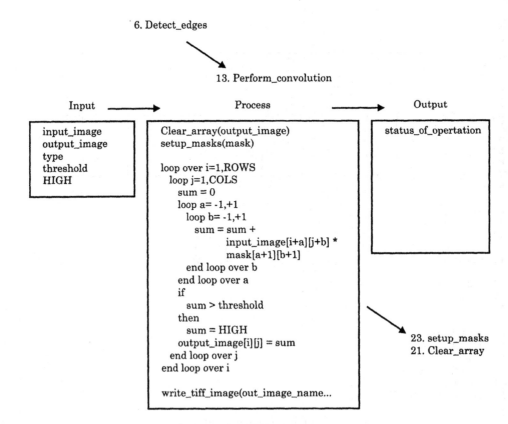

Figure 5.12   A HIPO detail diagram.

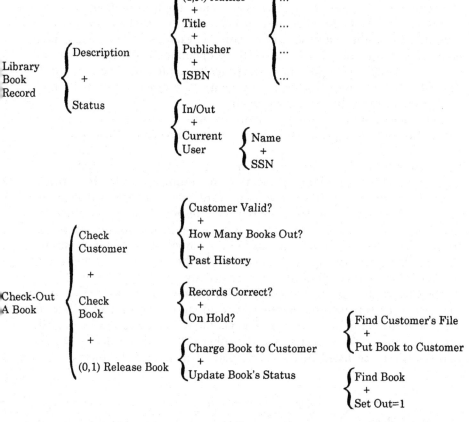

Figure 5.13 Two Warnier–Orr diagrams that represent data structure (top) and actions (bottom).

has one or more authors, a title, a publisher, and an ISBN. Each of these can break into more detail. *Status* contains an in/out indicator and the name of the current user. The current user has a name and a Social Security number (SSN).

The second diagram represents actions. When the library system needs to check out a book, it checks the customer's records, checks the book's record, and releases or does not release the book. Each action has more detailed actions. The diagrams can represent decision points, alternatives, and iterations.

Warnier–Orr diagrams are good for diagramming everything from entire systems to subroutines. The associated Warnier–Orr method is well suited to designing and documenting data-oriented business systems.

State-Transition Diagrams. State-transition diagrams illustrate how actions move a system between states. A program has many states, such as executing a subroutine or displaying a screen or menu. Figure 5.14 shows a state transition diagram for a program. The ovals are states, the lines with arrows represent movement between states, and the characters next to the lines are the inputs that cause the state transitions. For this example, when in the main menu, a user input of 1, 2, or 3 causes the program to display the corresponding menu. An Esc key input causes the program to prompt for exit confirmation (then an "X" causes system shutdown). Any other input at the main menu state displays the main menu again.

State-transition diagrams give visibility to the elements of time and change, in contrast to previous diagrams, which show data and action.

CRC Cards. Class Responsibility Collaboration, or the more familiar CRC, cards are an effective tool for representing and testing classes in object-oriented development. Figure 5.15 shows a CRC card. The name field is the name of the class, the knows and does fields are the responsibilities, and the with field is the collaboration. The responsibilities are the methods or active routines of the class. The collaborations are the names of the other classes this class needs to perform significant activities in the system. The other classes provide information or perform a needed activity.

The CRC cards make classes visible, which allows people to act out or test the system. Each person holds one CRC card, and a coordinator calls out a scenario or use case for the system. The people walk around the room acting out the scenario. They meet or use the other CRC cards needed in the scenario—only those listed in the with part of their card. Problems are in-

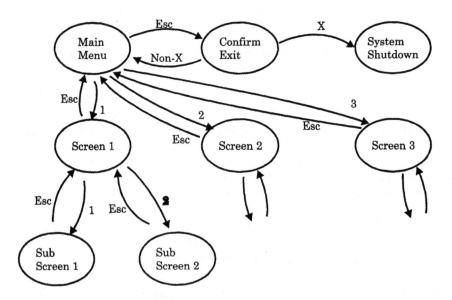

Figure 5.14   A state transition diagram.

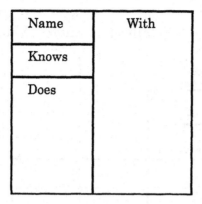

Figure 5.15   A CRC card.

evitable, but at this point they are easy and inexpensive to correct (Ambler, 1995; Constantine, 1995; Wilkinson, 1995).

CRC cards provide an active, participatory form of visibility. They also allow end users to work with developers. This enjoyable interaction means much to the system's development and eventual use.

Sequence Diagrams. Sequence diagrams show the interaction among different parts of a system. They also show the sequence and timing of the interactions. Figure 5.16 shows a sequence diagram for the software components that control an engine. The system components are listed across the top of the diagram. The vertical lines represent the passage of time for each of the components. The labeled and directional horizontal lines represent messages or signals that the components send to one another. The notes on the left side of the figure highlight important timing constraints.

Figure 5.16 shows how the system controller interacts with the fuel controller and a couple of monitors. There are many requirements documented in this simple figure. For example, the fuel controller is required to open the fuel valve only after being commanded to do so. It cannot open it under any other circumstances. The system controller is required to obtain the system's pressure every five seconds or less. The system is required to close the fuel valve in less than half a second after its pressure becomes too high.

A sequence diagram is an excellent method of capturing many pieces of information in one small place. I once worked on a system that had three major components. These components communicated with about thirty different messages in specific sequences under strict time constraints. These requirements were scatted among several hundred pages in half a dozen different documents. After long study, I was able to condense these hundreds of pages to one sequence diagram on a poster. That poster enabled us to understand the structure of the system during a much-needed upgrade project.

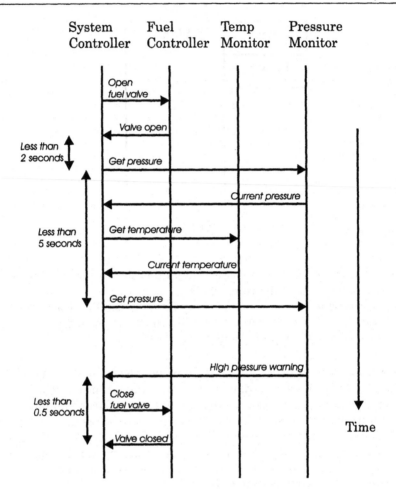

Figure 5.16   A sequence diagram.

Volere Requirements Shell. The fundamental visibility tool in the Volere method is the requirements shell. This is a white 5" × 8" card with field labels printed on it. The white color of the card caused one user to name them "snow cards." Anyone who has attended one of the Robertsons' classes on the Volere method knows that nickname.

The requirements engineer pencils in sentences and phrases next to the field names while analyzing and managing the requirements. The cards also provide the final information when it is time to write the requirements document. The requirements engineer acquires the information on the requirements shell while conducting user interviews about business events and use cases. The main fields on the requirements shell are:

Description: The intent of the requirement. This contains the user's words as to what is required. These are often vague and loose words.

Rationale: The reason behind the requirement's importance. This states why the requirement is important to the user.

Source: Who wants this requirement. The source of the requirement is important. Question will arise later, and it is quite helpful to know whom to ask.

Fit Criteria: Quantified, testable goals that the system must meet. The tester uses these goals to determine if the system passes. In many respects, this is the true requirement.

Customer Satisfaction: A number from 1 to 10. This is a measure of how happy the client will be if you deliver. This helps rank the requirements when the resources needed to implement every requirement are not available.

Customer Dissatisfaction: A number from 1 to 10. This is a measure of how upset the client will be if you don't deliver. This also helps rank the requirements when the resources needed to implement every requirement are not available.

The requirements shells are great tools. First, they are handy. You can grab a bunch of them and go talk to some users. At the same time, a colleague can grab a bunch of them and talk to other users. Second, they are physical manifestations of requirements. Each person can hold a requirement in their hand, and there is something about this that communicates well. Finally, these cards are easy to see. You can pin them to a wall, group them, rearrange them, merge them, split them, and so on.

Requirements Verification Traceability Matrix (RVTM). The RVTM is a table that traces a requirement from its inception through design, implementation, and test. Appendix B describes the RVTM in detail. For now, the RVTM is a visibility tool for the requirements that have been gathered and accepted for the requirements document. At this time, you enter the requirement name and number in the RVTM.

5.2.11 The Software Requirements Specification

Once the requirements are understood, they must be documented. This changes the requirements to visible products that people can review, discuss, and improve. The requirements are documented in a *Software Requirements Specification* (SRS).

The SRS describes the problem facing the customer. It can include photographs, videos, prototypes, screen displays, text, software diagrams, mathematical equations—whatever best communicates the problem. In theory, a designer should be able to create a solution using nothing but the SRS. In practice, this rarely occurs. Aim to make the SRS as complete, accurate, and descriptive as possible.

As I described earlier, the two activities in requirements engineering—analyzing the problem as requirements and documenting the problem—are not sequential; understanding the requirements will not be finished before documenting begins. How often you go back and forth depends on the people and the product.

Because the SRS is the functional baseline for the project, neither the customer nor the developer (typically the joint creators of the SRS) can change the SRS without the other's approval. Changing the SRS will require the project manager to gather other Configuration Control Boards and trace through the impacts to the project.

General Elements of a Good Document. Visible software requires documentation, whether that is online documents, Web home pages, built-in help systems, sketches, or plain old words on paper. Throughout this book, I describe documents that should be in a software project during particular development stages.

Always consider several questions when creating a document (Blum, 1992):

- *What is its function?* If the document should teach a user how to do something, it must be detailed, procedure oriented, and have plenty of graphics. The form is extremely important.
- *What is the management view?* If it is a structure chart that only the programmers will use, management does not care about the form of the document as long as the programmers understand it and it is kept secure for programmers to use five years from now.
- *Who are the readers?* This is probably the most critical question. End users need documents that are easy to access and help them do relevant tasks; managers need brief documents that explain how the software relates to the business; programmers need technical details.
- *What conventions must it follow?* Individuals cannot select their own document format. The CM plan (described in detail in Chapter 2 and Appendix B) describes the local conventions (single space, double space, ASCII, Postscript, TeX, version numbers in the header, and so on).

Avoid creating a document to satisfy a checklist. If a document is not necessary, don't create one. If it is necessary, it requires diligence from its creators and reviewers. Michael Jackson (Jackson, 1995) prescribes precision in all documents because "vagueness is one of the most common defects in software . . . [and] the reason for our frequent failures." Precision does not require a desktop publishing system and color Postscript printers. Expensive tools and technology do not make good documents; hard work, conscientious people, and good processes do.

Jackson also calls for "active critical inquiry," not passive acceptance from readers and reviewers. The reader should always be skeptical, not accepting the document at face value, but seeking proof in what the writer intended. Readers should always try to separate what they expect from what they see.

Choosing the SRS Author. Is it better to have the customers or developer write the SRS? In an ideal world, the customers should write the SRS. They know what they need. Why waste time dictating it to a developer? The customer can write the SRS, mail it to a developer, and have the developer design and build software. Unfortunately, this approach breaks down in practice because people do not write well enough to communicate their needs. Face-to-face discussions are inevitable.

There are distinct advantages to having the customer writing an SRS. The customer-written SRS will be general and define needs as the customer sees them, typically without technical solutions. This is a trait of a good SRS. The customers' ignorance of technical solutions keeps them out of the problem description. The customers' SRS will also talk about the goals of the customer instead of tasks.

The customer-written SRS is similar to a ConOps (concept of operations, described earlier) or a request for proposal (RFP). Because the ConOps is the customer's view of the software, it is written so that all customers can understand it. The RFP is commonly used when a customer does not have any software-developing capability (government agencies are good examples). The customer writes the RFP, distributes it to several software developers, and the developers return proposals for building the software. The RFP describes the problem without hinting at any solutions. The goal is to have software developers submit ideas for solutions. The customer decides which combination of solution and developer will serve him best.

Most developers would rather have the customer write the SRS, but when they see a customer-written SRS, they tend to change their minds. The developer's SRS is technical and specific—a reflection of how they think. Developers are also looking ahead to design and testing, and it is easier to design software and create tests given a technical, quantitative SRS, relative to a general, qualitative one. Establishing a functional baseline is also easier with a technical SRS.

But although the developer-written SRS makes the rest of the project easier, it is usually insufficient. Most developers cannot walk into a room full of customers and write a concise SRS on a chalkboard. There are too many unknowns, and the developer can steer the requirements in the wrong direction.

The best approach is actually a hybrid one, in which the customers write their version of the SRS and then the developer writes a final SRS. The customer's SRS can be a ConOps or an RFP. The customer's SRS introduces the developer to the problem, which gives him more insight into the situation and hence a better chance to write a good SRS. Rarely can a developer write an SRS without first reading a customer-written SRS. The exception is when the developer knows the customer and the customer's business before a project begins.

Types of Requirements to Include. An SRS must include a variety of requirements, both explicit and implicit and stated and unstated. *Explicit requirements* are stated directly by the customer. The customer will never approve an SRS that does not include them. These are the objects, functions, and states the customer deems most important.

Derived requirements are also stated but have been added by the requirements engineers. For example, consider software that must multiply and divide complex numbers. Multiplication and division are explicit requirements. The engineer can derive the requirement to also add and subtract complex numbers, since addition and subtraction are building blocks for multiplication and division.

Take care when putting derived requirements in the SRS. They can cause confusion and distrust. Customers may not understand why a requirement is there when they did not ask for it. The math example is easy to explain, but most cases are not so simple. If given too many derived requirements and too few explanations, customers can become suspicious that you are padding the requirements to make the project (and the final bill) bigger.

Some requirements are *unstated* (assumed) and need not be listed in the SRS. For example, software for banks must perform all functions required by law. Customers will not read these regulations, so it is unnecessary to repeat them in the SRS. You should, however, include a special section in the SRS that refers to other documents listing such requirements.

The SRS should also contain *what-if* requirements. These state what the software should do if the environment exceeds expected behavior. Suppose someone withdraws $1,000,000 from an automatic teller machine. This should never happen because the machine has limits on the amount of cash it will dispense (usually a few hundred dollars). But what if noise on the communication line makes the transaction *look* like $1,000,000? What should the banking software do (nothing, report an error, shut down, call the police)? What should file system software do when someone tries to write a file bigger than the disk drive?

What-if requirements generally come from the developer. It is unusual for the customer to consider such requirements. Customers focus on what the software should do under normal circumstances. The developer must raise the subject and then work through issues with the customer. Skip what-if requirements at your peril. The environment will always exceed expectations; if you ignore this, the software could do some crazy things—all of which you will be blamed for. Remember, the burden in requirements is with the developer.

In the same manner, the developer should work with the customer on the user interface. Do not put subjective terms like "user friendly" in the SRS. Such items will cause arguments when the heat is on. Instead ask: Who is a typical user (age, education, experience, etc.)? How long will a typical user need to learn to use the software? Will the user be able to remember how to use the software? Must he use it daily or weekly to retain knowledge? Will he always need to refer to the manual? How long should basic operations take? Do they require attention or can they be run overnight? How will the average user judge the software? Will the size and feel of the keyboard mean more than the display colors or the time required to learn to use them?

The developer must ask this seemingly endless string of questions. The customer will want you to stop asking questions and just "do the job." Use the statement from Weinberg given earlier: "I'm a professional and I'll excuse myself from a job before I will do something I cannot support professionally."

The developer should also specify the "-ilities" in the SRS—utility, usability, maintainability, adaptability, installability, portability, and understandability, as well as simplicity, security, and so on (described as part of software quality views in Chapter 2). Software that delights the customer but requires a programmer to install it will not sell. Software that sells but is confusing internally and expensive to maintain will not have a successful second version. Use the requirements visibility techniques given earlier to define the attributes and constraints. These will give you the "-ilities."

Length Issues. Should the SRS be brief and to the point or long and detailed? A short, brief SRS has several advantages. People can read it without growing tired, and alert readers comprehend more. It also gives the designers more flexibility. A long SRS may overconstrain them by describing the problem in so much detail that they are forced into a particular solution.

However, lack of detail also causes designers to make assumptions. Different people make different assumptions, and the differences eventually result in errors. When the customer and developer understand the problem well enough to intelligently constrain the designers, the SRS should be detailed and perhaps even require a certain product. However, use detail carefully so as not to restrict creativity.

The best approach is a mix of short and concise and long and detailed. Be brief and vague when it does not matter what the designers choose. Be detailed and restrict the designers on consensus points—when everyone agrees that the designers should go in this direction. State the restrictions and vagueness explicitly. "This portion of the SRS contains fine details because the customer and developer strongly agree on this part of the problem." Likewise, "This portion of the SRS is vague because the customer and developer feel this part of the problem could use some extra creativity."

The detailed or vague question should prompt you to use techniques like the Gilb chart (described earlier) to transform the question into a quantification. Numbers, equations, and formal notations are also useful. Replace "the software must respond to the user quickly" with "the software must respond to the user in less than two seconds."

Many software attributes are qualitative by nature, and transforming them to a quantitative form requires work (but work that is well worth it). Write a qualitative statement and examine the nouns, verbs, adjectives, and adverbs. (In Chapter 2, I gave some techniques and pointers that explain how to identify fuzzy language.) Break these words into details that have numbers. This is like assigning constraints to the attributes, as I described earlier. Use footnotes, appendices, and references to other documents. For example, in "the software must respond to the user quickly," the key words are software, respond, user, and quickly. Question these words. Does software mean the entire software system or just the parts that interface with people? Does respond mean finish an operation or flash a message? Does users mean all users or just the secretaries and clerks? Should the software respond differently to engineers, managers, and lawyers? Is "quickly" two seconds or half the time required by the current software? Asking these and other questions can transform "the software must respond to the user quickly" to the chart in Figure 5.17.

Checklist of Desired Characteristics. Figure 5.18 lists the characteristics every SRS should have (Davis, 1994), some of which I have already touched on. Even if your SRS does not reflect every one, you should at least consider

Type of User	Type of User/Software Interaction	Type of Response	Time (seconds)
Clerk	Login	Successful Login	< 2
		Error Message	< 1
	Deposit Entry	Entry Accepted	< 3
		Processing Message	< ½
		Error	< 2
Engineer	Matrix Addition	Processing Message	< ½
		Operation Complete	½ to 10
	Circuit Analysis	Error in Description	< 2
		Processing Message	< ½
		Operation Complete	1 to 20
Lawyer	Name Search	Processing Message	< ½
		Name Found	1 to 10
		Name not Found	1 to 10

Figure 5.17   Quantifying "the software must respond to the user quickly."

. Correct
. Unambiguous
. Complete
. Verifiable
. Consistent
. Understandable by the Customer
. Modifiable
. Traceable
. Design Independent
. Annotated
. Usable during O&M Phase

Figure 5.18   Desired characteristics of an SRS.

all of them. Correct carries two meanings. The first and most obvious is technical accuracy. If the software must perform a task in five seconds, the SRS must state five seconds—not four to six. The second meaning is that every requirement must satisfy a customer's need. A correct SRS does not have any extra requirements.

An *unambiguous* SRS has only one interpretation. English contains many words with multiple meanings. Such words cause confusion. Use words with obvious meanings or use words in an obvious manner. Numbers are not so ambiguous. This is another reason to quantify as much as possible.

Being *complete* has several parts. The SRS is complete if it includes everything the customers want. That is, the developer and customer will not need to add any features during design or coding. If a requirement is not understood completely, the SRS should state when the requirement will be known, e.g. "the format of the report cover sheet will be determined at the quarterly meeting on 1 June." Complete also means that every section, figure, table, page, and so on has a number. All necessary information not contained in the SRS is referenced. Every term is defined. Figure 5.17 is an example of how to quantify terms such as "user" and "quickly." Finally, the SRS includes all inputs and outputs for the software. Specify ranges of data (32 to 212 degrees), legal and illegal types of data (a–z, A–Z), and outputs that indicate errors (< 5 words spelled incorrectly).

The SRS is *verifiable* if every requirement in it can be verified. Chapter 9 describes the relationship between requirements and testing. The developer must be able to prove the software either does or does not meet each requirement. This is common sense and professionals must ensure this.

On the other hand, many requirements cannot be verified. Suppose the requirement is that the software must pilot a manned spaceship to Mars and back safely. How can this requirement be tested other than during the first trip of the manned spaceship? Exceptions to the verification rule occur frequently, but should not occur thoughtlessly.

To be *consistent,* the SRS cannot contradict any earlier documents, unless those documents were incorrect and the SRS states that explicitly. The SRS also cannot contradict itself. The style should be consistent. Do not denote paragraphs with numbers in one part and letters in another. Do not call the software "the product under consideration" in one section and "the software being written" in another.

Being *understandable by the customer* is self-explanatory. The customer and the developer are the Configuration Control Board for the functional baseline, and the SRS is the functional baseline. Customers cannot control changes to something they do not understand. In most cases, only a select group of customers is involved in the SRS, and only these customers need to understand it. Remember, the more customers who can understand the SRS, the more minds that can contribute to the problem, and the better the SRS.

The SRS must be *modifiable.* Requirements change, and the SRS must change with them. Anticipate change while writing the SRS—write it as you would a piece of software. Use the equivalent of defines, includes, logicals, and subroutines. Have a complete table of contents and index. If the memory requirement for a procedure changes, it should be easy to find every occurrence of that requirement in the SRS. Once again, quantities are easier to modify.

The SRS must be *traceable.* Traceability takes two forms. First, the project staff, notably the project manager and the configuration management staff, must be able to trace every requirement to its origin. Second, the readers of the design document should be able to trace each design element back to a requirement in the SRS. Numbering every requirement helps in this process. Using a database program (described later) is essential when requirements grow into the hundreds and thousands. Hypertext documents, cross-referenced spreadsheets, tables, and footnotes can refer to preceding and succeeding documents. People will trace back and forward through the SRS, so make their job easier. The RVTM mentioned earlier is an immense help in this area.

The SRS is *design independent* if it does not constrain the solution to be created. I touched on the relationship between requirements and design earlier in this chapter. Use techniques like bringing in outside consultants to help ensure design independence.

An *annotated* SRS states the relative importance of each requirement. All requirements are not created equally. Work with the customer to find the few requirements that will deliver the most value, as described earlier in the design by walking around technique. Time boxing and other processes (described in Chapter 7) emphasize this. At the very least, annotate each requirement as E, D, or O for essential, desirable, or optional (more on annotating individual requirements later).

The SRS should be *usable during operation and maintenance.* Chapter 10 describes the challenges unique to software maintenance. Users a decade after development will claim the software is broken when the problem is simply that everyone has a mistaken idea of what the software should do. A good

SRS will tell outsiders (and that is everyone 10 years down the road) when the software is broken and when someone wants to add to it. There is a big difference between the two and in how the O&M team handles them. Writing for the future is difficult, but not impossible. Bring in complete strangers to review the SRS. They will see it as the O&M team will see it in the future. If they misunderstand it, the O&M team will too, so fix the SRS now.

The SRS should be *signed* by the stakeholders. This is an important step in preparing the requirements document. If people have worked on something and believe in it, they should put their name on it. This is more difficult than it may sound. I have had great difficulty in convincing people to pick up a pen and scribble their name on a piece of paper. People fear being called on later to defend something they signed. There is much uncertainty involved in requirements as we gather and document them early in the project when we know the least. One way to reduce the fear of signing an SRS is to also admit in writing the predicament we are in during the requirements activity.

Karl Weigers suggests putting a paragraph below the signature line (Weigers, 1999). This information states our situation and also assures people that this need not be the final word on requirements. The paragraph states:

> I agree that this document represents our best understanding of the requirements for the project today. Future changes to this baseline can be made through the project's defined change process. I realize that approved changes might require us to renegotiate the project's costs, resources, and schedule commitments.

The final characteristic of an SRS is not listed in Figure 5.18: the SRS must fit the people, process, and product. An SRS for passenger airplane software (product) must be exactly right. That SRS should not spend pages emphasizing this when the developers (people) have 20 years of experience in this field. The SRS in a waterfall project (see Chapters 6 and 11) must be complete before moving on, whereas the SRS in an evolutionary project can have holes in it for several evolutions. Standards can help you write the SRS, as I describe later, but they are not a substitute for thinking about the 3Ps. Each SRS will deviate from the standard in some way. The people, process, and product determine what is and is not an appropriate deviation.

Expressing Requirements. The heart of the SRS is the requirements. A requirement can be expressed with input/output specifications, examples, or models. I/O specifications describe the software's behavior by showing the required output for a given input. Business software often concentrates on final reports—output. Real-time control software usually monitors a system being controlled—input. Other types of software deal with inputs and outputs equally. The difficulty in specifying inputs and outputs is that there are usually too many of them. The combinations quickly explode into an unmanageable size.

Another way to express a requirement is with examples. Examples are not precise specifications, but software is often applied to situations that are not precise. Examples convey information about the software's context and environment as well as its behavior. Scenarios are a type of example because they demonstrate typical software use. A videotape of customers performing their jobs is an excellent use of examples. Examples are similar to the ConOps described earlier, but they differ because they show developers the problems the customer faces without offering a solution.

Modeling is the best method of expressing a requirement in certain situations. A mathematical model is an equation (or set of equations) that describes a software system. Equations describe an image-processing operator precisely and completely. This is also true for digital signal processing applications and financial calculations. Functional models, like the software diagrams presented earlier, provide a mapping of inputs to outputs. Other types of models are useful in describing requirements (timing, grammar, and so on).

Take care when using models. A model implies precision, so do not use a model when the situation is not precise. Define the range of parameters in the model. If the parameters exceed the range, the model should respond in a safe manner. Do not let the model drive the software design. A model can be an excellent way to describe a problem and a very poor way to describe a solution.

Another potential problem with models is that users may not understand them. The requirements engineer interviews the user and goes back to his office to draw some diagrams like those shown earlier in this chapter. The next day, the requirements engineer goes back to the user and shows him the diagrams. The user, dazed and confused, nods and mumbles a few things that the engineer interprets as yes. That doesn't work well.

One way to work through this confusion is to use the natural language modeling approach of Sharp (Sharp, 1999). The requirements engineer creates a series of yes/no questions from his diagrams. He takes these to the user, asks the questions, and records the answers. He then gives the questions (no answers) and diagrams to a different engineer. The second engineer uses the diagrams and answers the questions. If the two sets of answers do not match, the requirements engineer has found something that is incorrect or unclear. In many cases, the two sets of answers will not match. This is because people make assumptions when they create diagrams, ask questions, and answer them. This technique causes the requirements engineer to go through the work one more time. The extra effort is worth it.

Regardless of form, each requirement should include elements of five content areas:

1. *Functionality.* Describe what the software will do (calculate interest, control the air conditioner, and so on). Include an introduction to the function, inputs, processing, and outputs.

2. *Performance.* How fast or reliably will the software perform its functions? Almost all performance requirements should be stated as quantities (2 msec, six significant digits, 32 Kbytes of memory, 2,000 hours).

3. *Design constraints.* Sources of constraints include complying with standards and hardware limitations. These and others limit the user interface, operating system, type of computer, programming language, and so on.

4. *Attributes.* These are the "-ilities" discussed earlier.

5. *External interfaces.* Explain how the software will interact with people, hardware, other software, and communications systems. The software must fit into the existing business systems.

5.2.12 Database Support

Software projects often have hundreds and thousands of requirements. Tracking this many requirements with a word processor alone is not a good practice. An alternative is to store requirements in a database system. Capable, inexpensive database packages are available for all platforms.

Using a database has several other advantages, including easier tracing, modification, and SRS writing. Tracing back and forward through baselines is a critical task in managing a software project, as I describe in Chapter 2 and Appendix B. Each requirement in a database can have several backward and forward pointers leading to previous and succeeding documents and baselines. These pointers transform a tedious and difficult task into a trivial one. People can concentrate on the substance of the project instead of on its mechanics.

Requirements change, and using a database makes changing them easier and less error prone. A requirement typically appears in several places in documents. Any change to the requirement means locating and changing it in each place. A database holds the requirement in one place and points to the various documents in which it appears, so a change is automatically replicated.

Database packages have report writing capabilities that can help you write parts of the SRS and other documents. A capable package and a skillful user can reduce the difficulty and increase the flexibility of writing requirements documents. (One of the best practices is to use specialists, as I described earlier.) Store all facets of the requirements (functionality, performance, and so on) in one place.

5.3 USING CM

Requirements are the major part of the functional baseline. Placing them in the baseline is a straightforward process that follows the directions in the CM plan (see Chapter 2 and Appendix B). The project manager presents the requirements (the SRS) to the *functional baseline Configuration Control Board.* Assisting in the presentation are the users and developers, who gathered the requirements and wrote the SRS.

The CCB should accept the SRS into the functional baseline without debate if the requirements gathering team (users and developers) has kept its superiors appraised of the requirements process and contents. If the team has not maintained visibility, they can expect problems that will require several visits to the CCB.

Requirements changes are inevitable. As I described in Chapter 4, requirements typically grow about 1% per month in a healthy project. Many projects experience much greater growth. The right way to handle that change is through the CM plan. This means the right people study all proposed requirements changes and report their findings to the CCB. The CCB, the people most knowledgeable and interested in this part of the project, decide what to do. The proposed changes, study findings, and decisions are visible to everyone.

The wrong way to change requirements is to let anyone change anything at any time. I have seen the resulting chaos in these situations. The project may produce software at some time, but no one can predict when, what software will eventually come out, and at what cost.

Controlling changes to requirements according to the CM plan is difficult and unpopular. People complain about bureaucracy and threaten to quit when they disagree with the decisions, but given the alternative of chaos and unpredictable cost, it is best to find a way to work through this resistance.

A key approach is to manage the timing of requirements changes. In the requirements change spectrum, one extreme is to bring every request for change (RFC) to the CCB when it arrives. This could require as many as three or four CCB meetings every week. The overhead for the meetings would be prohibitive. The other extreme is to allow RFCs twice a year. The CCB would not meet often, and overhead would be low, but users would grow frustrated and feel that management wasn't listening to their desires. The right timing for changes is somewhere in between. Exactly where depends on the project's people, process, and product. If the people don't know the product well, a learning process will be needed. The CCB would meet more often (twice monthly). Have the CCB meet as often as possible without wasting money; tell the users and developers how often this is, and keep your word. Never call off a CCB meeting when someone has an RFC in hand. That will kill trust and morale and will make the rest of the project almost impossible.

The project manager must maintain discipline and allow CM to do its job: The people are in place (CCB, CM staff), the CM plan has been drafted, and the documentation (SRS and baseline) is being managed. At times, I have been tempted to help things along under special circumstances, nearly always with bad results. CM worked when I followed the intended CM process.

5.4 USING STANDARDS

IEEE Std. 830-1998 is an excellent model for writing an SRS (IEEE, 1953) if you are new at it. If you have written dozens of requirements documents, the standard will probably not offer any new insights. However, most developers are not this familiar with writing SRSs and will find the standard invaluable in helping them include all the necessary information. The writers had hundreds of years of combined experience writing SRSs. They have already made all the mistakes and overlooked details that came back to haunt them later in their projects. Following the standard will eliminate these common mistakes.

Figure 5.19 shows the outline of the SRS recommended in IEEE 830-1998. This outline resembles the other IEEE standard documents I discuss in other chapters.

Introduction. Section 1, the introduction, provides an overview of the SRS. The purpose is to describe the document's intended readers and explain why it exists. *Scope* describes and limits the software being produced. For example,

1. Introduction
   1.1 Purpose
   1.2 Scope
   1.3 Definitions, Acronyms, and Abbreviations
   1.4 References
   1.5 Overview

2. General Description
   2.1 Product Perspective
   2.2 Product Functions
   2.3 User Characteristics
   2.4 General Constraints
   2.5 Assumptions and Dependencies

3. Specific Requirements
   see next figures

Appendices

Figure 5.19 SRS outline as recommended by IEEE Std. 830-1998.

"this SRS discusses the D-Word word processor that will be used by the secretarial staff of the Baton Rouge office of Acme, Inc." *Definitions, acronyms, and abbreviations* defines the terms in the SRS and often references other documents. *References* gives a complete list of documents referred to in the SRS (like the references section at the end of each chapter in this book). *Overview* briefly describes how the rest of the SRS is organized.

General Description. Section 2, the general description, discusses items that influence the SRS. It makes understanding the requirements easier. *Product perspective* describes how the product fits into its world. Software is usually part of a larger business system. Provide a diagram showing how this particular piece of software fits in the bigger picture. *Product functions* is a high-level brief summary of the software's intended functions. *User characteristics* discusses aspects of the customers that influence this piece of software. It is not a detailed essay on the customers. *General constraints* lists or refers to high-level constraints for the software, such as government regulations and hardware platforms. *Assumptions and dependencies* discusses items that influence the software, but may change. For example, the developers may assume that government regulations are going to change on January 1 because they have always changed on that date. However, if the regulations do not change on that date, the project will change dramatically.

Specific Requirements. Section 3, specific requirements, states the requirements in detail. It is the largest, most important section of the SRS because it contains everything needed by the developer to design software that will satisfy the customer. Do not hesitate to attach other visibility artifacts, such as videotapes, photos of screen prototypes, posters, and sketches. There are no rules to break; use what works.

Section 3 may take several formats. Figures 5.20 through 5.23 show four possible ways to organize it. Each method contains elements of the five areas in Section 2, but each emphasizes a different facet. These examples are by no means exhaustive. I include them to show how to include everything that is necessary and emphasize what is important. Think about your project, its people, process, and product, and use a method that best communicates the requirements.

Figure 5.20 takes a straightforward approach. Each functional requirement is listed with its introduction, inputs, processing, and outputs. The external interfaces come next. The section concludes with performance requirements, design constraints, attributes, and other requirements. "Other requirements" is for items that are necessary but do not fit well anywhere else.

The method in Figure 5.21 attaches the external interfaces to each functional requirement, which is useful if each required function has unique external interfaces. Software that controls a processing plant is an example. Each software subsystem controls a different type of machine and has vastly different external interfaces.

3. Specific Requirements

3.1 Functional Requirements
  3.1.1 Functional Requirement 1
    3.1.1.1 Introduction
    3.1.1.2 Inputs
    3.1.1.3 Processing
    3.1.1.4 Outputs
  3.1.2 Functional Requirement 2
    ...
  3.1.N Functional Requirement N

3.2 External Interface Requirements
  3.2.1 User Interfaces
  3.2.2 Hardware Interfaces
  3.2.3 Software Interfaces
  3.2.4 Communications Interfaces

3.3 Performance Requirements

3.4 Design Constraints
  3.4.1 Standards Compliance
  3.4.2 Hardware Limitations
  ...
3.5 Attributes
  3.5.1 Security
  3.5.2 Maintainability
  ...
3.6 Other Requirements
  3.6.1 Data Base
  3.6.2 Operations
  3.6.3 Site Adaption

Figure 5.20 SRS Section 3—Method 1.

Figure 5.22 shows a method that attaches the performance, design constraints, and attributes to each functional requirement. This is appropriate when these items are different for each function. The external interface requirements for the entire software system follow. A word processor could fit this situation. Every function (editor, spell checker, formatter) has the same external interfaces (one user, disk, operating system), but different performance requirements.

Figure 5.23 shows a method that allows different external interfaces, performance, design constraints, attributes, and other requirements for each function.

3.1 Functional Requirements
 3.1.1 Functional Requirement 1
  3.1.1.1 Specification
   3.1.1.1.1 Introduction
   3.1.1.1.2 Inputs
   3.1.1.1.3 Processing
   3.1.1.1.4 Outputs
  3.1.1.2 External Interfaces
   3.1.1.2.1 User Interfaces
   3.1.1.2.2 Hardware Interfaces
   3.1.1.2.3 Software Interfaces
   3.1.1.2.4 Communications Interfaces
 3.1.2 Functional Requirement 2
 ...
 3.1.N Functional Requirement N
 ...

3.2 Performance Requirements

3.3 Design Constraints

3.4 Attributes
 3.4.1 Security
 3.4.2 Maintainability

 ...
3.5 Other Requirements
 3.5.1 Data Base
 3.5.2 Operations
 3.5.3 Site Adaption

Figure 5.21   SRS Section 3—Method 2.

The report writer in a database package can write Section 3 in any of these or other formats.

As you can see, although IEEE Std. 830-1998 is neither light nor exciting reading, it can be tremendously helpful.

5.5   KEY THOUGHTS IN THIS CHAPTER

If the requirements are wrong, designing, writing, integrating, and testing software are done in vain. The two major steps in requirements engineering are to analyze the problem and document it. Analysis does not end before documentation begins. The requirements engineer will move between the

3. Specific Requirements

3.1 Functional Requirements

   3.1.1 Functional Requirement 1
     3.1.1.1 Introduction
     3.1.1.2 Inputs
     3.1.1.3 Processing
     3.1.1.4 Outputs
     3.1.1.5 Performance Requirements
     3.1.1.6 Design Constraints
       3.1.1.6.1 Standards Compliance
       3.1.1.6.2 Hardware Limitations
       ...
     3.1.1.7 Attributes
       3.1.1.7.1 Security
       3.1.1.7.2 Maintainability
       ...
     3.1.1.8 Other Requirements
       3.1.1.8.1 Data Base
       3.1.1.8.2 Operations
       3.1.1.8.3 Site Adaption
       ...
   3.1.2 Functional Requirement 2
     ...
   3.1.N Functional Requirement N
     ...

3.2 External Interface Requirements
   3.2.1 User Interfaces
     3.2.1.1 Performance Requirements
     3.2.1.2 Design Constraints
       3.2.1.2.1 Standards Compliance
       3.2.1.2.2 Hardware Limitations
       ...
     3.2.1.3 Attributes
       3.2.1.3.1 Security
       3.2.1.3.2 Maintainability
       ...
     3.2.1.4 Other Requirements
       3.2.1.4.1 Data Base
       3.2.1.4.2 Operations
       3.2.1.4.3 Site Adaption
       ...
   3.2.2 Hardware Interfaces
   3.2.3 Software Interfaces
   3.2.4 Communications Interfaces.

Figure 5.22   SRS Section 3—Method 3.

3. Specific Requirements

3.1 Functional Requirement 1
    3.1.1 Introduction
    3.1.2 Inputs
    3.1.3 Processing
    3.1.4 Outputs
    3.1.5 External Interfaces
        3.1.5.1 User Interfaces
        3.1.5.2 Hardware Interfaces
        3.1.5.3 Software Interfaces
        3.1.5.4 Communications Interfaces
    3.1.6 Performance Requirements
    3.1.7 Design Constraints
    3.1.8 Attributes
        3.1.8.1 Security
        3.1.8.2 Maintainability
        ...
    3.1.9 Other Requirements
    3.1.9.1 Data Base
    3.1.9.2 Operations
    3.1.9.3 Site Adaption
        ...

3.2 Functional Requirement 2
    ...

3.N Functional Requirement N

Figure 5.23   SRS Section 3—Method 4.

two—analyzing, documenting what he sees, talking with the customer, adjusting his original view, and repeating the process.

Problem analysis consists of requirements gathering and a thorough study of the requirements gathered. Requirements gathering and analysis is just as difficult as writing software. It requires identifying what must be learned and who has the information, gathering and analyzing the information, and checking and rechecking everything. The requirements engineer is key to this process. Select him with care. He must have a mixture of stamina, tenacity, patience, and tact.

One-on-one customer interviewing is a good way to elicit requirements. Use the five steps of effective interviewing: prepare, introduce, interview, close, follow up. Meetings are also useful. Be sure to follow proven meeting principles such as preparing attendees, organizing the meeting logically, and keeping it focused.

People-intensive tasks like requirements engineering can cause tense situations. Take care to be respectful and truthful. Avail yourself of the sage advice of Gerald Weinberg on diffusing such situations.

Evolve requirements by listing all functions, attributes (characteristics desired by the customer), and constraints and then combining them. Take care not to design while gathering requirements unless both you and the customer know the product very well. Document proposed design solutions but save them for the design stage.

Visibility techniques are vital during requirements engineering. During problem analysis, they help everyone see the customers' ideas. During documentation, they provide numerous diagrams of perspectives and make them available to the customer and the entire project team. Avail yourself of the many, many techniques out there, both group and individual. Facilitated meetings are especially helpful because they take you through requirements engineering from start to finish. The result is a complete requirements document.

There are many ways to make the problem and requirements visible. Draw a sketch and write a concept of operations. Know why the business needs the system, what it will do for the business, and what limitations there are at work. Understand each item under discussion as either an object, a function, or a state.

Requirements are documented in a *Software Requirements Specification*. The SRS represents everything the developer needs to create software that will satisfy the customer. In preparing the SRS, ask yourself: What is its function? What is the management view? Who are the readers? What conventions must it follow? It is best if the customer first writes the SRS and then the developer finalizes it.

The requirements are the major part of the functional baseline. Gaining approval of the functional baseline CCB will not be a problem as long as the users and developers who gathered and documented the requirements have kept everything visible. The key to successful CM is to follow the CM plan. The plan outlines the people, process, and product; has the support of the project's executive sponsor; and saves the project manager from making controversial decisions.

Follow the IEEE Std. 830-1998 to make sure the SRS does not omit important information.

REFERENCES

S. Ambler, "Using Use-Cases," *Software Development*, July 1995, pp. 53–61.

B. Blum, *Software Engineering, A Holistic View*, Oxford University Press, London, 1992.

B. Boehm, "The Art of Expectations Management," *Computer*, January 2000, pp. 122–124.

T. Buzan, *Use Both Sides of Your Brain*, 3rd. ed.,' Penguin Books, New York, 1991.

W. Carnes, *Effective Meetings for Busy People*, IEEE Press, New York, 1987.

P. Coad, "Working Out Dynamics with Scenarios," *Software Development*, October 1995, pp. 38–50.

L. Constantine, "Software by Teamwork: Working Smarter," *Software Development*, July 1995, pp. 36–45.

A. Cooper, "Goal-Directed Software Design," *Dr. Dobb's J.*, September 1996, pp. 16–22.

A. Davis, "Requirements Engineering," in *Encyclopedia of Software Engineering*, J. Marciniak, ed., Wiley, New York, 1994, pp. 1043–1054.

A. Davis, "The Art of Requirements Triage," Computer, March 2003, pp. 42–49.

E. Derby, "The ROTI Method of Managing Meeting Effectiveness, www.stickyminds. com, Esther Derby Associates, Inc., www.estherderby.com, xxxx.

D. Gause and G. Weinberg, *Exploring Requirements: Quality Before Design*, Dorset House, New York, 1989.

T. Gilb, *Principles of Software Eng. Management*, Addison Wesley, Reading, MA, 1988.

T. Gilb, "Level 6: Why We Can't Get There from Here," *IEEE Software*, January 1996, pp. 97–98.

R. Glass, *Facts and Fallacies of Software Engineering*, Pearson Education, Boston, 2003.

E. Gottesdiener, *Requirements by Collaboration: Workshops for Defining Needs*, Reading, MA, Addison-Wesley, 2002.

IEEE, *ANSI/IEEE Std 830-1998*, in *IEEE Recommended Practice for Software Requirements Specifications*, IEEE Press, New York, 1993.

M. Jackson, "Critical Reading for Software Developers," *IEEE Software*, November 1995, pp. 103–104.

S. Kaner, *Facilitator's Guide to Participatory Decision-Making*, New Society Publishers, Gabriola Island, British Columbia, 1996.

N. Karten, *Managing Expectations*, Dorset House Publishing, New York, New York, 1994.

N. Karten, *Communication Gaps and How to Close Them*, Dorset House Publishing, New York, New York, 2002.

S. Maguire, *Debugging the Development Process*, Microsoft Press, Redmond, WA, 1994.

J. Marciniak (Ed.), *Encyclopedia of Software Engineering*, Wiley, New York, 1994.

S. Robertson and J. Robertson, *Mastering the Requirements Process*, Addison-Wesley, London, 1999.

G. Rush, MG Rush Systems, Inc., www.mgrush.com, xxxx.

P. Schenck, *Identifying and Confirming User Requirements*, Learning Tree International, Reston, VA, 1994.

J. Sharp, "Validating Software Requirements," *Crosstalk*, November 1999, pp. 25–30.

S. Smith, www.stevenmsmith.com, xxxx.

G. Weinberg, *Quality Software Management: Vol. 1: Systems Thinking*, Dorset House Publishing, New York, 1992.

G. Weinberg, *Quality Software Management: Vol. 2: First- Order Measurement*, Dorset House, New York, 1993.

K. Wiegers, "Customer Rights and Responsibilities," *Software Development*, December 1999, pp. 34–37.

N. Wilkinson, *Using CRC Cards*, ACM Press, New York, 1995.

J. Wood and D. Silver, *Joint Application Development*, 2nd edition, John Wiley & Sons, New York, 1995.

R. Zahniser, "Design By Walking Around," *Communications of the ACM*, October 1993a, pp. 114–123.

R. Zahniser, "SST: System Storyboarding Techniques," *American Programmer*, September 1993b, pp. 9–14.

R. Zultner, "Blitz QFD: Better, Faster, Cheaper Forms of QFD," *American Programmer*, October 1994, pp. 24–30.

Chapter 6

Planning

In the last chapter, I discussed requirements, noting that requirements, planning, and risk management (the next chapter) are closely intertwined. During requirements, you primarily gain information about the product's intended use and its intended users. During planning, you use that information to decide the best way to develop the product. During risk management, you identify areas of risk and a way to manage them. As requirements change, so do plans and risks. As risks change, so do plans and requirements.

Planning is a significant area for balancing the 3Ps. A plan requires knowing the people who will be on the project. It is impossible to plan without understanding what process is best for a project. Finally, planning must consider the product to ensure that the right resources are allocated.

The first major step in planning is to choose a development process that will fit the product and people. The second major step is to derive tasks and a way to execute them according to the process model chosen.

Planning is also concerned with visibility. If there is no consensus on the big picture—the project's context—no effective planning can be done. Planning exercises make individual thoughts explicit and available to the entire group. They break a general idea into specifics: a "big project" becomes "a 10,000 staff-hour, $2 million project."

Configuration management helps the project manager navigate the many changes that happen to a plan during a project. Wise project managers will replan at regular, frequent intervals. It is easy for the new plans to confuse everyone and cause the project manager to spend his time and energy running around reassuring people. Wise project managers will also use configuration management to place the plan in the functional baseline (see Chapter 2 and Appendix B) and keep the many changes controlled and visible.

The Software Project Manager's Handbook. By Dwayne Phillips.
ISBN 0-471-67420-6 © 2004 IEEE Computer Society

Finally, standards play a significant role in planning. The IEEE's standard states what should be in a project plan and how to arrange the contents. Several all-inclusive military and commercial standards also help with the extremely difficult task of planning a project and documenting that plan.

6.1   ELEMENTS OF A GOOD PLAN

In planning, we attempt to predict a software project. You cannot produce a large, complex software product successfully without planning. A plan tells everyone what you *want* to happen, not so much what you expect to happen. Planning is a software management, not a software engineering, task. Perhaps this explains why software people (usually computer scientists and engineers) tend to avoid and even disdain it.

Planning and its close partner, estimation, are where many of us kill our projects before we begin. This is because of the expectations that come with planning. Suppose a software project starts and ends six months later with a good product. If the project was planned to last six months, this is a great project. If the project was planned to last four months, this was a failure. Nothing changed in the project, but the expectations created by the plan changed peoples' perception of it. Glass (Glass, 2003) feels that poor estimation is one of the two biggest problems in software projects (the other is problems with requirements). Jones (Jones, 1998) states:

> It is an interesting phenomenon that most of the major over runs and software disasters are built upon careless and grossly optimistic cost estimates. . . .

The problem is not just with the expectations that come with poor estimates and planning. People behave differently when they know they are behind schedule. We hurry, try shortcuts, and panic. These things only introduce more defects into the product and cause the project to fall farther behind schedule.

Planning is concerned with business goals. Solutions must serve the business in a timely and economic manner. They must accurately represent what the software people can do for the business. Many software project plans fail to consider that businesses operate on commitments (Humphrey, 1989, 1995). The business commits to delivering a product to its customers on a date for a price. If it fails to keep the commitment, the customers go away—and no customers, no business; no business, no need to worry about software projects.

McConnell (McConnell, 2000) frames the topic of planning in these terms:

> Thus, the primary purpose of software estimation is not to predict a project's outcome; it is to determine whether a project's targets are realistic enough to allow the project to be controlled to meet its targets.

Given this, planning is an attempt to determine if the business is ready to start a project. If the plan and estimate show the project is out of line with the current situation, the business does not begin the project.

The plan tells when the product will be ready and how much effort (money) is required. If it costs $1 million to build the product, and your business can sell 1,000 copies, will your customers pay $1,000 per copy? Will the product be ready for the spring show?

A plan requires three basic items, each of which I describe in more detail later:

1. *Task list.* Tasks are the building blocks of a plan. As Figure 6.1 shows, each task has inputs (everything required before the task can start) and produces outputs. The task is not complete until a review approves the outputs.
2. *Resources.* As Figure 6.1 also shows, each task requires some amount of time, people, and equipment.
3. *Task network.* A task network shows task precedence. It lets you verify that each task receives its prerequisites from previous tasks and sends its outputs to another task. If the prerequisites are not present, create tasks to build them. If the outputs go nowhere, eliminate the task.

Planning does not just happen. It requires time, effort, and resources. If you don't allow time for planning, the project will be behind schedule from day one. A key question is "How long does it take to do this?" *Estimation*, predicting the size of a product and a task's duration, is probably the most difficult part. The foundation of estimation (predicting the future) is *metrics*, the record of past actions.

There are many do's and don'ts in planning. Here are a few I have learned:

- *Do use metrics.* The Personal Software Process (PSP; Humphrey, 1995; more on the PSP later) calls for recording the time required for all tasks

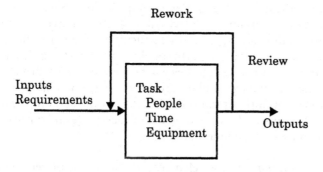

Figure 6.1 The elements of a task.

in minutes (not weeks, days, or hours). Another source (Neuhardt, 1996) describes recording everything a person does in minutes for several weeks. Many think this is too much detail, but analyzing such a record will show what the person actually accomplishes in a day. Most of us are interrupted dozens of times. We can write 30 lines of code per hour, but to tell how many working hours are productive, we need metrics. If an organization does not know how long it took to build their last product, they cannot plan for the next one.

- *Do create plans that succeed.* For example, minimize dependencies on outside groups because they will let you down. Give your people ample time and resources.

- *Do allow some preliminary design.* Builders cannot answer "How long will it take to build a house?"' but they can answer "How long will it take to build a two-story, four-bedroom, three-bath, double-garage house in Temple City, California?" Those qualifiers come from preliminary design.

- *Don't accept arbitrary plans unless you can negotiate the product.* A manager will say, "I want a new accounting system, and you should be able to do it (read "will do it") in six months." What is "a new accounting system"? Why six months? What will happen in six months? Accept an arbitrary plan only if you can have some flexibility in the product. If the manager really needs a new accounting system in six months, give it to him, but select the highest priority user requirements that can be satisfied in that time. Henry (Henry, 2002) sets this situation into simple sets of inputs and outputs. The required accounting system is an input. The plan to create it is an output. Yelling, threatening, etc. does not change the output; only changing the input changes the output.

- *Don't play estimating games* (Thomsett, 1996). Instead of dictating plans, some managers play games with the developer's estimate. The most common game is to double the developer's estimate. Sometimes the manager thinks the developer has already doubled the estimate, so he halves it. Some developers who have already played these games quadruple their estimate so that when the manager halves it, the estimate will still be double. Another game managers play is "trap the developer." The manager typically gathers a group of project stakeholders and invites them and the developer to discuss, say, a company picnic. The manager then casually asks the developer for his thoughts on the new project. The developer lays out his thoughts trusting that they will be viewed as a rough guess. He later finds that the manager and the group have converted his guess to a firm plan. Savvy developers respond "We have not worked out the details of the plan. Any answer I give now would be inaccurate and misleading, and these people deserve better than that."

Figure 6.2 summarizes the elements of a good project plan with WWWWWHH: who, what, where, when, why, and how (Boehm, 1996).

. Objectives - *Why* is the system being developed?
. Milestones and Schedules - *What* will be done *When*?
. Responsibilities - *Who* is responsible for a function?
							Where are they organizationally located?
. Approach - *How* will the job be done technically and managerially
. Resources - *How* much of each resource is needed?

Figure 6.2	WWWWWHH planning.

The planning process has endless variations on these basics. Figure 6.3 shows one of them (Sigal, 1993). In *define objectives,* you list the products (software, test software, user's manual, and so on) and the company's goals. The products are the starting point of planning. Goals help everyone make the countless decisions that arise in planning. Create this list in a facilitated objectives meeting similar to that described in Chapter 5.

In *plan the work* and *test the plan,* you create the first draft of the plan and then look for errors. The draft lists the tasks needed, who will do them, and so on. Did the plan consider everything? Does everything fit?

Analyze risk and *define controls* are part of risk management, which I cover in detail in Chapter 7). In brief, analyze risk looks at what could possibly go wrong. Define controls attempts to prevent unpleasant surprises during the project.

Figure 6.4 shows another view of basic planning (Thayer & Fairley, 1994). The objectives and goals are the project's desired outcome in products, delivery dates, improved marketplace position, better skills, and so on. The strategies are set at the business enterprise level and are high-level approaches for a successful project. For example, all projects below $1 million will qualify for the Capability Maturity Model Level 2 (CMU/SEI, 1995) and those above $1 million will follow Level 3. Policies are set at the project level and help people make decisions. For example, everyone will work 40–45 hours per week and be in their offices from 10 AM to 2 PM on Tuesdays and Thursdays. This helps a supervisor decide what to do when someone must take his child to the doctor on Wednesday and his product is due on Friday.

The next three activities (possible courses of action, planning decisions,

. Define Objectives
. Plan the Work
. Test the Plan
. Analyze the Risks
. Define Controls

Figure 6.3	One variation of WWWWWHH planning.

. Set Objectives and Goals
. Develop Strategies
. Develop Policies
. Determine Possible Courses of Action
. Make Planning Decisions
. Set Procedures and Rules
. Develop Project Plans
. Prepare Budgets
. Conduct a Risk Assessment
. Document Project Plans

Figure 6.4   Another variation of WWWWWHH planning.

and procedures and rules) look at the particular project in detail. A project can have more than one possible course of action. Explore the possibilities. Use decision-making and documenting techniques such as the decision-making table (see Chapter 4). The procedures and rules are specific methods of doing tasks in the project. For example, one person will always be at the management information center (MIC) from 8 AM to 6 PM on normal working days.

The project plan and budget are tied together. The plan contains the tasks, a network of tasks, the time required, and the schedule. The budget is the total cost of all the tasks and resources. It must include the cost of computers, copying machines, office space, travel, training, and food and drink for the MIC.

During risk assessment, you should examine all the work and look for possible problems. Determine how the problem would damage the project. Plan how to prevent the problem and handle it should it occur.

The final activity is to document or record the plan. Use visibility techniques. Put everything in the MIC where everyone will see it. Use the IEEE standard described later in this chapter for documenting plans (IEEE, 1998).

Documenting objectives, goals, policies, strategies, and so on, may sound like bureaucracy. Indeed, many firms have used such things so much that people are cynical about them. State the reasons behind the decisions in a project. Make them visible. Do not assume that everyone knows that this project is using a new GUI library because next year all projects in the company will use it. People will not understand this unless you state it clearly. If they do not understand decisions, they will not support them and make them work.

Common themes run through these and other variations of planning basics: Get organized to plan. Start with the end in mind. State clearly what will guide the project. Create a network of tasks. Look for errors and risks. Keep everything visible. Start with a blank piece of paper and a pencil. Sketch everything for yourself in a context document. (More on these later.)

6.2 BALANCING THE 3PS: SELECTING THE PROCESS

The basic software process breaks a problem into smaller, easier problems. Developers build small solutions and combine them into a software system. New techniques are often simply ways to repackage basic processes. They are admissions that today's problems are more difficult than they were 30 years ago (or they are recognition that higher-performance hardware has created more difficult software problems). Today's problems frequently require iterations and evolutions of basic processes, but the processes themselves have changed little.

Figure 6.5 shows the waterfall, iteration and evolutionary processes expressed as a V-chart. (The introduction to Part 2, The Development Life Cycle: Early Stages, describes how all software processes are some variation of the V-chart.) At the top of the figure is the classic *waterfall* process, a straightened-out V, one long line sloping down from left to right. The waterfall gets its name because the process flows down the steps like falling water. The waterfall model is criticized because many people assume that one step must be 100% finished before the next begins, which assumes that the users and developers understand the problem perfectly and iteration is not needed. In practice, this is rarely the case.

The next two diagrams illustrate the *iteration* process, delivering a product in increments. The users know what they want and are anxious to have something working. They want product functionality a little at a time. Iteration also allows developers to learn while building. The first of these two diagrams shows iteration with only one development team. The V-chart begins on the left and proceeds down to the breakpoint (X). At this time, the developers have finished the requirements and high-level design and have a plan to build the system in three increments. The dotted line ending with a 1 shows the start of the first iteration. The developers perform the low-level design, build and test the low-level modules, and perform the integration and test. This ends with the first delivery to the user.

Note how the process line drops straight down from this point. There is no need to gather requirements and perform high-level design again. The second iteration proceeds just like the first and ends with the second delivery. The second delivery integrates its functions with that given by the first. The process line again drops straight down to where the third iteration begins. It proceeds just like the second and integrates its results with the product the users are using.

The second iteration diagram shows iteration with three development teams. The V-chart begins on the left and again proceeds down to the break-

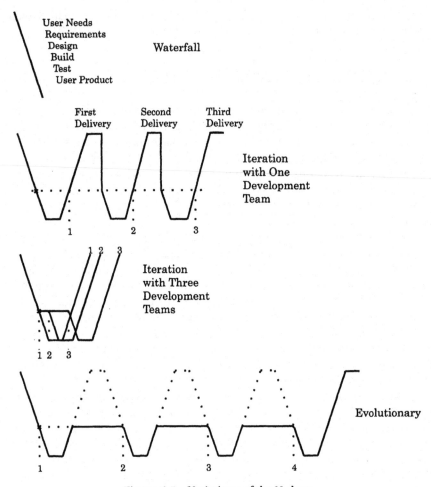

Figure 6.5 Variations of the V-chart.

point (X). Here, the developers know the requirements, high-level design, and how to build the product in three parallel increments. The first development team begins the first iteration at the breakpoint and proceeds as described above. The second development team begins the second iteration shortly after the first, and the third team begins thereafter. Each development team delivers their functions in a usable, but not complete, system. A short time later, the next team integrates their functions with what the users have, and the process ends with a complete system. Using parallel development teams can save time if enough people are available. It requires having a better plan in place at the breakpoint, however, and does not allow as much time for learning.

Are Software Problems Unique?

Some people believe software differs from hardware in more ways than you can count. Developing and maintaining software is simply one form of problem solving. The only way it differs from other problem-solving exercises in the workplace is that no physical laws govern its behavior: There is no law similar to a physical law that governs, say, a material's resistance to electron flow and the resulting drop in voltage. Actually, the greatest difference between software and hardware is attitude—the attitude that causes people to throw out centuries of proven, problem-solving exercises.

A software project should be run in much the same way as a basic engineering project. There is a problem, a solution comes to mind, and you implement it. As problems become more difficult, the solution process also grows. The first step is analyzing the problem to gather all the details. Several high-level solutions come to mind, with one solution being best for the circumstances. The solution has several parts. You gather the parts, assemble them, test them, and use them on the problem.

Problems change with time, so their analysis must also change. Considering and testing solutions can prove the analysis wrong. The parts of a solution may not fit together because the design was faulty. Once the solution is assembled, the problem has disappeared or no one wants to solve it anymore.

Somewhere along the way, software people forgot how to do basic engineering projects.* Some never knew how. I once believed strongly in the novelty of software. I believed that a software project was sitting down and coding solutions to problems. Time and trouble have taught me otherwise.

---

*T. Gilb, "Level 6: Why We Can't Get There from Here," *IEEE Software*, Jan. 1996, pp. 97–98.

The last diagram in Figure 6.5 shows the evolutionary process. In this case, the users are not sure what they want, so the developers build a little, listen to the users, build a little, listen to the users, and so on. The project ends when upper management decides that the users have enough system or that there is no more money left in the budget.

In this diagram, the V-chart begins on the left and again proceeds down to the breakpoint (X). At this point, the users and developers understand the high-level, but not the detailed, requirements. Building the system now would be a major leap of faith because it might be the wrong system. The first evolution begins at the dotted line labeled 1. The developers proceed with the parts of the high-level requirements the users have the most confidence in. They perform high-level design, low-level design, and build the code modules. The integration and test activities proceed up the right side of the V just far enough to give the users an experimental system to help them learn. The developers have also learned much about this application, what is possible, and how difficult it is to give the users what they want. This helps the developers revise the high-level requirements at the breakpoint, and the second evolution begins. Each evolution gives the users and developers more knowledge and grows the software into a full system. At some point, upper management decides to stop the evolutions, and the right side of the V proceeds to the top yielding a final system.

Another way to view iterative and evolutionary processes is in terms of baselines (see Chapter 2 and Appendix B). In the waterfall diagram, the requirements are the functional baseline, the design becomes the allocated and design baselines, the code is the development baseline, and so on up to the user product, which is the operational baseline. In the iteration diagrams, the functional and allocated baselines are known at the breakpoint. The first iteration creates the design, development, product, and operational baselines. The operational baseline remains the same while the developers create the second versions of the design, development, and product baselines. The operational baseline changes to its second version at the second delivery. In the evolutionary process, the functional baseline is incomplete at the breakpoint. The first evolution creates allocated, design, development, and product baselines. Each subsequent evolution updates the baselines with new knowledge, and the final evolution adds the operational baseline.

Given that there are process basics and variations, the question that comes to mind is how do you choose a process? The concepts of people, process, and product are one guide to answering that question. Another perspective comes from Alistair Cockburn (Cockburn, 2000). Cockburn's underlying principles in selecting a method are:

1. A larger group of people needs a larger methodology.
2. A system whose undetected defects will produce more damage needs more publicly visible correctness.
3. A relatively small increase in methodology adds a relatively large increase in cost.
4. The most effective way to transmit ideas among people is face-to-face interaction at a whiteboard.

Cockburn is an advocate of agile methods (described later) or the use of iterations. He, however, is one of the best spokesmen for the ideas of selecting a process to fit the product.

6.2.1 Prototyping

A popular and useful software process is prototyping. As I described in the last chapter, *rapid* prototyping is an excellent technique for learning nonfunctional requirements—requirements that deal with the look and feel of software (a Windows interface) as opposed to its basic functions (calculating loan amortizations). This technique, which is driven by the desire to save money, occurs near the top of the V-chart's left side. In straight waterfall models, developers could gather requirements and go through the entire project only to learn that the system they built was not what the users had in mind.

Be cautious with rapid prototyping. Users see the screens on day one and can assume the system will be ready in a week. Emphasize that there is nothing behind the screens. Although it is easy to superimpose an icon of a satellite on top of a world map, designing, writing, and testing software that will coordinate, control, and track the orbits of a fleet of satellites requires many months. One way to avoid this misunderstanding is to use paper prototypes. Instead of generating a user interface on the computer, do the same on large sheets of paper. The users can work through the paper to learn if they like the idea. The paper greatly reduces the chance that the user assumes the real system will be ready really soon.

Also be careful that hardware and systems people don't misunderstand your use of the word "prototype." A prototype airplane actually flies. It is a prototype only because it was not built on an assembly line. If you casually mention prototypes to aircraft people, they may assume that your prototype has all the code working behind the screens.

There are two basic types of prototypes: the throw-away and the evolutionary. In *throw-away* prototyping, developers use a demonstration tool or language. Once the users agree on the prototype, the developers throw away the code and build the product using a real programming language.

In *evolutionary* prototyping, developers use the code from the prototype in the final system. Today's visual tools are making this approach more attractive.

6.2.2 *Rapid Application Development*

Rapid Application Development (RAD) employs the best available people and processes to yield a product with the features most valuable to the customer in the quickest manner. Many people have described RAD in different terms (Bayer, 1994; Keuffel, 1995), and many products are advertised as RAD tools. RAD was an early example of agile methods (discussed later).

RAD concentrates on customer, product, and process. The *customer* focus discovers the 20% of what the customer wants that delivers 80% of what they need. This usually begins with customer surveys that aim to shorten the list of wants. Rank the customer desires, tear them apart to find the core requirements, and follow this with a JAD process (see Chapter 5 for more on JAD).

Show the customers a product (a prototype if nothing else) soon after the JAD session. Let them play with it while you and your team sit back and watch. Avoid the temptation to do the driving. Always keep the level of customer involvement high. Also remember that a customer's attention span is typically short. Maintain the momentum. If customers lose interest, they will not use the final software system, and the project will fail.

The *product* part of RAD emphasizes only essentials to enable rapid delivery—no frills. Bring the customers a product quickly.

The *process* part emphasizes throughput (rapid delivery again), but not at the expense of sound engineering. The process is iterative or evolutionary (Figure 6.5) and provides a product to the customer in a series of deliveries. The first deliveries have limited functionality, but are delivered rapidly. This keeps the customers involved and gains their confidence and trust. They eagerly expect two more functions next week because you have delivered two functions a week for the last month. These periods are known as *time boxes* (more on time boxes in Chapter 7).

Continuous application engineering characterizes the series of deliveries. The evolutionary style is not sloppy; it is not coding without thinking. It requires that early products be built with interfaces to modules that do not exist. This is difficult and cannot be done without applying and reapplying the best techniques of software engineering.

RAD is actually a variation of the V-chart that resembles the third diagram in Figure 6.5. The basic process and configuration management baselines are the same. The real difference in RAD is the people.

RAD is possible only if the development team has the right people. Because RAD emphasizes rapid delivery, the people on a project that follows the RAD process must be experts in narrowly defined areas. Use a customer survey expert to write and evaluate the customer survey. Use a JAD expert to run the JAD session. Use a GUI building expert to generate prototypes. Keep the development team small. This means fewer lines of communication, which means fewer, shorter meetings.

A short schedule increases the difficulty of a product, which requires more capability from people or process or both. Experts using the best software engineering techniques provide that capability.

Whenever possible, physically or virtually colocate developers and customers. No one will wait until next month's flight to the coast to ask a question or resolve a misunderstanding. Physical colocation carries its own set of problems. Easy access to someone can turn into endless interruptions. Keep everyone available, but also teach and exemplify courtesy and respect.

6.2.3 Microsoft Process

Everyone wants to know how Microsoft remains a high-profile, successful software company. In the last couple of years, Microsoft has publicized their process (McCarthy, 1995; Sherman, 1995) and although they have a few good techniques, they do not offer anything new to the technical world. Their real strength is in their business and marketing strategies.

The Microsoft process is based on the three dimensions of quality shown

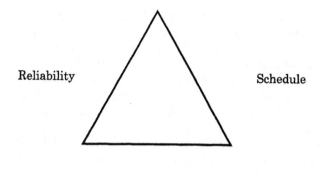

Reliability

Schedule

Feature Set

Figure 6.6 The Microsoft process: three dimensions of quality.

in Figure 6.6. *Reliability* is how good the product must be before shipping. *Feature set* is the product's definition (the requirements), and *schedule* is the ship date. The relative importance of the three changes with the product. Entertainment products must ship before Christmas, but do not need to be as reliable as a spreadsheet.

Many have complained that Microsoft ships software containing known errors. Yes they do, but the software works well enough for the vast majority of intended users. Most users don't care if their word processor crashes their single-user PC once every thousand hours (or every two years). They will just reboot the PC and go on. Therefore, Microsoft will not work into the long tail of the 90/10 rule-of-work curve (see Figure 5.1 in Chapter 5) to eliminate this fault. "Good enough" software is a variation of the test completion measure. Shipping a product that contains errors is not new; it's just that you hear more about errors in a Microsoft product.

A project begins with a vision statement, written by the marketing group that discusses the product's market positioning, key features, price range, desired shipping date, and so on. The vision statement focuses the entire team on the objectives and helps everyone think about the same thing. Next comes a product specification that describes in detail how the product will work. The development team builds a schedule that is based on the product specification. They divide the product into features, group the features into feature sets, and build the feature sets.

Microsoft emphasizes testing during development instead of at the end. A tester is assigned to every couple of programmers. The programmers and testers begin on the same day with the same specification. The testers use it to write the tests for the code the programmers are writing.

Once in the development phase, Microsoft builds the product every day. The product comprises a core with feature sets added to it. Each programmer works on a different feature set. When the programmer has one feature of the set ready, he links his code into the daily build. A daily *smoke test* follows the build. The smoke test briefly exercises all the product features. If the product breaks or "smokes," it is relatively simple to find out why. If the product worked yesterday, but doesn't today, the person who added his feature to the build has some work to do. The smoke test itself evolves in its coverage and sophistication as the product evolves.

The principle behind daily builds and smoke tests is called "synchronize and stabilize" (Cusumano & Yoffie, 1999). The daily build synchronizes everyone by placing them at the same point each day. Once the product passes the smoke test, it is stabilized. This process has several advantages. It reduces risk because the leaps of faith are only a day long. If the system collapses, the project needs to back up only one day to reach a point at which everything worked. This is a theme of daily builds. Bring the system to a known, good state and keep it there by adding features in small, low-risk steps. Daily builds boost morale. The product works on day one—the people are successful. Each day the product grows and keeps working, the people keep succeeding. Success breeds success and the people go home each day on a high note.

Another notable technique in the Microsoft process is *mentoring*. Each new programmer is assigned a mentor. The new programmer and the mentor read every line of code the other writes. This helps the new programmer learn from someone who knows, helps the mentor monitor the progress of the newcomer, and the mentor learns a few things from a fresh mind.

A word of warning: The elements in the Microsoft process are not new: iterations, evolutions, and builds have been done by others for years. Following the Microsoft process alone will not ensure success. Microsoft has had technical catastrophes on some of its major projects (big cost and schedule overruns). The best lessons to learn from them are in business strategies, not software process. I suggest reading Jim McCarthy's text (McCarthy, 1995) for more insights in this area.

6.2.4 Spiral Process

The spiral process model combines elements of many process models into a swirling spiral. Originated by Barry Boehm (Boehm, 1988), the spiral model has been modified by others including the Software Productivity Consortium (SPC) (Charette, 1994) and Boehm in a later work (Boehm, 1996).

The spiral is an excellent choice in high-risk projects, such as pure research and development, projects that depend on unproven technology, and projects in which failure could put the company out of business. Figure 6.7 shows a general spiral process. Each cycle begins in the upper-left quadrant with objectives, constraints, and alternatives. The *objectives* are what the team hopes to accomplish in that cycle. The *constraints* are the limitations on resources. The *alternatives* are various ways to meet the objectives given the constraints.

The second quadrant (moving clockwise) contains risk analysis and proto-

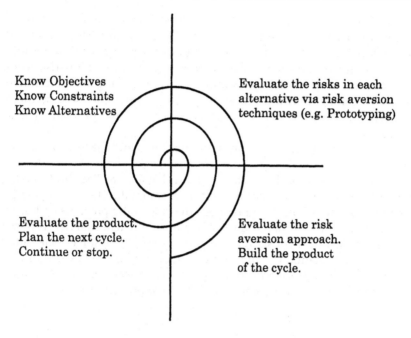

Figure 6.7   General spiral process.

typing. It begins with the alternatives produced in the first quadrant. The developers use prototypes to analyze each alternative's risks and gain more insight.

The third quadrant begins with an evaluation and decision. There are objectives and several alternative paths to the objectives. Each path has risks the developers know and understand. The developers choose an alternative and build the low-risk product for the cycle. In early cycles, the product is a concept of operations (see Chapter 5) or an early requirements document. In later cycles the product is a detailed requirements document, a detailed design, and, finally, the software system itself.

The final quadrant is concerned with the next cycle. The developers create a plan for the next cycle, review the plan carefully, and make a decision. They can revise the plan and review it again, accept the plan and begin the next cycle, or stop the project.

The third option demands serious consideration. The project is using the spiral model because of high risk. The current cycle may have taught the developers something (the technology is insufficient, the algorithms are immature, and so on) that warrants canceling the project. If the developers choose to accept the plan, the next cycle begins and the steps repeat. The objectives for the cycle produce new constraints, alternatives, risks, prototypes, and, finally, a new product.

The spiral is a process of processes because it contains elements of the basic waterfall and its iterative and evolutionary variations (see Figure 6.5). The spiral is a series of learning cycles. In each cycle, the developers identify and study risks, using iterations and evolutions. Cycling continues until the developers understand the problem well enough to write a low-risk requirements document. The final cycles build the system using a simple waterfall process. The straightforward process is possible at the end because the previous cycles have helped the developers understand the problem. The leap of faith is gone.

Figures 6.8 and 6.9 show Boehm's original spiral and the SPC variation, respectively.

Note the last cycle of the Boehm spiral in Figure 6.8. The third quadrant, the one in which the product is built, is a waterfall. The developers have learned about the problem and reduced the risk in the previous cycles. They are now ready to build the product in a simple, efficient manner. If they are not ready to do this, they should use another cycle to resolve issues and be ready. The third quadrant of the next-to-last cycle of the SPC spiral in Figure 6.9 uses a waterfall process for initial product delivery. That model assumes another complete cycle is needed before the final product is ready.

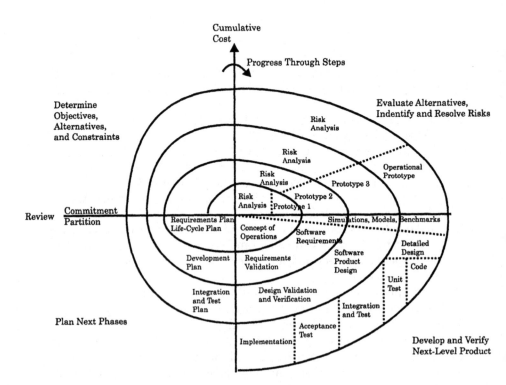

Figure 6.8   Boehm's spiral.

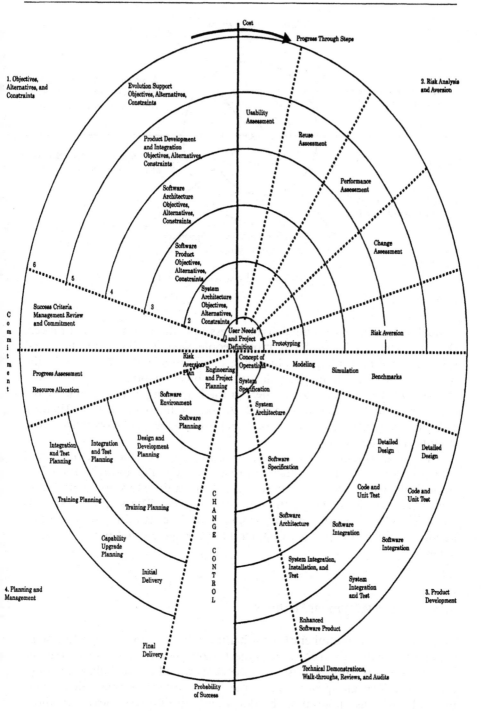

Figure 6.9 The Software Productivity Consortium's spiral.

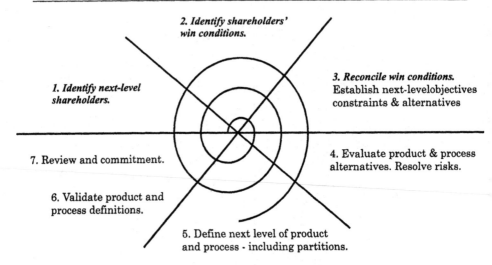

2. Identify shareholders' win conditions.

1. Identify next-level shareholders.

3. Reconcile win conditions.
Establish next-levelobjectives
constraints & alternatives

7. Review and commitment.

4. Evaluate product & process
alternatives. Resolve risks.

6. Validate product and
process definitions.

5. Define next level of product
and process - including partitions.

Figure 6.10   The win–win spiral.

Boehm later modified the spiral process into the win–win spiral process
(Boehm, 1996). The problem most people were having with the spiral
process was establishing the objectives, constraints, and alternatives in the
first step. The win–win model attacks this problem by introducing the Theory
W (win–win) approach (Ross, 1989) at the beginning of each spiral. Figure
6.10 shows this addition with steps 1, 2, and the first part of step 3 (italics).
These techniques help the developers and users agree on the objectives, constraints, and alternatives.

The spiral process provides ample opportunity for the developers and
users to learn about the product and reduce uncertainty and risk. The cycles
through the spiral also give management opportunities to stop the project in
a planned manner if the technology is insufficient. The stopped project is
not a failure and neither are the people on it. That is a big boost to those
people on their next project. Chapter 11 describes a spiral project in more
detail.

6.2.5   Agile Development Methods

In the late 1990s, a number of consultants and practitioners began to discuss
common experiences in software project management. A trend in these discussions was a reaction against processes that created detailed plans and large
documents. This group of people came to advocate what was called "light"
methodologies as opposed to the document- and process-"heavy" methodologies. Each light method had its own details, but they all emphasized evolving products through a series of short iterations.

We are uncovering better ways of developing
software by doing it and helping others do it.

Through this work we have come to value:

Individuals and interactions over processes and tools

Working software over comprehensive documentation

Customer collaboration over contract negotiation

Responding to change over following a plan

That is, while there is value in the items on
the right, we value the items on the left more.

Kent Beck	James Grenning	Robert C. Martin
Mike Beedle	Jim Highsmith	Steve Mellor
Arie van Bennekum	Andrew Hunt	Ken Schwaber
Alistair Cockburn	Ron Jeffries	Jeff Sutherland
Ward Cunningham	Jon Kern	Dave Thomas
Martin Fowler	Brian Marick	

Figure 6.11   The Agile Manifesto.

In February 2001, a group of these advocates met and wrote the Agile
Manifesto (Manifesto, 2001). They coined the term "agile" as opposed to
"light." The debate now became "agile methods" versus "planned methods."
The manifesto is shown in Figure 6.11. The principles behind the manifesto
are:

Our highest priority is to satisfy the customer through early and continuous delivery of valuable software.

Welcome changing requirements, even late in development. Agile processes harness change for the customer's competitive advantage.

Deliver working software frequently, from a couple of weeks to a couple of
months, with a preference for the shorter timescale.

Business people and developers must work together daily throughout the
project.

Build projects around motivated individuals. Give them the environment
and support they need, and trust them to get the job done.

The most efficient and effective method of conveying information to and
within a development team is face-to-face conversation.

Working software is the primary measure of progress.

Agile processes promote sustainable development. The sponsors, developers, and users should be able to maintain a constant pace indefinitely.

Continuous attention to technical excellence and good design enhances agility.

Simplicity—the art of maximizing the amount of work not done—is essential.

The best architectures, requirements, and designs emerge from self-organizing teams.

At regular intervals, the team reflects on how to become more effective, then tunes and adjusts its behavior accordingly.

There is little that is new in the manifesto and its principles. This author expressed similar ideas in the "management secrets" of Chapter 1 in the first edition of this text. Many others, including Royce (Royce, 2000) expressed such ideas clearly and in print. I applaud the agile methods advocates for highlighting such concepts as iterations, people talking to one another instead of trying to communicate just through documents, and being colocated with the customer. Many of these advocates blush when told they have created something new and wonderful. They often reply that their practices are common sense.

The following discuss some of the principles behind three of the agile methods: extreme programming, SCRUM, and lean software development.

Extreme Programming. Extreme programming (XP) is a method for small-to-medium-sized teams developing software in the face of vague or rapidly changing requirements. Kent Beck (Beck, 2000) created this method that takes commonsense principles and practices to extreme levels.

One of the drivers of extreme programming is the cost of change in software projects. The cost of change rises exponentially with time. Beck wanted the cost of change to rise little if any with time. He contends that this is possible if we have (1) simple designs, (2) automated tests, and (3) an attitude of constant refinement of design.

The physical environment for the extreme programming team is important. Everyone sits in one big room with some private areas and some public areas. The private areas allow people to think alone quietly. The public areas allow for pair programming (described below) and for groups of people to solve problems together. The room has lots of wall space where people can gather at whiteboards and pin cards to the walls.

The following describe the extreme programming practices.

The planning game. Determine the scope of the next release by combining business priorities and technical estimates. The business people decide what they want and establish the priorities. The technical people create estimates and detailed plans. A business person writes a story on a story card (index card) describing something the system should do. The technical people estimate the time required to implement the story. The business people take the story cards with estimates and decide what cards to implement in the next release. The technical people tell the business people when they can deliver. Next, the technical people divide a story into tasks and write task cards with estimates of time. Programmers volunteer to perform tasks.

Small releases. Put a simple system into production quickly by releasing new versions on a short cycle. Each release should be as small as possible and contain the most valuable business requirements.

Metaphor. Guide all development with a simple shared story of how the whole system works.

Simple design. The design should be as simple as possible at any given moment. People remove complexity as soon as they see it. The design strategy is (1) start with a test, (2) design and implement just enough to pass the test, (3) repeat, (4) if you see a chance to make it simpler, do it. With this strategy you will do something very simple the first time and make it more flexible the second time (refactoring). If you never have a second time, you don't pay for flexibility you don't need.

Testing. Programmers continuously write unit tests and then program until all tests pass. Users write tests that show that features are finished. Write the test first and then write the code. Any program feature without a test does not exist.

Refactoring. Programmers restructure the system without changing its behavior. This removes duplication, simplifies the design, adds flexibility, and improves communication. The refactored code passes all the tests without changing any of the tests. When programmers see a simpler design, they make the change. This is all based on the idea that things will change. If they won't, you do the design once and you're finished (a waterfall).

Pair programming. All code is written with two programmers at one workstation with one keyboard and one mouse. The person with the keyboard is thinking about the best way to do this code immediately. The other person is thinking about bigger issues. There is a constant dialog between the two people.

Collective ownership. Anyone can change any code at any place in the system at any time. Every person is responsible for everything they see.

Continuous integration. Integrate and build the system every time a task is finished. This may be many times a day. You need some good tools that allow automated tests and testing.

40-hour week. Never work overtime two weeks in a row. The goal is that everyone should be fresh and eager to work every morning and tired and satisfied every evening. Overtime is a sign of a serious problem on the project.

On-site customer. A customer sits with the team full-time to answer questions. If the customer does not want to commit a person to this task, the software probably isn't worth building.

Coding standards. Rules emphasize communication among programmers through the code. Given that people program in pairs and can see and change any code, it is important that everyone program in the same style.

Extreme programming is a variation of the evolutions described earlier. The team tackles parts of the system being developed. The planning game, story cards, and small releases all reflect this general strategy. They also reflect the "management secrets" shared in Chapter 1.

Extreme programming will not work for everyone in every case. If a customer insists on a big complete specification before programming begins, XP won't work. You cannot use XP with 100 programmers or 50 programmers or maybe not with 20 programmers. You cannot use XP if the situation means that each round of integration testing takes 24 hours. You cannot use XP if all the programmers cannot sit in one room.

SCRUM. SCRUM is an all-at-once approach to software engineering created by Ken Schwaber (Schwaber, 2001). People perform the activities of requirements, design, prototype, and acceptance all at the same time or concurrently. SCRUM (a scrum is a team pack in the sport of rugby; everyone in the pack works together to move the ball down the field) is based on having a customer work with the team to choose what parts of a system to implement. It is appropriate in the face of vague or changing requirements.

The customer has a backlog of features he wants in the system. The team gathers with the customer and decides what features will add the most value to the product that can be completed in 30 days. Once the customer decides on these features, the team plans how to do them. The team works hard for 30 days to add the features. This 30-day period is called a sprint. Once a sprint begins, no one can add or subtract features.

The team holds daily scrum meetings led by the scrum master (Schwaber, 2000; Rising, 2000). The meetings last 15 to 30 minutes, and during a meeting, each person answers three questions:

1. What have you completed since the last meeting?
2. What obstacles got in your way?
3. What do you plan to accomplish before the next meeting?

The lists of tasks (what has been accomplished and will be accomplished) are critical. These keep the team members focused on the project. People will lose focus from one day to the next without something that helps them focus. The daily scrum is that device that keeps the focus.

No one solves problems in the scrum meeting. The scrum master notes the issues, but small groups of people solve them on their own afterward. This is efficient, as two people meet later to solve a problem that involves the two of them. No one else spends a minute of time listening to that discussion. The only people who meet are those that are directly involved. That is a principle of SCRUM: only those involved in the work have a say in the work. Interested people may sit and watch, but they do not participate and interfere.

The scrum master does not act as a traditional project manager. He is present for the benefit of the development team, rather than the team being there for the benefit of the manager. The scrum master focuses on two things:

1. Finding and removing anything that is obstructing the team.
2. Keeping the team focused on building the most important software.

This differs from traditional management. Most managers slow their development teams. They don't try to do this, but do it by asking for reports, holding status meetings, asking for presentations, going to offsite meetings, and all number of other activities that seem to fill the day. The scrum master focuses on letting the team do the work and removing all obstacles.

SCRUM works when the members of the team are devoted to building the product for the customer. The simple idea is that people come to work and work all day on the product. Nothing gets in their way because the "manager" is removing those things. This may not work in all organizations. Some people cannot, either emotionally or legally, give up control of a project. They must have the traditional status meetings and reports. The organization demands 20% of everyone's time every day for various activities. The system gets in the way. SCRUM works, but it requires a culture that differs from most.

At the end of each sprint, the team gathers for a sprint review. They discuss what went well and wrong as well as their thoughts for the future. The customer meets with the team and describes the items in the backlog that are most important. The team estimates what they can do in the next sprint, and the process repeats itself.

SCRUM works best when the team has fewer than ten members. Schwaber reports that projects have used hundreds of people and the SCRUM process. These projects break the product into pieces that a ten-person team can build.

It should be apparent that SCRUM is another variation of building a product in increments. The 30-day sprints limit the size of the increment. Also apparent is the important role that the customer plays in selecting what to build in each sprint.

Lean Development. Lean software development is the creation of the Poppendiecks (Poppendieck & Poppendieck, 2003). They have adapted the concepts of lean development from other industries to software development. Their method concentrates on delaying decisions until people have the information necessary to make them. It seems to be a contradiction, but delaying decisions often speeds development. This is because if a customer waits to make a decision until he has the right information, he is far less likely to change that decision later. Changing the decision only introduces rework and delay.

There are seven principles of lean software development. These are:

1. *Eliminate waste.* Waste in software development comes in the form of wasted work and wasted time. There is no need to create documents that no one will ever read. There is no need to switch among a number of tasks and waste time in the switching. There is no need to waste knowledge by inefficient hand-off through documents when face-to-face interaction will do much better. Lean methods eliminate waste by focusing on the flow of value from request to delivery. If a customer wants something, what steps do we take to deliver it? We usually have a number of interfaces and transitions among teams of people. The Poppendiecks emphasize having a self-contained team complete all activities in a development cycle. This eliminates all the interfaces.

2. *Amplify learning.* Learning takes place via experiment. The developer should hypothesize what might work, perform an experiment, and learn from the result. Learning occurs faster with more experiments, and experiments come through iterations. The Poppendiecks recommend many short, full-cycle iterations to build a product.

3. *Delay commitment.* This is the concept of delaying decisions was mentioned earlier. Decisions should be based on known information instead of estimates. The known information comes with waiting.

4. *Deliver fast.* Everyone wants to do this. The trouble is how? The answer offered is simple in principle: do what you know to be correct right now without delay. Common delays include attending several weekly status meetings, not having a computer on a desk when a new employee arrives, not bringing in a needed person because Human Resources hasn't done the paperwork, etc. These are common delays that I have encountered many times. Fast delivery demands that we do what is necessary to remove these obstacles.

5. *Empower the team.* To go fast and keep the flow of value moving, the team needs to have the authority to make decisions. A key support to this is that they also have received the necessary training and leadership. The team working on the problem is better equipped to make the decisions than anyone else.

6. *Build integrity in.* The Poppendiecks attribute two types of integrity to a product. The first is perceived integrity. This is when the product delights the customer. Perceived integrity comes about with clear and frequent communication between the customer and the developers. The second type of integrity is conceptual integrity. This is when all the parts of the software work together to form a smoothly functioning system. This comes about with a good flow of information among the developers.

7. *See the whole.* We build whole software products. It is true that we build them by first building small parts and them combining those parts. Too

often, however, we can focus so much on the small parts that we forget the whole product. The Poppendiecks encourage holding people accountable for what they can influence in addition to what they can control. Designers influence programmers who influence testers who influence technical writers, and so on. The goal is for everyone to take more responsibility and ensure that the entire product delights the customer.

Once again, it is apparent that lean software development is a form of building a product with evolutions. The Poppendiecks have formed a solid philosophical foundation for a method that emphasizes the value, flow, and people in a project. The developers strive to keep the value flowing to the customers as fast as possible.

6.2.6 Process Improvement Mechanisms

Every software organization and individual should share one goal: Do it better tomorrow than you did today. This is process improvement and it is the reason you have processes in the first place. Every software organization and individual should establish some process for every project. Study the process via metrics, keep the good, throw out the bad, and experiment to find better ways of doing things.

This is straight out of the TQM script and has been said so many times in so many ways that many people have become cynical about it. But although the basic idea has been twisted and misused, it is still valid.

The key measure of process improvement is *return on investment*. If spending $10 saves $2, the ROI is -$8. If spending $5 saves $12, the ROI is +$7, and that is worth the effort. Inspections, testing early, configuration management, and so on, cost time and money, but have a positive effect on ROI. Do not make changes for the sake of change; make them for a positive ROI.

There is a catch-22 in process improvement. The typical software organization has no idea how much it costs to produce a unit of software. If they adopt some practices and calculate a cost per unit of product, they have nothing to compare it to. They have no idea of their improvement or ROI.

If you are in that category (and I have been there), start small. If historical data on product size exists, use it. Lines of code is not a perfect measure, but it's a start. Look at product cost in terms of staff hours and average salary. Calculate a rough starting point of productivity. Measure tasks, effort, cost, and product. Compare these project by project with the rough starting point. The comparison will indicate improvement.

If your organization has some past data, look at texts by Larry Putnam and Ware Myers [Putnam & Myers, 1992, 1997] to obtain a productivity index. Use this as your starting point for comparisons.

Software organizations worldwide are improving, and they have the projects and metrics to show their improvement and ROI. If your organization, no matter how good it may be, is not improving, it is losing ground. It will lose contracts, market share, and lay off employees.

In recent years, there have been several major trends in mechanisms to achieve and measure process improvement. Here I describe several of the most popular: the PSP, TSP, CMM, CMMI, and best practices. On close inspection, you will find nearly all the best practices from various sources in the CMM. People look at the CMM and see a strict waterfall. People hear about the DoD's sponsorship of the CMM and perceive bureaucracy. These are unfortunate misconceptions. Put politics and semantics aside and just use it. I have used the CMM, and it works. The CMM has its faults and several top experts have expounded on them (Jones, 1996), but it is a complete package. It begins at zero and builds up your organization while allowing you the freedom to choose the details that fit your culture.

Personal Software Process. The Personal Software Process (PSP) (Humphrey, 1995) was created by Watts Humphrey, an architect of the CMM (Humphrey, 1989). The PSP concentrates on improving an individual's ability to write more software, with fewer errors, in less time, predictably. It is important because of what it teaches about software development and how it helps software projects with more capable people.

The message of the PSP is to do what works. The method is a disciplined application of analysis, metrics, and statistics. What works is whatever the metrics and statistics indicate. The programmer uses a basic process and records how long each task requires in minutes (not hours or days). This shows how much time is required to produce a program of size X and lets you predict how much time you will need for the next program of size X. It also shows which practices or processes work; that is, which ones yield more product in less time, and which do not.

The PSP's metrics permit analysis and allow improvement. Start simple. Record how long it takes to do tasks; track errors and their fixes. If a person or a group is doing tasks better and working faster than others, learn from them. Metrics can reveal much about individual capabilities. However, beware of using them to single out individual performance. One of the main rules of metrics etiquette (Grady, 1992) is don't even *hint* at measuring individuals for either reward or punishment. Instead focus on process and teamwork. First, if people feel that metrics are an attempt to single them out, they will lie in their metric reporting. Second, and more important, one person seldom does all the work on a project. Individual software stars exist, but bright stars are surrounded by huge areas of darkness. Top software producers succeed by raising the level of everyone via good processes, effective management, and teamwork.

The PSP is based on experience. Humphrey has followed his own advice by adjusting the process according to the results of dozens of projects he and his students have completed. However, Humphrey's text is not for the casual reader. It is a workbook complete with homework assignments. It emphasizes statistics and can be downright boring. I wasn't thrilled when I first picked it up, but I worked through it, discovered I had many poor personal habits, and accepted needed change. I now design software and test the design before coding, read the code before compiling, track defects, and analyze all my data. The numbers showed me how to improve. I now write more software in less time with fewer errors. All I started with was a willingness to change.

Figure 6.12 shows how Humphrey takes the programmer from the present process to the full PSP in five steps (PSP 0 to PSP 2.1). PSP 0 begins by recording how long it takes to do every task in minutes. Many will argue that this is extreme. The best response is a statement by Capers Jones (Jones, 1996): "The number one root cause of cancellations, schedule slippages, and cost overruns is the chronic failure of the software industry to collect accurate historical data." You get much more accurate productivity data by breaking a task into minutes than by listing what you accomplished in a week or even a day.

The second key task of PSP 0 is defect recording. The programmer documents every error, including when it was committed, when it was found, and the time required to correct it. The PSP concentrates on preventing errors or catching them early. Documenting the errors proves that finding and fixing errors is the most time-consuming task in software (Jones, 1996). It also shows that we make more errors than we would like to admit.

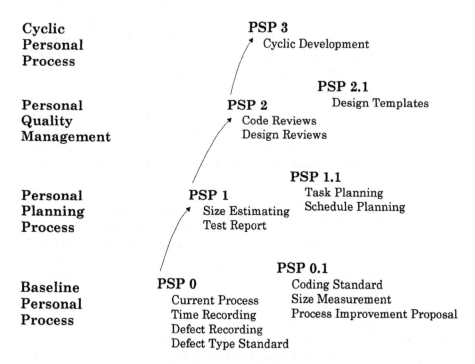

Cyclic Personal Process	**PSP 3** Cyclic Development	
Personal Quality Management	**PSP 2** Code Reviews Design Reviews	**PSP 2.1** Design Templates
Personal Planning Process	**PSP 1** Size Estimating Test Report	**PSP 1.1** Task Planning Schedule Planning
Baseline Personal Process	**PSP 0** Current Process Time Recording Defect Recording Defect Type Standard	**PSP 0.1** Coding Standard Size Measurement Process Improvement Proposal

Figure 6.12   The Personal Software Process.

PSP 1 and 1.1 move into planning and estimating. The programmer uses past performance to estimate future tasks, combining tasks to build a project plan. The PSP emphasizes and teaches how to predict when software will be ready. Later in this chapter, I describe the PSP's estimating techniques.

PSP 2 and 2.1 add design and code reviews. They are effective and efficient at finding and removing errors. Reviewing your own work is difficult, so the PSP requires creating and using checklists for design and code reviews. Reviews take time, but have a high ROI. If errors remain in code until testing, the debugging time will be far greater than the review time. We all make mistakes. Before working through the PSP, I thought printing and reading code before compiling was a waste of time. I don't think that anymore. The PSP reviews are similar to cleanroom testing.

This type of basic discipline characterizes the PSP. The steps are high-level design, estimating and planning, design, design review, code, code review, compile, and test. This is a straight waterfall and works for projects that require one person and tens of hours. If the project is bigger, use PSP level 3.0, which iterates several PSP 2.1 processes.

The PSP follows the basic V-chart, so it has a clear connection with configuration management baselines. The individual programmer starts with requirements and works through the allocated, design, development, product, and operational baselines. It is all fairly simple, given the proper perspective.

The PSP is an excellent teaching tool because working through Humphrey's assignments proves the value of applying basic principles in a disciplined manner. The methods learned improve the capability of individual programmers. Better individuals make better teams and products. If you lead programmers, arrange training and time for them to work through the PSP.

Team Software Process. The Team Software Process (TSP) was also created by Watts Humphrey (Humphrey, 2000). The PSP (previous section) guides individuals in their attempts to improve their abilities and the Capability Maturity Models (next section) guides large organizations in their improvement programs. Left in between these two are small teams. The TSP addresses these teams of up to 20 people.

The TSP is based upon the PSP. Humphrey recommends mastery of the PSP before attempting to use the TSP, as many of the concepts of the PSP such as scripts, checklists, and forms carry forward. Many people don't like to use such items as they seem too prescriptive. It is difficult, however, to argue with the documented results of the method, and there is one certain property of the PSP and TSP—the people document what happens in detail so there is little to argue about the results.

Figure 6.13 shows the general process of the TSP. The concept is that the team builds a product through iterations or cycles. The team creates a core of the product during the first cycle and adds features to the core during each succeeding cycle. The TSP is similar to many of the agile methods mentioned earlier in this chapter.

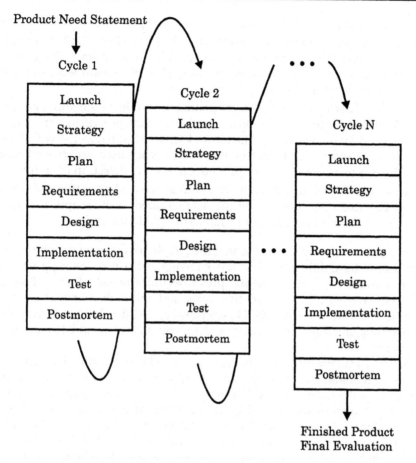

Product Need Statement

Cycle 1

Cycle 2

Cycle N

Figure 6.13 The Team Software Process.

Cycle launch. The launch helps the team begin each cycle. In the launch, the team decides on the roles each person will undertake (more on roles later) and what the team will attempt during the cycle.

Strategy. In this phase, the team decides on the basic strategy for the cycle. This includes creating a conceptual design of the product and making preliminary estimates on the product's size and the time required for the cycle.

Plan. The team plans in detail what they will do in this cycle. An important part of the team planning is to balance the workload among the members of the team.

Requirements. In this phase, the team produces the Software Requirements Specification. They also develop ways to show that their final product meets the requirements.

Design. The team produces the Software Design Specification in this phase.

Implementation. This is where the team builds the product. The TSP concentrates on standards, defects, defect prevention, and reviews. The goal of these ideas and the record keeping of the TSP is to learn ways to build products better in less time.

Test. This phase concentrates on integrating the product built and testing it. The goal of testing is to assess the product and the process that created it. Fixing defects comes next. The record keeping required in TSP will allow the team to analyze the defects they found, when they were created, and how the team can change its processes to prevent defects in the future.

Postmortem. The team ends each cycle with a review of what they did. They ensure that they collected all the data required in the scripts and then discuss what went wrong and what went right in the cycle.

An important part of the TSP is that the people on the team assume roles. Most people have difficulty with "just knowing" what they are supposed to do on a team. The TSP, therefore, prescribes roles ahead of time. People choose or are appointed to specific roles and fulfill them based on the scripts in the TSP. The roles are (1) team leader, (2) development manager, (3) planning manager, (4) quality and process manager, and (5) support manager.

The team leader's principal goal is to run an effective team. This includes helping individuals feel that they are part of a team and ensuring that they contribute to the team's efforts. The development manager is concerned with producing a high-quality product. The planning manager ensures that the team produces a good plan and then tracks their performance per the plan. The quality and process manager works to see that the team follows the TSP properly and produces a high-quality product. The support manager supports the efforts of the other team members by providing good tools, managing risks, and performing the configuration management tasks.

Like the PSP, the TSP can be mind-boggling at first. The method is full of detailed scripts, tables, and forms. Given its detractors, the TSP works for those who use it by the book. The concept behind the method is to use the process given the scripts, record data, look at the data, and change the process so that it works better for your team. It is hard to argue with that logic.

Capability Maturity Model. The emphasis on process began in the late 1980s with the CMM (CMU/SEI, 1995), which was created by the Software Engineering Institute of Carnegie Mellon University and sponsored by the U.S. Air Force. The CMM started as a method to assess the ability of a software contractor and evolved first into a process maturity framework and then into the CMM in its present form.

An organization begins the CMM by establishing a basic software process. This becomes part of the organization's culture, so they repeat the practices, sometimes in a different order, on every project. The organization then strives to improve its process. This philosophy says people are good and will build a good product if they are treated well and use the right process.

The CMM also teaches that organizations with mature processes produce better software consistently. Almost all software organizations have their successes—projects that delivered the product on time, within budget, with people ready to do the next project. Mature processes are repeatable. If an organization repeatedly performs a set of tasks on every project, it gains skill and confidence. This knowledge, this repeatable process, enables the people to deliver good products on time and within budget. Without a repeatable process, every project reinvents the wheel. Planning, estimating, scheduling, budgeting, and so on, are impossible.

The CMM was quite popular in the early 1990s (Yourdon, 1992), but has since lost some of its appeal. Many feel it requires too much documentation. It was also associated with the strict waterfall model or dismissed because it was too bureaucratic. The Microsoft process, described earlier, gained popularity, and software was either done the Microsoft way or the Department of Defense way, and who made more profit? Now agile methods and best practices—techniques that successful companies use—are eroding CMM use.

Figure 6.14 shows the CMM. It has five steps beginning with Level 1 and ending at Level 5. Most U.S. software organizations are at Level 1; fewer than 10 are at Level 5. What this says is that few organizations succeed consistently. In most organizations, a handful of people understand and use proven engineering and management practices, but successful practices are not used by everyone on all the projects.

Levels 2 through 5 contain *key process areas* (SEI, 1993a, b), which are similar to best practices, as I describe later. Using the SEI documents as guides, a software organization writes its own software process manual that covers all the process areas for a level, teaches its people how to use them, and uses them on every project. It takes one to two years to move up a level.

An organization can claim a CMM level only after an independent, outside group examines the organization against the SEI's criteria. Reaching a CMM level brings several benefits to the software organization. The biggest is the boost in morale. Because they know what they need to do on each project, people are freed from organizational worries and can concentrate on technical problems. Another benefit is that other organizations seeking a software contractor know that this organization has reached a level of proficiency because the CMM audit certifies it.

The CMM states what processes an organization must use, but does not dictate how to do them. For example, in Level 2 an organization must manage requirements. The CMM does not dictate a particular method of analysis or documentation. It merely stipulates certain requirements goals. You must document how you will accomplish them, train your people to do it, and have them do it on every project.

The previous paragraph seems to have been lost on many people. They criticize the CMM and laud other practices like agile methods without consid-

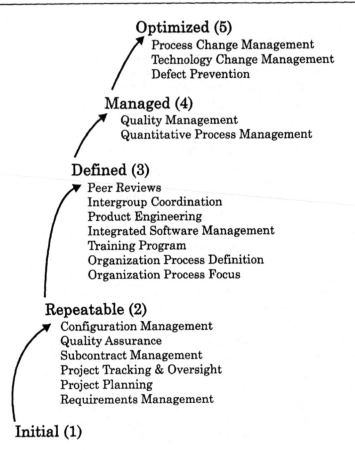

Figure 6.14 The Capability Maturity Model.

ering if the two areas are in agreement. Bill Curtis (Curtis, 2000) encourages the use of the CMM to enable agile methods. Advocates of agile methods want to develop software faster and survive in the face of changing requirements. Improving processes to go faster and managing changing requirements are two goals of the CMM, too. Having a process that is documented, taught, and used helps people to adjust to changes. The process is in place and known, so people don't have to think about it in the face of changing requirements and increasing demands.

Mark Paulk (Paulk, 2001), one of the CMM authors, examined extreme programming in light of the CMM. The practices of extreme programming fit well inside the CMM framework. Paulk's commentary on the situation reinforces that the CMM states what to do in general terms, whereas extreme programming is one particular method with a detailed description of best practices.

My personal experiences lead me to agree with Curtis and Paulk. I used the CMM in a lab with maintenance programmers. Some of the programmers wrote requirements and plans in pencil on the back of old source code print-outs. That was fine by the CMM. If anything, the individual agile methods re-strict individual variations more than the CMM ("If you are not doing pair programming you are not doing extreme programming").

All the processes and visibility techniques I describe here are allowed in the CMM.

Capability Maturity Model Integrated. The CMM described in the previous pages concentrated on process improvement for organizations working with software. That model led to the creation of several other models in areas such as systems engineering, software acquisition, and others. The proliferation of models began to cause problems in organizations that participated in these different endeavors. As a result, the SEI created a Capability Maturity Model Integrated, or CMMI. The goal was to provide a framework for enterprise-wide process improvement.

The CMMI has also grown in various forms. There are six different CMMIs in existence covering the different combinations of systems engineering, soft-ware engineering, integrated product and process development, and supplier sourcing. In addition, each model has a "staged" version and a "continuous" version. I'll restrict the discussion here to the systems engineering and soft-ware engineering fields.

The continuous representation of the CMMI (CMMI 2001b) uses capabili-ty levels to measure process improvement. This differs from the CMM de-scribed earlier. In the continuous representation, an organization chooses a capability area such as project planning and works to improve that one area. This CCMI defines the measures for the different levels of performance for that area. Thus, the CMMI allows an organization more freedom in deciding what to improve.

The staged representation of the CMMI (CMMI 2001a) uses maturity levels to measure process improvement. These maturity levels are like those used in the CMM. Figure 6.15 shows the maturity levels and their process areas. This is similar to Figure 6.14, and the process areas shown here are much the same as used in the CMM.

The CMMI uses the same principles as the CMM. An organization achieves a level of performance when an independent assessor examines their practices and grades them. The CMMI states what an organization should be doing in general terms and allows that organization to use whatever detailed proce-dures they deem best.

Like the CMM, the CMMI has been criticized as being too bureaucratic, too much like a waterfall, etc. As with the CMM, I feel many of these criticisms come from a lack of understanding. The commentaries of Curtis (Curtis, 2000) and Paulk (Paulk, 2001) hold true for the CMMI.

Best Practices. A recent trend and one that seems to be displacing the CMM, is *best practices* (Glass, 1995). The idea is to look at what the best people do

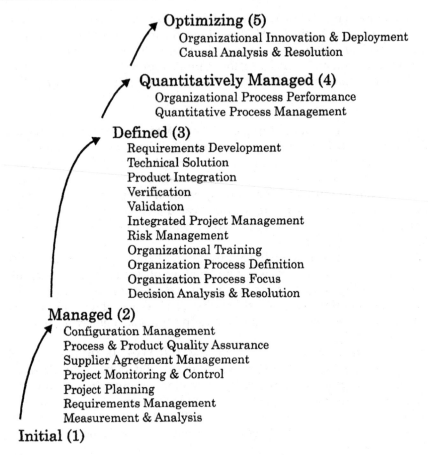

Optimizing (5)
Organizational Innovation & Deployment
Causal Analysis & Resolution

Quantitatively Managed (4)
Organizational Process Performance
Quantitative Process Management

Defined (3)
Requirements Development
Technical Solution
Product Integration
Verification
Validation
Integrated Project Management
Risk Management
Organizational Training
Organization Process Definition
Organization Process Focus
Decision Analysis & Resolution

Managed (2)
Configuration Management
Process & Product Quality Assurance
Supplier Agreement Management
Project Monitoring & Control
Project Planning
Requirements Management
Measurement & Analysis

Initial (1)

Figure 6.15   The Capability Maturity Model Integrated.

and repeat it. Best practices has a kind of grass-roots appeal—it is more practical and less bureaucratic than the CMM. But best practices and the CMM are not necessarily mutually exclusive. For example, a group within the U.S. Navy has formed the Software Program Manager's Network, creating their own list of best practices (Brown, 1996, 1999). The SPMN asserts that a big problem in software projects is an ill-equipped project manager. Their best practices are attempts to give quick, substantive help to project managers. The CMM looks at the software organization from a long-term perspective. It seeks to make proven software principles a part of the organization's culture.

At first glance, it may seem that with the SPMN the Navy is trying to duplicate the Air Force's CMM, but this is not so. The Navy group has done some excellent work and published several helpful pamphlets that are worth studying and using.

Figure 6.16 shows a compilation of best practices. (Brown, 1996, 1999;

. Risk Management
. User Manuals (as system specifications)
. Reviews, Inspections, and Walkthroughs
. Metrics (measurement data)
. Quality Gates (binary decision gates)
. Milestones (requirements, specifications, design, code, tests, manuals)
. Visibility of Plans and Progress
. Defect Tracking
. Clear Management Accountability
. Technical Performance Related to Value for the Business
. Testing Early and Often
. Fewer, Better People (management and technical)
. Use of Specialists
. Fight Featuritis and Creeping Requirements
. Document Everything
. Design Before Implementing
. Planning and use of Planning Tools
. Cost Estimation (using Tools, Realistic Vice Optimistic
. Quality Control
. Change Management
. Reusable Items
. Project Tracking
. Users - Understand Them
. Buy In and Ownership by Everyone
. Executive Sponsor
. Requirements

Figure 6.16   A composite list of best practices.

Yourdon, 1996; Jones, 1996). Figure 6.17 shows the same list arranged topi-
cally. Note how the CMM contains all the practices except those related to
people.

The practices in Figure 6.17 begin with people issues. The first three relate
to the business perspective I describe in Chapter 1: When at work, write only
software that people want. *Understand the users.* Who are they? What is their
level of education? How much experience do they have? What do they think
of computers? What do they think of you? Know what they need, what they
want, and what they will use.

This leads to *buy-in and ownership by everyone.* People—developers and
users—work better on a project if they own it, which is why small, new companies can produce good products quickly. Give your people the project and
let them make the decisions. This requires courage and skill from you as the
project manager, but it works. If people are told everything and nothing
comes from them, that is how they will work—nothing will come from them.

Technical performance related to value for the business means just what it says.
If the software project does not meet the needs of the business, the business
will fail, and you won't have to worry about following best practices.

People Issues
  Users - Understand Them
  Buy In and Ownership by Everyone
  Technical Performance Related to Value for the Business
  Executive Sponsor
  Fewer, Better People (management and technical)
  Use of Specialists
  Clear Management Accountability

CMM Level 2 Issues
  Document Everything
  User Manuals (as system specifications)
  Requirements
  Fight Featuritis and Creeping Requirements
  Cost Estimation (using Tools, Realistic Vice Optimistic)
  Planning and use of Planning Tools
  Quality Gates (binary decision gates)
  Milestones (requirements, specifications, design, code, tests, manuals)
  Visibility of Plans and Progress
  Project Tracking
  Design Before Implementing
  Risk Management
  Quality Control
  Change Management

CMM Higher Level Issues
  Reviews, Inspections, and Walkthroughs
  Reusable Items
  Testing Early and Often
  Defect Tracking
  Metrics (measurement data)

Figure 6.17   The composite list in Figure 6.16 arranged by topic.

The *executive sponsor* should be high enough in the organization to be above everyone on the project yet take a personal interest in the project's success. The executive sponsor does not work on the project day to day, but keeps an eye on it and steps in to help when necessary. Projects involve hard work over long periods. They wear people down, and tired people often concentrate on disputes instead of software. The executive sponsor, interested but not involved in the daily grind, can walk in with a good perspective and high energy. This helps settle disputes and renew the project.

The next two practices concern who is on the development team. Using fewer and better people means fewer communication channels, fewer misunderstandings, and fewer errors and error fixes. *Using specialists* also means getting work done more efficiently. Bring in specialists for short periods if necessary. Software projects comprise many different and difficult tasks. It is an accomplishment to become good at one of them, but silly to try to become good at all of them. When it's time to write a configuration management plan, bring in a specialist for two days instead of struggling with it for several weeks. If the customer needs to see some prototypes, bring in a prototype specialist, and so on.

The final people practice is *clear management accountability*. Managers are entrusted with the project and the lives and livelihoods of people. The manager must be held accountable for his actions. The manager's manager is responsible for watching what the manager does. I have seen too many cases in which managers abused their people, mismanaged their projects, and successfully laid the blame on everyone else.

The next group of practices is covered in Level 2 of the CMM. The first practice is to *document everything*. Visibility is important in software—taking one person's ideas and allowing other people to see them. This is the point of documentation. Documentation can be traditional reports and books, but it can also be videotapes, screen displays, posters, and sketches. The key is to record ideas and agreements so that others can see them. Documentation helps eliminate the "I thought you said." Instead, you can say "This sketch has our initials on it, so this must be what we agreed to." That's not bureaucracy; it's visibility.

The next three practices concern requirements. An excellent technique is having users write a *user's manual* for the system they want. The user's manual does not tell the developers everything (such as a calculation's number of significant digits of accuracy), but it does communicate much.

The next practice is simply *requirements*. It is hard to understand why, but some people still insist on attempting to build software systems without requirements. How a person can attempt a solution without understanding the problem is beyond me. I still remember my division chief (the executive sponsor of all my software projects) telling me in 1992 that "requirements are not part of our culture."

The third requirements-related practice is *fighting featuritis and requirements creep*. A change in requirements stops work and causes rework. Studies (Jones, 1996) show that requirements will grow about 1% per month. Higher rates of growth indicate a poor understanding of the problem. In these cases, use an evolutionary or spiral process to reduce risk and rework.

The next six practices concern planning and managing a project. The first two are closely related. *Cost estimation* means not letting someone dictate the project's cost and schedule. Start from scratch, build up a plan, work out the schedule, and total the cost estimate (more on estimating techniques later in this chapter). It is not an exact science, but it works. The process gives a justifiable plan (which tasks and in what order) and estimate (what each task will cost). *Planning* means not yielding to pressure to change the plan and estimate to fit someone's arbitrary figures. Someone reviewing your plan should show how they can reduce your figures. You can also reduce the size of the product to fit the desired plan and estimate.

The plan should contain quality and milestone gates. Quality gates are similar to the concepts in Gerald Weinberg's Public Project Progress Poster scheme (Weinberg, 1993). Each task in the project is a quality gate. The person performing the task says "I'm done." However, the project does not acknowledge this until others have reviewed the task's product. The review ensures quality and helps prevent disasters later on. *Milestones* are significant events in the project that indicate a gathering of key people to review the work done to date. Is the project fit to continue on its current path or should it change course or stop? The milestones in parentheses correspond to basic configuration management baselines.

Techniques for the *visibility of plans and progress* are described in detail in the next section. Put the plans and estimates in the management information center (MIC) so everyone can and does see it. The display of the plan is updated as the project progresses. Everyone knows if the project is on schedule, and everyone can help rescue areas that are in trouble. There are no secrets or surprises.

Updating the plan in the MIC falls under *project tracking*. The project manager, aided by status reports from the CM staff, knows the project's status. Because the tasks are quality gates, several people know when a task is finished. Key people know when major milestones are completed because they sat in the meetings.

These practices are simple, but they work. They are not mindless bureaucracy. In light of these practices, it is amazing to hear about projects that run out of control. Someone wakes up one day to discover a 12-month project is in its 24th month and no one knows how much money has been spent or how much more effort is needed to finish.

The final four practices in the CMM Level 2 group are basics. *Design before implementing* means fighting the urge to implement before thinking through all the requirements. Avoid "saving time" by jumping to code. As I describe in the requirements chapter (see Chapter 5), the result is typically more time, wasted time, and poor software.

Risk management asks "What could possibly go wrong?" Once you know this, ask such things as "What is the probability of something going wrong?" "How much will it affect the project?" "What would we do if it happened?" "How can we reduce the adverse affects?" "How can we prevent it?" Assuming that everything will work is a worst practice. Avoid it. Bad things happen on software projects; anticipate them. Chapter 7 describes some good risk management techniques.

Quality control (QC) includes everything that helps ensure the software does what is required. Visibility techniques are part of QC because they let people study and improve the ideas of others. The IDEA concept (inspection, demonstration, execution, and analysis) is at the heart of QC (Chapter 9 describes the parts of IDEA in detail). Good software does not just happen. It requires good practices applied by people with self-discipline.

Change management, the last of the practices in the CMM Level 2 group, is not the same as change prevention. Practice configuration management as discussed in Chapter 2 and Appendix B. Do not prevent or allow change without thought. Organize baselines and Configuration Control Boards and request and handle change in a planned and managed manner.

The final group of best practices is covered in CMM Levels 3, 4, and 5. In fact, many criticize the CMM for deferring these practices until higher levels. "How can you possibly omit such and such until level X? You won't reach that level for three years and such and such is essential today." This is a valid criticism when taken out of context, but the levels are in the CMM because people can absorb only so much change at a time. It would be great to bring in all the best practices at once, but that is hardly feasible.

Reviews, inspections, and walkthroughs (see Chapter 9) let people look at the work of others to find and fix errors early and remove misunderstandings.

Reusable items cut down on the new work to be done. Reuse is an excellent goal, but few people do it. It is difficult to capture work done to date, put it in a library, and make it easy to search, retrieve, and reuse. Source code is not the only item you can reuse. Aim to reuse parts of CM plans, requirements, designs, test scripts, and test data. Always think about reuse when building something for the first time. Ask what could be done differently that will make the item reusable. Also ask if something is available that can be reused to fit the current need.

Testing early and often is essential. Errors kill projects because, if found late, the cost of fixing them is far out of proportion to their value. Inspect, test, and review products early. Use visibility to get people thinking about the work of others.

The PSP emphasizes simple methods of *defect tracking*. Where were errors committed? Who found them? How? Where? When? How long did it take to fix them? What kind of errors were they? What practices will let us find them earlier or prevent them? These are difficult questions, but the answers are available and valuable.

Process Improvement and Change. One thing that holds for all types of process improvement is that they require people to change the way they think about things and do things. There are excellent sources of material available regarding the affect of change on people. Some of these materials have been written by people in the software field.

One factor about change in a software organization is that the people who must change the most are the managers (Derby & Rothman, 2001). Most of the process improvement models involve pushing authority and responsibility down to lower levels in the organization. Teams make their own plans, track their own progress, change their own processes, etc. The manager must adjust to these changes and act more in a supporting role and less in a controlling role. This is hard for many of us managers to accept. It feels that we are losing our power and authority as "the boss," and many of us worked hard for years to become the boss.

Change is not easy. A model for change helps us understand what we and others are experiencing during change. Such models make change easier to accept. One excellent model—the Satir change model [from Derby & Rothman (2001) and many other sources]—is shown in Figure 6.18. This shows how performance varies as people move through the stages of a change.

Life feels comfortable or at least familiar in the old status quo, but change enters the picture through a foreign element. This alters the existing situation and throws us into chaos. One such change might be a team adopting the SCRUM method. The manager now becomes a scrum master; he no longer controls the process but instead concentrates on removing obstacles. The tools and techniques he used previously don't work anymore. He is confused and uncomfortable. With time, the manager learns how to be a scrum master. He stops worrying about the old things and concentrates on his new role. This acceptance of his new role and tasks is his transforming idea. In the integration and practice phase, he takes that transforming idea and practices his new tasks. This is not easy, and there are setbacks, but the manager gradually raises his performance. He eventually reaches the new status quo where he knows what he is supposed to do each day; he does his tasks, and he grows comfortable with his new role.

There are several things that the Satir model of change should teach us. One is that change takes time. We do not move from our current process to a better process in one minute. We may need days, weeks, or months so there is

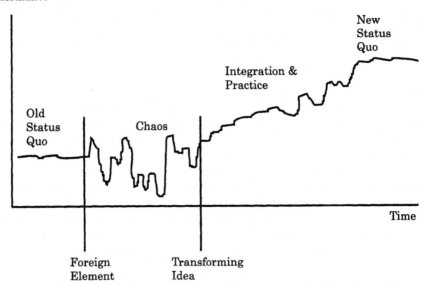

Figure 6.18   The Satir change model.

no benefit to trying to rush ourselves or others through a change. The second is that change brings a period of chaos. People will not enjoy this period and will complain bitterly. We shouldn't be surprised about these complaints and we shouldn't take them personally, as they are normal.

The manager should be prepared to work through change. Patience is a good tool to employ through a period of change. We should stay on course through the process improvement and work until we achieve it. There will be temptation and recommendations to go back to the old way. Expect these and work through them.

Given all the above, it is not surprising that another factor in process improvement and change is that people will resist. Dale Emery (Emery, 2001) has some excellent material on working with this resistance. He views resistance as a resource because it provides information that we can use to become more effective.

Emery has observed four factors that affect how people resist requests for change. The first factor is the expectations about the request for change. People may resist change based on their answers to three basics questions. These are (1) will I be able to do this; (2) if I do it, what will be the results; and (3) do I want those results? The second factor is the communication about the request for change. We may not explain the change or its reasoning well. Others may not explain their resistance well. We may all misunderstand one another completely. The third factor is the relationship among the people involved. People are not robots. Our relationships enter into a conversation before we say a word. The resistance given by people may have much more to do with the past working relationship than it does with the request for change. The fourth factor is the work environment. People may feel the requested change won't work *in this environment*. They might love the change somewhere else, but not where they work now.

Resistance to process improvement is natural and almost universal. A manager can receive it as a source of frustration or a source of useful information. The choice is ours.

Let's Go Faster. One of the fundamental goals of most process improvement efforts is to be able to produce software in less time. If an organization can maintain the quality of their products while going faster, they improve their position in the marketplace. Hale and others (Hale, Parrish, & Dixon, 2000) investigated what they call task assignment patterns and discovered that some simple yet not often used methods of going faster. They found that tasks take less effort (fewer man hours and thus less time) when you:

1. *Reduce concurrency.* This means letting one person work on a task alone. The concepts of pair programming (from extreme programming) and peer reviews are excellent practices, and the idea of reducing concurrency is not opposed to these. Reducing concurrency strives to let a small number of people work on a task instead of a large num-

ber. This reduces the amount of meetings and the amount of necessary communication. Every instance of communication provides an opportunity for miscommunication. Hence, it is best to minimize these opportunities.

2. *Increase intensity.* This concerns the degree of focus on a task. Do we perform a task daily or twice a year? If a person does a task daily, they will probably develop a high degree of familiarity with it. Hence, they can do it faster with higher quality. That is the person who should be assigned that task in a project. Another facet of intensity is the continuous time spent on a task. If a person works on a task full time until finished, they are more apt to work on it efficiently. If a person works on a task one hour per day for ten days, they are probably working inefficiently. It is best to assign a person one task and let them work on it until finished. This is not always the case, as a person could become stuck on a problem, but in most cases it is the best tactic.

3. *Reduce fragmentation.* This concerns the amount of switching among different tasks to fragment a person's day. Switching among tasks consumes time. If a person has two tasks to perform in a day, he will not spend four hours on each task. He will probably spend three hours on each task and spend two hours switching between them. This relates to the increasing intensity as discussed above. It is best to allow a person to work on one or two tasks in a day on a project. That allows them to do something different if they become stuck on a problem. Assigning three or four tasks to a person at one time, however, is inefficient and will hurt projects.

6.3   MAKING THE PROJECT VISIBLE: PLANNING TECHNIQUES

6.3.1   *Project Context*

The first thing I do on a new project is create a *project context document.* This document is for me and my development team only—no one else. A project context diagram structured as in Figure 6.19 is on the first page; the rest of the document discusses the diagram. The project context diagram is very different from the context diagram in Figure 5.7 (see Chapter 5). The context diagram is a high-level dataflow diagram. The project context diagram, on the other hand, shows the context or setting of a project.

As the figure shows, the left side of the diagram contains the names of the *customer, executive sponsor,* and our team (*producer*). The developers must know who is and is not the customer. Do not disdain outsiders who want to help, but know and listen to your customer first. The *customer and marketplace objectives* are the project's high-level goals. They are qualitative, not quantitative, and come from marketing or customer surveys. They will influence the *project requirements.*

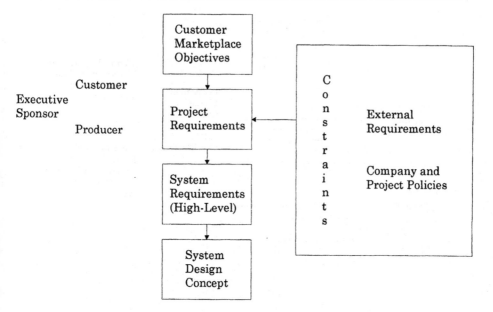

Figure 6.19 The project context diagram.

Also influencing the project requirements are the three items on the right. *External requirements* include compatibility issues and support required by others. The new system will not exist in a vacuum. It must work with existing systems and organizations. In the same way, the project must fit with *company and project policies*. Businesses have personnel work standards and rules. List these so that everyone knows what is influencing management's decisions. Finally, there are the project's *constraints*. Time, money, and equipment are limited. State the limitations and then challenge them ("if we buy SQL Super instead of using the same old Power team, we can save 3 months and $500,000").

All these items come together into the project requirements. These are what we want from the project, not the system. These requirements are qualitative and quantitative. They are an interpretation of the objectives in light of the constraints.

The final two blocks in the diagram are simple attempts at building the system on paper. The *system requirements* are what we want from the new system. The *system design concept* is a one way to achieve those desires.

Figure 6.20 shows a project context diagram for a new accounting system for Jones Inc. to give you an idea of how these blocks are filled in with project data (both the company and project are fictitious).

The project context diagram helps me gather my thoughts about the project, and put them on paper where I can see them. After I am satisfied that my ideas are clearly documented, I share them with the initial, small development team. We work over the diagram and refine it. The project context puts

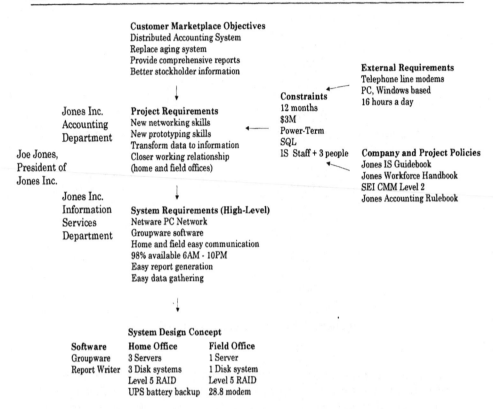

Figure 6.20   A sample context diagram for a fictitious project.

us all on the same track. We keep this document and share it with each new person who joins the project over weeks and months.

The ideas in the document are not concrete. Do not let the system design concept created in an hour constrain the project. Use it for what it is—a simple, quick tool to tell new development team members what the project is about in general terms. Keep this away from the customer, who can easily misinterpret your intent.

6.3.2   Creating a Task Network

A fundamental visibility technique in planning is creating a network of tasks and a PERT chart (see Chapter 4). The task network shows the tasks, who will perform them, the resources required, and how the project will create and combine intermediate products. A completed PERT chart gives the total resources required (people, time, money, equipment) and a schedule. Creating a PERT chart is a micro approach to project planning. It works from the lowest level of detail and builds up a complete plan.

A network of tasks is essential. It looks complicated, but can be created using the following steps.

1. *List all the deliverables (end products)*. The software is the most obvious but not the only deliverable. Other products include the user's manual and online help systems. Custom systems usually include a document for managers of users and one for system administrators. Some products will not be sent to the customer. These include a maintenance manual that describes the structure of the finished software and a set of test software to verify the product.

2. *Make a work breakdown structure (WBS) for each deliverable.* A WBS breaks a large work unit into smaller units and gives them structure. This mechanical process requires little thought (a little thought could probably automate it). There are several types of WBSs. One is the product-based WBS, in which you make seven task cards for each product:

1. Analyze the requirements for X.
2. Design at a high level for X.
3. Design at a low level for X.
4. Build components for X.
5. Test components for X.
6. Integrate and test components for X.
7. Test system for X.

Figure 6.21 shows an example. Across the top of the figure are four products for an accounting software package called D-Count (there should be more products, but this is sufficient for the example). Note the addition of a *system* product. Always add this to the product list because every project will have tasks devoted to the project itself. Make a task card for each task block. Use plain 3" × 5" or 5" × 7" cards or Sticky notes of this size. Each task card will eventually contain all the task elements shown in Figure 6.1. The example in Figure 6.21 will have 28 task cards. This is probably too many, but it's easier to discard tasks later than to think of ones you should have included.

3. *Lay out an initial task network.* Figure 6.22 shows the initial task network for the example in Figure 6.21. Tack or tape the task cards to the walls and connect them with yarn or string, or cover the walls with whiteboards, tape the task cards on the boards, and connect them by drawing lines on the boards with markers. Use large sticky notes instead of regular cards to make this easier.

The initial task network is structured around the three main products (D-Count software, test suite, and user's manual). These have horizontal strips of tasks associated with them. The three task strips join at control gates or milestones—junctions that stop the project and give everyone a chance to think before embarking on a new (expensive) flurry of activity. The task strips are parallel, which means tasks can be performed simultaneously if the people are available. Assign people to tasks at this time.

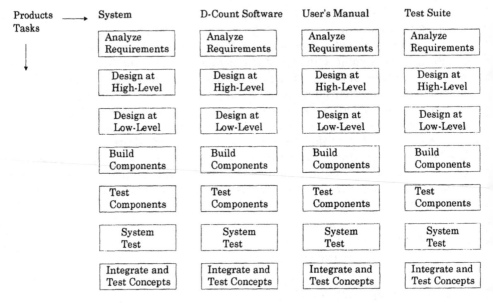

Figure 6.21   Sample work-breakdown structure.

Creating the initial task network requires some thought, but it is mostly a mechanical process. Put the tasks associated with each product in strips. Place a control gate after system high-level design, after the low-level design of each product, and before all the products are integrated.

4. *Refine the initial network.* This is the creative and difficult part of the process. Delete, add, combine, and rearrange the cards. Move them around and change their connections. Change the people, time, resources, inputs, and outputs on each card. Challenge the people refining the network. "Could your people outline the user's manual in three days?" "Won't you need to finish the design of the main routine before you design that subroutine? How can you do them in parallel?"

The refined network is the project's schedule—your commitment to everyone—and you must take it seriously. Allow for vacations, illness, and training. Give your people the time and resources they need to succeed.

Figure 6.23 shows the final version of the task network. Enter it into a project management software package. A dozen equally good packages are available. The software will generate a Gantt chart and more financial and management information than you could possibly use.

Document the decisions made during this step. The plan in Figure 6.23 shows that the user's manual will be written (top right) before the main part of the project begins. This is unusual. Why did the planners decide to do this? What were the alternatives? What factors pushed them in this direction?

Use the project management software to plot large, easy-to-read versions of

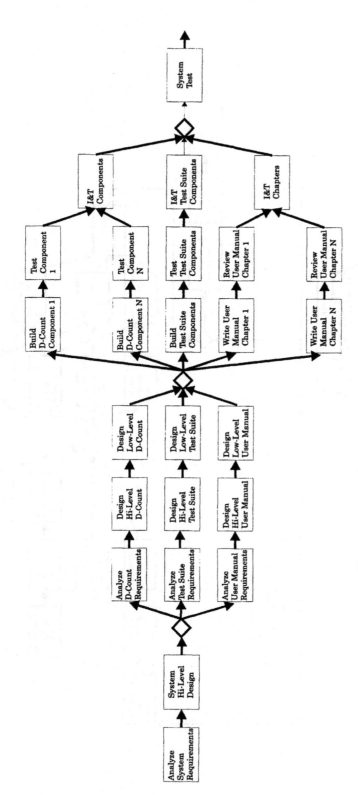

Figure 6.22 Initial task network for the example in Figure 6.21.

202

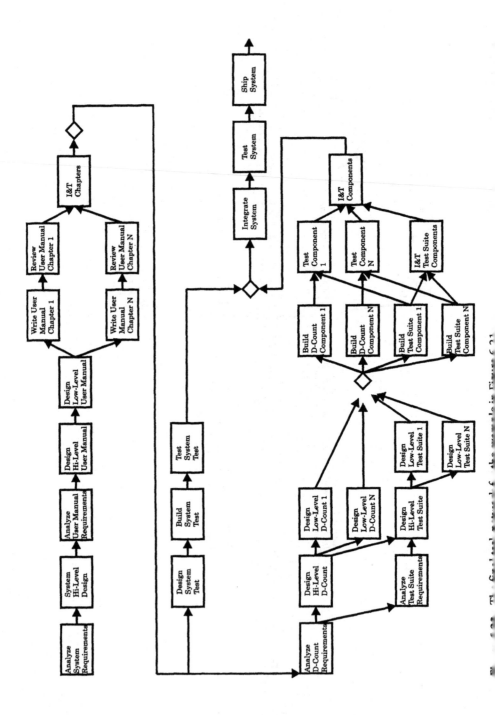

Figure 6.21. The factual network for the example in Figure 6.21.

the PERT and Gantt charts. Post them in the MIC. Explain them in detail to the people doing the work. The project depends on their meeting the schedule. If they see something wrong, listen and change the plan. Don't tell them they will just have to work harder. You will destroy your credibility and probably the project as well.

6.3.3 The Critical Path

A key part of managing a project plan like the one created in the previous section is identifying and managing the critical path. This is so important that basic project management is known as critical path management or CPM. When a task is on a project's critical path, a one-day delay in that task delays the project one day. Hence, it is important to keep those tasks on schedule to the detriment of tasks not on the critical path.

An example helps understand the concept of the critical path. In figure 6.24, a simple project comprises ten tasks. Each box shows a task with a task number, the name of the person performing the task, the start date, $(s = x)$, the end date $(e = x)$, and the duration $(d = x)$. The task dependencies are that task 9 cannot begin until tasks 3, 6, and 8 finish.

Figure 6.25 shows the same network of tasks with the critical path highlighted with dark task boxes. Any delay in tasks 1, 2, 3, 9, and 10 will delay the completion of the entire project. Note the "slack" label between tasks 6 and 9 and also between tasks 8 and 9. Those paths are not on the critical path of the project. If task 6 lasts nine days instead of five, that will not delay the end of the project. The same is true of all the tasks not on the critical path.

Knowing what is and is not on the critical path provides the project manager an opportunity to shift resources to maintain the schedule. Suppose Joe

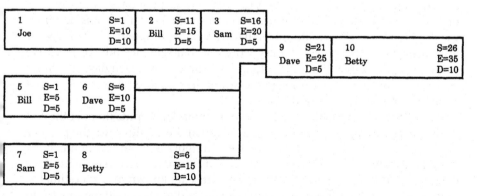

Figure 6.24 A simple project.

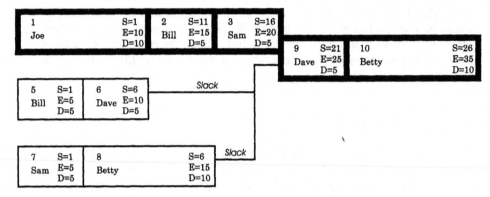

Figure 6.25   The same project with the critical path highlighted.

is having difficulty on task 1. This is on the critical path, so if Joe needs more than ten days to complete the task, the project will be late. You can step in and manage by having Bill and Sam help Joe on task 1. They can stop working on tasks 5 and 7, respectively, because there is some slack in the paths containing those tasks. Their help could keep Joe on schedule and thus the project on schedule. The same is true for all the tasks on the critical path. If the person working one of those tasks is having difficulty, you can stop work on other tasks and shift resources to keep the critical path moving.

6.3.4   *The Critical Chain*

A variation on critical path management that allows the project manager some freedom in planning and managing a project is the concept of critical chain project management (CCPM). The main concept of CCPM is to gather the buffer placed on each individual task and collect it in a big project buffer. For example, task 1 of Figure 6.24 is estimated to last ten days. For most people creating estimates, this is known as a 90% estimate. This means that if we were to attempt this task 100 times that we would complete it in ten days or less 90 of those 100 times. The key words of that sentence are "or less." We would probably finish that task in four days, three days, seven days, etc. Since we would almost always complete the task in less than ten days, we have put a buffer into the estimate of this single task.

CCPM collects these little buffers from every task and puts them at the end of the project in a project buffer. Figures 6.26 and 6.27 illustrate the process. Figure 6.26 shows the same tasks that were in figure 6.24. In this figure, however, the duration of each task was cut in half (five-day tasks were cut to three days, but that is close enough). These estimates are known as 50% estimates. This means that if we attempted a task 100 times that we would complete it in

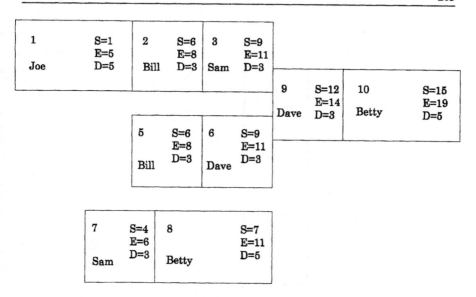

Figure 6.26 The first step in creating the critical chain.

less time than estimated 50 times and more time than estimated 50 times. For example, we would complete task 1 in less than five days half the time and in more than five days half the time.

The critical chain is the longest chain of dependent tasks. In this example, the critical chain comprises tasks 1, 2, 3, 9, and 10. These are the same tasks that were in the critical path of the previous section. The other two chains of tasks (tasks 5 and 6 is one chain and tasks 7 and 8 are the other chain) are known as feeder chains. This is because they feed into the critical chain.

Figure 6.27 shows the project schedule with three buffers added. The project buffer to the far right has been added to the end of the critical chain. The length of this buffer is 25% to 50% of the length of the critical chain. The two feeder chains have feeder buffers added to them. These two buffers are also 25% to 50% of the length of their chains.

Note that the schedule has decreased from 35 days in Figure 6.24 to 29 days. This is a decrease of about 10% to 15%. Most projects using the CCPM method have reduced their schedules about 15% to 25% compared to similar projects.

The CCPM method seems to work in reducing the length of projects. The question of why must come to mind. The same people are doing the same tasks with the only visible difference being that someone wrote a different number in the task duration on the schedule on the wall. How could that affect people? There are several reasons. One is that when people are given a 90% estimate (like in Figure 6.24) there is little or no reward for finishing early. If Joe finishes task 1 in seven days, what is he to do? He will most likely

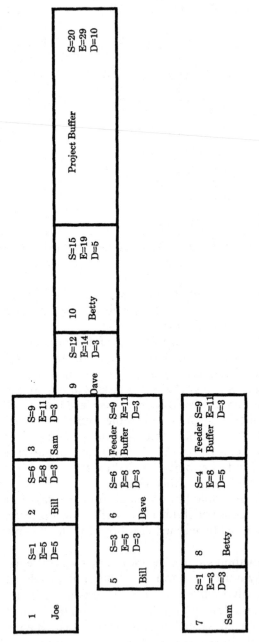

Figure 6.27 The second step in creating the critical chain.

take the next three days to check and re-check his work. Another reason is known as the Student Syndrome. If a student is given three weeks to complete a task that only requires three days, the student will often do nothing for two-and-a-half weeks and then work really fast to do the assignment. If Joe feels he can finish task 1 in seven days, he will find other things to do the first three days and then "get to work" on the task. These two reasons add up to the old saying that "work expands to fill the time allotted."

Another reason that CCPM reduces schedules has to do with multitasking. When a person works on more than one task, he spends time switching between those tasks. Instead of working on two tasks for four hours each, he will work on each task about three hours and take about two hours to switch between them. In the critical path example discussed in the previous section, the manager might have Bill and Sam help Joe with task 1 if Joe were struggling. Bill and Sam would be switching between their assigned tasks and helping Joe. That switching would subtract resources from the project without adding anything back. In CCPM, the manager would not ask Bill and Sam to work on several tasks at once, but would let Joe work on his task alone. If he took extra days to complete it, those days would come from the project buffer. That is the reason for its existence—to buffer the project from difficult tasks.

The previous paragraph provides a hint at what the project manager does using CCPM. Instead of shifting resources to the critical path when it is in trouble, the project manager manages the buffers (Zultner, 1999). The project manager keeps what looks like a checkbook of days. If someone finishes their task in less time than estimated, the project manager records that and adds the extra days to the buffer. He adds them to the project buffer if the task was in the critical chain and adds them to the corresponding feeder buffer if the task was in a feeder chain. In a similar manner, if someone needs more time than is estimated, the project manager records that event and subtracts days from the appropriate buffer. This checkbook gives the project manager a record of what is going well and not so well on the project. If the project buffer appears to be shrinking, the project manager will start working on contingency plans. If the buffer shrinks further, the project manager will start implementing those plans.

6.3.5 Cards on the Wall Planning

Cards on the wall is a working group technique to elicit requirements (see Chapter 5), but it is also an excellent tool for refining a task network (Phillips, 2001, 2002). Figure 6.28 shows people working a task network using this technique. The main benefit is that the participants own the plan, and when they own it, they will make it work. Therefore, involve people from as many groups (document writers, testers, programmers, users, and so on) as possible.

Figure 6.28   Cards on the wall planning session.

As the project manager, don't worry too much about the task network—that will get done. Instead, focus on the people. If someone is sitting back at the table, bring them to the wall. Suggest a few stupid ideas and move cards related to them to the wrong place. Push them into asserting their expertise to correct you. Make them work on the plan until they own it.

Prepare for the cards on the wall session in the same way you would prepare for a facilitated meeting (see Chapter 5). A cards on the wall session involves a number of people for one to five days. It costs money, so it deserves and requires forward thinking. Find a room off site to minimize interruptions. Ensure that it has ample blank cards, yarn, empty walls or white boards, tape, pens, paper, bathrooms, refreshments, computers, printers, and so on. Do not start until everyone arrives. Get a commitment from management that everyone will stay until finished. Do a warm-up exercise such as a task network for celebrating after the project.

This may seem like a silly gimmick, but it works. Some may ask "Can't one person just do the schedule and have others comment on it?" This approach might work, but the plan would always belong to the person who created it. It is "Bill's plan," not "our plan." When people own a plan, they work hard to see it succeed.

6.4   MAKING THE PROJECT VISIBLE: ESTIMATING TECHNIQUES

Estimation is predicting the size of a product or the length of a task. Most people do not estimate well, even though estimation is an essential part of planning. It's taken me years of successes and failures to evolve the following guidelines:

Know the purpose of the estimate and the desired accuracy. If someone needs the estimate for an informal discussion and it need be only within an order of magnitude, pause and give an answer. If the survival of the business depends on the estimate and it must be accurate within ±2%, an offhand reply would be disastrous. You are more likely to encounter the first example in practice.

Use prerequisites whenever they are available. Keep metrics from past projects and use a repeatable process. Metrics provide a reliable foundation for any estimation. Estimates without past data are dangerous. A repeatable process is a partner to metrics. If an organization always approaches software by doing analysis, design, build, and integration and test (or always does scenarios, prototypes, and iterations), its people know how much time each step requires. Consequently, they can predict how much time the same steps will require on the next project. Their discipline, mature process, and metrics allow them to make pretty good guesses.

If the prerequisites are not available, don't give up. Work harder by repeatedly dividing the tasks or products until they are small. Once small, estimation is much easier (almost anyone can estimate the time to write a "hello world" subroutine). The divide-until-small task is frustrating. Continually breaking down the problem produces the feeling of creating more problems instead of estimating how long the solution will require. Performing an unusual and difficult task always produces the temptation to fall back on a familiar task. Resist the temptation to start coding now (just solve it) and work through the problem at hand (estimation).

Be realistic. For most people, this means be pessimistic. Software people want to produce software. An optimistic estimate produces the opportunity to do so (the low bid wins the job). It can also mean a failed project (more time and money than estimated or working 80 hours a week for 40 hours pay).

There are two main types of approaches to software estimating: macro and micro. The Rayleigh model is an example of the macro approach; the Probe technique in the PSP is an example of the micro approach. Both use math, both are based on experience, and both work. Do not dismiss them as bureaucratic because they require a few hours to perform.

6.4.1 Rayleigh Model

The Rayleigh model gives you an overall project perspective to help ensure that plans for a project are realistic. Larry Putnam and Ware Myers (Putnam & Myers, 1992, 1996, 1997) developed this model from years of experience.

The model is based on the Rayleigh curve (named after the 19th century physicist Lord Rayleigh). As Figure 6.29 shows, the curve is the actual effort expended in a project beginning with design and ending with the delivery of a highly reliable product. The horizontal axis is time in the project. The vertical axis is the current effort in staff-months per month. The area under the curve is the total effort or staff-months of the project. This shows the cost (staff-months times dollars per staff-month).

The first vertical dotted line is at time T_D. This is where the software reaches initial operational capability (IOC). The second vertical dotted line is where the software reaches final operational capability (FOC). The area to the left of the first vertical dotted line is 39% of the total area, the area between the dotted lines is 39% of the total, and the remaining 22% is in the long tail to the right. Many people think they are done when the software works for the first time (IOC). This model states that they are not even halfway there. If they cut their staff at this point, the remaining 61% of the work will drag on for years.

The Rayleigh curve fits the staffing of large software projects. The curve begins when design does. The project needs only a few people at that time because there is only so much anyone can do. After the designers divide the design into parts, the parts need further design and division, so more people join the project. Coding begins to the left of the curve's peak, and staffing increases again. The software is ready for user testing near the curve's peak, the IOC. Testing involves the maximum number of people for the project. Staffing declines after testing as the testers and some programmers move on to other projects. The remaining programmers correct the errors found during testing. As the number of errors declines, so does the number of programmers. The software reaches an acceptable threshold of errors at FOC and is de-

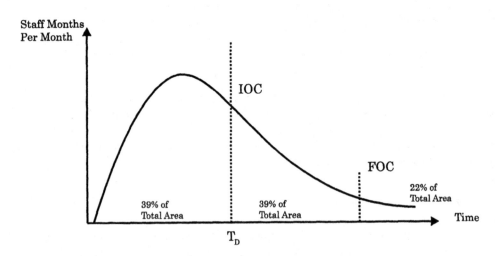

Figure 6.29 The Rayleigh curve.

livered. As the figure shows, however, 22% of the work remains in responding to the customer and supporting the product.

Figure 6.30 lists the equations for the Rayleigh model. The first equation (1), derived by Putnam and Myers, gives your organization's *productivity parameter*. The authors consider productivity to be more than just LOC divided by time. The productivity parameter is calculated from past project performance and indicates the organization's overall capability. The *product size* is the (often argued) lines of code (LOC) in the delivered software. This method requires using LOC, but there are methods for converting function points to LOC. *Effort* is the staff-years needed for the project. B is a special skills factor that ranges from 0.16 for products with 5,000 to 15,000 LOC to 0.39 for products with 70,000+ LOC (Putnam & Myers, 1992, 1997). This constant compensates for the differences in different size projects. (Larger projects have more people and require more communication. This means more meetings and more miscommunication, which can lead to more errors.) Time is expressed in years.

Next is the software equation. Notice that time (T) is raised to a power greater than one. This reflects the nonlinear nature of software projects. That is, software products twice as big require much more than twice as much time and money.

The software equation lets you calculate the time, effort, and cost of a project given your organization's past performance and the estimated LOC for the project. You merely insert the final LOC, the staff-years of effort, the time required in years, and the correct special skills factor B from a similar project and calculate the productivity parameter. Most organizations, even those without metrics programs, have these numbers. In the next section, I describe how to use the Probe approach to get an even more accurate estimate of the proposed product's LOC.

(1)   Productivity Parameter $= \dfrac{\text{Product Size}}{(\text{Effort/B})^{1/3} * \text{Time}^{4/3}}$

(2) $T_{Dmin} = 0.68 * (\text{Product Size/Productivity Parameter})^{0.43}$ in years

(3) $T_{Dmin} = 8.14 * (\text{Product Size/Productivity Parameter})^{0.43}$ in months

(4)   Effort in man years $= 15 * B * T_{Dmin}^{3}$ with T in years

(5)   Effort in man months $= 180 * B * T_{Dmin}^{3}$ with T in years

(6)   Cost = Man Months * \$/Man Months

Figure 6.30   Equations of the Rayleigh model.

Use the estimated LOC for this project and the productivity parameter just calculated to find the minimum T_D for this project. Equation (2) is for calculating T_{Dmin} in staff-years; Equation (3) lets you calculate in staff-months. The final step is simply to multiply the staff-months (or staff-years) of effort by the average cost of a staff-month (staff-year) for your organization.

Checking Proposals. As Figure 6.31 shows, these equations can help you check the validity of proposed plans and costs. The company here proposes to write an engineering software package with an estimated 300,000 LOC, which they hope to build in 18 months with 800 staff-months at a cost of $9.99 million (charging $150,000 per staff-year). The first calculation shows that their productivity parameter must be 31,481 to accomplish this. History says the average firm that produces engineering software has a productivity parameter of about 14,000 (Putnam & Myers, 1992, 1997). (Remember that the 31,481 is not as bad as it seems because the productivity parameter scale is nonlinear.) Assuming that the company is about average (which you can tell from past project performance), the 14,000 value gives a schedule and

Estimated   Size = 300,000 lines of code

Proposed   Time = 18 months = 1.5 years

                             Effort = 800 man-months = 66.6 man-years

                             Cost Rate = $150,000 per man-year

                             Cost = $9.99M

Required Productivity Parameter $= \dfrac{300{,}000}{(66.6/0.39)^{1/3} * (1.5)^{4/3}}$

                             $= 31{,}481$

Industry Average Productivity Parameter = 14,000

$T_{...} = 0.68 * (300{,}000/14{,}000)^{0.43} = 2.54$ man-years

Effort $= 15 * 0.39 * 2.54^{3} = 95.86$ man-years

Cost $= \$150{,}000 * 95.86 = \$14.4M$

Figure 6.31 Checking the validity of a proposal for an engineering system.

cost significantly higher than proposed. Use the 14,000 value and calculate the time, effort, and cost as shown. Do not accept this proposal. Explain the doubts and investigate to see if the company can justify the higher productivity parameter needed to meet their proposal.

Estimating Time Before Main Build. The Rayleigh model pertains to the main build parts of a software project (design, code, inspection, testing, and documentation). Figure 6.32 is another view of the Rayleigh curve that shows the relative times of phases before the main build. The first phase is what Putnam and Myers call the *feasibility study*. A few people analyze the requirements of the system, estimating the product size in ranges (minimum, expected, and maximum size). These sizes and the company's productivity parameter let you calculate T_{Dmin} as shown earlier. The feasibility study should last only one-fourth of T_D. The *functional design* phase is where a few more people perform the high-level design. They revise the estimate of product size and calculate a better T_D. This phase should last only one-third of T_D.

Planning Project Staffing. Figure 6.33 illustrates a 25,000 LOC project. The squared-off curve indicates that people are added to the project in whole units (no half or quarter people). This curve is for relatively small projects. Different curves are used for different size projects (Putnam & Myers, 1992, 1997). This curve is normalized so that the average project effort is 1.0 on the vertical axis and the time to reach FOC is 1.0 on the horizontal axis. The shape of the curve will always be as shown for this project size.

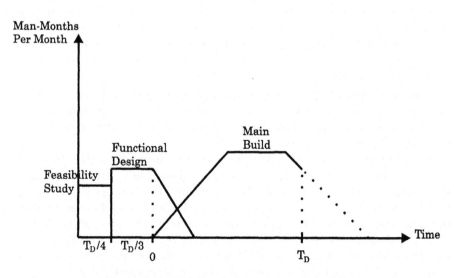

Figure 6.32 Relative time prior to main build.

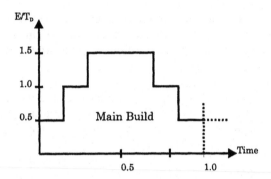

Past Data Shows
Productivity Parameter = $10,000/((20/(12*0.16))^{1/3} * (11/12)^{4/3}) = 5,142$

Expected Lines of Code = $(20,000 + 30,000)/2 = 25,000$

Minimum $T_D = 8.14 * (25,000/5,144)^{0.43} = 16.1$ months = 1.34 years

Effort = $180 * 0.16 * 1.34^{0.43} = 69.3$ man-months

Total Cost = 69.3 man-months * $10,000 per man-month = $6.93M

E/T_D = 69.3 man-months/16.1 months = 4.3 people

Time Length Ratio	Actual Time (months)	Rounded Months	Manpower Ratio	Actual Manpower (people)	Rounded People	Months
0.15	2.42	2	0.5	1.72	2	0-2
0.3	4.83	5	1.0	4.3	4	2-5
0.7	11.27	11	1.5	6.45	6	5-11
0.85	13.69	14	1.0	4.3	4	11-14
1.0	16.1	16	0.5	1.72	2	14-16
						16-20 2 people

Figure 6.33   Simple estimation model of a 25,000 LOC project.

Data from past projects leads to a productivity parameter of 5,144. The T_D calculation yields 1.34 years or 16.1 months, and the effort is 69.3 staff-months. Given our cost of $10,000 per staff-month, the total cost of the project is approximately $7 million.

If you replace the normalized numbers on the curve with actual ones, the 1.0 on the horizontal axis becomes 16.1 months (in this curve and for this size project, the IOC and FOC are the same). The 1.0 on the vertical axis is effort divided by T_D, or 4.3 people. The table at the bottom of the figure shows the conversions for normalizing to actual numbers. The first column is the normalized time numbers. Multiplying each by 16.1 produces actual time in months, which you then round off to get a practical number. The next three columns pertain to manpower. Multiplying the normalized numbers by 4.3 gives you the actual manpower, which you again round to whole numbers (people). The result is that two people will be the staff for the first two months, four people the next three months, six people the next six months, and so on. Two people will probably be needed to support the customer for four months after delivery.

A closer look at this example shows the dollars and cents value of process improvement. The cost ($7 million) seems expensive for 25,000 LOC. Start at total cost and trace backward. The cost is a simple multiplication of effort. The biggest contributor to effort is time raised to the third power. Cut the time and effort by streamlining the process and cost will fall dramatically. The time equation has a constant, the LOC, and the productivity parameter. Increase the productivity parameter and all the expensive numbers fall. If this rises from 5,144 to 10,000 (not that much as this is a nonlinear item), T_D would fall to 12 months, and effort would fall to 29.3 staff-months. The cost would be about $3 million instead of $7 million. Thus, a single, one-year project would save $4 million. Process improvement is expensive and time consuming, but as these figures show, it has a definite payoff.

The Rayleigh model delves into more topics than I can discuss here. It lets you calculate the proper staff build-up rates, peak staff time, defect rates, and so on. Read more about this model in books and papers by Putnam and Myers. Tens of years and hundreds of actual projects are the model's foundation. It is not theory. It works at work.

6.4.2 PSP's Probe

The Personal Software Process (Humphrey, 1995) uses Probe to predict the product's size and the required build time. In Probe (short for *Proxy-Based Estimation*), you substitute experience on similar past products and projects to predict future ones.

Figure 6.34 shows an overview of the estimating process. You combine the *basic design* for the product with historical size data (proxies) to *estimate the size* of the new product. The size estimate and *historical productivity* data (more proxies) let you *estimate resources*, including time. The next step is to put the tasks and times into a schedule (*make schedule*). Finally, you *execute the plan* to produce the product, feed back the actual size and time to the historical databases, and gather metrics. Metrics are crucial to the success of the process.

Figure 6.35 shows the elements of the *estimate size* step in Figure 6.34. This is the basic technique of taking an unsolvable problem and breaking it into smaller problems you can solve. The steps consist of dividing the product into small parts that are similar to parts from past projects. You can then use the actual sizes of past parts as estimates for the new parts. Finally, you adjust the estimate using information from past estimated and actual projects using linear regression.

Figures 6.36 and 6.37 give additional task breakdowns in estimating product size. Figure 6.36 shows a table that starts with data on past software. You

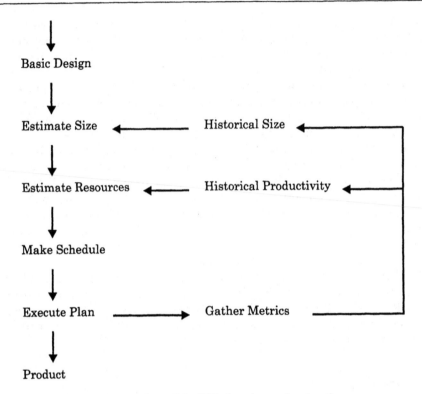

Figure 6.34   Overview of the PSP planning and estimating process.

then categorize parts of the software by function type and list them in the left column of Figure 6.37. The relative sizes of these parts form the column heads in Figure 6.36. You can then fill in the table with actual numbers from past projects.

The PSP uses lines of code to measure product size. Figure 6.37, a size-estimating table, shows subroutine categories and sizes in LOC. Many argue that subroutines are passé in an object-oriented world and that LOC is a bad measure of software size. I will not debate that here. My advice is to adapt Probe using whatever works—LOC, function points, number of data-entry screens, pages in a book, slides in a presentation, object classes, and so on—but be consistent throughout. Here I continue to use subroutines and LOC, but this is not the only scheme that will work with Probe.

To derive the table in Figure 6.37, you first design the product at a high level to produce a list of subroutines. You can then categorize each subroutine, decide on its relative size, and fill in the rightmost column with numbers from the table in Figure 6.36. Sum the rightmost column to get the *initial* estimate of LOC. The next step, linear regression, will produce the *final* estimate.

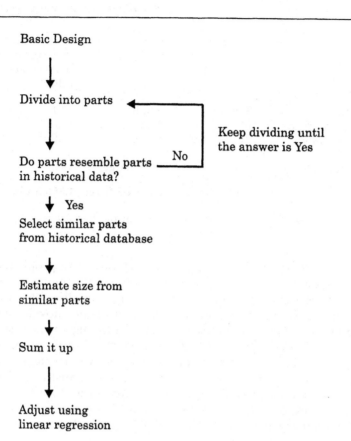

Figure 6.35 Overview of the "estimate size" step in Figure 6.34.

Relative Size Category	Very Small	Small	Medium	Large	Very Large
Calculation	8.3	42.1	75.6	99.6	136.5
Data	7.5	44.3	82.1	102.4	155.2
I/O	6.9	39.6	71.5	107.5	144.5
Logic	11.2	45.2	69.7	95.2	157.6
Setup	7.7	33.6	83.2	93.1	160.2
Text	9.5	51.2	77.9	89.6	141.6

Figure 6.36 Classifying historical data to determine product size.

Name	Category	Relative Size	Lines of Code from Historical Source Code Table
Main_routine	Setup	Small	42.1
File_open_and_create	I/O	Medium	71.5
Percent_remaining	Calculation	Large	99.6
...	...	...	...
Balance_summary	I/O	Very Large	144.5

Initial Total Estimated Size: 1,366.5 Lines of Code

Figure 6.37   A table for estimating product size.

Figure 6.38 shows the linear regression equations. Most people use a rule of thumb—add 40% to the initial estimate—to get this number. Linear regression arrives at a final estimate with more rigor and less subjectivity. Do not be alarmed if spreadsheets and handheld calculators provide answers in five minutes. Linear regression fits a straight line through data, as shown by the top half of Figure 6.39, a plot of the estimated LOC versus the actual LOC for five projects. Linear regression equations not only calculate the equation of the line passing through these points, but also the actual LOC that corresponds to the estimated LOC on the line. Anyone can draw a line on the graph that seems to fit the points. Linear regression provides a line that has the best fit for the points. The bottom half of Figure 6.39 shows the final estimates for several initial estimates.

The final step in Probe is to use linear regression to produce a time estimate from the size estimate. As Figure 6.40 shows the equations for the estimated size and the actual time of past programs. These equations can then be graphed in a way similar to size estimating. If estimated sizes of past projects are not available, use the actual size of past projects in these equations.

$$\text{Final Estimated LOC} = \beta_0 + (\beta_1 * \text{Initial Estimated LOC})$$

$$\beta_1 = \frac{\Sigma(\text{Estimated LOC}_i * \text{Actual LOC}_i) - n * \text{Estimated LOC}_{AVG} * \text{Actual LOC}_{AVG}}{\Sigma(\text{Estimated LOC}_i)^2 - n*(\text{Estimated LOC}_{AVG})^2}$$

for n prior projects

$$\beta_0 = \text{Actual LOC}_{AVG} - \beta_1 * \text{Estimated LOC}_{AVG}$$

Figure 6.38   Transforming the initial estimated size to the final estimated size using linear regression.

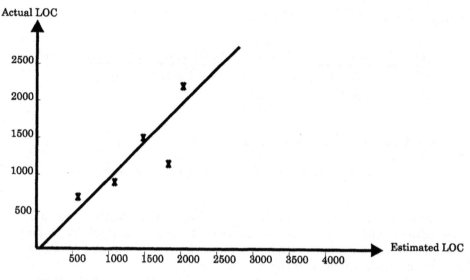

Data

Estimated	Actual
550	675
1100	795
1500	1450
1750	1200
2100	2315

$\beta_0 = 0.96$
$\beta_1 = -43$

Actual LOC = -43 + (0.95)*(Esimated LOC)
Calculated Values

Initial Estimate	Final Estimate
1000	917
2000	1877

Figure 6.39   A graph of linear regression for five projects.

Probe transforms a seemingly impossible estimating problem into small, possible steps. However, it does depend on data from past projects, which is one reason Humphrey teaches the PSP in steps, postponing its introduction until after the student has completed several projects. Use the PSP or some other means to begin recording size and time data. It will seem like bureaucracy, but it is the only way to provide the visibility you need to estimate and plan future projects.

Time Estimated $= \beta_0 + (\beta_1 * \text{LOC Estimated})$

$$\beta_1 = \frac{\Sigma(\text{LOC Estimated}_i * \text{Time Actual}_i) - n * \text{LOC Estimated}_{AVG} * \text{Time Actual}_{AVG}}{\Sigma(\text{LOC Estimated}_i)^2 - n*(\text{LOC Estimated}_{AVG})^2}$$

for n prior projects

$\beta_0 = \text{Time Actual}_{AVG} - \beta_1 * \text{LOC Estimated}_{AVG}$

Figure 6.40   Calculating estimated time from past project size in LOC.

Probe also transforms a qualitative rule of thumb (like add 40% to get a final estimate) into a quantitative, visible estimate. Because it is visible, people can work through it, understand it, and improve it. The graphs and equations give form and discipline to otherwise fuzzy ideas.

Humphrey created Probe to work with an individual programmer on one-person projects (the numbers in the examples here are from such projects), but you can easily extend this technique to multiperson projects. Probe can estimate the size and time of any task type (the number of slides in a presentation and the time to prepare it, the number of people to attend a meeting, the length of the meeting, and so on).

6.4.3   A Technique for Simple Estimation

This book is about approaches that work at work. Sometimes, the most powerful approach is also a simple one. I have found value in a straightforward estimation technique that does not require past data. Instead, it uses the idea of a low, high, and most likely estimate for any quantity (size, time, difficulty, and so on) (Putnam & Myers, 1992). Figure 6.41 gives the equations for this

Estimate $= \dfrac{\text{Low} + 4*\text{Most Likely} + \text{High}}{6}$ Total Estimate $= \Sigma.\text{Estimate}$

Standard Deviation $= \dfrac{\text{High} - \text{Low}}{6}$ Total Standard $=$ Square root$(\Sigma\,(\text{Standard Deviation})^2)$
Deviation

% Error $= \dfrac{\text{Standard Deviation}}{\text{Estimate}}$ % Error Total $= \dfrac{\text{Total Standard Deviation}}{\text{Total Estimate}}$

Figure 6.41   Simple estimation.

technique. The first produces an *estimate* from a low, high, and most likely ranking. The *standard deviation* for the estimate comes from the low and high estimates.

% error indicates the confidence in the estimate on the basis of the standard deviation and estimate. If this value is 20% or higher, the estimate needs more work. A large difference between high and low signifies too many unknowns. Break the item being estimated into smaller, more manageable, less risky parts and derive estimates for the parts. Repeat this process until the percentage of error is near 10%.

The final three equations show how to combine estimates for many parts. This gives a final estimate for an entire project as well as the percentage of error. Again, if the percentage of error is too high, rework the estimate.

This simple, quick, and effective estimating method works well if past data is not available. However, laziness should not be your motivation for using it if such data is available.

6.4.4   Judging an Estimate

Reviewing an estimate is a necessary part of planning. If the estimate is insufficient, you must revise it. Figure 6.42 gives a checklist for reviewing estimates (Park, 1996a). Figure 6.43 (Park, 1996b) provides a list that each organization should strive to meet in its estimating efforts.

Fairley (Fairley, 2002) discusses the quality of estimates in another light. He lists a dozen factors to consider when judging an estimate. The three I find most important are:

1. Distinguish between accuracy and precision. If your inputs are ± 20%, your estimates cannot be accurate to five decimal places.
2. Account for resource availability. People do not work 100% of the day. As mentioned previously in this chapter, switching among tasks takes

1. Are the objectives of the estimates clear and correct?
2. Has the task been appropriately sized?
3. Are the estimated cost and schedule consistent with demonstrated accomplishments on other projects?
4. Have the factors that affect the estimate been identified and explained?
5. Have steps been taken to ensure the integrity of the estimating process?
6. Is the organization's historical evidence capable of supporting a reliable estimate?
7. Has the situation changed since the estimate was prepared?

Figure 6.42   A checklist for reviewing an estimate.

Six Requisites for Reliable Estimating Procedures
1. A corporate memory (historical database).
2. Structured processes for estimating product size and reuse.
3. Mechanisms for extrapolating from demonstrated accomplishments on past projects.
4. Audit trails (values for the cost model parameters used to produce each estimate are recorded and explained).
5. Integrity in dealing with dictated costs and schedules (imposed answers are acceptable only when legitimate design-to-cost or build-to-cost processes are followed).
6. Date collection and feedback processes that foster capturing and correctly interpreting data from work performed).

Seven Indicators of Estimating Capability
1. Management acknowledges its responsibility for developing and sustaining an estimation capability.
2. The estimating function is supported by a budget and funds.
3. Estimators have been equipped with the tools and training needed for reliable estimating.
4. The people assigned as estimators are experienced and capable.
5. Recognition and career paths exist such that qualified people want to serve as estimators.
6. Estimators work with process improvement teams to quantify and track progress in software process improvement.
7. The estimating capability of the organization is quantified, tracked, and evaluated.

Figure 6.43   An organizational and capability checklist for reliable estimating.

time from a person's day, as do meetings (formal and informal). Also, people experience illness, take vacations, have babies, attend to relatives, attend training sessions, etc. We don't know the exact dates that these will occur, but we do know that they will occur, so we can plan for them.

3. Distinguish between estimates and commitments. I may estimate the time it takes to do something, but that does not mean I will do it in that time. If I tell you that I will do something in a period of time, that is a commitment. Often, people read an estimate and interpret it to be a promise or commitment. Check with people before assuming an estimate is a commitment.

6.4.5   Tailoring Techniques to the Process Model

Each project will use the basic task network, cards on the wall, and estimating techniques, but the order, time, and way in which they are used will vary across projects. Most of the variance stems from the process model being used.

In the next sections, I give examples of how you can tailor the use of these techniques to the particular process model. Each example revolves around a software company that employs 10 people. It has been doing banking applications for the last decade and has changed as the computing industry has changed (mainframes to networks of PCs, text-based interaction to GUIs). A primary customer is 80% of its business. The software company wants to grow by serving new customers. Assume that in each case you are the project manager.

Waterfall Project. Your primary customer wants a new report capability. This is similar to many of the projects you have done in the past. You and your customer know the product well, so you select the straight waterfall process.

Use the basic techniques in a straightforward manner. List the deliverables and create a work breakdown structure (WBS) for each (analysis, high-level design, low-level design, build, test, and integrate and test). Put these task cards on a wall in an initial task network. Hold a half-day cards-on-the-wall session to refine the task network. Use Probe to estimate product size for each task and the time required to build it. Sum these to get a total for the project. Use the Rayleigh model to check the validity of your estimate.

Execute the plan. This is a simple process for a simple product.

Evolutionary Project. A small, young accounting firm that heard about you through your primary customer asks you to develop a complete accounting system for their business. Your company is not familiar with accounting businesses and the accounting firm is not sure what they want and need.

This project requires an evolutionary process. Figure 6.44 shows three evolutionary plans. The top plan is the generic view of evolutionary projects using a series of V-charts.

The next plan is the first plan for the project. You must work down to the x to learn the customer's requirements. You can then design, build, test, and integrate the requirements in which the customer has the most confidence. That brings you to the second X, where work stops. The next area of the plan is unknown. At the second X, everyone will know more about the product, and work will continue with greater confidence. The endpoint of the project (far right) is known. Work will stop at that time or when the allotted funds run out.

Work out the details of this first plan. Treat this first, short evolution as a complete project. List the deliverables, make a WBS, lay out the initial task network, hold a cards-on-the-wall session, use Probe on each task, and check it all with the Rayleigh model.

Execute the plan until you reach the second x. At this point, everyone is smarter, and the project is far less risky. Calculate the time and money left to go before reaching the final limit. Decide if the project should continue.

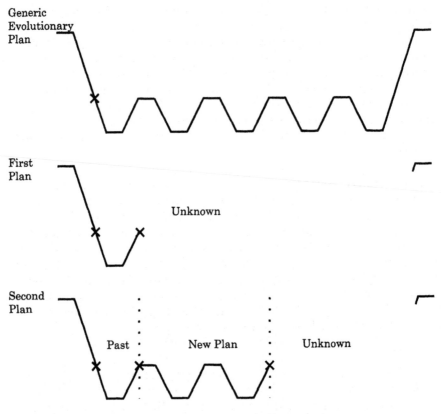

Generic
Evolutionary
Plan

First
Plan

Unknown

Second
Plan

Past · New Plan · Unknown

Figure 6.44   Planning an evolutionary project.

Maybe this is just not going to work, or maybe the customer knows enough
now to buy some shrink-wrapped applications.

If the decision is to continue, plan the next two evolutions. The second
plan (last diagram in Figure 6.44) shows this. Each evolution will design,
build, test, and integrate the requirements with the highest level of confidence. Treat these two evolutions as two complete projects. Start with the deliverables and a WBS and go through to Probe and the Rayleigh model.

Execute these two evolutions. This brings you to the third X in the second
plan. Determine the time and money left before the final limit. Is the customer satisfied with the current product? Are they so happy they want to extend the final limit? Are they so disappointed they want to quit now and cut
their losses? Answer these questions and make a decision.

If the situation is satisfactory, plan evolutions that will take the project to
the final limit. Treat each evolution as a project and reapply the planning and
estimation techniques.

This was a risky project with many unknowns—many invisible items. (See Chapter 7 for more details on managing risky projects.) A disciplined application of project basics removed the unknowns one at a time. The invisible became visible. The V-chart and the planning and estimating techniques let you work through the difficulties.

Spiral Project. A local, well-established printing company wants to expand their business by adding image processing, photographic processing, and graphics capabilities. At least they *think* this is what they want. They are somewhat uncertain, and you are uncertain about attempting the work. Your people know neither the printing business nor image and photographic processing. However, if this works, the printers will gain market share and your company will have a new, very popular line of business to offer customers. On the other hand, if it does not work, everyone will have wasted time and money and damaged their reputation. The two of you agree to approach this as partners and share costs.

This is a risky project that could fail at several distinct points. The spiral process is the best choice here because, as described below, it contains plans for several points at which management can decide to quit. Figure 6.45 shows a spiral for this project (see also the discussion of Figures 6.7 through 6.9). This is a generic spiral except for the products given in the third or lower-right quadrant. These are the desired products of each cycle. The first product is a concept of the final system. If the first spiral can produce a concept (every product in a spiral is a big if), the project can move on and your task becomes one of filling in the blanks. If not, stop the project. The second spiral attempts to find algorithms for image and photographic processing. If you can find these algorithms, you will attempt to write processing subroutines in the next cycle. If the processing works, the next cycle will explore how the users will use the system. Its goal is to determine the type of user interface required. If everything works in the first four cycles, the fifth cycle will be a straight waterfall process to build the system.

Begin planning by sketching the spiral. Estimate a time period and cost for each cycle. This is a rough estimate and gives everyone an idea of what the entire project might cost. Plan the first cycle as if it were a complete project whose deliverable is a system concept. Build a WBS and go through all the steps as in the previous examples. Limit the product so that the cycle will end before you spend too much time and money.

Execute the first cycle as planned. At the end of it, the fourth quadrant, plan the next cycle and update the rough plan for the entire spiral. Treat the next cycle as a complete project and work through all the planning and estimating steps. Review this plan and the history of the first cycle in detail. Was the product of the first cycle acceptable? How close were the actual time and expense of the first cycle to the estimates? Do you and your customer think this business opportunity is still worth pursuing? If it is, continue to the next

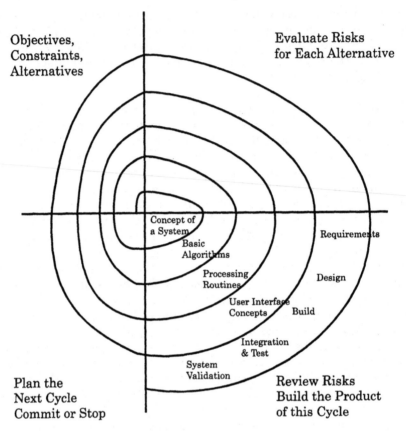

Figure 6.45   Planning with a spiral process.

cycle. If not, quit now. Everyone is smarter from the experience and no one has wasted too much time and money.

All the remaining cycles are like the first. Execute them as planned, plan the ensuing cycle, review everything, and decide whether to continue or stop.

The project may reach the end of the final cycle and deliver the new capabilities to the customer. It is entirely possible that a spiral project will stop somewhere in the middle. That is its nature. If the project stops, however, it will be because of a plan, not a disaster.

6.5   CONFIGURATION MANAGEMENT

The project plan belongs in the functional baseline. It fits here because requirements, planning, and risk management revolve around each other in timing and people. Project planning itself, however, does not fall neatly into one baseline like requirements and design because planning crosses many baselines.

There isn't much to say about putting the project plan into the functional baseline other than to do it, following the process set forth in the project's CM plan (see Chapter 2 and Appendix B). The functional baseline and the Configuration Control Board for that baseline already exist; as project manager, you need only initiate action.

That there is not much to say illustrates the simple power of CM. At this point in the project, the project manager does not have to search for people interested in maintaining the functional baseline. They are already designated in the CM plan as the baseline's CCB. All that remains to bring the product to the people is to follow the CM plan.

The project plan contains information that changes often, such as the task network. The project manager will need to reestimate the duration of tasks and the size of products at regular intervals as well as rearrange tasks in the network. However, the CM plan is designed so that the project manager and the CCB must exercise sound judgment in how they incorporate changes to the project plan. As tasks are completed—some on time, others early, and others late—the schedule changes. It is easy to enter schedule changes into a commercial product (Microsoft Project, Project Scheduler, and others). It is not easy to track every change. Attempts to do so have always frustrated me.

The CM plan empowers the CCB to control their baseline the way they see fit. A practical method is to put the project plan into the baseline monthly for projects longer than a year (twice monthly for shorter projects). The CM staff must keep copies of the plan for each month.

6.6 STANDARDS

All-in-one military and commercial standards are available to help project managers understand the necessary tasks. An IEEE standard can help in documentation.

6.6.1 All-in-One Military and Commercial Standards

I don't expect this to be a popular section. In fact, you may be tempted to skip it, but don't. Don't translate the section head as "All-in-one useless and commercial standards." Read a few pages. It may surprise you that practical all-in-one standards can be military as well as commercial. It is true that the military standards I describe have "expired," in that they are not legally required for every defense contract, but they are still required for many individual projects. They also include material that commercial projects can use. The fundamentals they prescribe and illustrate are still valid.

These standards have a different purpose from things like the CMM and best practices. The CMM describes a process that an organization follows on all projects. The military and commercial project standards tell what an organization should do on a single project. The standards also emphasize the format of needed documents, called DIDs (or data item descriptions), listing the table of contents and describing each section in great detail.

These standards do not give as much detail as some IEEE standards, but they are convenient. And being all-in-one, they are more consistent than the IEEE standards and shorter.

All-in-One Military Standards. The first significant military (Department of Defense, or DoD) software standard was DoD-Std-2167A (DOD-STD-2167A, 1988), which originated in 1988 to specify what a contractor was to do for the government on military system projects that contained software. Although it expired in 1994, many defense contractors still use it because their current projects are continuations of projects begun when it was active. Many defense projects continue 10 to 20 years after their standards legally expire. Figure 6.46 lists the tasks the contractor should perform.

Figure 6.47 is an often used DoD-Std-2167A chart that shows the products, reviews and audits, and baselines for each phase of a DoD-Std-2167A project. This is where criticism of the standard usually begins. Although it does not mandate a straight waterfall process, it does encourage it. Commercial software organizations dismissed DoD-Std-2167A quickly because of this bias. In reality, various DoD software projects failed because they did not vary the process when people, product, and common sense told them they should.

. Software Development Management
    System Requirements Analysis/Design
    Software Requirements Analysis
    Preliminary Design
    Detailed Design
    Coding and Unit Testing
    Component Integration and Testing
    Configuration Item Testing
    System Integration and Testing
. Software Engineering
. Formal Qualification Testing
. Software Product Evaluation
. Software Configuration Management
. Transitioning to Software Support

Figure 6.46 Tasks for in the DoD-STD-2167A all-in-one project management standard.

Phase	System Requirements Analysis	System Design	Software Requirements Analysis	Preliminary Design	Detailed Design	Coding and Unit Testing	Component Integration and Testing	Configuration Item Testing	System Integration and Testing
Deliverable Products	Preliminary System Specification	System Specification; System/Segment Design Document; Preliminary Software Requirements Specification; Preliminary Interface Requirements Specification; Software Development Plan	Software Requirements Specification; Interface Requirements Specification	Software Design Documents; Software Test Plan; Preliminary Interface Design Document	Software Design Documents; Software Test Descriptions (Cases); Interface Design Document	Source Code Listings; Source Code	Software Test Descriptions (Procedures)	Updated Source Code; Software Test Reports; Operation and Support Documents; Version Description Documents; Software Product Specifications	
					Developmental Configuration				
Reviews and Audits	System Requirements Review	System Design Review	Software Specification Review	Preliminary Design Review	Critical Design Review		Test Readiness Review	Functional and Physical Configuration Audits	
Baselines		Functional Baseline	Allocated Baseline					Product Baseline	

Figure 6.47   A chart for a DoD-Std-2167A project.

The next military software standard is Mil-Std-498 (MIL-STD-498, 1994). Introduced in December 1994, Mil-Std-498 is much more flexible than DoD-Std-2167A and includes more best practices. It allows and encourages using different process models and lets you tailor all tasks and documents to fit the project. The tailored standard ensures that "only necessary and cost-effective requirements are imposed on software development efforts."

Mil-Std-498 is an excellent guide to use on any software project—military or commercial. Figure 6.48 lists the required activities, which map quite well to CMM Level 3 and include most items on best practices lists. Two guidebooks are available for Mil-Std-498. One describes various ways to tailor the standard to processes, including iterative and evolutionary methods. The other explains the standard's concepts in detail (one page per concept as opposed to one sentence per concept in the standard itself).

Mil-Std-498 is also free. Although it expired in 1997, it will probably continue to be used for several more years.

All-in-One Commercial Standards. The DoD, along with other parts of the U.S. government, is moving away from government standards toward commercial ones. This is a general trend toward best commercial practices to make the government more productive and efficient.

The DoD has adopted the American implementation of the ISO 12207 standard in IEEE/EIA 12207.0, IEEE/EIA 12207.1, and IEEE/EIA 12207.2 (see

. Project Planning and Oversight
. Software Development Environment
. System Requirements Analysis
. System Design
. Software Requirements Analysis
. Software Design
. Software Implementation and Unit Testing
. Unit Integration and Testing
. Configuration Item Integration and Testing
. Software/Hardware Integration and Testing
. System Qualification Testing
. Preparing for Software Use
. Preparing for Software Transition
. Integral Processes:
    Software Configuration Management
    Software Product Evaluation
    Software Quality Assurance
    Corrective Action
    Joint Technical and Management Reviews
    Other Activities

Figure 6.48   Tasks for a Mil-Std-498 project.

References). Figure 6.49 shows the rather confusing evolution of military and commercial standards from 2167 to the present.

6.6.2 Documenting the Plan

All the various elements of planning and estimating must be gathered into a document. Without the document, the plan remains invisible and ineffective. The document does not need to be a traditional book. It can be a wall in a room, a collection of files on a computer, or drawer of loose-leaf sketches.

Document the plan using the content, and maybe the form, specified in the IEEE Std-1058 (IEEE, 1998). Hardworking, creative, and intelligent people put the standard together after years of effort. A plan documented according to the standard will contain the most important information produced by the planning efforts.

Figure 6.50 shows the format of a software project management plan written according to the standard. In many cases, the best practice is to have this document point to other documents, charts, or displays. You need not repeat material. The first parts are the title and front material. The *introduction* is an overview of the people, process, and product for the project. It also states how to change the plan and defines key concepts. This section is similar to material in the configuration management plan (see Chapter 2 and Appendix B). In fact, several parts of this plan and the CM plan will be similar.

Project organization describes how the people and process will be organized to produce a product. It shows the process model for the project (waterfall, evolutionary, spiral). It also discusses who's who in the project, their areas of responsibility, and their lines of communication.

Managerial process describes how the project manager will ensure that the project adheres to the plan. It contains constraints, policies, objectives, assumptions, and so on. It discusses risk management (see Chapter 7) and the

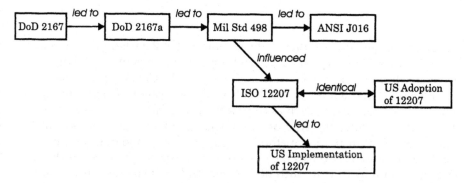

Figure 6.49 Evolution of military and commercial standards.

1. Introduction
   1.1 Project Overview
   1.2 Project Deliverables
   1.3 Evolution of the SPMP
   1.4 Reference Materials
   1.5 Definitions and Acronyms

2. Project Organization
   2.1 Process Model
   2.2 Organizational Structure
   2.3 Organizational Boundaries and Interfaces
   2.4 Project Responsibilities

3. Managerial Process
   3.1 Management Objectives and Priorities
   3.2 Assumptions, Dependencies, and Constraints
   3.3 Risk Management
   3.4 Monitoring and Controlling Mechanisms
   3.5 Staffing Plan

4. Technical Process
   4.1 Methods, Tools, and Techniques
   4.2 Software Documentation
   4.3 Project Support Functions

5. Work Packages, Schedule, and Budget
   5.1 Work Packages
   5.2 Dependencies
   5.3 Resource Requirements
   5.4 Budget and Resource Allocation
   5.5 Schedule

Figure 6.50   Format of the software project management plan according to IEEE-Std-1058.1.

staffing plan (described earlier in the section on the Rayleigh model). It also discusses how the project manager and upper management will obtain project status from the audits and status accountings the CM staff performs.

Technical process addresses the details of the software process, pointing to several other documents, such as commercially available texts and standards. The section specifies the type of computers, compilers, and component libraries as well as inspection methods, documentation standards, coding standards, and so on. It also lists the other documents to be produced, including standards on how to write such documents, and their contents. It concludes by describing the supporting organizations and their functions in the project.

These may include the CM staff, an independent verification and validation group, security staff, facilities maintainers, and technical writers.

The final section is "the plan." The task (work package) network is the foundation of this section, which points to the complete task network in a computer or displayed in the MIC. This is a good place to sum up the time, cost, and equipment scattered throughout the network.

The final sections are for other items that might be necessary, such as training, facilities, hardware procurement, security, and travel.

6.7 KEY THOUGHTS IN THIS CHAPTER

Planning attempts to predict what will happen in a software project. It is a difficult but essential part of producing software for a business. Estimating the size of a product and the effort required to build it is a key to planning.

Selecting a software process is a major part of planning. The fundamental software process model is the waterfall. Another is the evolutionary process, which is iterative and proceeds according to knowledge about the product gained in the previous "evolution." The spiral process combines the other models in a spiral pattern driven by risk management. The V-chart is a powerful diagram for observing process differences. Another process is the Microsoft process, which is characterized by daily builds and smoke tests. Study and select processes that fit your people and product.

Several mechanisms are available to measure process improvement, including the CMM, the CMMI, the Personal Software Process (PSP), the Team Software Process (TSP), agile methods, and best practices. The CMM and CCMI are sets of processes that everyone in an organization uses every day on every project. Such organizations are knowledgeable, disciplined, and succeed consistently. The PSP is related to the CMM and CCMI and helps an individual software engineer perform well in a repeatable and predictable manner. The TSP fills in the gap and helps teams of 20 people improve their processes. Best practices reflect activities that have proved successful in other companies. By repeating them, you improve your probability of success. The new movement that evolved the late 1990s is agile methods. These are specific forms of iteration and evolutionary processes.

Visibility techniques exist for both planning and estimating software projects. A project context document sets the stage for a project and its planners. A task network is the project's roadmap. To create the network, list all the deliverables (end products), make a work breakdown structure, lay out an initial network of tasks, and refine it. A cards-on-the wall session is an excellent group technique for refining the task network.

Techniques for making estimates visible include the Rayleigh model, which provides an overall perspective on a project, and the Probe method from the PSP, which uses historical size and time data to calculate estimates. You can also use a simple estimating technique based on a low, high, and most likely ranking if historical data are not available. You can use the different planning and estimating methods to plan a project using any process model.

Configuration management helps you as project manager place the project management plan into the functional baseline. This keeps the project's plan and organization visible. Putting the project management plan into the baseline is a simple and straightforward process as long as you follow the CM plan. If you surrender to pressure from impatient people and stray from the CM plan, everything becomes difficult. The CCB will decide how to incorporate the regular updates and reestimates of the plan into the baseline.

All-in-one military and commercial standards specify all aspects of a software project, and though not applicable to every project, contain helpful and proven techniques. The IEEE has a useful standard for documenting plans.

REFERENCES

S. Bayer and J. Highsmith, "RADical Software Development," *American Programmer*, June, 1994, pp. 35–42.

K. Beck, *Extreme Programming Explain: Embrace Change*, Addison- Wesley, Reading, MA, 2000.

B. Boehm, "A Spiral Model for Software Development and Enhancement," *Computer*, May 1988, pp. 61–72.

B. Boehm, "Anchoring the Software Process," *IEEE Software*, July 1996, pp. 73–82.

N. Brown, "Industrial-Strength Management Strategies," *IEEE Software*, July 1996, pp. 94–103.

N. Brown, "High-Leverage Best Practices: What Hot Companies are Doing to Stay Ahead," *Crosstalk*, September 1999, pp. 4–9.

R. Charette, "Risk Management," in *Encyclopedia of Software Engineering*, J. Marciniak, ed., Wiley, New York, 1994, pp. 1091–1106.

CMMI, *Capability Maturity Model Integration (CMMI SM)*, Version 1. 1, CMMI SM for Systems Engineering and Software Engineering, (CMMI-SE/SW, VI. 1), Staged Representation, CMU/SEI-2002-TR-002, ESC-TR-2002-002, December 2001a.

CMMI, *Capability Maturity Model Integration (CMMI SM)*, Version 1. 1, CMMI SM for Systems Engineering and Software Engineering, (CMMI-SE/SW, VI. 1), Continuous Representation, CMU/SEI-2002-TR-001, ESC-TR-2002-001, December 2001b.

CMU/SEI, *The Capability Maturity Model, Guidelines for Improving the Software Process*, Carnegie Mellon University-Software Engineering Institute, Addison-Wesley, Reading, MA, 1995; *http://www.sei.cmu.edu*.

A. Cockburn, "Selecting a Project's Methodology," *IEEE Software*, July August 2000, pp. 64–71.

B. Curtis, "Building Accelerated Organizations," *IEEE Software*, July August 2000, pp. 72–74.

M. Cusumano, D. Yoffie, "Software Development on Internet Time," *Computer*, October 1999, pp. 60–69.

E. Derby and J. Rothman, "Manager, Heal Thyself: Improving Software Processes Means Changing Management Processes," *Cutter IT Journal*, October 2001, pp. 24–34.

DOD-STD-2167A, *Military Standard, Defense System Software Development*, U.S. Department of Defense, 29 Feb. 1988, Commander, Space and Naval Warfare Systems Command, ATTN: SPAWAR-3212, Washington, D.C., 20363-5100.

D. Emery, "Resistance As a Resource," *Cutter IT Journal*, October 2001, pp. 35–43.

R. Fairley, "Making Accurate Estimates," *IEEE Software*, November December 2002, pp. 61–63.

R. Glass, "In Search of Self-Belief: The 'BOP' Phenomenon," *Computer*, January 1995, pp. 55–57.

R. Glass, *Facts and Fallacies of Software Engineering*, Pearson Education, Boston, 2003.

R. Grady, *Practical Software Metrics for Project Management and Process Improvement*, Prentice-Hall, Englewood Cliffs, NJ, 1992.

J. Hale, A. Parrish, and B. Dixon, "Enhancing the COCOMO Estimation Models," *IEEE Software*, November December 2000, pp. 45–49.

D. Henry, "Software Estimation: Perfect Practices Makes Perfect," *Crosstalk*, June 2002, pp. 28–30.

W. Humphrey, *Managing the Software Process*, Addison-Wesley, Reading, MA, 1989.

W. Humphrey, *A Discipline for Software Eng.*, Addison-Wesley, Reading, MA, 1995.

W. Humphrey, *Introduction to the Team Software Process*, Addison-Wesley, Reading, MA, 2000.

IEEE, IEEE Standard, ANSI/IEEE Std 1058-1998, *IEEE Standard for Software Project Management Plans*, IEEE Press, New York, 1998.

IEEE/EIA, *Industry Implementation of ISO/IEC 12207:1995—Standard for Information Technology—Software Life Cycle Processes.*

IEEE/EIA, *Industry Implementation of ISO/IEC 12207:1995—Standard for Information Technology—Software Life Cycle Processes—Life Cycle Data.*

IEEE/EIA, *Industry Implementation of International Standard ISO/IEC 12207: 1995; Standard for Information Technology—Software Life Cycle Processes—Implementation Considerations.*

ISO/IEC, *Software Life Cycle Processes*, 1 August 1995; available through the American National Standards Institute, New York, www.ansi.org.

C. Jones, *Patterns of Software Systems Failure and Success*, International Thomson Computer Press, Boston, 1996.

C. Jones, "Software Project Management in the 21st Century," *American Programmer*, February 1998, pp. 24–30.

W. Keuffel, "People Based Processes: A RADical Concept," *Software Development*, 1995, pp. 27–30.

L. Leach, *Critical Chain Project Management*, Artech House, Norwood, MA, 2000.

"Manifesto for Agile Software Development," www.agilemanifesto.org, February 2001.

J. McCarthy, *Dynamics of Software Development*, Microsoft Press, Redmond, WA, 1995.

S. McConnell, "Sitting on the Suitcase," *IEEE Software*, May June 2000, pp. 5–7.

MIL-STD-498, *Military Standard, Software Development and Documentation*, U.S. Department of Defense, 5 Dec. 1994; http://www.itsi.disa.mil.

P. Neuhardt, "Medicine for the Estimation Flu," *American Programmer*, June 1996, pp. 36–41.

R. Park, "A Manager's Checklist for Validating Software Cost and Schedule Estimates," *American Programmer*, June 1996a, pp. 30–35.

R. Park, "Assessing an Organization's Estimating Capabilities," *American Programmer*, July 1996b, pp. 42–49.

D. Parnas, "Why Software Jewels are Rare," *Computer,* February 1996, pp. 57–60.

M. Paulk, "Extreme Programming from a CMM Perspective," *IEEE Software,* November December 2001, pp. 19–26.

D. Phillips, "Cards-on-the-Wall Sessions," *Software Development,* July 2001, pp. 53–56.

D. Phillips, "Project Planning: It's in the Cards," *STQE,* January–February 2002, pp. 26–31.

M. Poppendieck and T. Poppendieck, *Lean Software Development: An Agile Toolkit,* Addison-Wesley, Reading, MA, 2003.

L. Putnam and W. Myers, *Measures for Excellence: Reliable Software On Time, Within Budget,"* Yourdon Press, Englewood Cliffs, NJ, 1992.

L. Putnam and W. Myers, *Controlling Software Development,* Executive Briefing, IEEE CS Press, Los Alamitos, CA, 1996.

L. Putnam and W. Myers, *Industrial Strength Software: Effective Management Using Measurement,* IEEE CS Press, Los Alamitos, CA, 1997.

R. Ross and B. Boehm, "Theory W Software Project Management Principles and Examples," *IEEE Transactions on Software Engineering,* July 1989.

W. Royce, "Software Management Renaissance," *IEEE Software,* July August 2000, pp. 116–121.

K. Schwaber, "Against a Sea of Troubles: Serum Software Development," *Cutter IT Journal,* November 2000, pp. 34–39.

K. Schwaber and M. Beedle, *Agile Software Development with SCRUM,* Pearson Education, Upper Saddle River, NJ, 2001.

SEI-93-TR-024, M. Paulk et al., *Capability Maturity Model for Software, Version 1.1,* Software Engineering Institute, Pittsburgh, PA, 1993a.

SEI-93-TR-025, M. Paulk et al., *Key Practices of the Capability Maturity Model, Version 1.1,* Software Engineering Institute, Pittsburgh, PA, 1993b.

R. Sherman, "Shipping the Right Products at the Right Time," *American Programmer,* February 1995, pp. 15–21.

B. Sigal, *Software Project Management Tools and Techniques,* Learning Tree International, Reston, VA, 1993.

R. Thayer and R. Fairley, "Project Management," in *Encyclopedia of Software Engineering,* J. Marciniak (ed.), Wiley, New York, 1994, pp. 900–923.

R. Thomsett, "Project Pathology: A Study of Project Failures," *American Programmer,* July 1995, pp. 8–16.

G. Weinberg, *Quality Software Management: Vol. 2 First Order Measurement,* Dorset House Publishing, New York, 1993.

E. Yourdon, *Decline and Fall of the American Programmer,* Yourdon Press, Englewood Cliffs, NJ, 1992.

E. Yourdon, *Rise and Resurrection of the American Programmer,* Prentice-Hall, Englewood Cliffs, NJ, 1996.

R. Zultner, "Project Estimation with Critical Chain: Third-Generation Risk Management," *Cutter IT Journal,* July 1999, pp. 4–12.

Chapter 7

Risk Management

Software projects have problems, which should come as no surprise nor should it be viewed as a weakness. Projects have myriad complex relationships involving both people and objects. More things can go wrong with a software project than with any mechanical device ever built.

Potential problems are risks. These are things that may go wrong in the future. Lister (Lister, 1997) describes risk as follows:

> A risk is any variable on your project, which you may or may not have direct control over, that could take on a value within its normal distribution of possible values, that either endangers or eliminates the possibility of project success.

Given that problems are inevitable, risk management asks "What exactly could go wrong? And if it does, what is Plan B?" The collection of Plan Bs forms the *risk management plan,* which is part of the overall project plan (see Chapter 6). As I said in the previous two chapters, it is impossible to do any successful plan without considering risks. However, I consider risk management to be important enough to warrant a separate chapter, if for no other reason than to underline its importance. The software community has historically refused to take risk management seriously, viewing those who attempt to identify risks as pessimists, or even troublemakers. Indeed, I have seen a room get suddenly quiet when someone brings up "a concern." However, as projects get more complex and safety-critical systems are being developed in greater numbers, we can no longer afford to sweep risks under the carpet. Pretending that problems will not occur will not prevent them. And if you are not prepared, the project will probably collapse. If it doesn't, your people will be under the burden of continuous crisis management.

Study the risk management tasks in this chapter and in the references and use them.

Some people seem to enjoy taking on risky projects, perhaps led by the "no pain, no gain" life style. However, companies can rarely afford to continually take on high-risk projects.

A risk is a problem that has not occurred. The problem may never occur, but if it does, it can hurt or even destroy the project. Planning can help the more daring realize that when risks materialize, the project dies, and they may soon enjoy living on the edge in a very real way.

Part of this misconception about risk comes from confusion in terminology. An article by Art Gemmer (Gemmer, 1997) helps reduce this confusion and gives tips for managers to pull risk-related information from people. A risk is not an opportunity—they are related, but they are not the same. The common item is probability. A risk is an issue that has the probability of becoming a problem. In contrast, an opportunity is an issue that has the probability of becoming a bonus. When someone tells me they have an issue, I cannot assume it is bad (risk) or good (opportunity). I need to pull that information from them by asking questions.

Risk management is the set of tasks that address any potential problem. Risk planning helps weed out what is actually not a risk by asking the two core questions described earlier (what could go wrong and what do we do when it does?). The first question looks for anything that could fail and trigger a string of failures. The second question produces alternative courses of action if problems occur.

Risk management heavily involves the 3Ps. In fact, the possibility of problems becoming real depends on the relationships among the people, process, and product. If people who do not know a product are constrained by a straightforward process, for example, problems can occur.

Risk management is also a visibility practice because it changes qualitative ideas into quantitative terms. A statement such as "I'm concerned about the interface between our software and the package we're buying." becomes "There is a 30% probability that the interface will fail, and on a scale of 1 to 10, with 10 being the most damaging, the damage to the project will be an 8." Like other parts of the planning process, it takes the ideas out of one person's mind and puts them into documents or displays them in the MIC. Everyone can consider them and help find solutions.

The success of risk management depends on the proper use of configuration management. If the project manager follows the CM plan (see Chapter 2 and Appendix B), the risk management information falls into the functional baseline with the requirements and the project plan. It becomes visible to everyone, and can be changed only by the functional baseline's Configuration Control Board.

Standards for risk management also come into play indirectly as part of project planning. For example, risk management is addressed explicitly in the project plan documented using IEEE Standard (IEEE, 1998) (see Chapter 6).

7.1 A TASK OVERVIEW

Figure 7.1 is an often used task breakdown for what Barry Boehm calls "risk engineering" (Boehm, 1989). In Boehm's scenario, risk engineering consists of two main activities—risk analysis and risk management. Most organizations tend not to distinguish risk analysis from risk management, instead calling both sets of activities risk management. Indeed, risk analysis and management overlap in practice as ideas on how to manage a risk come to mind while identifying, estimating, and evaluating it. Also, the process of deciding how to manage identified risks usually uncovers new risks. Discussing the process is easier if you take it in steps. Although not shown in the figure, the process culminates in a risk plan—documentation about all the identified risks and the decisions made about them.

In describing risk management here, I do not follow Boehm's task breakdown step by step because the focus of this book is on the four principles introduced in Chapter 1. In the description that follows, however, I periodically refer to this task breakdown.

7.2 BALANCING THE 3Ps: UNCERTAINTY AND CHOICE

When something is certain, there is no risk involved. Unfortunately, real software projects contain many choices, few of which can be made with absolute certainty. Rarely is one alternative better than all others in all respects. Chapter 8 shows some decision-making and documenting techniques for quantitatively deciding among alternatives. But even the best choice usually has its problems and a chance of failing. This chance of failing is risk.

The 3P-intensive tasks in risk management (see Figure 7.1) include risk identification and risk planning, control, monitoring, directing, and staffing.

Risk Analysis
- Risk Identification
- Risk Estimation
- Risk Evaluation

Risk Engineering

Risk Management
- Risk Planning
- Risk Control
- Risk Monitoring
- Risk Directing
- Risk Staffing

Figure 7.1   Boehm's task breakdown for risk engineering.

7.2.1 Risk Identification

To manage risks, you must first identify them. This is the risk identification task in Figure 7.1. Risk identification is part of risk analysis, which is simply analyzing everything in the project to find risks. Some risks are common to many projects; others are project specific. Analyzing risks is much easier using checklists from past projects. This comes from record keeping (metrics) and is characteristic of a mature organization using a mature process. Start keeping records today. Perform project postmortems, create lists of lessons learned, and use these to analyze risks on future projects.

Esther Derby (Derby, 2000) provides a list of questions that help identify risks in any project before the project begins. Her questions are:

1. Do the customers and the developers agree on the project objectives?
2. Has the organization done a project like this before?
3. Has the team done this kind of work before?
4. Will the project be solving a new problem or using a new technology?
5. Is the technical infrastructure in place?
6. What is the relationship between the customers, the users, and the technology team?
7. Is the implementation target date based on realistic estimates?
8. Do you have the project management skills you need?

Risk analysis involves identifying risks by looking at their cause and location (why and where). This necessarily involves considering the 3Ps. Project managers often look only at the product as a source of risk. They ask the necessary product questions, but fail to ask people and process questions.

Three main causes of risk are lack of information, control, and time (Charette, 1994). *Lack of information* means an uncertain outcome. If people do not have all the information about a device, they cannot be certain they can write a device driver for it. They have some level of confidence, but it may be considerably less than 100%.

Lack of control occurs when people depend on others to deliver a product. If programmers cannot write the device driver until the device maker delivers a document describing the device, they are depending on the device maker to write the document and write it well. The programmers cannot control the device maker. Outside groups are no different—they make mistakes and occasionally fail to deliver products on time. These occasional failures introduce risk.

Lack of time is an all too familiar problem. People in a hurry make mistakes, cut corners, and compound an already difficult task. The programmers are certain they can write the device driver, but are not certain about writing it in just two weeks. If more time were available, the programmers could build their own device, write its manual, and then write the device driver.

Examine each risk carefully. Look for a lack of information, control, and time. If you find a shortage in two or three of these, the risk could kill the project.

Identifying risk is a subjective process, and the results depend on a person's perspective and experience. A system administrator, Bob, once wanted to make several major changes to the network in our computer lab. He planned to do this at 7 AM so that everything would be working at 8 AM when the programmers came to work. I saw this as a risk. The programmers saw it as a big risk. The system administrator saw no problems. My perspective was that if something went wrong, all the programmers would waste a day. The programmers, many of whom had lived through some of Bob's mistakes, saw this as another Bob disaster.

As it happens, everything turned out fine. The point is that the collection of perspectives worked together to ensure success. There were risks in this situation, but because the programmers and I expressed concern, Bob was extra careful and made no mistakes.

Figure 7.2 revisits the top risks list introduced in Chapter 4 (Figure 4.3) (Boehm, 1989) but this time shows how the risks fall in and across the 3Ps.

Ask questions to reveal risks. Questions that find people risks include "What if Dave's mother becomes even sicker and he has to leave for six months?" or "What if our other project won't give me the five graphics programmers they promised?" Process risk questions are "Should we include weekly progress reviews?" and "Does the schedule allow us to test the algorithms sufficiently?" Questions that find product risks include "What if the operating system delays the device driver calls?" and "What if the search routine requires three passes instead of two?"

In Figure 7.2, *personnel shortfalls* directly concerns people. People are the most important aspect of software development and maintenance. The best

People
Personnel Shortfalls

Shortfalls in externally
furnished components

Real-time performance
shortfalls

Straining Computer
Science capabilities

Developing the wrong
user interface

Gold plating

Process
Unrealistic schedules and budget

Product
Developing the wrong software functions

Continuing stream of
requirements changes

Figure 7.2 Top sources of risk according to people, process, and product.

resources you can have are people who know what they are doing, have the self-discipline to do it, and the courage to tell the truth to those who may want to hear otherwise. Sometimes you don't have the people you need for the job, and sometimes the people you do have perform below expectations.

Personnel shortfalls can be the source of the most critical risks. My introduction to risk management came a few years back when I was working on a failing project ($20 million spent, no product). Having just read Barry Boehm's book on risk management (Boehm, 1991), I went to one of the project's managers and proclaimed that using software risk management would have prevented his problems. He replied that what he really needed was "people risk management." The people on the project were not performing well, were not being managed well, and were hiding problems because of fear.

Next in the list of risk locations is *unrealistic schedule and budget*. This falls exclusively under process and is a direct result of poor or no planning (see Chapter 6). A project manager cannot let others dictate schedule and budget. It is not easy to hold that line, but accepting arbitrary time and cost constraints guarantees failure. Be realistic and conservative. Your people may later thank you for being pessimistic at this stage.

Developing the wrong software functions is related to product. Failure in this aspect also means trouble with people developing the functions and the process they use, but its main problem is in the product. The product does not do what the users need, and is destined to become shelfware.

The next three risk items are not so clearly related to people, process, or product, but can be influenced by two or three of the Ps. They also stem from requirements (see Chapter 5). It should be no surprise that requirements claim four of the nine sources of risk. Requirements are the project's foundation; if the foundation is weak, the project will collapse.

Developing the wrong user interface is affected by both people and product. It results when the team fails to work closely enough with the customer during requirements analysis. Building prototypes, iterating, and evolving help avoid these mistakes.

Gold plating is listening to the customer too much and adding in every minuscule feature they mention. Time boxing (described later) eliminates this by letting you select only the top requirements for implementation. The agile methods mentioned in Chapter 5 all use some form of time boxing.

Most software project managers are familiar with the *continuing stream of requirements changes*. The project falls into a state of perpetual pregnancy (Weinberg, 1995)—always in progress, but never giving birth. The developers never finish the product, so the product is a problem. The developers never finish because they have no process. They are not using configuration management to organize people. They are not discussing requirements in light of the project and the business and making informed decisions about growing or shrinking requirements.

The next item is *shortfalls in externally furnished components*. A major risk here is from lack of control, which is a process matter. But people can also contribute risk in the form of two strong emotions. The first is hope that the external group will supply the product on time. This hope can lull the team into a false sense of confidence and keep them from monitoring the external group as closely as they should. The second emotion is blame. People sense that the external group will not deliver as promised, yet they let it happen. The failure of the external group provides a scapegoat. No matter what happens, they can blame the other group. Blaming does not help a failing project. Do whatever is possible to reduce dependence on external groups (see Chapter 4). When using an external group, visit them often. Do not assume they will succeed. If nothing else, frequent visits will tell them how important their work is to your project.

Real-time performance shortfalls and *straining computer science capabilities* are again people and process issues. People become overly ambitious and overly confident in the power of computers to solve problems. Patience is not mentioned often, but is sometimes necessary. Hardware has advanced and should continue to advance rapidly. Do not build a special-purpose machine and write special software to get 30% more performance. Write simple, portable software and wait until next year when off-the-shelf computers will be 30% faster. Better processes would help the situation. Use a spiral process and run simulations in the early cycles to determine if the existing hardware is powerful enough. Use similar patience and techniques in the computer science risk area. It is not advancing at the rate of hardware, but it is advancing. Build prototypes, perform experiments, or use spiral processes—do whatever it takes to learn if something is possible before spending large amounts of time, energy, and money.

Some of these sources of risk will be less obvious than others. Look everywhere for risks (even in the mirror). Be critical and pessimistic. Is any algorithm, device, or person key to the project? Does anything need to perform at a critical level (size, speed, timing, coordination, and so on)?

Search for ambiguity among the project team. Have individuals privately answer a question about the project. Does everyone give the same answer? If not, something is ambiguous or not well understood, and that something is a risk candidate.

Identifying risks requires a fresh perspective, so bring in outside consultants or experienced people from other projects for a day. Once the risks are identified, classify them (people, process, or product) and note their causes and symptoms (Why is this a risk? How did we notice it?).

As I just mentioned, time boxing can reduce gold plating. Time boxing, created by Richard Zahniser, breaks the project deliverables into periods of time (Zahniser, 1995). Developers will do as much as possible until the time runs out. Project managers traditionally juggle cost, schedule, and performance. In time boxing, the schedule aspect is in complete control. The project *will* deliver function X by May 1, function Y by May 14, and function Z by May 21. Cost and performance fall into line. The team can do only so much on the product before time runs out. Time boxing essentially reduces the uncertainty in the project by putting limits on the end product. If the product delivered within a time box does not work, the loss is not catastrophic. It is only a relatively small amount of time and effort. The time box limits the leap of faith.

Once the developers know the features the users want (requirements), they rank them as nice to have, should have, and must have. They then build the must have features in a time box. This experience helps them define future time boxes, and they go through several more before delivering the final product. Feature ranking is a standard (old IEEE standard) practice in requirements gathering.

Zahniser emphasizes that time boxing works with the human tendency to stretch tasks to fill available time. If available time is shortened, even shortened artificially by a time box, people will do less stretching, and the project will have less risk from personnel shortfalls. Figure 7.3 helps illustrate this with the 90/10 rule. The first 90% of the work takes 90% of the time, and the last 10% of the work takes the next 90% of the time. The time box stops work when the first 90% is finished. It prevents wasting time in the diagram's long, inefficient tail (upper right corner).

Figure 7.4 presents another perspective on time boxing from Larry Putnam and Ware Myers (Putnam & Myers, 1992, 1997, 1996). The area under the humps is staff-months of effort (directly proportional to cost). Point t1 on the time axis is the minimum development time for a product. A product has a

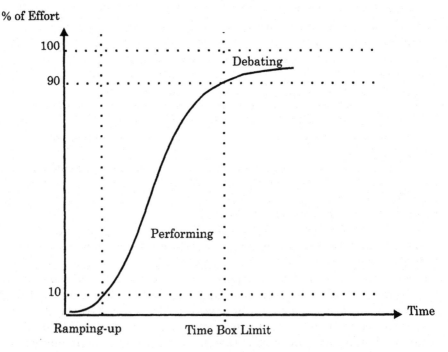

Figure 7.3 The 90/10 rule applied to time boxing.

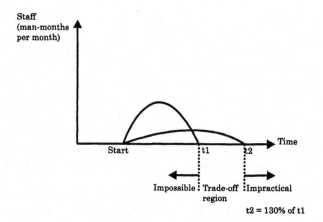

$$Size = Effort^{1/3} * Time^{4/3} * Process\ Productivity$$

Figure 7.4 · Limits on size and effort.

minimum time needed to build it, regardless of the people available (it still takes nine months for nine women to have one baby). To the left of t1 is the impossible region. Time t2 is at 130% of the minimum development time. It is impractical to plan on stretching the project beyond this, because the business needs the software. A trade-off region exists between t1 and t2.

The bottom of Figure 7.4 shows Larry Putnam and Ware Myers' software equation (see Chapter 6 for more on this). The process productivity number characterizes the developers' abilities. It can improve from project to project, but remains a constant inside a project. The effort is the area under the humps, time is the horizontal axis, and size is a measure of the product. Effort, time, and size translate to cost, schedule, and performance.

Notice the exponents and how time dominates the equation. A manager can alter staffing to move the time to finish a product within the time trade-off region. Small changes in time dramatically affect staffing and cost. For example, if the manager reduces the time from 120% of minimum to minimum, the cost doubles.

If time is important, don't buy time by adding people. Rather, cut features (find the 20% of the wants that meets 80% of the needs). Turn time into a time box, reduce the product to fit the time box, save money, *and* reduce risk.

7.2.2 Risk Planning

Risk management begins with decisions. Are the risks too many and too high to attempt the project? Do the aversion strategies provide a way around the risks? If the project is to begin, which aversion strategies will be used?

Once the project begins, someone must focus on managing the risks. This is difficult, since people are consumed with their own tasks and do not have time to worry about problems. In small projects, the project manager manages risk. In larger projects, say, those involving more than two dozen people and lasting more than one year, the project manager should designate a person or staff as a full-time risk manager. That person should have plenty of software development experience; experienced people have seen risks turn into problems. He should also continually question everything. His attitude should be realistic as opposed to optimistic and he must be emotionally detached from the product. Emotional attachment is great for the programmers, but it can blind people from seeing risk.

Begin risk planning by looking at the project's task network. Use visibility techniques to estimate and evaluate risks (described later) and then pinpoint each in the network of tasks. Create several risk aversion strategies (plan Bs) for each risk and assign each a probability. This new number is the probability that a problem will occur if the project uses the aversion strategy. Also estimate the cost in dollars of implementing the aversion strategy. These numbers let you calculate a risk leverage figure. The leverage from each aversion strategy is the ratio of the difference of the risk probabilities to the cost of the aversion strategy [(original risk − new risk)/cost]. The aversion strategy with the greatest leverage will be the one to use.

Plan how the risk aversion strategy would fit in the network if needed. When would symptoms of the risk first appear? When would the aversion strategy need to begin? When would you need to bring in consultants? Treat each risk aversion strategy as a small, complete project. Use the planning steps described in Chapter 6. In the best case, the plans will not be needed. In the worst case, they could save the project.

7.2.3   Risk Control

Once risk planning is complete, the risk manager (or risk management staff) must act to control risks. Risk control is being ready to manage the project if risks become problems. Robert Charette (Charette, 1994) lists seven ways an organization can approach risk management: (1) crisis management, (2) fix-on-failure, (3) risk mitigation, (4) prevention, (5) elimination of error, (6) anticipation of failure, and (7) management of change.

The first three are reactive. *Crisis management* is a contradiction in terms. There are no risks (problems that might occur), only catastrophes, and management focuses on survival. Bad things happen (people become ill and disks crash) and natural disasters like hurricanes, earthquakes, and fires can occur. All these events have a probability greater than zero, but an organization can identify, estimate, and evaluate them reasonably.

One step up from crisis management is *fix-on-failure*. This is the most prevalent approach. Management does not identify, estimate, or evaluate risks. A problem occurs and management fixes it. This works if the problem is not big and the fix does not require too much time, money, or effort. In too many cases, however, the problem is too big for this approach to work.

Risk mitigation has long been considered the best method of risk management. Management understands the risks in a project and reserves time, money, and other resources. These reserves serve as a buffer against problems if they occur. This is the typical estimate plus 50% just in case.

The final four (prevention, elimination of error, anticipation of failure, and management of change) are proactive. Proactive risk management is a better approach. *Prevention* manages risk by stopping it at the beginning of a project. This requires project managers to plan ahead and budget for risk.

The next step in improving risk management is *elimination of error*. This is also known as total quality management. An organization strives for process improvement (see Chapter 6). One way to reach this requires using mature processes such as those in Level 2 (Repeatable) of the SEI's Capability Maturity Model (see Chapter 6). At that level, an organization should be using the same processes to achieve the same success on different projects. Repeatable processes are predictable; predictable processes are certain, and where there is greater certainty there is less error.

Anticipation of failure comes as the organization continues to improve its processes. Errors occur infrequently, but still occur. The improving organization anticipates when they might occur, has a plan to deal with them, and handles them calmly when they happen.

The final step is *management of change*. Top organizations manage change that helps them take a proactive approach to risk. Proactive strategies require an organization to behave differently, which requires individuals to change. Change is difficult, and people will not accept dictated change. If change is treated as a process, however, it can be managed.

7.2.4 Risk Monitoring

Monitoring ensures that the organization is following the project and risk aversion plans. In particular, it watches carefully for the symptoms of the risks. Everyone is buried in day-to-day job details. They want the project to succeed without any major glitches. Their good intentions and efforts blind them to growing problems.

The risk manager must take a different perspective and hunt for problems. He must ensure that the aversion strategies are ready for the current risks and start preparing the aversion strategies for upcoming risks. The risk manager must do these tasks carefully. His job is contrary to everyone else's, and it will be easy for him to become the bad guy. If that happens, people could hide risk symptoms from the risk manager, which would lead to disaster.

The risk manager must speak openly about this contrary situation. He must explain the tension and emphasize that he does not want it to be personal. He must convey that he wants the project to succeed as much as the developers do. It will take hard work to convince others of this perspective and have them understand the role he plays in helping them and the project.

If the project is smaller, say a dozen people, the project manager will double as the risk manager. Be careful. If you are being tough on people as a risk manager, tell them why and how this role differs from your role as project manager.

Regardless of who serves as the risk manager, the project manager must monitor the situation to keep everyone on the same team. I typically speak with the risk manager and the developers together *and* separately, explaining how each person must do something different so that all of us can reach the same successful conclusion.

7.2.5   Risk Directing and Staffing

Risk directing is day-to-day risk management. The risk manager and project manager must work together to make risk management tasks a natural part of the project. Having people on staff to handle risks is a part of risk directing. The risk manager must see problems far enough in advance to have the right people on hand when needed. Risk aversion strategies typically use consultants or temporary employees and borrow employees from other projects. It takes time to bring these types of people into a project. This requires planning the risk aversion strategies and monitoring the project for symptoms of risk. These activities work together for successful risk management.

7.3   MAKING RISK VISIBLE

Visibility techniques in risk management include risk estimation, evaluation, and monitoring. Risk identification (from the previous section) risk estimation, and risk evaluation yield a set of risk analysis products that let everyone see the risks and give you a better chance to continue the project down the road.

7.3.1   Risk Estimating

To estimate the quantity of risk, I like to start with a classic equation:

$$\text{Risk} = \text{probability of occurrence} \times \text{consequence if it occurs}$$

The probability of occurrence is 0.0 to 1.0 and the consequence is an arbitrary range (1 to 10 or 1 to 100), with the higher number meaning more dire consequences. Another way to express the consequence is in dollars (to cost to fix the problem) or in time (the number of days needed to fix the problem). However, this subjective exercise alone can lead to faulty results.

As an example, consider a programmer named Joe. If Joe catches the flu, it will hurt the project. You assign a 0.3 probability of this event and an 8 of 10 as the consequence. Joe himself thinks a 0.03 probability is more accurate. He knows this is important and he won't become sick. Other programmers feel they are more important than Joe is on this project. They think a 3 or 4 of 10 would be the right consequence. Joe's manager, who gives Joe his annual salary increase, thinks Joe's importance is even lower.

Add time and money to improve the accuracy of your estimate. If better estimates of risk are necessary, build prototypes, run simulations, and bring in experts to add experience. Look at the risk's character, extent, and timing. *Character* describes if the risk is technical, political, economic, and so on. Extent deals with how bad the problem could be, how far reaching it is, and how many people it will affect. *Timing* describes if the problem will occur now or later, be short-term or long-term.

Returning to the example of Joe, look at the numbers available. How many sick days did Joe take last year? Will the project take place during flu season? How many times in the last 10 years has Joe had the flu? When Joe has been sick before, what was the actual impact on the project? Is Joe on the critical path of this project; that is, will a three-day absence cause a three-day slip? Take the time to do the research, find the real numbers, and reduce the effect of opinions.

7.3.2 Risk Evaluation

Evaluating risk consists of assessing the risk, ranking it, and determining risk aversion strategies. Assessing the risks looks at all the risks identified at one time. As mentioned earlier, identifying and estimating risks are subjective tasks. The results vary widely depending on who performs them. Assessment gives people a chance to reconsider each risk and the values assigned to them. This normalizes risk estimation. Once assessment is done, put the risks with the highest values (the product of probability and consequence) at the top of the list.

A key part of assessing risks is to select a risk referent for each area of risk. A *risk referent* is a threshold used to judge a risk. Any risk above its referent triggers an alarm. Referents come from the project objectives stated in the project context document and project management plan (see Chapter 6). Suppose a project objective is to introduce the programmers to a new set of math functions so that they will be ready for several projects next year. If the risk referent for this objective is 2.5 on a scale of 1 to 10, a risk related to the math functions that has a (probability (consequence) greater than 2.5 is unacceptably high. You must either reduce that risk or cancel the project. Although this task is also subjective, it does help put the issues in perspective. When risks exceed their referent, stop and study the issues carefully. This is not a simple decision point, but rather a threshold that requires some action.

Another way to evaluate a risk is via the "surprise factor" (Hall, 2003). Some potential problems turn into problems slowly while others do so quickly. Those that turn into problems slowly have a low surprise factor. For example, an employee may have a birth in the family and will take a few weeks off. That event has several months of warning. Potential problems that become problems with little warning have a high surprise factor. For example, an employee may experience an accidental death in the family and need to take a couple of weeks off to tend to family matters. There is not much warning of such an event.

Once you have assessed and ranked the risk, select risk aversion strategies, as described earlier.

7.3.3   Risk Analysis Products

At the end of risk analysis, the project managers should understand the top risks for the project. This means knowing each risk, its probability and consequence, cause, symptoms if it occurs, and its referent. It also means having several risk aversion strategies that include both preventive and corrective actions. Finally, it means knowing the probability, cost, and risk leverage for each aversion strategy.

Figure 7.5 is a summary of all the risk analysis products for the objective of introducing programmers to the new math functions (described in the last

Risks

Risk	Probability (0.0-1.0)	Consequence (1-10)	Product	Cause	Symptom
R1. Key people unavailable in time	0.5	9	4.5	Organization stretched too thin	Schedule delays
R2. Math library not ready	0.5	8	4.0	Lack of planning. This lib should have been ready two projects ago.	Cannot integrate product
R3. Training insufficient	0.5	5	2.5	Training budget too small	Too much OJT. Slow development

...

Risk Referent for R2
Project Objective - Gain experience with math library functions
Referent = 2.5

Figure 7.5 Summary of risk analysis for the project objective "introduce programmers to new math functions."

subsection). The first section of the figure lists the products of estimating the top risks. The figure shows only three risks, but the summary should contain at least the top 10. Each risk has a reference number (such as R1), a short statement (which can refer to another place for more explanation); the probability, consequence, and their product; and a cause and symptom.

The next section of the figure contains the evaluation results for each risk listed (the figure shows the information only for the second risk to save space). First is the referent, which gives the project objective related to the risk and the referent threshold. Next are at least three aversion strategies. Each strategy has a reference number, a short statement (refer to an explanation if necessary), a new probability, and the cost to implement the strategy. The final part shows the risk leverage calculations, which indicate the best aversion strategy.

Figure 7.5 fills nearly a page and covers only one risk. All told, you will need 10 to 20 pages, depending on the size of the project. This requires time and energy, but it is not mindless bureaucracy. When people can see the risks, they can work on the issues.

Figures 7.6 through 7.8 show other methods of listing risk analysis information. Figure 7.6 differs from Figure 7.5 in how it quantifies the consequence or impact of a risk. Instead of stating the consequence as a number from 1 to 10, this method states it as an impact in time or money. If the risk becomes a problem, the impact will be the loss of three months on the project, or $100,000.

Figure 7.7 is an isorisk chart resulting from risk analysis. An isorisk chart plots the probability of a risk against its impact. A line curves through the points to denote the risk referent. In this chart, the top risks are identified by plotting their probability against their impact in either time or money. The risk referent line divides the acceptable and unacceptable risks. The isorisk chart makes it easy to see all the risks facing the project.

Identifier	Name and number
Category	People, process, or product
Description	What would occur and why it would be a problem
Cause	Root cause of the risk:
	Control - lack of process definition
	Resources - lack of staffing, skills, etc.
	Time - lack of schedule
	Information - lack of knowledge
Time Frame	Period of time risk is most likely to occur
Chance	Probability of occurring
Impact Cost	Cost in money or time
Impact Description	Why you assigned that impact cost

Figure 7.6 Summarizing risk analysis information as a time and cost impact.

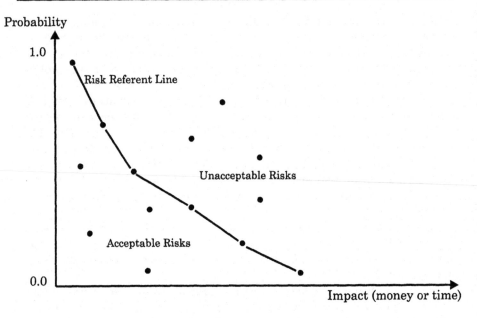

Figure 7. 7 An isorisk chart.

Figure 7.8 shows a method for listing risk aversion strategies. Again, by making aspects of the strategies visible to all project members, you avoid miscommunication about the time and procedure for implementing them.

7.4 OTHER WAYS TO MANAGE RISK

The preceding sections have described the classic methods of risk management. These are proven to work. However, they can overwhelm organiza-

Priority	Place in the top ten list
Identifier	Name and number
Description	What would occur and why it would be a problem
Strategy	Technique to employ to avert the risk (one or more)
	Accept - no action, just watch it
	Mitigate - take action to reduce probability and/or impact
	Transfer - get someone else to accept the risk
	Avoid - pursue a course to zero the probability
Activities & Status	Actions taken or will be taken to avert the risk
Cost	Cost in time or money of averting the risk
Trigger	Conditions that cause taking the aversion actions

Figure 7.8 Making risk aversion visible.

tions that have never managed risks in any form before. The following subsections provide three alternatives to start on the path to full risk management.

7.4.1 Testing

Almost all organizations test their software before releasing it. In doing so, they are practicing risk management (Estes, 2000). Testing is a risk management practice. The purpose is to find defects before the customer does. The possible defects are the potential problems. Testing contributes to risk management by giving managers information about the quality of the product.

In planning tests, a common question is "where are defects most likely to be in the software?" People test their software according to the answer to this question. After their testing is finished, have they found all the defects? The answer is no, which then brings the question, "If testing doesn't find all the defects, why do we test?" The answer is that the testing attempts to find the most likely defects. Note how this discussion contains the phrase "most likely" several times. Testing deals with probability, as does risk management. Hence, testing is a risk management practice that attempts to remove potential problems.

Understanding this concept is important for project managers. Testing reduces the potential that customers will find problems in the software, but never eliminates this potential. Believing that testing does eliminate the potential of later problems is foolish and quite risky.

7.4.2 Scenario Planning

Many people in the software industry disdain risk management if for no other reason than the name. If you try to introduce some of the formal risk identification, aversion, etc. practices, these people may openly revolt. One way to perform many of the classic risk management practices and avoid some of the resistance is via scenario planning (Russel, 1999).

In scenario planning, you guess multiple futures for a project and make high-level plans for each of them. People are comfortable with stories and scenarios. They have a realistic feel and are easier to create than the quantities discussed earlier in the chapter.

Imagining a future begins with a statement like, "I can see a future where in three months the math library company hasn't delivered, yet. That would cause us to sit around and wait."

An aversion strategy would come from the question, "If that future occurs, what would we do while sitting around and waiting?" The team members could throw out things they might do at that point in the project if they had a week with nothing to do.

Scenario planning helps people to realize that bad things may happen on the project. It prepares them mentally and emotionally so that when bad things happen, they don't experience as much denial and shock. They are more apt to go forward with their alternate plans.

7.4.3   Whiteboard Risk Management

This is an informal way to bring team members into risk management in the middle of a project. It is effective and has low overhead. The project manager starts whiteboard risk management by asking a few smart people into his office for a chat about the project. The discussion begins with the question, "What could possibly go wrong on the project next week?"

The people present will mumble a bit and think of a few things that could go wrong. Write these on the whiteboard. Most of these potential problems won't hurt the project as the team could take care of them in a day or two. Write these easy-to-handle risks on a piece of paper and erase them from the whiteboard. Don't throw the paper away as it contains useful information.

Now concentrate on the items still on the whiteboard. Ask, "What could we do to prevent these from happening?" Scribble the answers on the board next to the items.

Next ask, "What would we need to do if these potential problems occurred? What resources would we need?" Scribble these answers on the board and after the meeting start gathering the resources.

The final question is, "What will indicate that the potential problem is turning into a real problem?" Write the answer on the board and have the people present keep watch for those indicators.

In 30 minutes, with nothing more than a whiteboard, marker, and some smart people, the team has performed risk management for the next week. The formality was low, the communication and visibility were high, and the project is in much better condition.

7.5   CONFIGURATION MANAGEMENT

Because risk management is part of the project plan, its products belong in the functional baseline. There is little to add to the configuration management discussion from the planning chapter (Chapter 6). The Configuration Control Board exists, and the risk management plan states what to do. As project manager, you need only follow the plan diligently.

The risk management plan, or the risk management section of the project plan, will change during the project. The functional baseline CCB must control the changes. The basic information will not change.

The top-risks list should change regularly, such as monthly or even weekly. The CCB may choose not to control every change to this list. One method I have seen work is for the CCB to set a threshold for change. This relates to the probability × consequence calculations (see Figure 7.5). If the product of any issue in the list changes by 3.0 or greater, the CCB needs to know right away. If the product is less than the threshold, it can wait until a regularly scheduled CCB meeting.

7.6 USING STANDARDS

As mentioned earlier, risk management must be documented. Some organizations require a separate risk management plan, whereas others include this in overall project planning documents. Both the IEEE standard for project management plans (IEEE, 1998) (see Chapter 6) and the CMM have a section for risk management. The place is not important, as long as it exists somewhere.

List the risk manager and explain his role in the project. Who analyzed the project for risks? Tell what approaches they used and how they made decisions.

Document the products of risk analysis as shown in Figure 7.5. Explain how the risks relate to the project. Discuss the risk aversion strategies and how they address the risks. Give everything a reference number (R1, R2.AS1, and so on). Figure 7.5 is a short listing, but it is the result of much work. Point to other documents as well.

Create a risk management notebook, folder, or file cabinet to contain all risk management information. Identifying, estimating, and evaluating risks are subjective tasks. They involve discussions, opinions, trade-offs, and countless decisions. Document these using the visibility techniques described here and in Chapters 4, 5, and 6. Keep unofficial documents. These are not published in the formal sense of a contract deliverable, but they should exist, be well organized, and be easy to find.

7.7 KEY THOUGHTS IN THIS CHAPTER

Software projects commonly have problems. Risk management attempts to predict the problems and either prevent them or have a plan to minimize their effect. Risks—problems that have not yet occurred—stem from a lack of information, control, or time. Most of the critical risks come from personnel shortfalls, either because you don't have the people you need for the job, or because the people you do have perform below expectations. Most risks arise during the requirements stage.

Risk engineering analyzes and manages the risk in a project. Risk analysis identifies, estimates, and evaluates risks. The 3Ps are particularly important in risk identification and in all aspects of managing risk (risk planning, control, monitoring, directing, and staffing). Managing risk begins with planning, which involves creating risk aversion plans—what to do if the potential problems become real. The project manager monitors the project for signs of problems. If they occur, managers must direct risk aversion plans and provide people for them. Risk management approaches range from crisis management to the far-sighted management of change.

Visibility is important during risk estimation and evaluation. The estimate of a risk is its probability of occurring times the consequences if it occurs. The results of risk analysis can be made visible with various charts and graphs.

The products of risk management belong in the functional baseline. Use the configuration management principles discussed in Chapters 2 and 6 (also see Appendix B) for putting the project plan into the functional baseline. Allow the Configuration Control Board to use good business sense in deciding how to control regular changes in the top-risks list.

Risk management must be visible. Document all risk management activities in a separate risk management plan or as part of the project management plan. Use the IEEE standard for project plans to help you avoid reinventing the wheel.

REFERENCES

B. Boehm, *Software Risk Management*, IEEE CS Press, Los Alamitos, CA, 1989.

B. Boehm, "Software Risk Management: Principles and Practices," *IEEE Software*, January 1991, pp. 32–41.

R. Charette, "Risk Management," in *Encyclopedia of Software Engineering*, J. Marciniak, ed., Wiley, New York, 1994, pp. 1091–1106.

E. Derby, "Risky Beginnings," *Software Testing and Quality Engineering*, November December 2000, pp. 50–54.

D. Estes, "Year 2000 Testing: A Radical Perspective," *Cutter IT Journal*, February 1999, pp. 13–21.

A. Gemmer, "Risk Management: Moving Beyond Process," *Computer*, May 1997, pp. 33–43.

[Hall 2003] P. Hall, "Knowing the Odds," *STQE*, March April 2003, pp. 35–40.

IEEE, IEEE Standard, ANSI/IEEE Std 1058-1998, *IEEE Standard for Software Project Management Plans*, IEEE Press, New York, 1998.

T. Lister, "Risk Management is Project Management for Adults," *IEEE Software*, May June 1997, pp. 20–22.

J. Marciniak (ed.), *Encyclopedia of Software Engineering*, Wiley, New York, 1994.

L. Putnam and W. Myers, *Measures for Excellence: Reliable Software On Time, Within Budget*," Yourdon Press, Englewood Cliffs, NJ, 1992.

L. Putnam and W. Myers, *Controlling* Software Development, Executive Briefing, IEEE CS Press, Los Alamitos, CA, 1996.

L. Putnam and W. Myers, *Industrial Strength Software: Effective Management Using Measurement*, IEEE CS Press, Los Alamitos, CA, 1997.

L. Russel, "I Wish I'd Known that from the Start: Scenario Planning for Project Management," *Cutter IT Journal*, May 1999, pp. 13–17.

G. Weinberg, "Just Say No! Improving the Requirements Process," *American Programmer*, October 1995, pp. 19–23.

R. Zahniser, "Time Boxing," *Software Development*, March 1995, pp. 34–38.

PART 3

THE DEVELOPMENT LIFE CYCLE: MIDDLE TO LATE STAGES

In this section, I continue applying the four themes introduced in Part 1 to the rest of the development life cycle. This section focuses on how the 3Ps, visibility techniques, configuration management, and standards affect design, integration and test, and maintenance. Although maintenance is not strictly a development stage, many of the decisions made during development have a direct bearing on how easy or hard the product is to maintain or enhance later on. The chapters in this section are not as closely linked as chapters in the last section, but they are worth looking at as a unit to get a sense of how decisions made in one stage affect the product in other stages. Design influences the degree of difficulty of integration and testing. A modular design lets the team integrate the software logically. Because each module fits easily with the others, testing is more straightforward. Each test can be modular and self-contained like the software modules. The same holds true for the relationship of design and software maintenance. A modular design eases software maintenance; an overly complex design makes software maintenance an expensive nightmare.

The Software Project Manager's Handbook. By Dwayne Phillips.
ISBN 0-471-67420-6 © 2004 IEEE Computer Society

Chapter 8

Design

Design is about building a software system correctly. In the requirements stage, the team worked to define the correct system—the one the customer wants. Now, they must build the correct system correctly.

Design is to a large extent an exploratory process. People rarely sit down and design a product correctly the first time because they do not have enough information. Projects would be much easier if developers knew at the start what they know at the end. Design is about finding that foresight with the same 20/20 vision as hindsight. Use the design as a picture of the product to come. "Design" the product, document the design, and then analyze and fix it. Work hard to understand how the product to come will and will not satisfy the customer. Study past successes and failures to avoid what David Parnas calls "ignorant originality" (Parnas, 1996)—repeating mistakes or claiming some great new discovery when someone else has already discovered it. Both are wasteful.

Balancing the 3Ps is extremely important in design because difficult people issues can arise during this stage. Design is inherently creative and, thus, it is a somewhat artistic process that does not always fit neatly into a procedure. There are morale issues. Many creative people are offering solutions or parts of solutions, yet the business may be dictating significant design parameters, such as language, operating system, hardware, and user interface. The project manager must balance solutions with these kinds of limitations, paying close attention to abilities, the team's emotional barometer, and the design's fit to process and product.

Because design is both a process and an artifact, it is also both a visibility technique and a visibility product. Design constraints are set forth in the *Software Requirements Specification* (SRS; see Chapter 5). The SRS takes the idea for a solution out of one person's mind and places it before the group to consider and improve. Many of the diagrams and visibility techniques discussed in Part 2 apply to design.

Design spreads across three configuration management baselines: the functional baseline (the requirements), the allocated baseline (high-level design), and ending with the design baseline (low-level design). Proper CM is particularly important during this stage to avoid mixing up these baselines.

Standards come into play when the design is recorded in a *Software Description Document*. IEEE-Std-1016 (IEEE, 1998) is a good format for the SDD. It will help you form thoughts about the design and show you how best to express it. Experienced, creative, and knowledgeable practitioners wrote it. They already made all the mistakes, so use their hard-earned knowledge.

8.1   THE CHALLENGES OF THE 3Ps

Design involves creating many solutions to a problem, choosing one according to a set of criteria, and showing the chosen solution to others so that they can improve on it. Design is the creative part of a software project because it produces something that was not there before. This contrasts to the requirements stage, which is discovering what is there, and the coding stage, which builds what is specified.

There are three challenges to balancing the 3Ps: managing creativity, reducing design frustration, and correctly evaluating and selecting design alternatives. Because it is largely creative, design, more than any other part of software development, depends on the people doing it. People with experience in the product area can design solutions with a minimum of revisions and frustration. In all other cases (most of the time for most of us), design must be powered by well-chosen processes and various forms of iteration. The team must typically look at the problem several times from several perspectives before the "Aha!" happens.

8.1.1   *Managing Creativity*

Like all creative processes, design is messy. Its success rests largely on the degree of the designers' experience, iteration, and abstraction. Some try in vain to make it a straightforward exercise. Tools, techniques, and methods can help, but creativity tends to elude even the most organized project manager's attempts to box it. The wise project manager expects this and is flexible and patient.

Experience. Experience is key. The more experience a designer has, the more solutions he knows, and the wider the range of possible solutions he can offer for the current problem. This is why people are programmers before they are designers. Programmers learn solutions while gaining experience with software. Every designer needs to expand his toolbox of solutions. Designers must continually research and study software solutions to gain knowledge and experience.

Reusing previous designs is very difficult, and few organizations have been able to do it. Problems are different, and designs (solutions) usually do not solve different problems. There are, however, common elements among different solutions. Seeing the common elements and being able to use them in a cost-effective manner is a great challenge. The potential benefit is so great that we must all attempt to do this.

Some people, regardless of experience, do not make good designers because they cannot work with design's sloppy nature. Many excellent programmers, testers, and analysts, can work out problems, find problems or verify correctness, help people understand and communicate their problems, and monitor complex situations. They cannot, however, construct a solution. They cannot consistently find that creative spark.

Iteration. Iteration is one way to work through design frustration. Plan to design, review, and redesign. Create the first design to understand a problem and the second to solve the problem. This may seem costly, but the design is the software's foundation. It takes time and money to do it correctly. Refusing to invest in design will produce the same disastrous results as refusing to invest in requirements. Remember, the goal is to build the right product the right way. Place this redesign step in the project plan so that no one can say "We should do this once more, but we're already behind schedule, so we'll go with what we have."

During the redesign, review the problem and the first design critically. Find at least three major deficiencies in the first design. If you cannot see them, have someone else take a look. The deficiencies are there; it's just a matter of finding the right perspective to locate them.

Do not produce a second design by merely correcting the faults of the first. Examine the faults. Where do they lead? What do they indicate? Did you misunderstand the original problem? Did you fail to optimize a critical part of the solution? Did you design something that cannot be built? Is the design too complex or esoteric? Use this knowledge, start from scratch, and create a new, second design.

This process is similar to Frederick Brooks' (Brooks, 1975) advice—"Plan to throw one away; you will, anyhow"—a statement that has been debated since Brooks first made it in 1975. Of course, a business cannot build a $10 million software system, throw it away, and build a second $10 million system for actual use. However, a group of engineers can spend one week on a design, throw it away, and spend a second week on a second design. If you put this in the project's plan, you need not worry about exceeding the budget to do it.

Prototyping tools (see Chapter 5) can also help iteration by generating screens and scenarios that let designers more easily find the faults in the design. Use prototypes with caution, however, and do not make them too expensive to throw away.

Abstraction. Abstraction is the process of viewing a problem from different levels of detail. The first view sees the problem in large pieces. Each succeeding view sees each piece as small pieces and continues down to the lowest applicable level of detail. People cannot see a large problem by trying to see all the fine details at once. The large number of small details is overwhelming.

Using abstraction helps people think and create logical designs. Figure 8.1 illustrates a software system broken into levels of abstraction. The first thoughts of a design should be about high-level subsystems. Once the subsystems are understood, break each subsystem into modules. Repeat this process to break each module into a subroutine and, finally, design the inside of each subroutine.

Dividing a system into subsystems, modules, and subroutines is high-level design. Designing the inside of the subroutines is low-level design. I have seen many people sketch out the subsystem and module structure and proclaim, "Design finished. Programmers will fill in details."

This happens too frequently and reflects the tendency we all have to stay well within our comfort zone. Designers who were programmers first are much more comfortable programming. It is natural for them to want to end design and start programming. As project manager, you must be alert to this pattern. Adjust the process to achieve the desired product: a design complete at all levels of abstraction. I like to give designers a day's break after they complete each level of abstraction. This lets them recharge their creative energy before moving to the next level of detail.

Designing without using abstraction leads to failure. Often, a designer starts with the details of one subroutine in mind. He designs the details of the subroutine and tries to make the remaining 98% of the software system fit around the subroutine. He may eventually succeed, but 98% of the system will be hard to understand, build, and maintain.

Designing with abstraction is not necessarily the same in every case. Many software systems depend on the correct and efficient operation of a few subroutines. In these cases, designing this 2% of the software first may be the best approach.

Design by diving into an abstraction level. Start wherever is best, but design only whatever is necessary at that level, no more. I tend to prefer higher levels. Designing too much of a low level too early may be a waste of time. As the rest of the software system takes shape, the low-level design will need changing for the good of the system.

8.1.2 Reducing Design Frustration

Frustration is inevitable in design. In addition to the frustration of the technical issues in the design, designers must handle the "How's it going?" and "Is it too late to add feature X?" inquiries from customers.

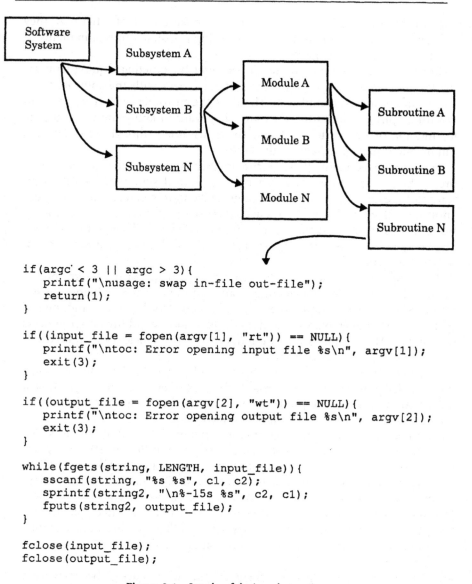

```
if(argc < 3 || argc > 3){
    printf("\nusage: swap in-file out-file");
    return(1);
}

if((input_file = fopen(argv[1], "rt")) == NULL){
    printf("\ntoc: Error opening input file %s\n", argv[1]);
    exit(3);
}

if((output_file = fopen(argv[2], "wt")) == NULL){
    printf("\ntoc: Error opening output file %s\n", argv[2]);
    exit(3);
}

while(fgets(string, LENGTH, input_file)){
    sscanf(string, "%s %s", c1, c2);
    sprintf(string2, "\n%-15s %s", c2, c1);
    fputs(string2, output_file);
}

fclose(input_file);
fclose(output_file);
```

Figure 8.1 Levels of design abstraction.

There are several ways to handle this interaction and reduce the frustrations in the design activities themselves.

Managing the Interaction of Customers and Designers. In theory, customers are not involved during design (or coding or testing). They drive the project during the requirements activities by stating what they need and what parts of the solution (design) they consider most important. After that, they are supposed to go away and leave everything not stated in requirements to the discretion of the designers.

Most customers are tired of developers after the grueling requirements activities and are glad to have no more involvement with the software's creation. Others are less complacent. These are the customers who have unusually strong opinions about the software. They want to know about, contribute to, and approve every design detail. These customers, though well-meaning, can be micromanaging pains in the neck.

How designers handle these customers means much to the success or failure of the project. If the customers participate in design, they own the software to a greater degree and have a larger stake in integrating it into their environment. They will want it to succeed. If the customers are pushed away from the design in a less than tactful manner, they will disown the software. They may not use the final software and could work to see that everyone labels it as a failure.

The best course of action is to let customers help during design, but to manage this carefully. The customer can give the designer valuable insight into how the product should meet requirements. On the other hand, he can cost time and money because he doesn't fully understand the design process or product. The designers may be reduced to 50% efficiency as they try to teach these things to the customer.

As project manager, watch the schedule and cost and balance these against the knowledge the customer brings. If the customer's insights begin to cost more than the schedule or project budget can tolerate, go to the project's executive sponsor and ask for some tactful intervention.

Another danger the customer brings is a stream of last minute changes. The CM section later in this chapter discusses this further. Briefly, designers should try to include as many ideas as time, money, and the CM plan will allow. Never short-cut the process given in the CM plan. At some point, designers must say "No more changes in this version, but we'll be sure to put these features into the next version." The challenges are to know when you arrive at this point, to inform the customer respectfully, to handle objections tactfully, and to keep your promise in the next version's design.

Rushing into Design. One of the biggest frustrations in design occurs when a project rushes into design before the requirements are done. People try to write the requirements in English as a book full of "will" statements (the software will calculate loan interest, the software will store data for five years, the software will have windows, and so on). This activity requires time, consumes dozens of pages in the SRS (Chapter 5), and wears out the requirements gatherers. They call it quits and declare the requirements done.

This situation illustrates two prevalent human traits. The first trait, mentioned earlier, is the tendency to do what is familiar and comfortable. For software programmers turned designers, this means speeding through requirements and design to get to the programming.

The second trait is a lack of knowledge. Writing requirements in English only is a mistake. Tom DeMarco (DeMarco, 1979) discussed the inherent weaknesses of the English language for specifying requirements. English is imprecise, wordy, redundant, and full of implications, connotations, and innuendo—which is why DeMarco's structured method contains little English and many dataflow diagrams, process minispecifications, and data dictionaries.

Appendix C steps through Ed Yourdon's structured analysis/structured design, or SA/SD, method (Yourdon, 1989), which is a refinement of DeMarco's technique. When I show the SA/SD method to experienced software practitioners, they commonly reply that the dataflow diagrams are design; the requirements are will statements. The frequency of this reply matches the frequency of troubled and failed software projects.

These troubled projects express requirements in English and design in requirements diagrams and leave everything else to the programmers. The programmers, in turn, make assumptions about design decisions that the designers never made. During integration, these two sets of design decisions collide and the resulting errors send the project into a downward spiral of code–text–fix code–test–fix.

As project manager, you must ensure that the team does the requirements-then-design process correctly. Follow a proven method like SA/SD. Dozens of equally appropriate techniques are available.

Make Designs Verifiable. Designs come from requirements, so like requirements, they must be verifiable. The design will lead to code, which will be tested. If the design has one large, do-everything module, testing individual functions will be difficult. The design should separate functions into loosely coupled modules so that testing will be logical and manageable.

Choose Structure Wisely. The structure or architecture is the arrangement of the units in the software. Any design with more than one subroutine has a structure. Think about structural issues like coupling, cohesion, information hiding, and modularity.

Coupling is a design property that states how much each unit depends on the others. Loose coupling means that the implementation of one unit does not depend on the implementation of another. Loosely coupled units are independent; you can change them without changing the others. As Parnas says (Parnas, 1996), "Independence that allows for graceful change should be the goal of a well-designed system." Loosely coupled units ensure that independence. Tightly coupled modules are appropriate only when you need the highest possible execution speed. I worked on a couple of supercomputer projects. Speed was so critical that we used the ultimate in tight coupling: no subroutines. All the code was in one main module. Use tight coupling only in case like this, where there are no alternatives.

Cohesion describes how well the statements inside a unit relate to one another. If the statements are related logically, the unit has high cohesion. This means the unit does one thing and one thing only. Consider a unit that inputs a matrix, inverts it, and outputs the result. It uses an algorithm that reads in only a part of the matrix, does some process, does some output, reads in some more, and so on. The three operations are mixed, and only the designer can understand how it works. The statements in the unit are related geographically on the page, not logically. Now consider breaking that unit into three units: input, processing, and output. The statements in each unit are related logically; all work to do the same operation.

In this simple example, it is easy to see the lack of cohesion, but designers and programmers make the same kinds of mistakes in more complex designs without being able to see the ramifications. Stop and consider cohesion. When rushed, it is easy to design a unit that will do three or four different operations. The designer loses perspective: he understands the system and cannot see how his design might confuse anyone.

Information hiding, an old and somewhat forgotten technique (McConnell, 1996), seeks to place or hide details inside an item that tell how that item works. These are details that the outside world does not need to know. This concept led to encapsulation in the object-oriented world. In Figure 8.1, for example, designers need not know the inside of Subroutine A to call it. If they do, they will write their own routines in a way that depends on the internals of Subroutine A. If the internals of subroutine A change, many other places in the software will also have to change.

Steve McConnell (McConnell, 1996) suggests three steps to using information hiding effectively. The first is to identify the design secrets to hide. The most common secrets are items that have a high probability of changing. The next step is to separate each design secret by putting it in its own unit (package, module, subroutine, class). The third and final step is to isolate or hide each secret so that if it does change, the change will not affect the rest of the software.

Ask what needs to be hidden. Asking this over and over promotes good design decisions at all levels. Common candidates for hiding include hardware drivers, file formats, complex data structures and logic, and business rules. A top candidate is any routine that is difficult and may need redesigning.

A classic case of failure to hide information was the Y2K problem (Jarvis et al., 1999). The error, handling years with two instead of four digits, was not hidden in one module. Instead, we spread it all over all our applications. Once we decided to correct this error, we had to go everywhere to try to find it and then fix it consistently. This was a design error, and many organizations paid dearly for it.

Modularity makes design less difficult by using information hiding and data abstraction. Information hiding hides important design decisions in modules; data abstraction uses this to give users an abstract view of data, as opposed to an implementation view.

For example, suppose a code module operates a queue data structure. Users can check how many members are in the queue and enter and exit it. The users do not know how the module implements the queue; they know only how to use it. The queue is an abstract data type. If the module changes the way it implements the queue, the users are not affected.

Data abstraction is what differentiates a modular design from a structured one. In structured design, the queue's implementation would be visible. That is, the users would know that the routines use a linked list, array, and so on to implement the queue. Changing the queue's implementation would require visible changes to several routines.

Modular and structured design work well together. Modularity keeps design secrets hidden, whereas structure shows the logical sequence of steps. The modules provide the software's main structure. The structured design is a secondary structure that helps everyone see how the software works and meets the requirements. Modular designs program naturally in languages such as Ada and Modula-2. Languages such as C, Basic, and Pascal work better with structured designs, although they can be used for modular designs as well (McConnell, 1993; Phillips, 1998).

Modular design also enables separated teams to develop software in parallel (Herbsleb & Grinter, 1999). One of the phenomena of the late 1990s was developing software around the clock. Organizations had team members on different continents where their different eight-hour shifts would end and begin continuously. The design allowed different groups to work in parallel. Each group finished their own modules, and the lead group would integrate them into a system. There are various ways to do this. One of the best is to have the integration group combine the modules from the different groups each day. This is not easy, but Internet and telecommunications technologies make it possible.

Designing for Reuse. Another frustration of design is that sinking feeling that you are reinventing the wheel. The current design is similar to the design of last year's project. It is just different enough to cause us to repeat the entire design process. If only we had made that last design more general purpose.

Completely original solutions are rare. They are usually similar to or combinations of existing solutions. Programmers have reused solutions for years by reusing code or using code libraries. In recent years, design reuse has gained attention under the title of patterns (Gamma et al., 1995). Architects and other engineers have reused designs for centuries, and this is finally spreading into software engineering.

The first and most important step in designing for reuse is to *decide* to design for reuse. Some claim that using method X guarantees a reusable design. This is simply not true. Poor designs are possible in any method, just as good reusable designs are possible in almost any method. The key is to proclaim reusability as a project goal by stating it in the project plan (see Chapter 6).

Once the attitude for reuse is set, look at the problem at hand. What is at the core of the problem? Is it banking, insurance, or airline reservations? Keep probing on deeper and deeper levels.

For example, many software systems are CRUD—create, retrieve, update, and delete. The prevalence of CRUD systems is evident in that most development environments (like the Microsoft Visual series) are optimized to build CRUD systems. A GUI allows the user to enter or create a block of information. An I/O system saves the information and later retrieves it for the user. The GUI lets the user update the information, and the I/O system saves it. The GUI and I/O system let the user delete the information. The basic elements are the GUI, information, and I/O system.

The designer needs to look at these elements to make them more general purpose than is necessary for this project. This means looser coupling, more information hiding, more iteration, more customer interaction, and more data abstraction. This points to the object-oriented approach and explains why reuse is an advantage claimed by its proponents. Remember, however, that using the object-oriented approach will not guarantee reuse (Fichman & Kemerer, 1997).

There is a danger in creating reusable designs and reusing designs. Design reuse can stifle creative thought. This is evident when designers are told to do something a certain way because "that's the way we always do it." The project manager needs to watch for this and balance the time and money saved with reuse against the cost of wearing blinders. The cost often takes the form of ex-employees—good designers who leave to find an organization that lets them use their creative abilities.

8.1.3 Evaluating and Selecting from Design Alternatives

Once several designs have been completed, reviewed, and revised, it is time to evaluate them and choose one. Have the designers propose at least three designs—three ideas to solve a problem. If not, ask them to work harder to get solutions. High-level designs do not require great time and expense. The project shouldn't have to triple its budget for design activities to have three candidate high-level designs.

Unlike creating solutions, evaluating design alternatives can be done step by step. Over the years, I have distilled an evaluation and selection method that uses Gilb charts (Gilb, 1988) and decision tables (see Chapter 4). It is simple, powerful, and it works at work.

The first step is to base design decisions on criteria, which the designers and you have selected before design begins. Having criteria before design is important; if the criteria come at the same time as the solutions, people will slant the criteria toward their favorite design.

McConnell (McConnell, 1993) developed a list of questions to ask in examining a design, which is given in Figure 8.2. Figure 8.3 lists what McConnell considers the characteristics of a good design.

Lists like Figures 8.2 and 8.3 are excellent starting points for thinking about the 3Ps of the project. Choose a small set of characteristics that are appropriate. Assign relative weights. Justify the characteristics and weights in writing. This will help people in the long maintenance years ahead.

To illustrate the evaluation and selection process, consider a project to replace an organization's digital signal processing software. The new DSP software will be used for at least five years. The new software is to be evaluated ac-

. Is the overall organization of the program clear, including a
   good architectural overview and justification?
. Are modules well defined, including their functionality and their
   interfaces to other modules?
. Are all the functions listed in the requirements covered sensibly,
   by neither too many nor too few modules?
. Is the architecture designed to accommodate likely changes?
. Are the necessary buy vs build decisions included?
. Does the architecture describe how reused code will be made
   to conform to other architectural objectives?
. Are all the major data structures hidden behind access routines?
. Is the database organization and content specified?
. Are all key algorithms described and justified?
. Are all major objects described and justified?
. Is a strategy for handling user input described?
. Is a strategy for handling I/O described and justified?
. Are key aspects of the user interface defined?
. Is the user interface modularized so that change in it won't
   affect the rest of the program?
. Are memory-use estimates and a strategy for memory management
   described and justified?
. Does the architecture set space and speed budgets for each module?
. Is a strategy for handling strings described and are character
   string storage estimates provided?
. Is a coherent error-handling strategy provided?
. Are error messages managed as a set to present a clean user interface?
. Is a level of robustness specified?
. Is a part over or under architected? Are expectations in this area set
   out explicitly?
. Are the major system goals clearly stated?
. Does the whole architecture hang together conceptually?
. Is the top-level design independent of the machine and language
   that will be used to implement it?
. Are the motivations for all major decisions provided?
. Are you, as a programmer who will implement the system, comfortable
   with the architecture?

Figure 8.2   Questions to ask in examining a design.

. Intellectual Manageability
. Low Complexity
. Ease of Maintenance
. Minimal Connectedness
. Extensibility
. Reusability
. High Fan-in
. Low to Medium Fan-out
. Portability
. Leanness
. Stratified Design
. Standard Techniques

Figure 8.3   Desirable design characteristics.

cording to the criteria in Figure 8.4. As described earlier, the managers, customers, and developers should have already decided on the criteria by this time.

The *functions* criterion indicates that the design must include all the needed DSP functions. The *initial cost* is how much it will cost to acquire the software by buying, building, or some combination of both. *Maintenance cost 5 years* is an estimate of how much it will cost to maintain the software over its five-year lifetime. *Portable* relates to how easy it will be to move the software to a new computer or operating system. Computers change drastically in five years and the software must adapt. The users develop new DSP operators regularly. *Customize* rates how well the software allows the users to mix operators to form new ones. *Five-year lifetime* relates to whether or not the software will be supported in five years. Companies that develop commercial software can go out of business, and thus no longer support their products.

The *weights* determine the outcome of the evaluation. In the example, they are somewhat arbitrary, but in practice, significant amounts of money hinge

Criterion	Weight (1-10)
Functions	10
Initial Cost	4
Maintenance Cost 5 Years	6
Portable	8
Customize	9
Five Year Lifetime	9

Figure 8.4   Design criteria for the DSP example.

Attribute	Scale	Test	Worst	Plan	Best	Now
FFT Functions	Number	Demonstrate	3	5	8	5
Filter Methods	Number	Demonstrate	5	9	13	9
Display Types	Number	Demonstrate	4	6	9	4
...	...	...				

Figure 8.5   A Gilb chart of the functions criteria for the DSP software example.

on them. Managers must choose the weights with great care and justify their choices in writing.

A set of Gilb charts will help the project manager, customer, and designers evaluate design alternatives. Figures 8.5, 8.6, and 8.7 are Gilb charts for the first three criteria in Figure 8.4. It is best to have one chart for each attribute, rather than combining several attributes into a single chart. That way, only the designers who need to evaluate that attribute need to see the various alternatives.

These charts show what the current situation provides (the "now" column) and the plan, best, and worst expectations for the new DSP system. Figure 8.5 shows some of the function categories. For example, the first class of functions is the FFT. The current DSP software has five types of FFT functions. The customers want five types in the new system, will accept as many as eight types, and will not tolerate any fewer than three types. The chart shows the same for filter and display methods.

This chart will direct the design evaluators when they compare various high-level designs. It tells the evaluators to give a low score to any candidate design that only has three types of FFT functions. It also states to give the same score to any candidates that have eight or more types of FFT functions.

Figure 8.6 also provides initial cost information to help people evaluate design alternatives. It directs the evaluators to give a low score to any candidate design that initially costs more than $150,000. Figure 8.7 provides the same type of information for the five-year maintenance cost.

Once the managers have the evaluation criteria and the designers have completed several candidate designs, the designers and customers must look at everything. In this example, there are four candidate high-level designs. The first is to write a complete DSP software system from scratch. The next two de-

Attribute	Scale	Test	Worst	Plan	Best	Now
Initial Cost	Dollars	Estimate	$150K	$125K	$75K	n/a

Figure 8.6   A Gilb chart of the initial cost criteria for the DSP software example.

Attribute	Scale	Test	Worst	Plan	Best	Now
Maintenance Cost 5 Years	Dollars	Estimate	$500K	$250K	$150K	$550K

Figure 8.7 A Gilb chart of the five-year maintenance cost criteria for the DSP software example.

signs are to purchase different commercial DSP packages (fictitious for this example). The fourth candidate is to purchase the source code of a DSP system and modify it.

Place all the Gilb charts and the designs on walls in a room and let people walk around and look at them. As discussed above, the Gilb charts help the evaluators compare the different candidate designs. Have everyone present to answer questions and explain. This is not a competition to see which design team wins. The entire business enterprise will win or lose based on the quality of the decision. Have everyone and every piece of information available for the evaluation.

The final step is to decide on a design. Use the decision table. Figure 8.8 shows a completed decision table for this example. The winning design is to purchase the source code for a DSP package and modify it.

The decision table is not the end of the process. Filling in a table is a mechanical procedure, and decision making is not mechanical. The decision table results often leave decision makers with an uneasy feeling that they've overlooked something. Review everything. Examine the criteria and their weights, and repeat the entire process if necessary. A quantitative, documented decision reduces politics and quarrels, but numbers can be misleading.

A decision table is a model, and models are not perfect. Although the decision table can guide us in making choices, we should not let the decision

Design Candidate	Criteria Weights	Functions X10	Initial Cost X4	Maintenance Cost 5 Years X6	Portable X8	Customize X9	Five Year Lifetime X9
Handwritten		10	1	2	8	9	10
Commercial Package #1		6	9	9	4	7	7
Commercial Package #2		7	8	8	7	6	3
Purchase Source Code & Modify		10	3	2	8	9	10

Figure 8.8 Decision table for the DSP software example.

table make our choice for us. There is a fine line here between a quantitative view and the people, process, and product. Be sure to walk it carefully.

An additional factor to consider in deciding among design alternatives is the change in technology with time. Highsmith calls this "the edge of time" (Highsmith, 1999). In addition to asking, "What is the best processing system (or whatever)?" ask, "What is the change cycle of this component?"

The operating system is one example of a component that will change with time. I have managed several projects where the almost annual change in operating systems broke our systems. We did not consider the change cycle in our design and planning. The best approach is to put markers in the project plan (the long-term project plan that includes the operations and maintenance phase) that coincide with the change cycle. Reconsider your design decisions at these points.

8.2   VISIBILITY—EXPRESSING THE DESIGN

Visibility techniques are important when expressing a design. The goal is to create a design description that is good enough for a programmer to take it and write software that satisfies the customer. The visibility techniques can help designers examine the problem, create solutions, choose one solution, and describe that solution to the programmers.

Design is similar to analyzing requirements in that the target is a design description. In Chapter 5, I showed how the target of requirements analysis is the *Software Requirements Specification*. The *Software Design Description*—both words and pictures—is the target of the design process. The designers should focus on these words and pictures as they attempt to create solutions.

8.2.1   Words

The keywords in software describe objects, functions, and states. In Chapter 5, I described how requirements are also expressed in these terms. Because the problem (the requirements) is expressed in these terms, it makes sense to keep the solutions (designs) in these terms as well. To quickly review, *objects* are things in the real world. Capture them with data in the software solution space. *Functions* are actions in the real world. Design corresponding functional subroutines for the solution space. *States* deal with condition, history, or timing. Design transitions, events, and time spaces into the software.

Different software systems will emphasize objects, functions, and states to different degrees. An accounting system will concentrate on objects (money) and functions (financial calculations) and may not care about states (overnight batch processing jobs). A chemical plant control system will concentrate on states (the time heat is applied to chemicals) and use simple objects (fluid level) and functions (open valve and close valve).

Ensure the design contains all three elements. If one or two elements are not important, reduce but do not eliminate them from the description. Do this thoughtfully, not arbitrarily. Explain why the element is mentioned only briefly.

8.2.2 Pictures

Software diagrams are usually the best way to express a design. Refer to the context, dataflow, SADT, Warnier–Orr, state transition, HIPO diagrams, structure charts, sequence diagrams, and CRC cards in Chapter 5. Use these and any other diagrams that will show a programmer what the software should contain. If the diagram does not help do this, don't force it. Also, earlier in this chapter (Section 8.1.2), I mentioned the need to avoid rushing into design. Do not take a dataflow diagram and say "look, the design is done." Work all the way through proven requirements analysis and design methods like those given in Appendix C.

Figure 8.9 shows how three design approaches examine the same situation (McConnell, 1993). The group of items at the top left of the figure represents the situation or *problem area*. Each item inside the problem area represents an operation or a data structure. The left column shows the structured approach (described in Appendix C). The first step in this approach is to pull out the most important thing. The next step is to find things for the next level. The process repeats until all the things are in the proper top-down hierarchy.

The center column shows the information-hiding approach, which follows the principles of modularity discussed earlier. This approach finds a thing and separates it as a secret, continuing until everything has been separated. Some secrets can be placed as parts of other secrets as in the lower-right corner. The right column shows the object-oriented approach. Things are pulled out as objects, and several things can be part of the same object.

The object-oriented approach provides the greatest potential for design reuse. In Figure 8.9, an object contains data and functions, which can be part of the solution across designs. However, as I mentioned earlier, only hard work—not a particular method—guarantees reuse.

Visibility via design diagrams is an excellent aid in reusing designs. Reuse requires finding the elements common to different solutions. These common elements are almost impossible to find if the designer cannot see the complete design. Design diagrams meet this need by making designs visible.

Software diagrams also play a role in the split between high-level and low-level designs. Dataflow diagrams and others are suited only for expressing some parts of high-level designs. HIPO and Warnier–Orr diagrams (see Chapter 5) work at all levels of abstraction and so can express low-level detailed designs.

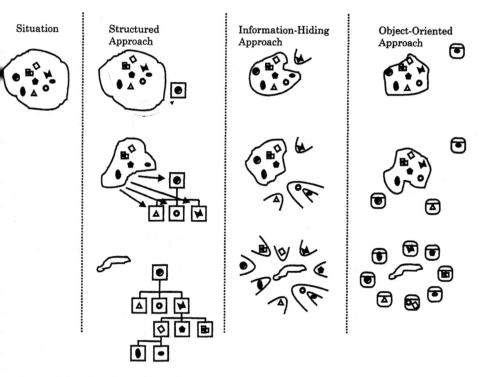

Figure 8.9 How the structured analysis/structured design, information-hiding, and object-oriented approaches look at the same situation.

Figure 8.10 shows how a HIPO diagram expresses low-level details (Fairley, 1985). The design details of the subroutine `perform_convolution` are written in structured English, a shorthand for expressing algorithms. There are many forms of the algorithm language. Some practitioners have refined this into specific design languages that have syntax checkers and compilers.

Figure 8.11 shows the same information as Figure 8.10, but in a Warnier–Orr diagram that uses the Warnier–Orr notation (Higgins, 1986). Warnier–Orr diagrams, used too infrequently in the United States, have the power to express all levels of functional and data abstraction.

8.3   DESIGN IN THE CODE

Another line of thought regarding design is whether or not to document the design anywhere. I have worked on projects where the engineers told me directly that, "the design is in the code." In some respects, this is true. The source code written by a programmer is not really the software. The software is an executable file that runs on the computer. The source code is something

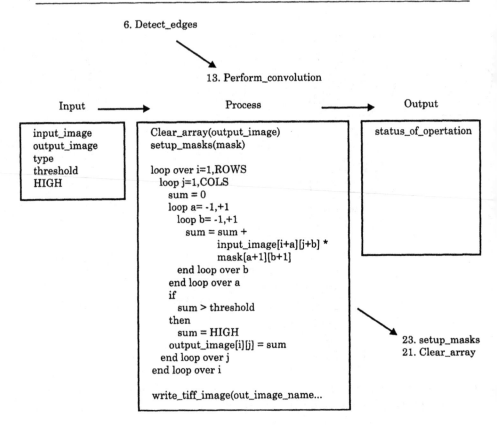

Figure 8.10 HIPO Diagram showing high- and low-level design.

that people can read that expresses what the executable file will do when run on the computer. Hence, the source code is a detailed design of the software.

One branch of this concept is design by contract (Kolawa, 2000). This is a structured way of writing comments in the source code file that expresses what the code should do. These design comments are in a standardized format so that people can understand them years after they have been written. The design by contract idea keeps the design in the same text file as the source code. This help to keep the design and the code consistent. This method works well as long as the text expression of the design is sufficient. Sometimes it is, but sometimes it isn't.

. I believe that a disciplined approach to keeping the design in the source code file may work. The key is to maintaining the discipline. It is easy for people to slip into an undisciplined style of expressing the design as well as disregarding it altogether. Once you tell programmers that they can keep the design in the code, they may skimp on the design text and revert back to a "code like hell" process.

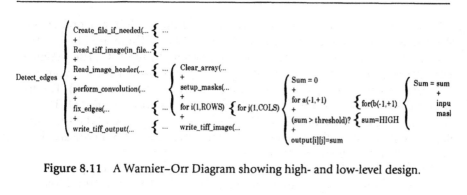

Figure 8.11 A Warnier–Orr Diagram showing high- and low-level design.

8.4 DESIGN AND PROCESS

At this point in the chapter, readers may be disenchanted with the concept of design as I have described it. This sounds like the classic waterfall process where the requirements are 100% complete before design begins, and the design is 100% complete before the coding begins. I don't believe that is the way people perform the requirements and design tasks in real life. We describe it that way because these activities should take place. The description is given only to provide the reader an idea of the nature of the tasks.

I discussed the various processes in Chapter 6, where I mentioned the strict waterfall as well as iterative and evolutionary processes. The agile methods mostly fell into the evolutionary processes. One theme of the agile methods is to evolve the product with a series of cycles. Each cycle, however, contains all the basic phases of requirements, design, implementation, test, etc. It is possible, and I recommend it, to evolve the requirements documentation and the design documentation while evolving the product. Also remember that such documentation does not always have to be in the form of traditional documents. Videotapes, web pages, cards on the wall, etc. are valid forms of documentation.

The design activities of the agile methods received much attention in the late 1990s and early 2000s. Ambler (Ambler, 2001 etc.) has written extensively about agile modeling. The main concept is that the design will change in each cycle of product evolution. That is the hardest thing for some designers to accept. They are accustomed to designing a product once and moving on to the next product. The agile methods, extreme programming in particular, emphasize changing the design as the customer and developers learn more information. This is called "refactoring."

I feel that some of the disagreement on "changing the design" and "designing once" comes from a misunderstanding of terms. In refactoring, a programmer may think of a simpler method to implement a module. He changes that code and is finished. The module behaves in the same manner as before, but it is different inside. This is redesigning "in the small," and it is not a complete high-level redesign of the product every week.

The evolving design in agile methods comes from two fundamental principles found in extreme programming (Fowler, 2001). These are (1) "do the simplest thing possible" and (2) "you aren't going to need it." The designer designs the simplest module that can pass the test written for it (recall the concept of writing the tests before writing the code from Chapter 6). The resulting design is not flexible, but that flexibility may not be needed. That is the point of the second principle. The designer does not spend the time and effort to create a flexible and reusable design when one is not necessary. That adds speed and efficiency to the process.

The agile form of design doesn't work for everyone and every product. As stated in Chapter 6, each particular agile method, like any method, has its limitations. Once way to combine traditional and agile design is to first create a high-level design that contains few details. The team fills in the details during each cycle of product evolution. This allows them to design modules that are simple. It also permits them to refactor modules at any time.

8.5   DESIGNING WITH COTS

People often use COTS (commercial off the shelf) products when developing systems. As personal computers became accepted in business, people realized that using them and their software in systems could save money. The developers were taking advantage of the marketplace. Software companies were selling many thousands of copies of their products, so they could amortize the development cost. System developers could buy a host of good products at a low price instead of writing all the code themselves. Why write an operating system for a million dollars when you could buy one for a hundred dollars? The U.S. federal government pushed the idea of using COTS in systems in the mid-1990s. The government wasn't the only organization adopting the craze to use COTS.

In the late 1990s, people began to discuss how using COTS was not always a good idea. Below are listed several of the problem areas with designing a system that employs COTS products.

Change. COTS products change often. Most software companies will release a new version of their product once a year, and some will do so more often than that (Brownsword et al., 2000). These short life spans can be a major problem with a system you design (Tracz, 2000). Sometimes, the COTS product changes between the time you finish your design and release your product. The short life span is critical if you are building a system that you want to last for more than two years. You will have to make updates to your system each year. Sometimes, the cost of these updates will equal your initial development cost.

Control. Users of COTS products do not control them (Brownsword et al., 2000; Alford, 2000). The software companies that develop the COTS products will change them when they want to and make the changes that they want. Many system developers have felt that they would be able to influence the software companies as to what changes went into the COTS product and when. The problem is that you are not a big enough customer to have such influence (Tracz, 2000). Let me personally emphasize this. The U.S. Department of Defense (DoD) is the single largest consumer of software and other IT products in the world, yet it is not a big enough customer to influence any but the smallest software companies.

Dependencies. COTS products depend on other COTS products (Brownsword et al., 2000). The other products must be present and must be installed in exactly the right directories. A change in one of these other COTS products could break the COTS product you need. If you don't change the supporting COTS product, some other supporting product may break. It is easy to be chasing these changes around in circles. Another factor in this is that many COTS products, like a personal computer, are not standard. There are differences in the details of personal computers. I have worked on projects in which we had to replace a personal computer and the replacement did not work. There was enough difference in the computers so that our application would not run. I have been on projects in which one personal computer worked, but another would not. The second computer would be the same model from the same manufacturer and even have a serial number off by just one number. That did not matter, as something was different enough to break our system.

Requirements. COTS products are made to satisfy a large market. They do a little of what everyone wants, so they probably won't meet your specific requirements (Tracz, 2000). This brings about a number of trade-offs. You must decide if the cost savings is worth not meeting requirements.

Licenses. A startling factor about COTS software is that you do not buy it. Instead, you buy a license to use it (Tracz, 2000). The license policies of various software companies can be quite restrictive. I worked on a project where the O&M people wanted to erase the disk of a laptop computer every six months, reformat the disk, and install the software again. The license policies of several software companies forbid this. The workaround was costly.

Some Suggestions. There are various things to do that ease some of the problems with COTS products. Alford (Alford, 2000) suggests (1) purchasing technical information on the product, (2) purchasing support from the software company, or (3) purchasing modification support from the software company. Another tactic is to test the COTS product just like testing software you write yourself (Tracz, 2000). These practices will cost money and time, and the reason for using COTS was to save money and time. Finally, Voas (Voas,

1998) suggests writing your own software instead of using COTS products. He encourages people to (1) write software in the form of reusable components and (2) write other software that integrates those components. If you use COTS software, you will perform step (2) to integrate the COTS. The idea is to write your components so you will have control over them.

When COTS Still Makes Sense. In spite of the above problems, there are still many situations where designing COTS into a system is a good idea. The following are some of these situations.

- *Quick turnaround.* You need to build your system quickly. Buy existing software components and integrating them can be done quickly.
- *Short lifetime.* You know that you will not be using your system for more than one year. Hence, you will not be hurt by the frequent updates that the software companies perform on their products.
- *Disposable systems.* You will use your system a few times and dispose of it. This occurs when systems comprise COTS software and hardware. The users take a system to the field, use it in a unique situation, and the system is no longer usable. This occurs relatively infrequently, but it does occur.
- *Little or no training budget.* If your organization does not train its users, COTS products are a good choice. The users already know how to use common applications because they used them in school or at home. Designing these applications into your systems lessens the need for training.
- *Large Operations and Management (O&M) budget.* If you have a large O&M budget, you can afford to update your system as often as the software companies update their COTS products. Since the O&M infrastructure and budget are in place, the initial low cost of COTS products fits well.

8.6 CONFIGURATION MANAGEMENT

As I mentioned earlier, design crosses three baselines. The design solves the problem stated in the requirements—nothing more, nothing less—so the design must be traceable to requirements and vice versa. That is, every entity in the design must correspond to a requirements item. The *functional* baseline captures the requirements in the *Software Requirements Specification* (SRS). The SRS is a statement of the problem, but it also contains elements of design in the form of constraints. More important, the requirements baseline points to everything in the other two design baselines. If something in a design baseline cannot be traced back to the requirements baseline, it should be deleted. A tool to help confirm this tracing is the requirements verification traceability matrix discussed later. If the design does not satisfy every requirement, it is incomplete. If it provides capabilities not required, it is bloated and must be trimmed.

The second baseline is the *allocated* baseline, which contains the high-level design—the major elements of the software architecture. This baseline allocates or assigns the software requirements to these major elements. Sample high-level elements include the GUI (graphical user interface), the operating system, the output processor, the number crunchers, and so on. The degree of detail in the high-level design stops here.

The third baseline is the *design* baseline. This contains the low-level or detailed design—the modules, subroutines, and internals of subroutines. The designers fill in all the details of the elements listed in the high-level design. They must include every detail the programmers will need to write the software. The individual requirements allocated to the high-level design elements flow down to these details.

Because design crosses multiple baselines, it is easy to become confused about what goes where. What types of people should be on each CCB? Should you have one design document or one each for the allocated and design baselines?

8.6.1 Configuration Control Boards

The requirements baseline is controlled by the *functional CCB*. Typical members are customers and senior managers—those who decide what the software should provide to the organization.

The *allocated CCB* comprises senior developers. These senior people are the ones who allocate the requirements to large design elements. Not many designers are involved at this point because there is little design work. The experience and expertise required is great. As discussed earlier, sometimes customers want to be involved in design. If this is the case, a customer representative should be on the CCB.

The *design CCB* comprises the senior designers who sit on the allocated baseline CCB as well as other designers. The other designers are the ones who designed the details into the large design elements. The volume of design work has expanded at this level while the expertise required has diminished. Again, there may be some customers working with the designers. If so, one or two of them should sit on this CCB.

8.6.2 Design Documents

A common question concerning the high- and low-level designs and their associated baselines is whether to put the two designs in one document or two. It would be nice to have two design documents to emphasize the separation of the two baselines and make it easier for the CM staff to keep them under control, but this is often not cost-effective. I find that during a software project, there are enough documents to write, track, and control. Consolidating the two design baselines into one document—the *Software Design Description* (described later)—reduces the count by one. Indeed, IEEE-Std-1016, as well as most others, prescribes only one SDD.

Combining two design baselines into one document usually takes the form of having a preliminary and final version of the SDD. The preliminary version holds the high-level design. If you use the IEEE's standard, the SDD will have holes in it or TBDs (to be determineds). You complete the final version by adding in the low-level details to fill in these holes.

Take care that the final version does not change the high-level design information contained in the preliminary version. The only differences between the two versions should be the amount of detail. Changing high-level information is an unauthorized change of the allocated baseline. Only the allocated baseline CCB can do that.

8.6.3 The CM Plan

Placing the design into the proper baselines requires following the CM plan's process, as you did when you put the requirements, project plan, and risk management information into the functional baseline (see Chapters 5, 6, and 7). Be patient with the people and resolve to follow the process so that the product's integrity will be guaranteed. Deviations from the process, no matter how well meaning, will lead to bad results.

The CM process becomes more of a challenge as the project moves into design. The project is moving forward in time and growing in cost. Changes to requirements during the requirements phase add cost to the project because work had to be repeated. That repeated work, however, had a relatively low cost. It meant altering the requirements baseline alone.

Requirements changes during the design activities mean changing two or three baselines. The repeated work and its cost are much higher here. As mentioned in Chapter 2, a requirements change means the high-level design must change, and that ripples down to a change in the low-level design. Three CCBs must examine and approve the changes.

The CM staff can help you trace the changes. Someone, usually a customer, requests a change to the requirements baseline. The CM staff traces the changed requirement to the major design elements that were allocated to the original requirement. Use your planning skills to estimate the time and money cost needed to change the allocated baseline. The CM staff next traces the high-level design change to the low-level design change in the design baseline. Estimate the cost to make that change.

Now you, representatives of the three CCBs, and the executive sponsor must decide, on the basis of the cost of the desired change, if the added value justifies the extra cost. This is a difficult decision and not one that the CM process can resolve for you. It does, however, make everything visible so that you can make an informed decision. You are not stranded in the middle of competing factions in a no-win situation. The CM plan tells you the process to follow, the products to gather, and the people to inform.

This process also works for those last-minute changes the customer wants. You can fall back on the no-exceptions strategy, but that is easier said than done. You will come under enormous pressure as the project progresses because each day it becomes more costly to make a change. Customers wanting that "one more change" do not see this; they want what they want.

As I described earlier, your people skills are critical during this stage. You must explain or teach the CM process without appearing patronizing. You must be firm without appearing stubborn. You must be flexible without appearing weak. In short, you must call on all your resources to do what is right for the good of the project and everyone involved.

8.6.4 Tracing Requirements

If the design does not meet a requirement, it is incomplete. A tool to help ensure completeness is a requirements verification traceability matrix (RVTM), a simple table that lists every requirement, the design element(s) that satisfies the requirement, and what part of the system test will validate that the software meets the requirement correctly. This tool was introduced in Chapter 6 on requirements.

Figure 8.12 shows a sample RVTM, which you and the CM staff typically create during the design development stage. The first column lists the numbers of the functional (FR#) and performance (PR#) requirements. We filled in these columns when listing the requirements. The second column lists the design element responsible for satisfying the requirement.

The third column states which code unit(s) (subroutine, method, etc.) will implement the requirement. The project manager will complete this column

Requirement	Design Element	Code Unit	Code Unit Test Element	Design Test Element	Requirement Test Element
FR1	Command interpreter			DTE1	RTE3
FR2	text reader			DTE4	RTE2
FR3	text formatter			DTE3	RTE4
...	...			...	...
PR1	Operating system			DTE6	RTE6
PR2	text data store			DTE7	RTE7
PR3	windows package			DTE2	RTE1
...	...			...	...

Figure 8.12   A sample RVTM.

during the coding phase of the project. The fourth column lists the test that will verify the code unit, and the project manager will complete it as those tests are written. The fifth column lists what part of the system test will verify the proper functioning of the design element. The last column shows what part of the system test will validate that the software meets the requirement correctly. The project manager and the CM staff are responsible for the RVTM. The CM staff controls it as part of the allocated (high-level) or low-level design baseline.

8.7   STANDARDS: WRITING THE SDD

The chosen design solution must be documented so that people can review, discuss, and improve it. As mentioned earlier, the design is described in a *Software Design Description*, which shows how the software will be structured to satisfy the requirements given in the SRS. This is a representation or model of the software. It must be sufficiently detailed for the programmers to write the needed software.

The SDD may be one or two documents as discussed earlier. Make this decision at the start of the project and inform everyone. Tell the designers how to split the baselines into two documents or how to keep them separate in one document.

Those writing the SDD should review IEEE-Std-1016 (IEEE, 1998). They need not follow the standard slavishly, but it is a good tutorial on what should be in the document. It can help you ensure that the SDD is complete.

8.7.1   *Contents*

The IEEE standard centers the design description around *entities*, or parts of the software system. A design entity is distinct design element that stands alone and can be tested alone. Entities exist at all levels of abstraction and can contain other entities. Every individual square in Figure 8.1, for example, is an entity. An entity can be a function, data structure, object, or class. The SDD describes entities by listing their properties and the relationships among them. It uses a set of 10 standard attributes for every entity, as shown in Figure 8.13. Attributes are characteristics or statements of fact about the entity that answer certain questions. The collection of answers is a complete description of the entity.

Identification is the name of the entity. It lets people refer to it without confusion. *Type* describes the kind of entity such as a subsystem, data structure, or class. *Purpose* tells why the entity exists. Design entities exist to satisfy requirements in the SRS. This attribute should point to the SRS; if it cannot, the design entity should be removed. The identification, type, and purpose attributes are high-level design information.

. Identification
. Type
. Purpose
. Function
. Subordinates
. Dependencies
. Interface
. Resources
. Processing
. Data

Figure 8.13   Set of attributes for each design entity.

Function tells what the entity does. If the entity is a function or group of functions, this attribute lists the input, process, and output. If it is a data entity, function describes the type of data it holds. *Subordinates* lists all the entities contained by this entity. The function and subordinates attributes are both high- and low-level design. During high-level design, the designers know the basic function of an entity and that it will call out subordinates. The details of the data and processing are not known. They are TBDs during high-level design and filled in during low-level design.

Dependencies describes the relationships this entity has with other entities. This entity may use or be used by other entities. Structure charts or object-oriented diagrams are good for depicting these dependencies. *Interface* describes how other entities interact with this one. These include calling methods and sequences or timing and protocols. It specifies the input and output parameters of calls, including their ranges, formats, and error codes and conditions. If the entity is a user interface, this attribute describes the fields or shows the screen prototypes. The dependencies and interface attributes are both high-level and low-level design. In contrast to the function and subordinates attributes, the team will know most of this information during high-level design.

Resources describes the items or resources used by the entity that are external to the software system being described. Software systems at work do not stand alone. They use code libraries, class libraries, operating system services, and hardware (notably disks, printers, and screens). This attribute details how, when, and why the entity uses these external resources. The resources attribute is both high-level and low-level design.

Processing has the greatest level of detail of all the attributes. It provides the rules the entity uses to achieve its function—the algorithm. As such, it provides insight into the function attribute. The processing attribute is both high-level and low-level design.

The last attribute, *data*, provides the nouns corresponding to the verbs of the processing attribute. It provides the greatest level of detail of the data in or used by the entity. The data attribute is both high-level and low-level design.

The SDD should contain every attribute for every entity. It is acceptable for an attribute to be "none."

8.7.2   Organization

The SDD must be accessible to a variety of users, each with a different perspective. Programmers are the most obvious users, but managers, testers, CM staff members, and customers also have reason to read and use the SDD.

The easiest form of organization for the SDD is to list each design entity with its 10 attributes. However, although this classic database approach is easy to write, it is not easy to read. As the number of entities grows, the SDD users will find it increasingly difficult to find the information they need.

IEEE Std-1016 accommodates users by providing four design views in the SDD. Each view is a subset of the entity attributes. Adding the four views provides the same information as listing all attributes for all entities. However, the information is easier for different users to find.

The four views are decomposition description, dependency description, interface description, and detail description. Figure 8.14 shows one organization of the design views and the attributes included in each view. Appendix A contains a sample SDD that uses a processor model, a task model, a structure chart, data dictionaries, and process specifications to present various views. These illustrations are from the structured analysis and design method presented in Appendix C.

The *decomposition description* shows how the designers divided or decomposed the software system into subsystems much like Figure 8.1. Each entity is identified by name, type, purpose, and basic function. These attributes describe the entity in general. The subordinates of each entity are also included. The decomposition description is a high-level view that is particularly useful for managers who need only this level of detail. It also has the detail and information the CM staff needs as they trace through baselines.

The *dependency description* describes the relationships among the entities. Its dependencies and resources attributes tell which entities need what other entities and external resources. This is a key view when considering changes to this or related CM baselines. A change to one entity may require changes to any other entities that use it or are used by it. The same is true of changes in external resources.

The *interface description* gives the external view of every entity through the interface attribute, which contains all the information needed to use the entity. Programmers use these external interfaces to write program calls to the entities. Testers use them to write test drivers. Designers use the interface attribute to design the internal details of each entity. If the SDD is split into high-level and low-level designs, this description will be the major part of the high-level description.

Design View	Entity Attributes
Decomposition Description	Identification Type Purpose Function Subordinates
Dependency Description	Identification Type Purpose Dependencies Resources
Interface Description	Identification Function Interfaces
Detail Description	Identification Processing Data

Figure 8.14 Recommended design views for the SDD.

The *detailed design* gives the internal view of every entity through the processing and data attributes. Programmers need this view to write the software. Testers can also use it to write white-box or structural tests. If the SDD is split into high-level and low-level designs, this description will be the major part of the low-level part.

Just as with requirements, a database program can help track the design. Large software systems will have hundreds and thousands of design entities with 10 attributes each. The report writing capability of a database package can easily put the right attributes into the four views. Edit the design through the database and let it write most of the SDD. Use a database specialist to help with these tasks.

Figure 8.15 is an outline or table of contents for an SDD. The first two sections are similar to the IEEE documents described in previous chapters. The final four sections contain the views just described.

8.8 KEY THOUGHTS IN THIS CHAPTER

Design builds the correct system correctly. For that reason, it is just as important as requirements. The main design tasks are to create solutions, select a

1. Introduction
1.1 Purpose
1.2 Scope
1.3 Definitions and Acronyms

2. References

3. Decomposition Description
3.1 Module Decomposition
3.1.1 Module 1 Description
3.1.2 Module 2 Description
3.2 Concurrent Process Decomposition
3.2.1 Process 1 Description
3.2.2 Process 2 Description
3.3 Data Decomposition
3.3.1 Data Entity 1 Description
3.3.2 Data Entity 2 Description

4. Dependency Description
4.1. Intermodule Dependencies
4.2 Interprocess Dependencies
4.3 Data Dependencies

5. Interface Description
5.1 Module Interface
5.1.1 Module 1 Description
5.1.2 Module 2 Description
5.2 Process Interface
5.2.1 Process 1 Description
5.2.2 Process 2 Description

6. Detailed Design
6.1 Module Detailed Design
6.1.1 Module 1 Detail
6.1.2 Module 2 Detail
6.2 Data Detailed Design
6.2.1 Data Entity 1 Detail
6.2.2 Data Entity 2 Detail

Figure 8.15   Outline of the SDD.

best solution, and document the chosen design. Designs must trace back to requirements; if they do not, they are either incomplete or bloated.

Balancing the 3Ps is difficult in design because like all creative processes, it does not lend itself well to procedure. Design depends more on the people than any other activity. Choose your design procedures wisely.

Design may cause many frustrations, but there are techniques to reduce them. Experience, iteration, and abstraction can help you manage creativity. Iteration means design, review, and redesign; abstraction lets you divide and conquer.

Carefully manage customers who want to participate in design. Don't rush from requirements into design. Make your design verifiable with a structure that uses loosely coupled, highly cohesive modules. Information hiding and modularity separate difficult parts of the design and make maintenance easier.

Designers should make every attempt to create designs that can be reused on different projects. First and foremost, set reusability as a project goal. Peel away the layers of the problem to discover its core; extend the core elements to make them more general purpose. Do not let the goal of design reuse stifle creativity.

The 3Ps also come into play as the team and customers evaluate different designs and select the best one. Visibility techniques are mostly about expressing the design in words and diagrams. Base the design choice on criteria established before the design process begins. Establish criteria and weights, expand each criterion, and use decision tables to make and document decisions.

Use software diagrams to express designs. Use only diagrams that are appropriate to design; avoid using requirements diagrams. HIPO and Warnier–Orr diagrams are excellent for expressing all levels of design detail.

Design crosses three configuration management baselines. Early design, the type that necessarily begins during the requirements stage, is captured in the functional baseline. High-level design is in the allocated baseline, and detailed design is in the design baseline. A requirements traceability matrix is a powerful tool to help trace the requirements from the requirements baseline through the allocated baseline down to the design baseline.

The final step in design is to document the chosen design in a *Software Description Document*. IEEE-Std-1016 can help ensure that your SDD includes all the required information in the most accessible form for the different types of people who must find and use the information.

REFERENCES

L. Alford, "Supporting Commercial Software," *Crosstalk*, September 2000, pp. 13–16.

S. Ambler, "Debunking Modeling Myths, *Software Development*, August 2001, pp. 51–53.

S. Ambler, "Tools and Evidence," *Software Development*, May 2002, pp. 65–66.

F. Brooks, Jr., *The Mythical Man-Month*, Addison-Wesley, Reading, MA, 1975.

L. Brownsword, P. Oberndorf, and C. Sledge, "An Activity Framework for COTS-Based Systems," *Crosstalk*, September 2000, pp. 8–12.

Structured Analysis and System Specification, Yourdon Press, Englewood Cliffs, NJ, 1979.

R. E. Fairley, *Software Engineering Principles*, McGraw-Hill, New York, 1985.

R. G. Fichman and C. F. Kemerer, "Object Technology and Reuse: Lessons from Early Adopters," *Computer*, October 1997, pp. 47–59.

M. Fowler, "Is Design Dead?" *Software Development*, April 2001, pp. 42–46.

E. Gamma et al., *Design Patterns, Elements of Reusable Object-Oriented Software*, Addison-Wesley, Reading, MA, 1995.

T. Gilb, *Principles of Software Engineering Management*, Addison Wesley, Reading, MA, 1988.

J. Herbselb and R. Grinter, "Architectures, Coordination, and Distance: Conway's Law and Beyond," *IEEE Software*, September October 1999, pp. 63–70.

D. A. Higgins, *Data Structured Software Maintenance, The Warnier–Orr Approach*, Dorset House Publishing, New York, 1986.

J. Highsmith, "Adaptive Management: Patterns for the E-Business Era, *Cutter IT Journal*, September 1999, pp. 24–30.

IEEE, ANSI/IEEE Std 1016-1998, *IEEE Recommended Practice for Software Design Descriptions*, IEEE Press, New York, 1998.

A. Jarvis, V. Crandall, and C. Snow, "Who is to Blame for the Y2K and Similar Bugs," *Crosstalk*, September 1999, pp. 23–27.

A. Kolawa, "Automating the Development Process," *Software Development*, July 2000, pp. 46–48.

S. McConnell, *Code Complete*, Microsoft Press, Redmond, WA, 1993.

S. McConnell, "Missing in Action: Information Hiding," *IEEE Software*, March 1996, pp. 127–128.

D. Parnas, "Why Software Jewels are Rare," *Computer*, February 1996, pp. 57–60.

D. Phillips, "Information Hiding in C via Modular Programming," *The C/C++ Users Journal*, January 1998, pp. 57–60.

W. Tracz, "Architectural Issues, Other Lessons Learned in Component-Based Software Development," *Crosstalk*, January 2000, pp. 4–7.

J. Voas, "COTS Software: The Economical Choice?" *IEEE Software*, March April 1998, pp. 16–19.

E. Yourdon, *Modern Structured Analysis*, Yourdon Press, Englewood Cliffs, NJ, 1989.

R. Zahniser, "Design By Walking Around," *Communications of the ACM*, October 1993, pp. 114–123.

Chapter 9

Integration and Testing

Integration is the process of combining software parts to form a complete software system. There are many ways to do this, and all include a form of testing. Software parts that work individually do not always work when combined. Testing is necessary to ensure that the whole works as well as the parts.

Testing is the last step in most projects. If two weeks are left in the project's schedule, and the project plan calls for six weeks of testing, developers will skip four weeks of testing so that they can end the project on time. How many times have managers said "Don't worry if we get behind schedule, we'll make it up in testing"?

This is one of the worst things you can do to the product. Testing proves that the software does what it is *supposed to do* correctly. It essentially breaks the software so that the team can fix it. It does not always result in error-free software, nor should it. Software does not always need to be error-free. Testing shows that the software works as well as desired. If everyone could do their job perfectly, it would not be needed. However, everyone on the project is human and therefore has likely made at least one mistake.

Integration and testing are all about the 3Ps. The project manager must select testing techniques that consider people, process, and product. Emotions can run high during testing. Programmers have invested part of themselves in the software and now someone is attempting to break it to discover its weaknesses. If errors mean a personal loss, programmers will fix tests so that errors are not found. Everyone can become stressed as they await the results of integration (what if it doesn't all fit together?) and testing, and they can become impatient with the testing process (haven't we found enough errors?).

Visibility is related closely to testing. If the developers have been using visibility techniques, it is relatively simple to determine if the software does

The Software Project Manager's Handbook. By Dwayne Phillips.
ISBN 0-471-67420-6 © 2004 IEEE Computer Society

what it should. This is because requirements and testing have a one-to-one correspondence; each visible requirement leads to one test.

Configuration management plays a surprisingly large role in integration and testing. Test artifacts span all the major baselines of a project. Tests have a one-to-one correspondence with all development stages. Test artifacts belong in the baseline that corresponds to each stage. The CM plan guides the project manager in keeping everything under control. The requirements verification traceability matrix (described in the last chapter) helps keep track of everything.

Finally, as in other stages, standards are useful for ensuring that the documentation—in this case test documentation—is complete. Each test should have a minimum of three documents, but some tests can require up to ten.

9.1 SOME I&T MYTHS

In this chapter, I depart somewhat from the organization of previous chapters, which began with the 3Ps principle. I do this because I believe integration and testing (I&T) is sufficiently misunderstood to warrant a rather detailed clarification. Below are some common misconceptions about the I&T development stage.

Myth 1: Testing is about running the software until you get the right answer. Most of the software community (including me for most of my career) has taken or continues to take this narrow view. In this type of testing, no one looks at the software until a test phase at the end of a project. You then have a flurry of test, fix, fix new errors introduced, test, fix, and so on. Unfortunately, there are so many buried errors that the test–fix routine spirals downward and often does not end until there is no time left in the project. Iterative testing is fine if some errors are steadily diminishing. In fact, you should plan for iterative testing, but not the kind that fixes two errors and introduces three more.

Myth 2: Thorough testing is too expensive for most projects. The traditional (read "wrong") testing approach just described requires from 50% to 75% of the development cost. People who have experienced this on several projects correctly point out that it is too expensive. What they fail to see, however, is that there is a wrong way and a right way to do testing. The wrong way causes the downward spiral just described. Sadly, because I've spiraled down that road too many times, I've learned that this type of testing is too expensive monetarily and emotionally. No wonder people who do this type of testing want to minimize the time they do it.

The right type of testing is what I call "looking at" the software. This approach, or IDEA testing (explained in a minute), spreads testing and reduces its cost by doing more work earlier in the project. The right way spends $25 early in the project and spends $50 on traditional (end-of-project) testing. The wrong way saves the $25, but spends $200 on end-of-project testing. The $25 spent the right way saves $125. This means the right way of testing actually makes money.

The "looking at" approach to testing has several dimensions that form the IDEA acronym: inspection, demonstration, execution, and analysis. *Inspection* means to read the source code. *Demonstration* means to run the software and watch it. *Execution* is running special test drivers to check for specifics. *Analysis* checks the software against hand-computed answers or answers from other computers. But even IDEA will not work well if you use it only at the end of the project. Use good processes throughout development. People analyze, design, and write software, making mistakes all along the way. If you inspect your requirements, designs, and source code as you go, you reduce a large percentage of errors. And, as the previous chapters emphasize, this means making these items visible so that others can study and improve them.

Myth 3: Testing ensures quality. Testing is mistakenly equated with quality assurance. In the best interpretation, an error-free test might prove that the software built is perfect, but it might also prove that the test is not suitable. However, it does not ensure that the right software has been built, which is a major quality component. That type of quality starts with requirements.

Myth 4: Testing is always a mechanical process. Many developers tend to think that testing is a "no-brainer." This is simply not true. First, finding errors depends on the oracle assumption—someone somewhere knows the correct answer. This is true in many common software applications (people know the Fourier transform of basic functions and the correct interest on a car loan), but how do you test software for applications where the correct answer is not known or impossible to calculate without the developed software? How do you test a weather-predicting program? How do you calculate the answer that only the world's most powerful supercomputer can produce?

Second, errors are not logical, disciplined, or systematic. What happens to the software when someone spills coffee on the keyboard? Does the random flood of characters just hang the system or does it prompt the system to start deleting important data? What happens when someone trips on the power cord and kills the computer? What about when characters are typed in numeric fields? Testers must anticipate a range of errors and test accordingly.

Myth 5: Error-free software is always the testing goal. We all want error-free software (that's what we were taught in college), but this is rarely the goal at work. Test until the error rate is below a threshold, not necessarily until there are zero errors. Think about the big picture and consider the costs and benefits. Microsoft rarely releases error-free business software, but most users don't care if the word processor crashes once a year. It is another matter if a crashed software system will cost a business $50,000 an hour. If you are developing a safety-critical system, such as a flight controller, and a failure will kill hundreds of people, zero errors, or at least a very small number, must be the goal.

Myth 6: Testing is a technical endeavor. Testing is an activity that supports the business. Again, this relates to looking at the big picture. The business managers of an organization decide when to ship the software (Rothman, 2000). The testers tell the business managers what type of testing they have performed and what they have found in the software. The business managers decide if the product is ready to ship. Many testers mistakenly feel they are responsible for the quality of the product that is shipped. Often, we succumb to pressure, real or imagined, to tell managers that all is well regardless of the situation. Testers need the courage to tell the truth and the contentment to live with the decision that business managers make.

Test completion is always a moving target because new errors are introduced during testing as programmers attempt to fix the errors the tests discovered. Some projects use "bebugging" or error seeding (putting bugs in as opposed to taking them out). Bebugging occurs after programming and before testing and indicates how many real errors are still in the software. Suppose you seed or insert 20 errors and testing finds 10 of the seeded errors and 30 other errors. You found half the seeded errors, so you probably found half the real errors. Continue testing until you find a satisfactory percentage of errors (then remove the rest of the seeded errors).

9.2   MANAGING THE 3Ps: PEOPLE

The "people" here are the developers and independent testers. It is easy for these two groups to become antagonistic. The programmers who wrote the software may take any errors found as a weakness in their creative abilities. The testers may become enamored with tests to find the last few bugs. If you have been practicing visibility techniques from the beginning of the project, errors should be accepted as part of the natural process of developing software. However, with some personalities, especially very creative people, resentment will be inevitable.

It is vital to keep the team working as a team. The programmers should know they make mistakes and not see them as personal problems. (Recall the "I make mistakes" part of the annual pizza lunch in Chapter 4.) Everyone, however, lapses and takes offense. The testers must realize that their actions can be interpreted as insults. Remind everyone how their actions and reactions can hurt one another and the project. Keep the project goal in everyone's mind. No one succeeds or fails alone.

Another morale issue is false optimism. Early testing finds many errors quickly. The team can be fooled into thinking that this rate of error finding will continue and that all errors will be uncovered soon. Figure 9.1 proves otherwise. The solid curve, the actual rate of finding errors, has a high positive slope early on. The dotted diagonal line extends the slope optimistically until it intersects point E—the time when you would have expected to find all the errors. That time, however, occurs much later, as the solid curve indicates. The optimistic line fools us.

Prepare the team early to expect this pattern. Share this figure and explain how the tests find the easy errors first, but after that, progress will slow. Be careful not to let the early, easy success lead to predictions of quick finishes and premature celebration plans.

Morale can be a problem in I&T if the project has used the wrong testing approach and you are mired in a test–fix–test–fix situation (see Myth 2 above). The project should be finished, but it isn't. The programmers are tired and dejected because instead of working on a new project, they are trapped in an endless cycle of error-catching in the old project.

As project manager, you need to step in and redefine success and failure. Use the weekly success strategy outlined in Chapter 4 and gain speed by slowing down. Let a programmer analyze the error he is fixing and hold a review to let him explain it to his peers. Do not attempt a fix until everyone agrees with the analysis. This is a requirements activity. Hold another review when the programmer is ready to propose a solution. Once everyone agrees with the approach, let him code it. Review the code before testing.

These reviews will point out the reported error as well as several unreported errors. Those extra errors will be there. If they weren't, the project would not be in trouble. With this method, the project team can count down to the predetermined acceptable number of errors. You stop the fix-two-errors-find-three-more cycle. The programmers succeed day by day and the morale problem disappears. Success breeds success.

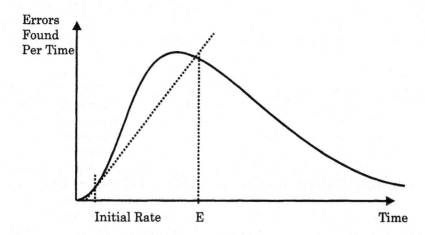

Figure 9.1 Rate of finding errors.

9.3 MANAGING THE 3Ps: PROCESS

The testing process can be full of surprises. The project manager must be alert to common testing problems and encourage the team to follow the IDEA approach to testing. Glass (Glass, 2002) has noted three underlying characteristics of testing and related activities. First, error removal, which is the final goal of testing, is a terribly complex activity. It consumes time, energy, and money, and we don't yet have an optimal approach to this problem. Second, there are many types of testing (I will describe some later) and these are necessary prerequisites for error removal, but even when we use them all we are still lacking in finding errors. Finally, inspections (code reviews and such as discussed earlier in the book) are an important supplement to testing. Inspections are one part of the IDEA approach.

9.3.1 Common Testing Problems

A project typically encounters at least one of four common testing problems:

1. *Unrealistic planning.* This is a failure to account for the inevitability of mistakes. Everyone on the project will make mistakes that will take time to find and correct. Allocate the needed time and people. The most common mistake is not to plan for a second round of testing. You can't test, fix, and move on. Plan to test, fix (with reviews as explained earlier), and test again.

2. *No test policy.* Nothing specifies how testing will accomplish quality on the project. People have their own ideas, which they don't share. This lack of visibility will result in chaos. Write a document or make a poster stating who will do what according to what standards. Place this on-line and in the Management Information Center (see Chapter 4 for more on the MIC).

3. *Mismatch of testing time and the 3Ps.* I touched on this in I&T Myth 5 earlier. Error-free software is rarely the goal at work. Think about the big picture. On one project, I was part of a team developing software for users who were true experts and made few mistakes while using the software. They also had their own staff of programmers to frequently modify the software. We had a high threshold of errors and spent about 1% of our time testing. Given the people, process, and product for that software, extensive testing would have been a waste of resources.

   Identifying and fixing the error-prone modules [McConnell 1996B] can help shorten test time. Most programs usually have a module (subroutine, class, subsystem, and so on) with more than its share of errors. An unusually high rate of errors indicates fundamental problems in the module. If the module has more than 10 errors per thousand lines of code, remove it, throw out the code, redesign the module from scratch, and recode it. This is often costly, but it will save time and money in the long term.

4. *Insufficient testing time.* As I described earlier, if the first phases of the project are behind schedule, the testing time shrinks. If impatient people rule the day, poor products go to the customer, the business suffers, jobs are lost, and families suffer. Cutting corners does not save time or anything else.

9.3.2 IDEA

IDEA (inspection, demonstration, execution, and analysis) is closely related to traditional testing. The demonstration, execution, and analysis (DEA) are the parts that form the traditional concept of testing. Inspection (I) is the added dimension (Phillips 2002).

To understand why, let me revisit the IDEA elements in more detail. Bypassing "I" for the moment, *demonstration* is watching the software run or using it (does it run or crash?). Using a new word processor is a demonstration. The user is not verifying any specific functions or testing the limits of the software; he is just running it. *Execution* employs special drivers to verify specific functions of a piece of software. Testers write the drivers as part of a plan of attack on the software. *Analysis* checks the results of the software against known answers. The answers can be computed by hand or come from a program and computer that produces the known, correct answer. Analysis can also use test driver programs like execution. An example of analysis would be to create a document with 10 known misspelled words. A spell checking program would need to find those 10 words to pass the test.

Inspection is reading the source code. Inspection can find errors that no other method can and is the most efficient testing practice. Watts Humphrey's Personal Software Process (Humphrey, 1995) (see Chapter 6) emphasizes inspection. I did not believe that inspecting source code before compiling it could save time, but working through Humphrey's exercises taught me otherwise.

Computer-assisted testing, such as compiling and executing, often leads us astray. A syntax error points to a specific line in a program and says "here is your error." Sometimes that is correct, but more often than not a problem such as a major logic error is located 10 lines above. The compiler message focuses attention on the line with the syntax error, which acts as a set of blinders to the big problem. Returning to the word processor example, a spell checker focuses attention on the spelling of a word, but in the same sentence you may have "they" instead of "the." You would have to read the entire sentence to discover that.

Proper inspection methods search for and (usually) find all types of errors in software. One pass through the code looks for syntax errors. The next pass examines proper variable types; the next pass logic; the next pass calculations; and so on. People perform inspections and bring their unique experience and intelligence to the table. Computers do not yet have the ability to analyze code the way people can.

Inspection also extends beyond source code and it is the only testing method that can. For example, inspection can find "Easter eggs" (Weinberg, 1995), features a programmer hides in the source code. The Easter egg is activated by an unusual input such as the user pressing the F1 and ESC keys. The input causes the software to take an unusual action such as crediting $1,000,000 to the programmer's Swiss bank account.

Some of you may be wondering why I have put material on inspection in multiple chapters. If so, you probably view inspection, walkthroughs, and the like as pertaining only to completed code. Consider Figure 9.2, which is based on data from real-world projects (McConnell, 1996). You are probably where "most organizations" are. However, as the figure shows, if you use IDEA to catch defects (up to 95%) early on, you will save time. In fact, "testing" in this way can save more development time than any single technique. This is a direct contradiction to how most people view testing.

When you rely on one big test at the end of development instead of using the IDEA concepts throughout, all the errors hit at once, and the developer cannot correct them because they are too intertwined. The best approach at that point is to start over, but that is impossible financially. So, organizations work around the errors and ship the software.

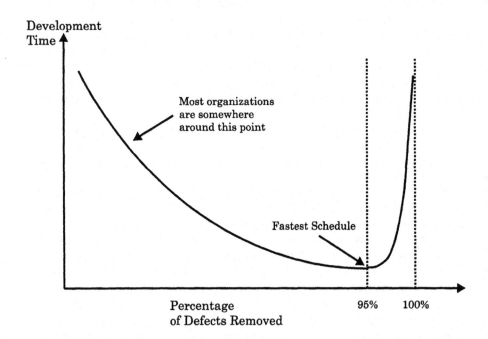

Figure 9.2   How removing defects early on saves time.

Ironically, the best way to speed development is to slow down. Use IDEA in the requirements stage. Analyze requirements using the techniques in Chapter 5 and review your understanding. Design a solution as described in Chapter 8, think about it, iterate, and design again. Code and inspect the code before running the compiler. This methodical approach reduces errors and speeds development.

Cynics will claim "we found the errors, but saved time by not removing them." People remove errors when they can. They leave only the errors that are too hard to fix—those made early in the project and not found until late. Use the IDEA techniques and find and correct errors early. If you can't, keep a record of all errors detected during development and after delivery. Be honest about whether the error was removed or left for someone else to work on at some other time.

Think about people, process, and product. Choose the elements of IDEA that are most appropriate for your people and product and work them into your process as best you can. Learn this technique and apply it to as many items in development as possible. Tom Gilb and Dorothy Graham have evolved a good inspection model (Gilb & Graham, 1993), which I described earlier in Chapter 4 (see also Figure 4.2). Remember, "you get what you inspect, not what you expect" (Conklin, 1996).

9.3.3 Verification and Validation

Verification and validation (V&V) go hand in hand with testing. In fact, if you are following the IDEA approach, you are doing V&V. *Verification* comprises a series of small tests to show that parts of the system are functioning properly. *Validation* comprises a set of tests to show that the entire system is what was desired. Verification answers the question "Did we build the system right?", whereas validation answers the question "Did we build the right system?"

An important aspect of V&V is *independent* verification and validation. IV&V (some read the Roman numerals and call this four and five) means that an outsider, someone who did not design or program the software, verifies the parts and validates the system. I strongly believe in doing both V&V and IV&V because of the dual nature of software testing. If I am testing software I wrote, I want to show the world that it has no errors. If I am testing software written by someone else, I want to break the software—find all the errors. Hiring an outside organization to perform V&V is expensive, but you generally get a higher-quality product.

9.4 VISIBILITY: TESTING TECHNIQUES AND DETAILS

The main job of visibility in testing is to make the weaknesses of the software being developed obvious to the development team. When everyone understands what the test is supposed to accomplish, they are more likely to accept the results and act on them without undue emotion. Visible testing avoids questions like "Where did they get those figures?" or "We never count things like that as errors." Make sure the team understands the tests and their function. Specific testing techniques you are most likely to use include black box, white box, integration, acceptance, and regression testing. Cleanroom testing is also a powerful technique, although it is seldom used.

Black box testing is the most often used because it tests software against its operating environment. *White box* testing tests the internal structure of the software, so it requires detailed knowledge of the software. *Integration* testing occurs when individual software modules are combined or integrated. *Acceptance* testing tests the entire software package. *Regression* testing occurs when correcting errors. This list is by no means exhaustive; I encourage you to read other sources (Myers, 1979; Beizer, 1995; Hetzel, 1988; Kaner, 1993).

9.4.1   Elements of Effective Testing

Take care to use high-quality testing. A test is a form of scientific experiment and it should have certain characteristics to ensure that its results are valid. One is repeatability. Computers are digital devices with discrete levels (1s and 0s). Repeating a software test under the same conditions should yield the same result. If the result changed, it is probably because the test changed. The cause of nonrepeatable tests is lack of visibility (poor documentation, poor plans and procedures, poor record keeping, poor CM). The result of nonrepeatable tests is wasted time. Different test results may cause testers to search for errors that do not exist in the software when in reality the errors are in the test itself.

Use the computer to help with repeatable tests. Computers are good at mundane, tedious, repetitive tasks like this. Write and use test scripts that generate input data, run the data through the software, and compare the result with known answers. Write a test procedure that states exactly how to apply the test script to the software. Test the script and the procedure with different people and situations to ensure that they are correct.

Test scripts are particularly useful for software being developed with a graphical user interface (GUI). The test script can bypass the GUI and exercise the number-crunching routines on a spreadsheet or the spell checker on a word processor. Use CM to save the test scripts and procedures. Once they work, they are priceless. Use a video camera to help test GUIs. Film the testers as they exercise the menus, buttons, and slides on a user interface. Compare these to the "right answer," perhaps a video the users made when they stated their requirements.

Another aspect of quality testing is the use of real-world input and output. These are the correct answers that come from existing systems. Use the test scripts to run the real-world input through the software being developed. The test output should match the real-world output. Take the real input and output from the operational baseline (the current system the users are using). This type of testing will ensure that the new system will not damage the business when it replaces the old system. Again, use CM to keep this data for future testing.

Be creative. Use whatever is available and works to permit repeatable tests. Think about people, process, and product; keep everything visible, and use CM. Testing means nothing if the test is not appropriate. Plan the testing strategy, write the plan (described later), and use it to review and improve your strategy. Write the test procedures. Review them to ensure they cover everything in the plan and are correct. Then, and only then, spend the staff hours to test the software.

Add a statement relating to quality to every statement you make about the product (Weinberg, 2002). Instead of saying, "the interface modules will be ready in three weeks," say, "the interface modules will be ready in three weeks with all the type-1 errors removed and half the type-2 errors still in place." This precise language will not give anyone a false impression about the quality of the product. It removes the ambiguity of the word "ready."

Involve testers early in the project, especially in early design reviews and meetings (Dedolph, 2001). The testers will bring a different perspective to the design process. Most designers know what should be in a product. Testers often know what should not be in a product and how these unwanted features seem to creep in. The testers can help the designers design the product so that it is easier to test. One simple way to design a product that is easier to test is to put each function into a separate module. The testers can check the function by testing that one module. Once it is proven to work, they are done with it. If the functions are mixed together, testing becomes much more difficult and time-consuming. Early participation by the testers also helps to establish a good working relationship that will pay dividends during the testing activities. The testers and designers will be able to communicate better if they know one another.

Testing is time-consuming and expensive. Take the time to do it right. I have seen competent, intelligent people spend millions of dollars because of poorly planned and implemented tests.

9.4.2 Black Box Testing

Black box testing tests the function of software. It treats software as something contained in a black box. How the software does what it does is unknown and unimportant. The only thing that matters is that the software does what it should.

There are many types of black box testing. Here I cover test readiness, error guessing, user profile, boundary values, finite state machine, and cause–effect graphing.

Test readiness. Black box testing should always begin with a test readiness test (sometimes called ad hoc or trial-and-error testing). This answers the question "Is the X function present (ready for testing)?" This question may seem like a waste of time: Function X must be here because we are here to test it. But to testers, building and delivering software is a complex task, and it is easier than you think to omit a function from a delivery. I worked on a project that received a software delivery twice a year. Each delivery contained 200 functional units. The first part of our acceptance test checked for the existence of each one. If all were present, ensuing tests checked the proper functioning of each unit. Missing functions mired the first couple of deliveries. This lapse ended when the producer started running our test readiness test before shipping the software.

Error Guessing. In this test, the tester uses his experience to guess where an error might be. This goes back to the need for creativity and thought during testing, described earlier (see I&T Myth 4). Error guessing comes from the school of hard knocks and should be part of any black box testing.

Risk-Based Testing. Testing is a risk reduction activity (Sherer, 2002) (see Chapter 7 for a description of risk and managing risk). Given some software that has not been tested, there is a high probability that the software contains defects. Testing the software helps find defects to be removed, so it reduces the probability that users will find the defects. All defects are not equal, as some mean much more to users than others. Risk-based testing concentrates on items that are critical to the users (Goldsmith, 1999). Answer the basic questions, "What must work correctly?" and "What cannot fail?" Write that software early in the project and test it thoroughly.

User Profile Testing. Also known as random testing, this procedure focuses on how the users use the software and what errors are important to them. Errors are inevitable. User profile testing asks "Will the errors become evident in normal use and bring grief to the users?" If not, forget about them. This may seem lazy, but it is actually a wise use of resources.

The difficulty in user profile testing is learning what parts of the software the users use all the time and what errors will give them trouble. Once you know this, testers can generate test inputs to test those areas. One method is to work with the state transition diagrams (Poore & Trammel, 1997). These show how the software will transition from one state to another. It is also helpful to have the probabilities of these transitions labeled. For example, a user of a word processor will transition from the edit mode to the file save and open mode more often than to the column setup mode. Therefore, testing the file save and open transition is more important. Another method is to analyze the use-case scenarios (McGregor & Major, 2000; Whittaker, 2000). These will reveal what uses are most important to the users.

Voas (Voas, 2000a, b) proposes a unique way to learn how users use software and what should be tested the most. His method is to have the developer pay an independent lab to insert code in the product that will monitor and store information on usage. The independent lab distributes the modified software to users and then reports to the developer. This information is clean in that it shows how users really use the software and not what the managers of users report. The managers of users often report how they think their employees should use software. These two reports often differ greatly.

Boundary Values Testing. This part of black box testing falls under *equivalence partitioning*, a method to divide or partition the possible input values into meaningful regions. Testing uses one value from each region rather than using several values from one region and ignoring the others. For example, suppose the software simulates water in a chemical plant. Water freezes at 0°C and boils at 100°C, so meaningful partitions are below 0, from 0 to 100, and above 100. Test the software with one value from each partition. If the software works at 12°C, it should also work at 55°C, so don't waste time testing at both places.

Also test the software at the boundaries and one-off boundaries. In the water example, this means testing at 0°C, 100°C, 99°C, –1°C, 1°C, and 101°C. Errors commonly occur at these one-off locations. Finally, test at the highest and lowest theoretical temperatures that water could reach, which is the upper limit in software testing.

Finite State Machine Testing. Most software packages can be considered state machines. They have known conditions or states and they transition between them. This type of testing exercises the transitions from one state to another. For example, each menu in a user interface is a state. While at the main menu, pressing "r" transitions to the report menu state, pressing "a" transitions to the accounts menu state, pressing ESC transitions out of the program, and so on. Test each state and its transition to every other state. Also use invalid inputs (press Alt-r instead of r) to ensure that unwanted transitions do not occur.

Cause–Effect Graphing. In this method, the tester organizes all possible combinations of inputs (causes) and outputs (effects) of a program. It helps organize the concepts in other black box techniques as well, such as equivalence partitioning and finite state machines. In the water example just described, suppose the software also simulated relative humidity, with three ranges or partitions of humidity to go along with the three temperature ranges. There are nine possible combinations of the temperature and humidity partitions, and these nine situations dictate how the software should behave. List the nine causes in a table with nine associated effects. Use the table to create and test for each cause–effect combination. Several causes will produce the same effect. Some causes and effects will be "don't care." Cause-effect graphing is a systematic way to organize test cases. It gives more visibility to the process and helps ensure your testers don't miss something.

9.4.3   White Box Testing

White box testing (sometimes known as clear box testing) tests the software's structure. How the software does what it does (its structure) is known and is important. Elements of importance in white box testing are coverage and branch and condition testing.

Coverage. The ideal is to exercise or cover every statement and every possible path through a program. There are almost an infinite number of paths through a program, however, so the aim of white box testing is to provide the best coverage possible within the constraints of time and money.

Branch and Condition Testing. In branch testing, also called decision testing, the goal is to traverse every path through a program. One way is to draw a flow chart or control chart of the code module. The first test exercises one path through the flow chart. The next test exercises a path through the flow chart that differs from the first. Parts of the two tests may traverse the same path, but some part of the two paths is different. This process continues until the tests have covered every part of the flow chart. Note that this does not cover every possible combination of paths through the flow chart, just every path.

Condition testing is more detailed than branch testing. Suppose a subroutine contains if (a > 0 AND b < 0) then ... else ... This contains two branches (then and else), so branch testing would use two tests to exercise both branches. This contains a compound condition with four possibilities (false–false, false–true, true–false, and true–true), so condition testing would use four tests to exercise this condition.

Look at branch and condition testing. Analyze the structure of code in light of these two processes. Your goal is to test everything without wasting time by repeating test cases.

9.4.4   Combining White Box and Black Box Testing

Black box and white box testing look at the same thing from different perspectives. They are both necessary, but using them independently can waste resources. When testing the lowest-level unit of code, first use code inspection. Next, use black box testing. Then, analyze what parts of the structure the black box test did and did not cover. Use white box techniques to cover those cases.

If you are testing executables delivered to you, white box testing is not possible. Use black box testing with extra diligence and care.

In practice, it is best to alternate between black and white box testing. Figure 9.3 shows how this happens during I&T activities. The left column lists an activity that precedes a test. This runs up the left side of the V-chart (see Part 2 introduction, Chapter 6, and Figure 9.13). It follows the logical code, test, integrate, test, integrate, test, and so on. The center column describes the test performed. Testers commonly test the inside of a unit and then the outside of the unit, and, finally, combine that unit with others to produce a larger unit. The process repeats itself with the larger unit. As the right column shows, this process alternates white box and black box tests.

9.4.5 Integration Testing

Integration testing has five forms—bottom-up, top-down, sandwich, big bang, and build—each of which has its own advantages and disadvantages. As always, consider these processes in light of your people and product. Follow the guidelines on when and how to write test plans and procedures. Figures 9.5 through 9.9 illustrate the different approaches using the simple program in Figure 9.4, in which a main routine calls two subroutines that in turn call other routines.

Preceding Activity	Test	Test Type
Programmer codes subroutine	Test internal structure of subroutine	White box
Tester tests subroutine	Test subroutine	Black box
Combine subroutines into subsystem	Test interfaces of subroutines	White box
Subsystem becomes a unit	Test subsystem	Black box
Combine subsystems into system	Test interfaces of subsystems	White box
Systems becomes a unit	Test the system	Black box

Figure 9.3 Alternating black box and white box testing.

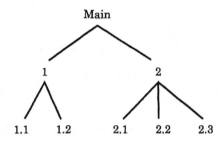

Figure 9.4 The structure chart for the I&T examples.

Bottom-up. In this classic I&T approach, analysis and design break a problem into smaller problems and solutions. The small parts of the solution are written as code modules (subroutine, class, package, and so on), and testing verifies each code module individually. The bottom-up approach combines the modules into subsystems, which are tested; the tested subsystems are combined into larger systems, and they are tested, and so on. Figure 9.5 shows this testing order. The bottom-up process is simple and works well when your people understand the product they are building.

Top-down. Top-down I&T is similar to bottom-up but it starts with a fully tested main routine and works down. Tests add one code module to the main routine and test this combination. The process continues adding individual modules to the program and testing it. Figure 9.6 shows this testing order. Each new integration has a test. The top-down process works when your people are not quite as sure about the product, but the risk is not too high (see Chapter 7 for a discussion of risk and risk management). This process is similar to what many agile methods use.

Sandwich. Sandwich I&T combines the bottom-up and top-down approaches. The bottom-up part combines and tests individual code modules into subsystems. The top-down part tests the main controlling subsystem. The sandwich

1. 1.1
2. 1.2
3. 2.1
4. 2.2
5. 2.3
6. 1.1, 1.2, and 1 together
7. 2.1, 2.2, 2.3, and 2 together
8. All the above with main and test together

Figure 9.5 The bottom-up I&T order for the chart in Figure 9.4.

1. main with stubs for 1 and 2
2. add 1 to main and test together
3. add 2 to above and test together
4. add 1.1 to above and test together
5. add 1.2 to above and test together
6. add 2.1 to above and test together
7. add 2.2 to above and test together
8. Add 2.3 to above and test together

Figure 9.6   The top-down I&T order for the chart in Figure 9.4.

process then adds and tests the bottom-up subsystems one at a time. Figure 9.7 shows this testing order. This straightforward process works well when your people know the product, but the product is too large to use either top-down or bottom-up exclusively (it would be too time-consuming).

Big Bang. The big bang I&T tests each code module individually. The next step combines all the modules at once and tests the whole, as shown in Figure 9.8. The big bang approach is risky. It is also the most efficient process if everything works right the first time. However, this is the exception. Typically, the big bang test reveals so many errors that no one knows where to start. A flurry of confused fixing and testing ensues. Often, the remedy is to stop and go back to the bottom-up approach. I don't recommend the big bang process unless your people know the product exceptionally well.

Build. The build I&T starts with a core system and adds a set of functionally related modules one at a time in a series of builds. This process grows the system's capability in a conservative, low-risk manner. The builds can be short and simple or long and complex. Figure 9.9 illustrates the big bang I&T with

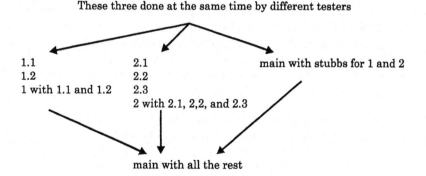

These three done at the same time by different testers

1.1	2.1	main with stubs for 1 and 2
1.2	2.2	
1 with 1.1 and 1.2	2.3	
	2 with 2.1, 2,2, and 2.3	

main with all the rest

Figure 9.7   The sandwich I&T order for the chart in Figure 9.4.

1. main with stubss for 1 and 2
2. 1 with stubbs for 1.1 and 1.2
3. 2 with stubbs for 2.1, 2.2, and 2.3
4. 1.1
5. 1.2
6. 2.1
7. 2.2
8. 2.3
9. 1 with 1.1 and 1.2
10. 2 with 2.1, 2.2, and 2.3
11. main with all the rest

Figure 9.8   The big bang I&T order for the chart in Figure 9.4.

four builds. A large analysis system could begin with a data-collection function. Users would exercise this and collect data for six months. After technical and cultural acceptance, the next build would add data-processing functions. The next build, six months later, would add data-analysis functions. This process is also similar to what many agile methods use.

Because of the recent publicity given to Microsoft's "daily builds" (McCarthy, 1995), many believe that builds are a new technique. In reality, the build process has existed as long as software has existed. The process is an admission that your people are building a product that is not well understood and is therefore difficult. The build process works well in these cases because it allows for learning and for growing the product with a minimum of risk.

9.4.6   Acceptance Testing

The final test in a project is the acceptance test. This is the validation part of V&V, as described earlier. A successful acceptance test means the customer begins to use and find value in the product. The product should be at the agreed-on error threshold (signifying test completion) before the acceptance test begins. In well-run projects, the acceptance test is more like a demonstration or a "look how well we've done" exercise.

Acceptance tests should show the product's capability, stability, resistance, compatibility, and performance, as well as its stress points and structure. *Capability* means the product works correctly once. *Stability* means the product

1. Build 1 - main, 2, and 2.1
2. Build 2 - add 2.2 and 2.3 to build 1
3. Build 3 - add 1 and 1.1 to build 2
4. Build 4 - add 1.2 to build 3

Figure 9.9   The build I&T order for the chart in Figure 9.4.

works correctly again and again. A spell checker should run on an open document over and over without crashing the system. *Resistance* is resistance to failure, which means bad data should not kill the software. Attempting to run a spell checker on a file of the wrong format (an executable file for example) should yield an error message—not a hung system. *Compatibility* means the software interfaces with other system software and hardware. Software typically must fit into existing systems and cultures. *Performance* means the software must be as fast, as small, as accurate, as safe, as portable, and so on, as promised. *Stress* testing finds where the software will break. How many users can simultaneously log onto an operating system before it crashes? This is also known as qualification or *qual* testing. *Structure* testing examines and exercises the system's internal processing logic.

The acceptance test must prove all these to the waiting customer. Give the acceptance test a little extra excitement and showmanship. It is the last test you and your team will see, so you may be tired and feel like getting it over with. It is, however, the first test and demonstration that many customers will see. Do something to excite them about your product so that they will carry that excitement to their workplace and use the software.

9.4.7 Regression Testing

Regression testing begins when users or testers find an error. The error is corrected and leads to a new test case that ensures the error is gone. This new test case becomes part of the software's complete test suite. Future testing includes the test case and ensures that the software does not degenerate or regress to the previous error state.

Actual errors are the basis of regression testing. This is good because regression testing prevents real-world errors from recurring and wasting your time. This is bad because errors already found can take attention away from undetected errors and give a false sense of security. The point of regression testing (and any repeatable test) is to have a set of tests scripts and procedures that test the software. Keep these tests accessible and easy to repeat. Run the tests whenever any change is made to the software. Add cases to the test suite to cover any errors found in or made to the software.

9.4.8 Cleanroom Testing

Cleanroom testing is a complete development process rather than a single testing technique. Its concepts, however, can teach valuable testing techniques as well as ways to specify, design, and write software that is easier to test. Cleanroom testing emphasizes statistical quality control, the absence of test and fix, the mathematical mapping of inputs to outputs, box-structured design, and inspection to produce zero-defect software. People either love it or hate it. I had no use for it until someone explained it in terms I could understand. I hope to do the same here.

Figure 9.10 shows the three teams involved in cleanroom testing and their basic tasks. The *specification team* creates a specification for the software product while breaking the software into increments. Cleanroom testing employs an incremental process in which each increment is 5,000 to 20,000 lines of code. This is an admission that the product is difficult enough, or the quality expected is high enough, to warrant building it in steps.

The *development team* designs and codes an increment using box-structured design and functional verification. They pass the increment along to the *certification team* without once compiling or executing it. This is where opponents of cleanroom testing scoff. Why not use a compiler? Climb out of the academic tower and get back to the real world. My thoughts ran along those lines (still do to some extent), but please read on and consider what cleanroom testing has to offer.

Box-structured design emphasizes breaking the problem into a hierarchy. Each unit or box (probably a subroutine) performs one simple, easily verified function. These functional units are called by control routines written in a manner that emphasizes their logic. Cleanroom testing emphasizes software whose correctness can be proved mathematically. This mathematical proof claim always confused me. However, this is not math in the sense of regular algebra ($ax^2 + bx + c$), but in the sense of Boolean algebra (AND, OR, NOT). Like the cause–effect mapping in black box testing, this technique uses Boolean algebra to map the input cases to the output cases. The correctness of software written in this manner can be verified by careful, diligent inspection. What's more, this type of writing and inspection costs less than code, test, fix, test, fix, and so on. Coding before thinking is outmoded.

The development team inspects and verifies the code they write. This is the ultimate use of visibility. Everything is written and given to the group for examination. The certification team compiles and tests the software by running test cases. If the certification team finds errors, they pass the increment back to the development team. If all is well, they roll the increment into the growing product. The certification team uses statistical use specifications (as in the user profile testing element of black box testing), the functional specification, and the performance specification to create their test cases. Their goal is scien-

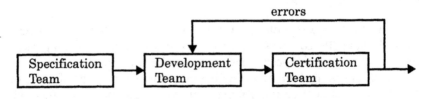

Figure 9.10   Cleanroom testing teams.

tific, not seat-of-the pants, software testing. The team emphasizes statistical quality control to track every aspect of the errors they find.

The next two figures show how cleanroom testing concepts can help in writing and testing software. The figures are code segments taken from a utility program that formats raw text into paragraphs and pages for printing. The code segment prints a title, date, and page number in the page header. Figure 9.11 shows the first method used to implement this in C. Using an

```c
if(the_page_number[0] != '\0'){
    if(the_title[0] != '\0'){
        if(the_date[0] != '\0'){
            sequence number 7
            ...
        }
        else{
            sequence number 5
            ...
        }
    }
    else{
        if(the_date[0] != '\0'){
            sequence number 3
            ...
        }
        else{
            sequence number 1
            ...
        }
    }
}
else{
    if(the_title[0] != '\0'){
        if(the_date[0] != '\0'){
            sequence number 6
            ...
        }
        else{
            sequence number 4
            ...
        }
    }
    else{
        if(the_date[0] != '\0'){
            sequence number 2
            ...
        }
        else{
            sequence number 0
            ...
        }
    }
}
```

Figure 9.11 Unstructured code sample of if–then–else.

if–then–else style, it examines the contents of the title, date, and page number strings and calls sequences of routines accordingly.

Figure 9.12 shows code influenced by cleanroom testing concepts. The title, data, and page number strings are either empty or contain text to be printed. The first step examines the strings and sets a Boolean variable to 1 or 0. The rest of the code reads like a Boolean logic table. There are three variables, so there are eight distinct cases.

The code samples in Figures 9.11 and 9.12 accomplish the same result, but the cleanroom code is more logical and mathematical. It is much easier to see the eight situations the code handles. It is possible to inspect this code, prove that it covers all mathematical possibilities, and verify its function.

```c
title = 0; page = 0; date = 0;
if(the_title[0] != '\0')        title = 1;
if(the_page_number[0] != '\0')  page = 1;
if(the_date[0] != '\0')         date = 1;

if(page == 0  &&  date == 0  &&  title == 0){
    sequence number 0
    ...
}
if(page == 0  &&  date == 0  &&  title == 1){
    sequence number 1
    ...
}
if(page == 0  &&  date == 1  &&  title == 0){
    sequence number 2
    ...
}
if(page == 0  &&  date == 1  &&  title == 1){
    sequence number 3
    ...
}
if(page == 1  &&  date == 0  &&  title == 0){
    sequence number 4
    ...
}
if(page == 1  &&  date == 0  &&  title == 1){
    sequence number 5
    ...
}
if(page == 1  &&  date == 1  &&  title == 0){
    sequence number 6
    ...
}
if(page == 1  &&  date == 1  &&  title == 1){
    sequence number 7
    ...
}
```

Figure 9.12 The code in Figure 9.11 logically structured using cleanroom testing.

Cleanroom testing concepts will help you write, inspect, and test software at work. It will not solve all the problems in the software world, and I am not convinced that the development team should go without a compiler. Its heavy reliance on inspection goes a step beyond the techniques in the PSP (Humphrey, 1995). You also do more thinking, designing, and inspecting than with other methods. On the other hand, it forces you to work smarter and that saves time and improves quality.

9.4.9 Test-Driven Development

A key part of the agile development methods discussed in Chapter 6 is how testing fits into the development process. One of the fundamentals of agile development is test-driven development (TDD). This is important enough that Kent Beck, the creator of extreme programming, wrote a separate book on this topic (Beck, 2003)]. TDD has three basic steps:

1. Red—Write a test that doesn't work, and perhaps doesn't even compile at first.
2. Green—Make the test work quickly, committing whatever sins are necessary in the process.
3. Refactor—Eliminate all the duplication created in merely getting the test to work.

Beck provides a number of examples in his text to highlight the emphasis on simple and quick in the Green step. For example, if a routine is to multiply two values, the test might be to pass the routine the numbers 2 and 5, expecting the routine to return the result of 2 times 5. The first version of the routine simply states something like

```
return(10);
```

This would pass the test written in the Red step. In the Refactor step, you would write a more flexible multiplication routine. One like

```
return(input1 * input2);
```

This example stretches the point a bit, but it illustrates the concept of implementing only exactly enough (Bedunah, 2002) to fulfill the requirements of the test. One of the principles of TDD and extreme programming is to do just enough and go on. I have seen many people on many projects put "hooks" into software where they could later add features that users were sure to want. In the end, however, the users never wanted those features, we never hung them on the hooks, and we wasted much time and effort.

Beck (Beck, 2002) also encourages TDD to improve the lives of the testers and developers. The traditional method of performing all the testing at the end of a project places enormous stress on those people performing the test. The organization wants to ship the product on schedule and they have slipped along the way to testing. They are a month behind, so they want to cut testing from six to two weeks. The testers are under pressure to say, "Its okay, ship now" though they feel otherwise. With testing driving the development, each test is created in the first or Red step. There is no pressure-packed rush to test at the end of the project.

The developers also enjoy a better life using TDD. In the traditional method, the programmers write code and wait for the defect reports to come back from the testers. Their life from this point to the end of the project consists of patching the software until it passes the tests. This patching, though it does make the software "correct," degrades many of the quality measures of the code. Therefore, the programmers end the project by "messing up" their code. In TDD, however, the code begins simple and sometimes crude, as the example above showed. As the project progresses, the programmers see the quality of the code improve.

TDD is not appropriate for every situation. It does, however, fit well in many situations. As with all processes and techniques, think about the people and product and choose the process.

9.5   CONFIGURATION MANAGEMENT

CM plays a major role in testing because testing spans all the major CM baselines. This may be hard to understand at first, but as you read further, it will hopefully become clear how testing relates to all development activities and thus how test artifacts span multiple baselines. (Chapter 11's sample projects also emphasize this correspondence.) The CM staff and project manager can use a requirements verification traceability matrix to help them track these relationships.

9.5.1   *How Testing Relates to Other Activities*

There is a one-to-one correspondence between requirements and testing. If the requirements state that the software must calculate the square roots of numbers, testing must run a few square root problems. This is common sense. What is not as obvious is that as soon as the requirements are stated, a tester (someone not involved with stating the requirements) should start writing the test plan using nothing but the requirements. This ensures that the test will check these requirements.

This one-to-one correspondence extends to all development activities. Figure 9.13 shows this concept in the classic V-chart. The left side of the V resem-

User Need   User Test

   Requirements   Test System

      High-Level Design   Test Subsystems
      (subsystem requirements)

        Low-Level Design   Test Subroutines
        (subroutine requirements)   (external test)

          Build Each Subroutine   Test Subroutines
                            (internal test)

Figure 9.13 How testing relates to development activities.

bles the basic waterfall model of development, breaking the problem into smaller, more detailed problems. The right side of the V combines or integrates solutions to build a system that satisfies the user's needs.

The process starts with user needs and breaks those into system requirements. The high-level design states solutions to those requirements, and the low-level design breaks the solutions into more specific solutions (subroutines). The bottom of the V is the greatest detail—the source code for each subroutine.

The right side of the V is a series of integrations that combine small solutions into larger ones. Each integration step includes a test to verify that the result performs correctly. Suppose, for example, the users need a basic software calculator (+, −, *, /, %). That means the user or acceptance test will have a checklist that contains +, −, *, /, %. The user test is written as soon as the users express their preferences. The requirements state the accuracy, fault conditions, and user interface for the calculator. A system test is immediately written that checks the accuracy, fault conditions, and user interface. The high-level design states the requirements for each subsystem (one for +, one for -, and so on). When the high-level design is complete, a test is written for each subsystem. The low-level design states the requirements for each subroutine. When that stage is finished, someone should immediately write a test for each subroutine and test it per the test plan. The next step is to integrate the subroutines into subsystems and test per their test plans. In other words, go back up the right side of the V.

Every task in the chart has an inspection attached to it. Users and developers inspect the user needs in a meeting. This ensures that +, −, *, /, and % are the only things the users need (no trig functions). Developers inspect the requirements, high-level design, low-level design, and source code. Test writers inspect their test plans and procedures. The team looks at everything as soon as it is created so that they can catch their mistakes right away. As I described earlier, waiting until the end of the project to look at the software is disastrous.

9.5.2 *Controlling Test Artifacts*

Now we are ready to see how the testing artifacts span the baselines. Figure 9.14 adds the baselines to the V-chart of Figure 9.13. First look at the requirements on the left side of the V. The gray line leads across the V to the system test (labeled "Test System") and shows that the requirements are in the functional baseline. We first saw this in Chapter 5. Also included in the functional baseline are all the testing artifacts related to system test. The artifacts include the plans, procedures, and reports discussed later and the scripts, data, and other testing aids discussed earlier.

Planning for the system test begins as soon as the functional baseline CCB accepts the requirements into the functional baseline. While the designers work on the high-level design, the test planners start planning the system test. When finished, the test planners submit the test plan (see the next section on documenting tests) to the functional baseline CCB. The test plan becomes part of that baseline and is controlled by the CCB using the CM plan (see Chapter 2 and Appendix B). Next, the test planners write the procedure for the system test and send it to the functional baseline CCB. The results of the system test are the final elements placed in the functional baseline.

The same holds true for the other tests on the right side of the V. Everything related to "Test Subsystems" goes into the allocated baseline via the corresponding CCB. Everything related to "Test Subroutines (external test)" goes into the design baseline via the corresponding CCB. Everything related to "Test Subroutines (internal test)" goes into the development baseline via the corresponding CCB. Finally, everything related to "User Test" goes into the development baseline

The CCBs for each baseline control the test artifacts using the process in the CM plan. If the testers want to change the test procedures, they approach the appropriate CCB and request the change. They present their reasons for

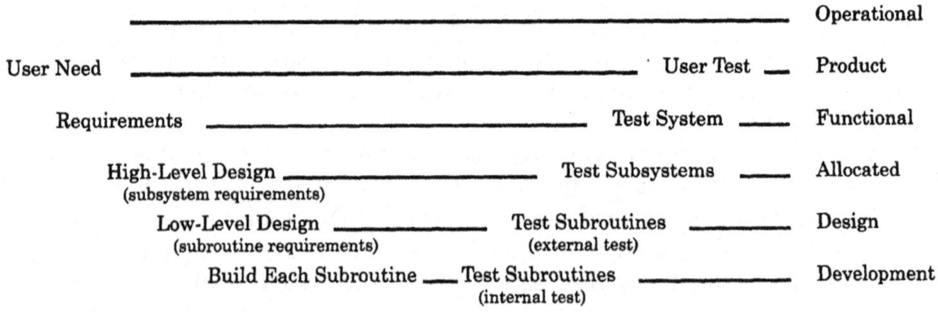

Figure 9.14 Relating tests and baselines.

the change, the project manager presents the cost of accepting and rejecting the change, and the CCB makes a visible decision.

Controlling test artifacts is just as important as controlling requirements, design, and anything else. Every part of the system test traces to a requirement. A part of the test should not change if the corresponding requirement does not change.

The project manager must resist the temptation to let "a few little parts" of the test change. Follow the process in the CM plan every time. As with other CM issues, I have followed the CM plan and bypassed it. Following the plan brings less pain and costs less time and money.

9.5.3 Using the Requirements Verification Traceability Matrix

Part of the testing process is to continue the requirements verification traceability matrix introduced in the last chapter. The RVTM can take several forms when testing information is added. The RVTM in Figure 9.15 extends the matrix in Figure 8.12 by showing code units, the test for code unit test elements, and the types of testing (I, D, E, or A) .

As in Figure 8.12, the first column lists the functional (FR#) and performance (PR#) requirements. The design element column lists the design element that meets that requirement. The code unit column states which unit (subroutine, method, and so on) will implement a requirement. These first three columns have traced down the left side of the V-chart.

The code unit test number states which small code unit test will verify the code unit and what type of testing it will use. The design test element column states what test will validate the design element. The requirement test element column states which part of the final system test will validate the requirement. These three columns are tracing up the right side of the V-chart. There could be a column for every test performed in the project. The test methods

Requirement	Design Element	Code Unit	Code Unit Test Element		Design Test Element		Requirement Test Element	
FR1	Command interpreter	get_options()	CU1	I	DTE1	D	RTE3	I
FR2	text reader	read_text_line()	CU3	E	DTE4	E	RTE2	A
FR3	text formatter	format_text_line()	CU6	D	DTE3	I	RTE4	E
..	...	...	...	...	...	...	...	...
PR1	Operating system	DOS	CU7	E	DTE6	I	RTE6	D
PR2	text data store	N/A	CU9	D	DTE7	D	RTE7	E
PR3	windows package	Fred's windows	...	A	DTE2	E	RTE1	A
..	...			...	...	...	...	...

Figure 9.15 The requirements traceability matrix in Figure 8.12 with testing information.

columns state the type of test (inspection, demonstration, execution, or analysis) that will be used in the system test.

Any blanks in the testing columns show an incomplete test plan. Blanks mean that we are not validating that the system does something the users want. The value of the RVTM is that these omissions are obvious. Projects with a hundred or more requirements often miss a requirement in testing. Without an RVTM, it is impossible to catch these mistakes.

As discussed in Chapter 8, the project manager and the CM staff continue to be responsible for the RVTM, maintaining it as part of the allocated or design baseline.

9.6   STANDARDS: DOCUMENTING THE TEST PLAN

"I tested the software" means something different to everyone who says and hears it. There must be something visible that describes the test and the result of the test. IEEE-Std-829 is IEEE's vision of testing and documentation (IEEE, 1998). As Figure 9.16 shows, it requires eight document types: test plan, test design specification, test case specification, test procedure specification, test item transmittal report, test log, test incident report, and test summary report. How many of these you use depends on the people, process, and product. If you are developing the flight control software for a 747, these eight documents are the minimum. Most of us, however, can get by with the three core document types: test plan, test procedure specification, and test summary report. I use "document types" instead of "documents" deliberately. These three could be documents, videos, sketches on a poster, or whatever works.

Test Plan. The test plan states the general approach to testing. It is the design of the test. Suppose we need to test the performance of number-crunching software on a new workstation and compare that to its performance on an old supercomputer. There are several ways to do this. One is to port all the software to the workstation and run the two machines side by side. Another is to port a small percentage of the software and run this side by side. Yet another approach is to write a small amount of completely new software that contains computations similar to the software in question and run this side by side. Each approach has its strengths and weaknesses.

The test plan will describe the chosen approach and why the team thinks it is best. The level of detail should be no more than is necessary to convince everyone that you are on the appropriate path. Use the decision making and documenting techniques discussed in Chapter 8. Remember the one-to-one correspondence between requirements and tests and begin writing the test plan and procedure as soon as the requirements are finished.

If possible, have people other than your programmers write the parts of the plan that involve checking the design and code. Do not wait until the day be-

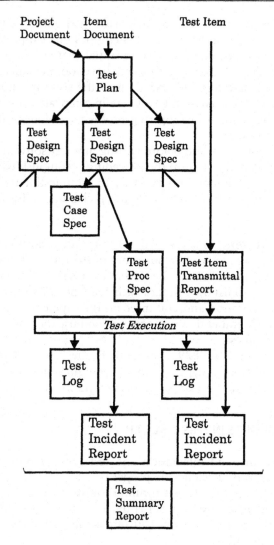

Figure 9.16 Types of test documents recommended by IEEE-Std-829.

fore a test begins to start thinking about how to test something. Think about people, process, and product. Make the decision clear and visible to everyone.

Review the test plan before writing the test procedure. Use the inspection techniques described earlier. Challenge the decisions described by the test plan as they have a lasting effect on the project. Do not proceed until the test plan is what the project needs.

Test Procedure Specification. This specification contains step-by-step instructions on how to run the test. It should contain everything needed to permit almost anyone to run the test unassisted. It should be similar to the old Heathkit* assembly instructions. Each step does one simple thing. The margin next to the step contains a place to initial that you have performed the step. It is difficult for the test procedure to have too much detail.

A good test procedure states exactly how the software should react to inputs and lets anyone exercise the software in a repeatable, dependable manner. This is crucial when investigating problems and ensuring that fixes do not break the software.

Review the test procedure before writing any test software or performing the test. Ensure that the steps in the procedure accomplish what the test plan intended. These documents and reviews add up to testing the test. The test is an intellectual product. Just like everything else in a software project, tests must be tested.

Test Summary Report. This summary of test results should inform everyone of both the general and specific outcomes of the test. It should state that the workstation performed 50% of the tests at least 80% as fast as the supercomputer. It should also list the result of each test (the FFT software required 300 msec on the workstation and 200 msec on the supercomputer). When creating the report, remember that management will use the test results to plot the course of the business.

Read and use IEEE-Std-829. It explains Figure 9.16 in detail and the purpose of each document type. Although you may not need all eight, you should understand and use the concepts behind them.

9.7   KEY THOUGHTS IN THIS CHAPTER

Several myths surround integration and test (I&T). Noting and explaining these myths helps understand the proper way to integrate and test software. The myths include: (1) testing is running software until you get the right answer, (2) testing is too expensive, (3) testing ensures quality, (4) testing is a mechanical process, (5) error-free software is the goal of testing, and (6) testing is a technical endeavor.

The 3Ps play a large role in I&T. Programmers and testers can become antagonists. Morale can be a big problem if the people are caught in a downward spiral of code–test–fix–code–test-fix. Redefine success and create a process with which people succeed weekly.

Common process problems in I&T include unrealistic planning, no test policy, mismatching tests, testing time, and the 3Ps. A process that must be

---

*I have learned that many readers may not remember the Heathkits. These were kits that contained parts for a device ranging from a clock to a large-screen television. You would buy the kit containing parts and instructions and build the device yourself. The instructions contained great detail. Each instruction step told you to do one thing. In the margin next to the instruction was a place to put a check mark showing that you had performed that one simple step.

included in I&T is IDEA: inspection, demonstration, execution, and analysis. Use these early and often in the project to prevent a testing nightmare at the end. Employ verification and validation in testing. Verification is a series of small tests that verify small parts of software. Validation is a set of tests that determines if the system is what the users wanted. Use independent people to perform verification and validation to obtain a higher-quality product.

The main job of visibility in testing is to make the weaknesses in the software plain to all. Use black box, white box, integration, acceptance, regression, and cleanroom testing. Types of integration test processes include bottom-up, top-down, sandwich, big bang, and builds. Use quality engineering practices in testing. Tests should be repeatable, so create reusable test scripts and test data.

Configuration management is surprisingly critical to I&T. Testing spans all the baselines in a project. There is a one-to-one correspondence between testing and requirements (and design levels and code). The V-chart illustrates how this works and why tests belong in baselines. An important tool in keeping everything organized is the requirements traceability matrix.

Maintaining high-quality, visible tests require documentation. IEEE-Std-829 shows how to document tests properly, listing eight types of documents needed in safety-critical systems. Most development projects need only three basic types: test plan, test procedure specification, and test summary report. The test plan states the general approach to testing. The test procedure specification contains step-by-step instructions on how to run a test. The test summary report tells everyone both the general and specific outcomes of the test.

REFERENCES

K. Beck, *Extreme Programming Explained: Embrace Change*, Pearson Education, Upper Saddle River, NJ, 1999.

K. Beck, "Testing in XP," *Cutter IT Journal*, August 2002, pp. 24–26.

J. Bedunah, "Introducing Test-Driven Development," *STQE*, January February 2002, pp. 16–17.

B. Beizer, *Black-Box Testing: Techniques for Functional Testing of Software and Systems*, Wiley, New York, 1995.

P. Conklin, "Enrollment Management: Managing the Alpha AXP Program," *IEEE Software*, July 1996, pp. 53–64

M. Dedolph, "Why Testers Should Participate in Early Reviews," *STQE*, March April 2001, pp. 79–80.

T. Gilb and D. Graham, *Software Inspection*, Addison-Wesley, Reading, MA, 1993.

R. Glass, "A Satisficing Approach to Software Testing in a Many-Flawed World," *Cutter IT Journal*, July 2002, pp. 13–17.

R. Goldsmith "Plan Your Testing," *Software Development*, April 1999, pp. 35–39.

B. Hetzel, *The Complete Guide to Software Testing*, QED Information Sciences, Wellesley, MA, 1988.

W. Humphrey, *A Discipline for Software Engineering*, Addison-Wesley, Reading, Mass., 1995.

IEEE, *ANSI/IEEE Std 829-1998, IEEE Standard for Software Test Documentation,* IEEE Press, Piscataway, NJ, 1998.

C. Kaner, *Testing Computer Software,* Van Nostrand Reinhold, New York, 1993.

J. McCarthy, *Dynamics of Software Development,* Microsoft Press, Redmond, WA, 1995.

S. McConnell, *Rapid Development,* Microsoft Press, Redmond, WA, 1996.

J. McGregor, M. Major "Selecting Test Cases Based on User Priorities," *Software Development,* March 2000, pp. 26–31.

G. Myers, *The Art of Software Testing,* Wiley, New York, 1979.

D. Phillips, "A People-Satisfying IDEA," *Cutter IT Journal,* July 2002, pp. 26–30.

J. Poore and C. Trammel, "Bringing Respect to Testing Through Statistical Science," *American Programmer,* August 1997, pp. 15–22.

J. Rothman, "No More Whining," *Software Testing and Quality Engineering,* September October 2000, pp. 79–80.

S. Sherer, "Consider the Consequences: Risk-Based Testing Strategies," *Cutter IT Journal,* pp. 12-16, August, 2002.

J. Voas, "Will the Real Operational Profile Please Stand Up?" *IEEE Software,* March April 2000a, pp. 87–89.

J. Voas, "Developing a Usage-Based Software Certification Process, *Computer,* August 2000b, pp. 32–27.

G. Weinberg, "Just Say No! Improving the Requirements Process," *American Programmer,* Oct. 1995, pp. 19–23.

G. Weinberg, "Playing Quality Chicken," *STQE,* January February 2002, pp. 55–56.

J. Whittaker, "What is Software Testing and Why is it so Hard?" *IEEE Software,* January February 2000, pp. 70–79.

Chapter 10

Software Maintenance

Software maintenance comprises all activities that help people use software. Often disdained, it universally consumes more people, time, and money than any other software activity. Little has been written about it, few universities teach it, and most people didn't enter the software field to do it. This is unfortunate because it can be exciting, rewarding, and, most of all, educational. In the four years I did it, I was able to see a large variety of software in a short time. I worked with software written by many people from different cultures and companies. I learned what worked, what did not work, and what cost money in the long term.

Maintenance, like development, requires thinking about people, process, and product. Software maintenance is usually a long-term situation in which a group of maintainers work with the customers for years. There are fewer unknowns, and the people know the product well. Therefore, the process can be simple. Do not, however, let the familiarity stop the thinking. Know your customers, their business, and their culture. Strive to fit in their business and help them use the software.

It is particularly important to understand maintenance phases. Make the tasks and their products visible. IEEE-Std-1219 is an excellent maintenance roadmap. Configuration management may even be more important in maintenance than in development because the boundaries between baselines are less defined.

In short, everything about the four principles that pertains to development applies to maintenance, and maintenance has its own set of issues as well. Like testing, maintenance is not well understood. For that reason, as I did in the testing chapter, I begin this chapter with some clarification of the topic.

10.1   WHAT IS MAINTENANCE?

There are three basic types of software maintenance: adaptive, perfective, and corrective. Some people consider emergency to be a fourth type. *Adaptive* maintenance involves changing software to adapt to a changing situation such as new regulations or business opportunities. *Perfective* maintenance seeks to improve the software by, say, adding a better user interface or making operations faster. *Corrective* maintenance is fixing a problem in the software. Many think that corrective maintenance is the only type, but it is actually only about 25% of all software maintenance. *Emergency* maintenance is fixing something immediately to avoid dire consequences, such as the loss of life, property, or livelihood. Emergency maintenance can cause trouble later because people tend to ignore any established procedure in the interest of fixing the problem right now.

10.1.1   Maintenance or Development?

In the past, there was a clear break between development and maintenance. Today's development practices blur that boundary. Maintenance is now thought of as continued development. In the Microsoft process (described in Chapter 6), developers build a tiny product on day one and build on it daily. In essence, development starts and ends on the first day with the rest being adaptive and perfective maintenance. Microsoft proudly issues regular updates to products. These are maintenance updates. Some may disagree with this assessment, but the trends toward iterative and evolutionary development and agile methods are more like software maintenance than software development.

Software maintenance is a viable alternative to development. Starting with a blank sheet of paper and developing new software is expensive. Only occasionally is starting from scratch the best approach. Reusing, modifying, and maintaining existing software make more sense in most cases because you are capitalizing on an investment instead of throwing it away.

Deciding when to create software and when to modify existing code is a business decision that requires careful analysis. Software can be improved through maintenance, but it can also be degraded if poorly modified. If poor modification has gone on for some time, the software may no longer be reusable.

10.1.2   Maintenance Activities

Software maintenance involves several closely related activities. It is important to understand the different activities before delving into details (Blum, 1992). *Forward engineering* is traditional development starting with requirements and going through design, coding, testing, and delivery. *Reverse engineering* involves analyzing existing software to understand its structure, components, and functions—how it works. *Redocumentation* seeks to understand and then document software that lacks documentation. *Design recovery* is a subset of reverse engineering that documents the design or overall structure of software by studying the code. Reverse engineering, redocumentation, and design recovery are key tasks in understanding existing software.

Restructuring changes the internal workings of the software while leaving the external properties the same. *Reengineering* is an internal and external overhaul of the software. This reclaims or reuses as much of the software as possible, adds new software, and puts it all in a new implementation. Restructuring and reengineering change existing software after it is understood.

Refactoring, discussed in Chapter 6, is similar to *restructuring* and *reengineering*. The goal of all these activities is to improve the software in some form while leaving much of the software the same. *Refactoring* and *restructuring* are the closest to one another. Both strive to improve the internal workings of the software while leaving the external behavior unchanged. Proponents of agile methods argue that *refactoring* is done during development whereas *restructuring* is a maintenance activity. On the other hand, agile methods advocates also lean toward the idea that development and maintenance meld into one continuous activity.

10.1.3 Why Use Configuration Management?

The CM activities discussed in the previous chapters and Appendix B continue during software maintenance. This is another surprising aspect of maintenance. Though most people think the only thing to control during maintenance is the source code (development baseline), all the baselines still exist. The Configuration Control Boards (CCBs) for each baseline exist, but do not meet as often. The CM staff is smaller than during development, but performs the same tasks.

CM helps maintain the integrity of the software in all types of maintenance. Corrective maintenance usually means correcting source code. This involves the development baseline and its CCB. Perfective maintenance usually involves changing the design and code so the software can do something better. This involves the allocated, design, and development baselines. Finally, adaptive maintenance adds new requirements so the software can adapt. This involves all the baselines.

10.1.4 Why Is It So Expensive and Difficult?

Software maintenance is *expensive* because it requires that people work for years, and software people are expensive. The next logical question is why does it require people working for years? I can explain that with the simple Phillips law of software half-life: Software outlives hardware.

Many types of software prove this law. Some word processing programs were written in the 1970s to run on 8-bit processors under the C/PM operating system. Those word processors now run on personal computers that are thousands of times more powerful than the original platform. The software, modified many times in major ways, has outlived eight generations of hardware.

Software maintenance is *difficult* for two reasons. The first is that customers are demanding. They want (too many) changes. They are creative and if someone will listen, they will ask for what they want. This calls for management. Management must step in, look at the requested changes, and make decisions. What is the return on investment? How will it improve the performance of employees? How will it affect the customers? The CM staff must trace through the baselines and provide the information necessary for the decisions.

The second reason for the difficulty of software maintenance is that most software is not written to be maintained. Most developers have neither maintained software nor paid for software maintenance. They write software as a writer, not a reader. In this chapter, I describe techniques that will help you write more maintainable software.

10.1.5   Why We Should Not Neglect Maintenance

People tend to neglect software maintenance. The greatest example of this is how we neglected adaptive maintenance on time and date functions and caused the Y2K problem (Thomsett, 1998). I was caught in what seemed to be a simple update to a system to make it Y2K compliant. As usually happens when we think something is simple, it was a down-to-the-wire nightmare. We had neglected to update the operating system of a computer system for a couple of years. When we moved to the Y2K-compliant operating system (OS), we learned that our compilers would not function properly. We went to the compiler vendors only to learn that they had dropped their product line for that OS. Now we had a Y2K-compliant OS with no compilers. We had to find and install new compilers before we could do anything else. Now, six months into a simple update, we were ready to look at the source code of our application. We soon learned that the original design had allowed date-related code to be scattered throughout the system. We made changes in dozens of places. The best thing to do would have been to reengineer the system, but we were behind schedule and didn't have time to do that.

My Y2K experience, and probably that of many others, showed how neglecting maintenance always catches up with us. The biggest reason for this neglect relates to the attitude toward maintenance discussed in the next section. We know we should change something, but we put it off until tomorrow. The trouble is that tomorrow will come, and it usually comes at a time that we least expect. Adaptive maintenance becomes emergency maintenance, and we don't have the time to reengineer the software. Instead, we patch it quickly and hope that tomorrow will stay away for a while.

10.2 BALANCING THE 3Ps: MANAGING THE MAINTAINERS

Software maintenance relies on people even more than development. It is also harder on people, which may be why few programmers jump at the opportunity to do it. The prevalent feeling about maintenance is that it's all the work and none of the fun.

A big challenge in managing maintainers is to reverse this poor image. As I mentioned earlier, corrective activities (repair) are only about 25% of all software maintenance. Emphasize that most of the maintainer's time will be spent on adaptive (making software new) and perfective (making software better) maintenance, which is very creative. Compensate people for software maintenance work. Maintainers are not second-class programmers, and should not be paid as such. Highlight the learning that occurs in maintenance work.

Staffing is another challenge. Who should do maintenance? Many organizations select people who are either new or not wanted on development projects. This is a business mistake. Software maintenance is where the money is (see Section 10.4). It is a good business opportunity, and management cannot afford to waste it. It is also a people mistake. Inexperienced people do not learn much from other inexperienced people. Also, those assigned to maintenance aren't blind. They will look around and see who else is assigned to maintenance. They will see what the organization thinks of maintainers, and they will either quit or become demoralized.

A good strategy is to make a low-energy developer a maintainer. Low-energy developers are those who were present during the product's development (attended meetings, worked on parts of the product) but did not work the 50-hour weeks to finish it. High-energy developers are generally too burned out on the product to maintain it. The low-energy developer knows the product and has enough energy left to maintain the product.

Another good strategy is to rotate people between development and maintenance. This is somewhat inefficient, but it can boost morale. Everyone does everything, and no one is a second-class programmer. It is also an effective training tool. Everyone has the opportunity to learn and appreciate both sides of the development/maintenance fence. Developers experience what it's like to reverse-engineer and change clever or complex software. They understand the reading side of writing software. This makes them better developers.

Steve McConnell (McConnell, 1997) has proposed another way to balance the work between maintenance and development. He advocates having two teams of people working on a product at the same time. The first team concentrates on incremental updates to the product. They perform classic software maintenance, adapting the product to the marketplace and correcting errors reported by users. The second team starts with a blank sheet and builds the next major release of the product. These major releases should come every three to four years. This strategy—two full teams working at the same time—sounds expensive. In some ways it is, but it is a proactive approach that reduces risk to the product line. It can keep current users happy while allowing a team to look to the future.

Regardless of the strategy, assign at least two people to every maintenance task (Fairley, 1985). First, it is good to have a backup for vacations, sickness, and other absences. Second, and more important, it keeps ideas flowing and maintains visibility and accountability. One person assigned to a product can easily go dark or hide the smell. People need someone else to ask questions, inspect their work, and contribute ideas.

10.3 BALANCING THE 3Ps: MANAGING THE PROCESS

Software developers can help themselves by creating easier-to-maintain software. Software as a product differs from, say, the company's fax machines, because the maintainers are also the developers. The goal should be to develop long-life software—software that is inexpensive over the long term. Such software has two parts: itself and everything else.

To produce long-life software, the development team should aim for five main goals:

1. *Clear and simple design.* Easy-to-maintain software typically has an easy-to-understand design. Use the principles of modularity, information hiding, and abstraction (see Chapter 8). Break the problem into smaller problems whose answers are easier to grasp. Constantly ask how to make the design simpler. Bring in outsiders to ask these questions during inspections. Look for areas that confuse, frustrate, and waste time for them, and improve those areas.

2. *Clean, readable code.* The code should also be clean, clear, and easy to read (Hunt, 2002). Reading is the key because this is exactly what maintainers will be doing. Keep logically distinct parts of the code separate. Do everything to help the maintainer a decade from now. Use outsiders just as you would in design inspections. This follows from the extreme programming concepts of simplicity and refactoring.

3. *Complete and readable documentation.* The everything-else part of long-life software includes the documentation and all the visibility artifacts. The CM baselines should be traceable, as described in Chapter 2 and Appendix B. Documenting decisions is particularly important. Decision documentation explains to maintainers why the software is as it is. The

reasons for the decisions tell them what caused the software. Situations change with time, which in turn change the reasons behind design decisions. Maintainers often omit needed changes because they are not sure why the developers did something. Decision documentation tells them why and lets them improve the software.

The developers should write a manual that explains the software to the maintainers. Have designers and programmers compile this information. If you have a version description document (see Appendix B), that will work. If not, copy the essential diagrams from the SRS and SDD as well as source code comments and put these into a file folder or three-ring binder.

4. *Use of standards.* The standards need not be legal documents, but they should exist and everyone should follow them. Proper use of standards means the code and all the documents are consistent, and everything is easier to find and read. Have the designers document the design with standard figures and notations. Do not make the maintainers learn a new notation for every figure. Make the maintainer's job easier, even when it makes the developer's job harder.

5. *Complete, easy-to-use test suite.* Develop a complete, easy-to-use test suite using the guidelines in Chapter 9. Keep good copies of the tests, test data, and instructions on how to conduct and interpret all the tests. The maintainers will use these time and time again. Every modification, and there will be hundreds if not thousands, should include testing the software to demonstrate that it still works. Reinventing a test for every modification is the ultimate in inefficiency. Test-driven development, discussed in Chapter 9, provides a good test suite for use in maintenance.

10.4 BALANCING THE 3Ps: MAKING THE MOST OF THE PRODUCT

Most people agree that software maintenance is expensive. What they sometimes don't see is that software maintenance is also an opportunity to earn money. The software maintenance business does not have a large profit margin, but it is a low-risk, steady endeavor that keeps people employed and teaches them much about software.

Maintenance can consume 80% to 90% of the total life-cycle cost of software. It is hard to imagine, but this large percentage is invisible. It happens while the developers are off developing another software system.

Figure 10.1 shows an optimistic estimate of the staff hours and cost of a software system over nine years. In this example, 10 people work one year to develop the software ($1.5 million). The developers leave and maintenance begins. One programmer maintains the software during years two through four, and the cost rises with the programmer's salary.

Year	1	2	3	4	5	6	7	8
Persons	10	1	1	1	4	1	1	1
$K/Persons	150	150	165	180	200	220	250	280
Total $K	1500	150	165	180	800	220	250	280

Figure 10.1 Optimistic estimate of development and maintenance cost for a software system.

Maintenance costs shoot up in year five because the customer wants an overhaul of the software. Every three or four years, either a major event occurs or minor events accumulate to cause a major revision. Maintenance returns to one programmer a year for years six through eight. Year nine sees another major revision requiring four people.

After only nine years, the $1.5 million software has incurred $3.2 million in maintenance costs. So even an optimistic version of maintenance cost is 68% of the total life-cycle cost. The original developer might have seen the first one or two years of maintenance, but moved on to something else and missed years four through nine. These years and their costs were invisible.

Figure 10.2 shows a realistic example. Here, major revisions occur in years four and seven and require the same effort as the original development. It now costs more than $5.6 million to maintain a $1.5 million product—80% of the life-cycle cost. Even this realistic example might be optimistic: a product that cost $100,000 to develop in the 1970s could cost $10 million to maintain today.

Given the cost of maintenance shown in these examples, it is easy to have a mistaken impression about maintenance and software quality. It seems that if software is good, maintenance should be cheap, but that is wrong (Glass, 1998). If the software is good, people will use it often. When people use software, they find things in the software that could be improved and they find ways to use the software that the developers didn't anticipate. These activities spur adaptive and perfective maintenance. If the users don't like the software, they throw it away and no maintenance is necessary. Hence, good software requires more maintenance and maintenance expense than poor software.

In light of these figures, it would be foolhardy for an organization to assign its newest, weakest people to maintenance. Typically, where there are profits to be made, successful companies put their best people forward.

Year	1	2	3	4	5	6	7	8
Persons	10	1	1	10	1	1	10	1
$K/Persons	150	150	165	180	200	220	250	280
Total $K	1500	150	165	1800	200	220	2500	280

Figure 10.2 Realistic estimate of development and maintenance cost for the same software system in Figure 10.1.

To make software maintenance a long-term, profitable business, the maintenance group must keep the software usable—this means the customer must choose to use it instead of asking for a new piece of software. If the maintainers do well, the customer will keep the software and the software maintenance contract. If the maintainers do poorly, the customer will hire a different group to develop new software. There are worse things than spending $800,000 in year five to maintain the software. One is to pay someone else $2 million in year five to develop new software.

10.5   VISIBILITY: UNDERSTANDING THE MAINTENANCE STAGES

Software maintenance begins when there is an issue with the people and software. As Gerald Weinberg says (Weinberg, 1992), the issue could be software, documentation, training, or just a user who wants to do his job a different way. Do not jump to the conclusion that a major software change is required. Think. Study the issue with the customer. Only when you are sure that software is involved should you move to change it.

Over the years, I have found that IEEE-Std-1219 (IEEE, 1998) is invaluable as a guide to the straightforward application of basics. It goes way beyond documentation, providing a complete start-to-finish treatment of software maintenance. For this reason, I cover it in the rest of this chapter, rather than waiting until the last section to cover standards, as in previous chapters.

Figure 10.3 summarizes the entire process outlined by IEEE-Std-1219 and shows how the products flow between tasks. Figure 10.4 shows the main stages in the IEEE standard process as a V-chart (see introduction to Part 2 and Chapter 6). This maintenance process saves money (Lerner, 1993) because it follows the simple adage of leaving something better than you found it. In describing this process, I will frequently refer to earlier chapters—a testimony to how much software maintenance resembles development.

As Figure 10.3 shows, the IEEE process begins with a modification request (MR). Other names for this are request for change (RFC) or discrepancy report (DR). Whatever the name, use a standard form that follows configuration management principles. The MR is a short (often one page), customer-written requirements document.

10.5.1   Identification and Classification

The primary objective of the identification and classification phase is to validate the MR by ensuring that it is complete, unambiguous, and written in a way that maintainers can understand. If necessary, the maintainers or the customer rewrites the MR.

Toward the end of identification and classification (although not specifically shown in the figure), the validated MR undergoes preliminary analysis.

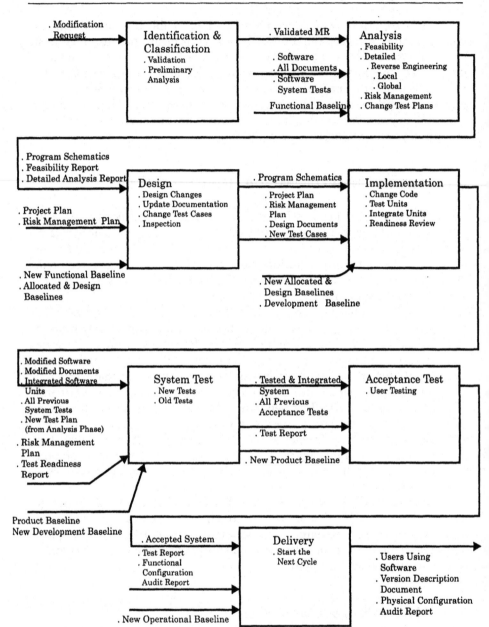

Figure 10.3   Summary of the maintenance process outlined by IEEE-Std-1219.

Problem/Modification   Delivery
Identification and Classification
             Analysis   Acceptance Test
                   Design   System Test
                       Implementation

Figure 10.4 V-chart of the main stages of maintenance as set forth in IEEE-Std-1219.

At this time, maintainers give the MR a name; set its priority; and classify it as adaptive, perfective, corrective, or emergency. They also estimate the resources (time, people, and so on) needed to fulfill the MR. This estimate is not a plan, and no one should have the impression that it is a firm commitment.

10.5.2 Analysis

During analysis, maintainers choose whether or not they will improve the software or allow it to deteriorate. Unless there is a business reason not to, choose to improve the software product. If all is well—the software was written well with high internal quality, good documentation, good configuration management, and all the other elements of long-life software—analysis will be short and inexpensive. Unfortunately, this is the biggest "if" in software. More time, energy, and money is spent on analysis—up to half the maintenance resources—than in any other maintenance phase. The "if" usually turns out to be an "else," so all the re-'s (reverse engineering, redocumentation, restructuring, reengineering, and design recovery) are needed.

IEEE-Std-1219 breaks analysis into two parts. *Feasibility* analysis is a first look at the software in light of the MR, an attempt to understand the high-level modification requirements. The product of feasibility analysis is a feasibility report that describes the impact the modification would have on the software, any alternative solutions, and the modification's costs and benefits.

Detailed analysis takes a closer look at the MR and expands on the elements of the feasibility report. The requirements for the modification become firm and detailed; the alternative solutions become a detailed modification plan (see Chapter 6 for project planning); and test plans and procedures (both black and white box) are formulated (see Chapter 9 for test plans and procedures).

The major task in detailed analysis is to identify what parts of the software require modification. Maintainers must understand the software using the list of development products sent into the analysis box in Figure 10.3. Acquiring this understanding can easily be the bulk of the detailed analysis task. How do you find the date calculation you are supposed to change if the source code is the only visible representation of the software?

This is frustrating, expensive, and wasteful—but it's a great teacher. Nothing communicates the value of clear design, code, and documentation better than a dig through clever, complex source code. The next time programmers complain about updating documents or writing "stupid" (meaning "clean") code, remind them of the curses they screamed while trying to understand someone else's software.

Reverse engineering is a tedious task under these circumstances. I recommend using one of the many good reverse-engineering tools available to analyze code and generate tables and diagrams that can help you understand the software. As always, make sure the tool fits your people, process, and product.

In IEEE-Std-1219, reverse engineering is viewed in terms of program schematics. These are building blocks used to understanding the software in the same way that schematic diagrams help us understand electrical systems. Program schematics show a software unit with its input, process, and output.

As Figure 10.3 shows, reverse engineering consists of local and global analysis. *Local* or "in the small" analysis begins by identifying units or sections of source code. A unit is a logical partition of the source code. Ideally, one subroutine is one unit. In poor designs, often there are several units in a subroutine or a unit may span several subroutines. Whatever the case, the reverse engineer needs to document the software as it is. Once the unit is identified, describe its operation with a functional or process specification using structured English (see Chapter 8). Now, combine the unit, its specification, and its input/output to form the software schematic. This is similar to the building blocks of the HIPO diagram, described in Chapters 5 and 8.

Global or "in the large" analysis creates an anatomy of the complete software system. The first step is to create linear circuits. Each linear circuit forms a program application by lining up the software schematics input/output to input/output. An example linear circuit would be the software schematics needed to create a program application such as calculating interest on a loan. The final step of global analysis places all program applications (all linear circuits) in one diagram. This is the complete program anatomy. It looks like a large HIPO diagram or structure chart (see Chapter 5).

IEEE's view is only one interpretation of reverse engineering. Content is more important than semantics. Whether you use program schematics, formal units, and linear circuits or another set of terms does not matter as much as matching the reverse-engineering approach to the people, process, and product.

As Figure 10.3 shows, the analysis phase produces many documents (bottom left of the design box). This is a crucial phase for documentation because much of the software becomes understood and documented for the first time. The documents produced here will make the next modification easier and less expensive. Following IEEE-Std-1219 will help you raise the quality and lower the maintenance cost of your software because it gives people who did not write the software a model for explaining it to others who also did not write the software.

The next task in the analysis phase is *risk management*. Software maintenance changes software that customers are using. It changes working software, and there is a risk that the change will break the software. Perform the risk management steps described in Chapter 7. Document the risks in the risk management and project plans.

The last task in the analysis phase is to *change the test plans* as required. If the requirements have changed, this will trace to a change in design and then in code (see the RVTM in Chapters 8 and 9). You will need to validate that the modified software meets the modified requirements. This means modified testing, so change the test plans.

10.5.3 Design

During design, maintainers *design the changes* needed to fulfill the MR. This design phase is similar to the design phase in development projects (Chapter 8) except that maintenance design has far more constraints because it must fit into an existing product.

As Figure 10.3 shows, the documentation from analysis (left of the design box) is the input to design. A major design task is to *update the documents* to reflect the design changes. This means updating the designs and test cases. Because designers note the changes needed in the source code, maintainers must also *change test cases* in the test plan. The additional information makes it possible to fill in the missing details on the project plan. During this time, the project manager must take care to monitor risks and keep the risk management plan up to date.

The detail added during design conveys what specific source code the programmers will modify. The program schematics created during analysis provide the designers visibility. They can see where everything is and where to add, subtract, and modify code. Everything is organized, visible, and people can review and improve it.

The design phase closes with *inspections* and reviews. Implementation is about to begin, and it does not matter how well programmers perform if they are being told to make the wrong changes. The designs, project plan, risk management plan, and test cases all come under scrutiny.

The result of design becomes the new allocated and design baselines.

10.5.4 Implementation

Programmers *change the source code* during implementation. For many software maintenance organizations, implementation is the only activity. They attempt to validate an MR, analyze and understand the software, design the change, and implement and test it all at once—which is one reason maintenance costs so much.

Once the changes are finished, the programmers *test the units* using the test cases from maintenance design. They then *integrate the tested units* and build the modified software into a new version.

Implementation ends with a *test readiness review* to ensure that modified software is ready for independent testing (testing by those other than the programmers and designers). The software coming out of implementation becomes the new development baseline.

10.5.5 System Test

During this phase, an independent testing group tests the complete modified software system in both *new and old tests*. The group may be people from outside the organization or people within the organization who were not involved in analyzing, designing, or coding the changes. The group tests the system using the test plans changed during analysis, as well as test cases accumulated during the software system's life. The tests have two main goals. The first is to demonstrate that the changes fulfill the MR. The second is to prove that the changes do not break the rest of the software system. This phase contains the many testing contradictions and challenges described in Chapter 9. The testers produce the usual test reports when finished. If the software passes the system test, it becomes the new product baseline.

10.5.6 Acceptance Test

As in system test, the acceptance test tests the complete software system, but this time in *user testing*. Allowing users to test the software in a safe environment is as close to using the modified software at work as possible without risk to the business. If the users accept the software, it becomes the new operational baseline.

10.5.7 Delivery

The final step in software maintenance is to have the customers use the software on the job. Also, the software is not the only product. If maintenance was adaptive, the software now performs new functions, so the user manuals are different and training may be needed. The installation procedures may be different. The software documentation (*Software Requirements Specification, Software Development Document*, and so on) is certainly different. Make sure the CM staff controls everything and keeps copies in a safe place that is easily located.

The change in documentation relates to an important part of maintenance that I call "document what you touch." Many people (Rajlich, 2000) have found themselves in the maintenance mode with little or any current documentation. We are staring at a large and undocumented mess and wondering what to do first. One approach is to stop all work and write several books about the current software. That will provide a complete set of documents for future maintenance activities. I don't advocate that approach, as the software users are left with no updates to the software for a long time.

The "document what you touch" approach causes you to do just what the name says. When you touch a section of code, you document what you understand about it. I was once in a maintenance situation where a hardware and software system was installed about ten years prior to my arrival. Many changes had been made in ten years, but the original documentation was all that was on hand. No one had saved any information about any of the changes, so the documentation was worth little. I documented each small thing that I touched and kept the documentation in a file drawer. At the end of two years, about 90% of the system was documented. Those who followed after me had documentation that helped them find their way through the system.

The current maintenance project ends when customers receive the modified software. If the project was conducted properly, the software is better, not worse, than it was before. Customers can do important tasks differently and more effectively than they could before.

Software maintenance never ends, so this phase includes *starting the next cycle*. Whereas the delivery ends the current maintenance project, it also begins the next one. The maintenance people keep helping the users use the software. Their help will lead to the next modification request.

10.6 CONFIGURATION MANAGEMENT

Configuration management is critical in software maintenance. Maintenance projects are all about change, and change control is one of the four main CM activities (see Chapter 2 and Appendix B). Maintenance projects are also about communication and coordination, another key CM activity.

All the day-to-day management practices from Chapter 4 apply to software maintenance. The modification has a visible plan; the project manager collects status, compares the plan and status, and takes corrective action. Everyone should continue to record the time it takes to do every task because, as in development, these metrics will aid future projects.

The software maintenance activities must follow a CM plan. This may be part of the maintenance policy document or a separate document. A well-written CM plan can carry over from development to maintenance with little modification. Regardless of format, the CM plan must be available and followed strictly. Software maintenance can turn to chaos quickly. Stay organized and stay with the plan.

The CM people follow the guidelines in Chapter 2 and Appendix B. As a maintenance project manager, you are responsible for everything. Rely on CM to keep track of details. Appoint a CM staff, usually one person or one person part-time, to lead the CM activities. Each baseline has a Configuration Control Board to control its contents. The people on each CCB will be different from those who served during development. Those people have probably moved on. The CCB members in the maintenance project will, however, represent the same groups (management, users, developers, and so on).

10.6.1   Keeping Baselines Straight

As Figure 10.3 shows (bottom arrows), the CM baselines are the inputs and outputs of every phase of software maintenance. The existing requirements, design, code, and system are the basis for the functional, allocated, design, development, product, and operational baselines. CM maintains existing baselines; well-practiced software maintenance creates absentee baselines, and CM must hold it all together. The CM staff must provide the baselines as inputs and carefully control the modified output baselines. Maintainers frequently work on several MRs simultaneously, and it is easy to mix up baselines. The result is almost always disastrous.

For example, the analysis phase often changes the software's functional or requirements baseline because the user typically wants a new or different function. Make sure the functional baseline CCB studies and approves these changes. The analysis phase also creates documentation that does not exist. These new documents become part of the functional baseline. Another area of potential mix-up is the design phase, because the new design changes the allocated and design baselines. Again, be sure the corresponding CCBs consider and approve these changes. Finally, changing the source code during implementation creates a new development baseline. The programmers are the development baseline CCB and control its content.

One way to avoid mix-ups is to start each MR on the correct baseline. IEEE-Std-1219 (see Figure 10.3) begins the MR at the requirements or functional baseline, but this is not always the case. In an adaptive change, the software must change to meet a new situation—usually a new requirement. The functional baseline is the starting point for the modification. A perfective change, however, warrants improving how the software does something. This means changing the design and may either be a high-level (allocated baseline) or low-level (design baseline) design change. A corrective modification indicates a mistake in the software, which could be in any baseline. The analysis phase must find the mistake and determine which baseline is the starting point.

10.6.2   Managing Releases

A crucial task of the project manager and the CM staff is managing software releases. If this is done well, the users are happy and remain users. If not, the users look elsewhere for software. Whenever possible, do several MRs in one version. Releasing a new version for every completed MR is inefficient because each time you must interrupt the customers' work for installation and training. No matter how many changes customers request, they still find the process of implementing that change confusing and frustrating. Weekly releases are one extreme. I've worked at this extreme and it is hectic. The circumstances were very demanding, but once we were organized for it, we became accustomed to it. The other extreme is to hold MRs for a year before releasing a version. A good frequency is about twice a year.

The optimum release frequency depends on what you have promised the users. Talk to them and decide the frequency by balancing the cost to the maintainers and the benefit to the users. Release software precisely as promised. If the users can depend on release dates, they will learn to time their MRs accordingly. Meeting agreed-on deliveries keeps users satisfied.

10.6.3 Pacing the Process

Software maintenance can be managed to make it efficient and predictable, but not if you hurry along and cut CM corners. Shortcuts reduce quality and eventually result in longer, not shorter schedules. In addition, errors introduced during software maintenance anger customers. They decide that the software is no longer maintainable. They terminate the maintenance contract (fire you) and initiate a new development (hire someone else).

Software maintenance struggles with "deterioration dynamics" or "software decay" (Rajlich & Bennet, 2000)—the philosophy that change weakens a product. A product, like software, has a certain structure. If that structure changes, the software is not as strong or secure as the original. This relates to the concept of technical debt. As the software deteriorates, each succeeding change becomes more difficult and expensive. The technical debt eventually reaches a point where changes are almost impossible.

I believe that deterioration need not accompany maintenance. In fact, with disciplined, courageous management, maintenance can improve software. Don't hurry through maintenance. Chapters 5 through 8 describe techniques for responding to pressure from both upper management and the customer. If you capitulate to requests to do things the wrong way, you have only yourself to blame for the result. I have been in places where everyone wanted quick fixes because it had always been done that way. I was able to change that slowly through persistence and time. We gradually progressed from quick and dirty fixes to CMM level 2 (yes, the CMM works in software maintenance, too). This came as we showed the customers the long-term value of doing it right. This was difficult and the accumulated stress and fatigue pushed me on to another job. In Chapter 1, I said that we have only recently begun to do maintenance that improves software. It's time to throw out the old processes and approaches that kept us from that goal for so long.

10.7   USING STANDARDS

The IEEE standard for software maintenance [IEEE 1219-1998] shown in Figure 10.3 addresses the management and execution of software maintenance activities. Like the other IEEE standards, IEEE-Std-1219 was written by experienced professionals who have already made all the mistakes. It stresses the disciplined application of fundamentals. Read it. Even if you do not follow it strictly, it contains information worth knowing. It works at work.

I also recommend using a maintenance policy document on maintenance projects, which you can pattern after the IEEE standard. The four years I worked on maintenance were much easier because we had such a document. The policy document states the project's purpose and goals as well as detailed procedures. On development projects, this type of information is in the project plan (Chapter 6). Maintenance differs from development in that the maintenance project does not have one large beginning and one large end. Each MR initiates a small project, so there are many beginnings. It is wasteful to write a new project plan for each one. The maintenance policy document helps new project members, briefs management, and keeps customers abreast of progress.

Using the IEEE-Std-1219 forces you to pay attention to the project's quality. The familiarity that exists on software maintenance projects can lead to the belief that changing the software is easy. Believing this increases the probability of making mistakes (Weinberg, 1992). Follow the process stated in the maintenance policy document on every change. Shortcuts only decrease quality and increase costs.

10.8   KEY THOUGHTS IN THIS CHAPTER

Everything about the four principles that pertains to development applies to maintenance, and maintenance has its own set of issues as well. Software maintenance is often a viable alternative to development. However, if the software has been poorly modified for some time, it may no longer be reusable.

Maintenance is generally misunderstood and mismanaged. The three main types of software maintenance are adaptive, perfective, and corrective. (Emergency maintenance is an unofficial fourth type.) Types of maintenance activities include forward engineering, reverse engineering, redocumentation, design recovery, restructuring, and reengineering.

Because software outlives hardware, maintenance can consume up to 90% of the software's total life-cycle costs. This means that software maintenance is an excellent business opportunity. Software maintenance is difficult because customers are demanding and most software is not written to be maintained. Because of these factors, maintenance work is hard on people, and management must be creative in staffing maintainers.

Making maintenance visible requires understanding the various maintenance phases and their inputs and outputs. IEEE-Std-1219 is a good roadmap of the software maintenance process.

Configuration management is critical. All software maintenance activities must follow a CM plan whether that plan is carried over from development or created from scratch. CM baselines are in the inputs and outputs of every maintenance phase. Changes do not always begin at the same baseline. Identify the correct baseline and use the proper Configuration Control Board to monitor changes. Software can deteriorate during maintenance, but you can prevent this with disciplined, courageous management. Resist the urge to take CM shortcuts. The resulting chaos will only keep you in the maintenance project longer.

Record the principles of the standard in a maintenance policy document that will guide all maintenance efforts. The IEEE-Std-1219 allows maintainers to improve the software through reverse engineering and redocumenting. Write a maintenance policy manual following the IEEE standard to keep the project status visible.

REFERENCES

B. Blum, *Software Engineering, A Holistic View*, Oxford University Press, Oxford, 1992.

E. Fairley, *Software Engineering Principles*, McGraw-Hill, New York, 1985.

R. Glass, "Maintenance: Less is not More," *IEEE Software*, July August 1998, pp. 67–68.

A. Hunt, "Software Archaeology," *IEEE Software*, March April 2002, pp. 20–22.

IEEE, IEEE Std 1219-1998, *IEEE Standard for Software Maintenance*, IEEE CS Press, Los Alamitos, CA, 1998.

M. Lerner, "Software Maintenance Crisis Resolution: The New IEEE Standard," *Software Development*, Aug. 1993, pp. 65–72.

S. McConnell, "Annualized Software Delivery," *IEEE Software*, January February 2000, pp. 103–104.

V. Rajlich and K. Bennet, "A Staged Model for the Software Life Cycle," *Computer*, July 2000, pp. 66–71.

V. Rajlich, "Incremental Redocumentation Using the Web," *IEEE Software*, September October 2000, pp. 102–106.

R. Thomsett "The Year 2000 bug: A Forgotten Lesson," *IEEE Software*, July August 1998, pp. 91–95.

G. Weinberg, *Quality Software Management: Vol. 1, Systems Thinking*, Dorset House, New York, 1992.

PART 4

APPLYING THE PRINCIPLES

This section has only one chapter, but it should be enough to give a flavor of how the four principles interact in different projects. You will see many common themes as well as uses that are specific to a particular process.

Chapter 11

Cookbook

This chapter walks you through three projects, each of which uses a different process model—waterfall, evolutionary, or spiral. It also discusses some other software projects (a spreadsheet, a web site, and an agile project)—the type often seen at work, but rarely discussed in a book on software project management. I created this chapter for those who have read the preceding chapters, have learned many things, but now have more questions than when they started. Software project management is a practical endeavor with practical questions. Where do you start? What is the first step and the next and the next and so on?

I call this chapter "Cookbook" because it lists the ingredients and steps described so far and combines them into projects that need "only" competent designers, programmers, testers, and configuration managers to succeed—if managed the way I describe. The project descriptions will refer to sample documents that I provide in Appendix A for the first project. However, although the text in these documents relates specifically to the first project only, their form can fit almost any project.

The projects contain many documents—some will say too many. It is true that I work for the U.S. federal government and that government work typically requires more documentation than private industry, but that's not why I put in so many documents. Documents are visibility, not bureaucracy. As I've emphasized in preceding chapters, documents let people see and work with the thoughts of others.

The documents in this text are paper-based because that is the medium of a book. The project documents can also be sketches, posters, videotapes, and so on. Use what works at work, but provide visibility.

Much of this chapter is my opinion, which is based on the experiences of others who have already made mistakes and succeeded and my personal experience doing the same. After a statement of each project's situation, I offer my interpretation of how to proceed. There are many ways to succeed in a project and many more ways to fail. These descriptions are not necessarily roadmaps. Just as there are many recipes for a tasty chocolate cake, there are many ways to complete a successful project. Read these examples and think about how to do them differently and still succeed. Try sketching your own diagrams and ideas.

There are no absolute rules, only guidelines. For years, I tried to find a project management rule book only to discover that none exists. How strict the guidelines should be is a matter of choice. Think and do what works at work. When in doubt, err on the side of formal, structured, disciplined practices. Skipping steps or omitting documents incurs risk or raises the chances that potential problems will become real. If the project fails, people will ask why you skipped such and such. Skip only when you are confident the project will succeed anyway.

Use the four basic principles I have described throughout this book: the 3Ps, visibility, configuration management, and standards. Review the best practices, the Capability Maturity Model (CMM), and Personal Software Process (PSP) in Chapter 6. (Because much of this chapter will draw from Chapters 5 and 6, this is the last time I refer to them in this chapter; citing them whenever they are relevant would be cumbersome.) Appendix B, a tutorial look at configuration management across the development life cycle, and Appendix C, a description of Ed Yourdon's structured analysis/structured design (SA/SD), are also useful references for this chapter.

I view each sample project in terms of the V-chart. Although some may view this diagram as too simple or too much like a waterfall, I use it because it contains all the process basics. It has valuable features like showing the one-to-one correspondence of requirements to tests. The evolutionary and spiral project examples show how the V-chart can be varied to provide all the flexibility a project manager will ever need.

Each project description begins with the available people and the product they must build. It then shows you how the particular process fits these two. You may not always have this situation. The process and product may be dictated, and you must choose the people. Chapter 2 gives several examples of how you can juggle these three factors.

The key to all these projects is the people. Pay attention to them. Establish and maintain a good work environment. Talk to everyone every day. Watch out for those times when morale can drop. Look for drops in morale at times when it should be high.

The examples strive to keep everything visible. They assume that you create a management information center (MIC) at the start of the project and that you document everything and put it in the MIC. The examples also assume that you use configuration management daily as described in Chapter 2 and Appendix B. All the projects assume that you capture baselines and manage them, use Configuration Control Boards to make informed decisions, and have a CM staff who can identify and control the products and provide everyone information via status accountings and audits.

For each project, I provide project detail figures that show the activities people will perform and the products they will create. Make charts and figures like these when conducting a project. Because they provide perspective and context for the project, they are the quickest way to show someone where the project is today and where it is going tomorrow.

One last thing: as I mentioned in the preface to this book, software does not run in a vacuum. Therefore, a software project manager can expect to be involved in a fair amount of hardware design and procurement. If you are lucky, the company will have a separate hardware manager. Your job then becomes one of using good people skills and visibility techniques, such as extending the MIC to the hardware designers. However, in my experience, the software project is saddled with the hardware design as well. That means you either do the hardware design or supervise those who do. Nonetheless, software is the driver. Buying the hardware is relatively cheap and simple. The trick is buying the right kind of hardware and making the software work with it.

11.1 ESSENTIALS

The following project examples contain mountains of information, but not everything. Some activities, products, and principles are basic to every project. Time and space do not allow me to mention them wherever they belong specifically in the examples. Instead, I briefly review them and tell you generally where they belong.

11.1.1 Use Journals and Decision Records

The project manager should keep a journal (paper or electronic) and make entries about the project daily. This is the project's history, so note who did what on what date. Projects can become frantic and overwhelming. It is easy to forget details that seem trivial but later become important (what was the name of that consultant who knows how to fix this problem?). Spend five to ten minutes a day keeping a journal.

Also keep a decision book. A decision book documents the decisions a person makes during a project. It describes the question, the alternatives, the decision, and the reason one alternative was chosen instead of the others. If needed, include a complete decision table as illustrated in Chapter 8. Countless decisions are made during a project, so document them. Your decision documentation will become more valuable with time, especially when maintainers try to understand why the developers did what they did.

11.1.2   Perform All CM Activities

Perform all the CM activities described in Chapter 2 and Appendix B. The examples mention the baselines, but they omit many other important CM activities. Identify everything, control all the products, obtain status via status accountings, and perform audits. For example, when a workstation vendor delivers a workstation (spiral project example), the CM staff must perform a physical audit to ensure that it is delivered as ordered. The project team cannot put their hands on it until this is done. Use CM to enhance coordination and communication on projects.

Write visible memoranda for each control gate, where major decisions are made. Do not assume that everyone will hear about the decision. Write a memorandum that states the control gate decision and its reasoning. Post this in the MIC to make it visible and public.

11.1.3   Manage Day by Day

As project manager, this is your most important focus once the project begins. Create and maintain a good work environment, gather status, analyze the situation, and take action. Gather the right types of information, plot it, and keep the plots visible and public in the MIC. Use earned value tracking and the other status indicators described in Chapter 4.

11.1.4   Use Standards

Use the IEEE standards to perform tasks and write documents. Remember, when in doubt go by the standard. Write four or five software requirements specifications using the standard. Once you become experienced in writing such documents, you can change your approach to fit what works at work, but until then, use the standard. Write the documents well. The many documents written during a project are useless if people do not read and understand them. Chapter 2 offers some guidelines on how to write more effectively.

11.1.5   Conduct a Retrospective

The final task of every project is to conduct a project retrospective as discussed in Chapter 4. You, the team, and the lead customer should go off site for a day to discuss the project. What did you learn? What went wrong? What went right? The most important question is how can we do it better next time? That puts the focus on process improvement and the return on investment.

11.2 OPT: A WATERFALL PROJECT

The first project uses the often-maligned waterfall process, which steps through requirements, design, code, integration, and test in sequence. The waterfall process is criticized because it does not permit feedback or iterations. This is true, but the waterfall is the most efficient process when your people know the product they are building.

Some may feel that this first project is too easy and not like the projects they tackle at work. Please be patient—the second and third projects are more complex. Also, both easy and hard products depend on the experience of the people building them. I have never built a product like the one in this example, so I would not be able to use a waterfall process. However, the people at Acme Inc. are experienced in this product type, so for them the waterfall is the best process.

11.2.1 Context

Your name is Rachel Widmark. You head the seven-person Information Services (IS) department in Acme Inc.—a 100-person company that makes flower arrangements for hotels. The people in the IS department work on payroll and office automation issues (word processing templates, spreadsheets, and so on). They also write software occasionally to simulate management issues.

Acme has many different customers with many orders daily. Six clerks handle all the orders. They answer the telephone, write the orders on 5″ × 7″ cards, and ensure that the orders eventually go out to the customers. Everything is done with pencil and paper. Customers are beginning to complain that Acme's phone lines are always busy.

Acme wants to build a basic CRUD (create, retrieve, update, and delete) system for the clerks. The clerks write the same information repeatedly. For each customer, they write the necessary information on a card when the customer calls, on a form for the flower arrangers, and on a form for the billing people, the delivery people, and so on. Acme needs hardware and software that will let the clerks type the information only once while on the telephone and then instruct the system to do all the repetitive work. The goal is to reduce the clerks' time and errors so that they can increase the number of orders and Acme can hire more people.

11.2.2 Project Details

Figures 11.1 and 11.2 show this project. You and the president are calling "OPT" (order processing and tracking). Figure 11.1 is a simple diagram of the waterfall process in a V-chart. Between each project phase (waterfall step) is a

Operations   Operations
User Need   Demonstrate to Users
User Requirements   Validate User Requirements
Developer Requirements   Validate Developer Requirements
High-Level Design   Integrate and Test
Low-Level Design   Test Units
Build Units

Figure 11.1   Diagram for the OPT (waterfall) project.

control gate. The control gate is a review or major milestone, where the managers stop the project and check everything. The project does not move on to the next phase until the managers approve the work to date.

I strongly recommend you draw figures like Figures 11.1 through 11.6 for every project you manage. They show who is doing what and when to produce what. Use big pieces of paper to have complete diagrams. The large diagrams were broken into pages for the format of this book. They would be much better as one big diagram.

Phase	User Need	User Requirements	Developer Requirements
Activities	. Users and management for software to help them at work . Exec sponsor agrees and signs memo starting the project . PM writes context document . PM, lead customer, and exec sponsor write CM plan . PM builds MIC . Think about 3Ps . Select team members	. Think 3Ps . Choose a process . RM Pre top ten list . Write Pre SPMP . Write Conops with users . Write User's Manual . Write test plan 0 per User's manual . Write test procedure 0	. Gather and analyze requirements . Write SRS . Write test plan 1 per SRS . Write test procedure 1 . Capture functional baseline
Control Gate Question	N/A	Do we know who will build what for whom?	Have the users made their bes effort to express the problem?
Question	Who is who and what does everyone need?	What is the problem as seen by the users?	What is the problem as seen b the developers?
Products	User statement of need Exec sponsor memo Context Document CM Plan MIC	Pre SPMP Conops User's Manual Test Plan 0 Test Procedure 0	SRS Test Plan 1 Test Procedure 1 Functional Baseline

Figure 11.2   Details for the OPT (waterfall) project.

Phase	High-Level Design	Low-Level Design	Build Units
Activities	. Do pre design . Cards on the wall planning . RM top ten list . write SPMP . Create a hi-level design . Write SDD 0 . Write Test Plan 2 per SDD 0 . Write test procedure 2 . Capture Allocated baseline	Create low-level design Write SDD 1 Write test plan 3 per SDD 1 Write test procedure 3 Capture design baseline Manage day by day	. Write software units . Inspect code as necessary . Manage day by day
Control Gate Question	Does everyone understand the problem fully?	Have we expressed the high-level solution as best we can?	Do we know everything we need to know to write the software units?
Question	How will we solve the problem at a high-level?	How will we fill in the details of the solution for this evolution?	How do we write the code?
Products	SPMP SDD 0 Test Plan 2 Test Procedure 2 Allocated Baseline	SDD 1 Test Plan 3 Test Procedure 3 Design Baseline	Software units Unit development folders

Phase	Test Units	I&T Units	Validate Developer Requirements
Activities	. Perform test procedure 3 (outsiders) . Write test 3 report . Control resulting units . Manage day by day	. Integrate tested software units. . Perform test procedure 2 . Write test 2 reports . Control resulting integrated units . Manage day by day	. Perform test procedure 1 . Test integrated subsystems (requirements writers or outsiders) . Write test report 1 . Control resulting software . Capture development baseline . Manage day by day
Control Gate Question	Are the software units ready to be tested by outsiders?	Are the integrated software units ready to be tested by outsiders?	Are the integrated units ready to test against the developer's requirements?
Question	Do the software units perform per the low-level software design?	Do the integrated software units perform per the high-level design?	Do the integrated subsystems meet the developer's requirements?
Products	Correctly functioning Software Units Test 3 report	Correctly functioning integrated units Test 2 reports	Test report 1 Development Baseline

Figure 11.2   (continued; also see next page).

Phase	Validate User Requirements	Demonstrate to Users	Operations
Activities	. Test integrated units (user requirements writers) . Perform test 0 procedure . Write test 0 reports . Control resulting integrated units . Manage day by day	. Train the users . Let the users use the software safely . Executive sponsor writes memo . Capture product baseline . Manage day by day	. Install the software on the job . Capture operational baseline . Perform software maintenance activities . Project post mortem
Control Gate Question	Are the integrated subsystems ready to test against the user requirements?	Are the products ready for the users to use?	Are the products ready to work at work?
Question	Do the integrated subsystems meet the user requirements?	Did the developers meet the user's needs?	Is the business working at work?
Products	Test 0 Reports	User accepted software Executive sponsor memo of acceptance Product baseline	Operational Baseline Happy Users

Figure 11.2 (continued).

Figure 11.2 provides the details of the project. Each column of the table describes a phase from Figure 11.1. The *activities* rows list the actions performed during that phase. The *control gate question* rows contain the key question asked during the control gate that precedes the phase. The phase will not begin until everyone answers yes to that question. The *question* rows contain the general question that phase seeks to answer. The *products* rows contain what the project produces during the phase.

The following paragraphs describe the phases in Figure 11.2. Although not shown in the figure, there is an initial operations phase (upper left in Figure 11.1) that shows Acme's situation before the project begins. There is no software and the business is suffering because of it.

User need. At some point, the people at Acme began to grow weary of doing everything with pencil and paper. They knew something about computers from home use and felt there was a better way to do business. This feeling eventually took the form of the clerks' manager asking the president of Acme for software.

The president agreed there was a problem and saw how software could help the business. He was the one who decided to have your department create a system to meet this need. His position in Acme and his interest in the project make him the perfect executive sponsor for the project. He asks you to manage the project. Your first official act is to ask him for a written memorandum (see Appendix A) that states what you and the IS department are supposed to do. That memorandum is the project's first visibility product; it tells everyone who is doing what for whom and under what authority.

Your first unofficial task is to talk with the clerks—your customers. How do they feel about computers coming into their jobs? Many of them are probably afraid and could resist this project to the bitter end. Time and familiarity can reduce this anxiety. Visit with them daily and ask for their help.

Your second official act is to talk with the executive sponsor and the clerks' manager, who is your lead customer. After these discussions, you write a context document (see Appendix A) for you and the rest of your department. The context document will guide the work throughout the project.

At this point, you and the CM staff must write the project's CM plan using the guidelines in Chapter 2 and Appendix B. Appendix A gives the CM plan for this project. The CM staff is one member of the IS department. You explain the CM plan to the executive sponsor, president, and lead customer (the clerks' manager). All three of you sign the plan and agree to abide by and enforce it.

This is also the time to build the MIC so that everyone at Acme can see how the project is progressing. Display the memorandum from the executive sponsor and the CM plan (with big signatures).

The next step is to begin thinking about the people, process, and product. Do the people know about this type of product? What processes have they used?

Select the core team members from the IS department. Everyone in the IS department will help on the project at one time or another. Four people, however, will work on the project full time. Designate these people and place their names in a prominent location in the MIC.

Spend time with the people in the IS department who are not core members of this project. They may feel left out and like second-class citizens. Assure them that they are still important to the health of the company. You need them all the time to keep the company running while you are working on this project. Do whatever you can to bring them into the project as often as you can.

You will use some consultants on this project to augment your staff because you don't have enough people to work the project *and* keep the company going. Explain this to everyone in the IS department. It is easy for people to feel that the consultants will take their jobs. If people feel this way, they will work to see that the consultants and the project fail. Reassure everyone that the consultants are here for the project and then they are gone.

The user need phase ends with a control gate. You, the executive sponsor, and the lead customer meet and discuss who will build what for whom. Details include who in the IS department will talk to which clerks to obtain what specific information. The three of you must agree on these points or the project will fail. People will waste time gathering the wrong information, and you will build the wrong system, Acme will suffer, and it may lose people instead of gaining them.

User Requirements. During the user requirements phase, you attempt to learn and document what the clerks want. The main task of the project team during this phase is to spend time with the clerks to learn their jobs and how a new system can help them. Continue to think about people, process, and product.

Once you know the product and the people, choose the process. Draw a V-chart like that in Figure 11.1, which will form the basis for the general project plan. Time-box or limit each phase in the chart using data from similar past projects. If such data is not available, work harder. Break down the phases into tasks and the tasks into smaller tasks, continuing until you know the tasks well enough to make reasonable estimates. This gives everyone a general idea about the project's length and cost. Emphasize to everyone that this is a general idea. If the final project is within an order of magnitude of this estimate, it is a good estimate.

You can also begin risk management activities (see Chapter 7). You should know a few things about the people, process, and product, so you should be able to see a few potential problems. Put these on a first draft of the top-risks list.

It is also time to start the software project management plan (see Figure 6.41 for the IEEE-Std-1058 format). The first few sections concern company policies, goals, and structure and the basic process model. You already know these items, so go ahead and paste them into the document.

The first complete document in this phase is the concept of operations, which describes the software as the users see it. It is a user-driven operational document, as opposed to a developer-driven technical one. Sit back and let the users talk, act out scenarios, pretend to take telephone orders, and go through their daily routines. Appendix A gives the ConOps for this project. The ConOps can assume many forms; this is only one of them.

The users drive the ConOps, which shows why you need their help. The good will you built in your first unofficial task is important here. If you have talked to the users every day, they have some knowledge of and trust you. They will tell you what you need to know. If they have never seen you before, they will not feel comfortable talking to you, especially if they have suspicions about the project. In such a case, invest your time wisely by spending it with the users. Gaining their trust and insights is the most important thing you can do.

A logical next task after the ConOps is to begin the user manual (Weiss, 1985), which will drive the designers and programmers. Use display screens or flip charts to step the clerks through the software. Lay out a main screen with options. When the clerks press 1, they should see screen X (literally). To send a request to the delivery department, the clerks will do A, B, and C. You should be able to write all this information at this time.

The user manual imposes requirements on the software, so a corresponding test is needed. Remember, there is a one-to-one correspondence between requirements and testing, as Chapter 9 described. The project team writes a test plan and then a test procedure based on the user manual (test plan and procedure 0—there will be four sets of tests in this project, numbered 0, 1, 2, and 3). In the V-chart, the *validate user requirements* phase of the project is opposite user requirements. Testers will run the test written now during that phase to ensure the final software does everything the user manual says it will.

The user requirements phase ends with a control gate. Meet with the executive sponsor, the lead customer, several representative clerks, and the project team to ensure that the requirements for the software as seen by the clerks are understood. The project team states what they think the clerks want. The clerks correct them as needed and vote yes on the control gate only when they are satisfied.

Developer Requirements. This phase of the project captures the requirements for the software as seen by the project team. The information the clerks provide is not sufficient for designers and programmers to build the software. The clerks stated how many calls they receive a day and what they write down for each call. The project team translates that into bytes, baud rates, operating systems, user interfaces, memory, printers, networks, and so on.

The product of this and the previous phase is the *Software Requirements Specification* (SRS). The project team must take the user requirements and break them into greater detail. The resulting technical document should be almost good enough to pass over a cubicle wall to a designer (I don't recommend just handing one over, but it's worthwhile to get close to that quality.) Appendix A gives the SRS for this project.

The SRS, like the user manual, imposes requirements on the software, so the project needs a corresponding test. The project team writes a test plan and then a test procedure based on the SRS (test plan and procedure 1). In the V-chart, the *validate developer requirements* phase is opposite the developer requirements. Testers will run the test written now during that phase to ensure that the final software satisfies the SRS.

Talk with the lead customer and some of the senior users while you are writing the SRS. You will need the lead customer's approval during a control gate at the end of this phase. If the control gate is the first time the lead customer sees the SRS, you are in trouble. You will fail the control gate and spend another week talking about and changing the SRS. Let the lead customer know what you are doing and what is in the SRS as you write it. Maintain communication and trust with the customer at all times.

It is now time for the CM person to capture the functional baseline. This will contain all the products to date (ConOps, user manual, SRS, and test plans and procedures 0 and 1). Have the CM person put the original of the baseline in a safe place and display a copy in the MIC. The functional baseline Configuration Control Board consists of you, the executive sponsor, and the lead customer.

This phase also ends with a control gate. Meet with the lead customer and project team to discuss the SRS. The lead customer must ensure that the SRS does not steer the software away from what he wants. The designers will design software on the basis of the SRS and user manual. They must state their understanding of these products. If the writers of these products have a different understanding, the two must reconcile their differences. Design cannot begin until everyone agrees on the requirements—no solutions until you know the problem.

High-Level Design. In this phase, the project team will design a solution at a high level and plan the project in detail. The first step is a preliminary design. The designers spend at most one day sketching out the software's basic subsystems. Each subsystem will have a name and functional responsibility.

The preliminary design lets you plan the project in detail (as opposed to the broad planning done during the previous phase). Treat each subsystem as a product and create a work breakdown structure (WBS) for each. Set up an initial network of tasks from the WBS and work on it until the project team agrees on a final task network. The task network will include tasks you have already performed (write CM plan, write user manual, and so on). You performed tasks that were not planned officially, but that is acceptable; the front-end of projects is not that exact. From this point, however, the project will have a plan and you and the team need to follow it. Use the techniques from the Personal Software Process to estimate the size of each product and duration of each task. Work on these estimates with the project team until they commit to meeting the estimates. Do not create the estimates yourself and tell the project team what they will do. If they do not own the estimates they have no stake in seeing them succeed. Display the final task network (PERT chart) and the corresponding Gantt chart in the MIC. These fill in all the details of Figure 11.1.

Now complete the risk management tasks. Examine all risks and write the top-risks list.

Finish the SPMP. All the policy, planning, resource, and risk information is available. Appendix A contains the SPMP for this project, including risk management information.

Once planning is done, create a high-level design for the software. This fills in the details of the preliminary design done earlier. Use basic design principles of abstraction, coupling, and information hiding and use software diagrams. HIPO charts would probably suffice for this project. The high-level design must address all the requirements in the SRS. Place the high-level design in an SDD (SDD 0). Appendix A contains the SDD for this project. SDD 0 is the high-level design only. SDD 1 adds low-level design.

High-level design work does not require everyone's time. It is best for a couple of people to do this task because the ideas are at a high level of abstraction and having too many opinions is not helpful. Do not, however, lock out people. The programmers will eventually make the high-level design work. Let them see the design while the designers are creating it. Ask their opinions and have them think about implementation details. Let them gain part ownership so that they will work to see the design succeed.

SDD 0 imposes requirements on the software, so, once again, the project needs a corresponding test. The project team writes a test plan and then a test procedure based on SDD 0 (test plan and procedure 2). The SDD states that "subsystem X interfaces with subsystem Y and performs functions A, B, and C." The test plan and procedure verify that the final subsystem X performs as designed. In the V-chart, the *integrate and test* phase of the project is opposite the high-level design. Testers will run the test written here during that phase to ensure the software subsystems satisfy SDD 0.

It is now time for the CM staff to capture the allocated baseline. This will contain all the products since the functional baseline (SPMP, SDD 0, and test plan and procedure 2). This baseline also goes in a safe place and a copy is displayed in the MIC. The allocated baseline Configuration Control Board comprises you and the designers.

The phase ends with a control gate. Meet with the designers and programmers to discuss the SPMP and high-level SDD. After the control gate, the detailed project plan will become public. Therefore, everyone who has a task in that plan must agree that they can complete that task according to the plan. The designers must ensure that the high-level design addresses every requirement in the SRS. If it does not, future work will only multiply the omission.

Low-Level Design. In this phase, the project team will create and document the low-level or detailed design of the software. They begin with the high-level design in SDD 0, which specifies subsystems. Their final product will be specifications for the lowest level of software units (probably subroutines). This product must have enough information to allow programmers to write source code. Once again, let the programmers look at the low-level design while it is taking shape. Encourage them to take ownership of the design so that they will work to see it succeed. Place the low-level design in another SDD (SDD 1).

As before, SDD 1 places requirements on the software, so the project needs a test plan and procedure (test plan and procedure 3). SDD 1 states that "software unit X has input parameters A, B, and C and output parameters D, E, and F, and performs functions G and H." The test must verify that the final software unit X satisfies that specification. In the V-chart, the *test units* phase of the project is opposite the low-level design. Testers will run the test written here during that phase to ensure that the software units satisfy SDD 1.

The CM staff captures the design baseline. This will contain all the products since the allocated baseline (SDD 1 and test plan and procedure 3). This baseline again goes to a safe place and a copy is displayed in the MIC. The design baseline Configuration Control Board is made up of you and the designers.

A control gate ends this phase. Meet with the designers, and programmers to discuss SDD 1. The programmers will take the software unit specifications in SDD 1 and write source code, so they need all the information to do that. The programmers and designers must agree on the content and meaning of SDD 1. Any misunderstanding will cause the programmers to write the wrong code.

Time Out! What if We Misunderstood? The discussion of the waterfall project so far should raise questions. What if we misunderstood something? What if we made a mistake in the developer requirements? What if the users have a new idea about their job and the software? Why don't we show the users some prototypes before we start designing and coding?

These questions bring up the bad side of the waterfall model. You must have everything correct before leaving a phase for the next one because looking back is almost impossible. In this project, the product is easy. It doesn't have these nagging questions. There will be no need to back up, because there will not be any misunderstandings or additional thoughts that change the requirements. In this project, the people do not find it hard to develop the product and the product is not hard to develop. This is the only time to use a waterfall process.

The users and developers have been working in the product field for years and know all the details. The users can express their desires clearly on the first try and the developers know exactly what they are trying to say. This is all quite efficient.

The other two projects in the cookbook are for products the people do not understand well. Those examples will show how the other processes allow for learning but also introduce inefficiencies.

Build Units. Resuming the OPT project details, you come to the build units phase, in which the programmers write source code from the specifications for the software units (subroutines) in SDD 1. While doing this, the programmers create unit development folders (see Chapter 4) for each unit. The UDFs will contain the specification, source code, and, later, the test results.

Talk to the programmers every day one on one. The build phase is when the software becomes a reality or fails. Do not allow anyone to mumble that all is well when they are struggling. Remember the "I make mistakes" speech. Look for puzzled faces and bring in helpers when necessary.

The programmers will inspect and test the units. These activities are to ensure that the units function correctly on the inside (the white box testing described in Chapter 9). Their task is to prepare the units for others to test in the next phase. Emphasize that people make mistakes, which is why the programmers must inspect one another's code during this phase. If the code is incorrect in the next phase, it will be sent back to this phase. Moving back a phase to correct an error is expensive.

The phase ends with a control gate. Meet with the programmers to discuss the status of the software units. The programmers must convince you that the software units are ready to hand over to someone else for testing. The goal is to have the units pass the test the first time. The project team wants to avoid the test–fix, test–fix cycles.

Test Units. This phase begins the ascent up the right side of the V-chart in Figure 11.1. Each phase on this side involves combining parts and testing them. Activities on the left side broke the problem into smaller parts and produced a test for those parts; the activity on the bottom of the V-chart built a small solution. It is now time to test the solution, combine it into a bigger solution, test that, and so on.

The test units phase involves outside testers. It would be great to bring in outside consultants to do this, but it is sufficient to have programmers on the project team test the units written by other programmers. Watch out for the antagonism that can develop. Programmers can take it personally when other programmers find errors. Programmers can rub it in when they find errors. Keep the team a team. If there is bad news, first confirm it and then deliver it personally and carefully.

The testers use test procedure 3 written during the low-level design phase and document test results by writing test report 3.

If a software unit fails its test, it is sent back to the programmer and the build-units phase. This is an unwanted exercise, as I described earlier. When a software unit passes its test, have the CM staff capture it. Make sure the UDF has the correct copy of the correct software. It should also contain the software's specification from SDD 1, its test from test plan 3 and test procedure 3, and the test results from test report 3.

The phase ends with a control gate. Meet with the programmers and testers to ensure that *all* the software units have passed all their tests. You can't move the project to the next phase if only *most* of the units have passed.

Integrate and Test. The project team will combine the software units into subsystems and test them during this phase. The subsystem specifications are in SDD 0 and their tests are in test procedure 2. The testers—programmers who did not write the units—run the test and put the results in test report 2.

If any subsystem fails its test, it is sent back. Again, watch out for possible antagonism among programmers and testers. As you go further up the right side of the V-chart, it becomes increasingly expensive to back up and correct mistakes. Any change to anything on the left side of the V-chart must ripple down that side and back up the right side. The project team may need to repeat low-level design as well as programming. Revising the low-level design also means revising the tests for that design as well as the code in the software units.

The phase ends with a control gate. Meet with the programmers and testers to ensure that *all* the software subsystems have passed all their tests. You can't move the project to the next phase if only *most* have passed.

Validate Developer Requirements. The project team will combine the software subsystems into a complete system and test it against the developer requirements during this phase. The developer requirements are in the SRS and the test is in test procedure 1. The entire project team runs the test and puts the results in test report 1.

If the software system fails the test, the project team has big problems. Finding, let alone correcting, the problem may take weeks. Correcting any problems may mean revising the high-level design, low-level design, or code.

The CM staff captures the development baseline. This contains all the products since the design baseline (software units, subsystems, complete system, and test reports). This baseline again goes to a safe place and a copy is displayed in the MIC. The development baseline Configuration Control Board comprises you and the programmers.

The phase ends with a control gate, in which you meet with the entire project team. In the next phase you must show the clerks that the software is ready for them. This is a big step. The software must work. Developers can forgive each other's mistakes because they've made them, too. The clerks, however, may not be sympathetic. Some of them still may not want the software. Those who do, expect the software to work in just the way they conveyed to the developers weeks earlier. The project team must ensure that they and their software are ready.

Validate User Requirements. The project team, in cooperation with the lead customer (the clerks' manager), will test the complete system against the user requirements during this phase. The user requirements are in the user manual and the test is in test procedure 0. The project team and some clerks run the test and put the results in test report 0.

If the software system fails the test, everyone has a big problem. Correcting problems at this late phase is very expensive. If you have led the project team through the V-chart with care and discipline, major problems should not surface here. If, however, you coasted along, especially in the control gates, you may have a bad surprise.

A control gate meeting with the president (executive sponsor) and lead customer (clerks' manager) ends this phase. All of you must decide if the software is ready for the clerks to use in a practice setting. As long as the software agrees with the manual—and that was the object of the test in this phase— everything is ready.

Demonstrate to Users. This phase prepares everyone for putting the software on-line at work. The project team places the software in a setting that is as close to being on the job as possible. They train the clerks on the software by going through the user manual step by step. The clerks learn the software and how they will use it at work.

It is important at this time for the project team to help the clerks. The team's attitude can make or break the entire project. If the clerks do not like the software system, they will not use it, and the project will be a waste. When the users balk at the system, and they will at some point, don't let the project team back away and say "We gave them everything they wanted and they don't like it." Instead, encourage them to step in with a positive, helpful attitude. They must show the clerks what is happening, how to use the software, and how it will help them.

When the lead customer feels the clerks are trained, he should let both you and the executive sponsor know. The executive sponsor then writes a memorandum of acceptance. This memorandum quickly appears in the center of the MIC for everyone to see. Making success visible is important.

The CM staff captures the product baseline. This contains all the products since the development baseline (user-accepted software). This baseline again goes in a safe place. The product baseline Configuration Control Board comprises you, the executive sponsor, and the lead customer.

The final—and perhaps most important—control gate of the project occurs here. If you, the executive sponsor, and the lead customer pass this control gate, the software will go on-line. If the software is not ready, the clerks will fail at their jobs, customers will become angry, Acme will suffer, and people will lose their jobs. Wait for the next phase until all three of you are certain you are ready to take that leap.

Operations. This phase is where the project team installs the software and the clerks use it at work. Once the software is installed and operational, the CM staff captures a copy of that and places in it the operational baseline.

The project team disbands and goes back to their regular jobs in the IS department. The software goes into software maintenance. Changes to the software come through a regular software maintenance process (see Chapter 10).

Even though the project team disbands, they are not finished. The users will find problems. Some of the problems will be with the software and some will be personal. The users will call on the project team. It won't matter who has been designated to maintain the software; the users will call on the people who delivered it to them. Coach these people not to say "Don't talk to me, I'm done with that. Talk to someone else." The software project can still fail after final delivery. Everyone must continue to work with the users. Everyone must understand this will happen and have the patience and energy to work with it.

The final task of this project is to conduct a project postmortem as discussed earlier. You, the team, and the clerks' manager (lead customer) should go off site for a day to discuss the project. What did you learn? What went wrong? What went right? The most important question is how can you all do better next time? That puts the focus on process improvement and the return on investment.

11.3   SYSTEM UPGRADE: AN EVOLUTIONARY PROJECT

This project uses an evolutionary process, in which the product is delivered in stages. Evolving is a newer, more popular style of project. As the example will show, it is a way to deal with a product that is difficult for the people building it. The product has too many unknowns for it to be delivered all at once. Evolutions let people learn about each unknown one at a time.

In describing the System Upgrade project, I follow the same format I did for the waterfall project and borrow heavily from it. I do not describe each phase in as much detail or delve into as many people issues, and I do not provide sample documents. However, most of the phases are similar to those in the previous project, and the previous descriptions and document models apply for the most part.

11.3.1   Context

This project has the same company, Acme Inc, and the same personnel—you, selected people from the seven-person IS department, the manager of the clerks (lead customer), and Acme's president (executive sponsor).

However, this time, the clerks are using a basic text-based computer system with a central minicomputer and a terminal for each clerk (as opposed to pencil and paper in the previous project). The clerks are proficient with this system. The IS department built the existing software for the clerks.

The president of Acme Inc. wants you to provide a new software system. Everyone feels that a graphical user interface (GUI) will raise productivity because the clerks will be able to point and click many operations instead of typing everything. Several industry studies support the utility of a GUI, so Acme has decided to go with it. A GUI will require a new operating system on the same central minicomputer. It will also require new terminals. The new terminals will plug into the existing system with no problems (really). While making these changes, the president and clerks' manager have a few new functions they want you to include.

11.3.2   Project Details

Figures 11.3 and 11.4 show the details of the System Upgrade project. Figure 11.3 is a simple diagram similar to Figure 11.1, except that here the basic V-chart has three smaller V-charts in the middle. The smaller V-charts are the evolutions. Figure 11.4 is similar to Figure 11.2, giving details of the many phases in Figure 11.3. As before, each phase ends with a control gate.

Operations. The operations phase of this project is different from that of the previous project, which began with no software. This one begins with a soft-

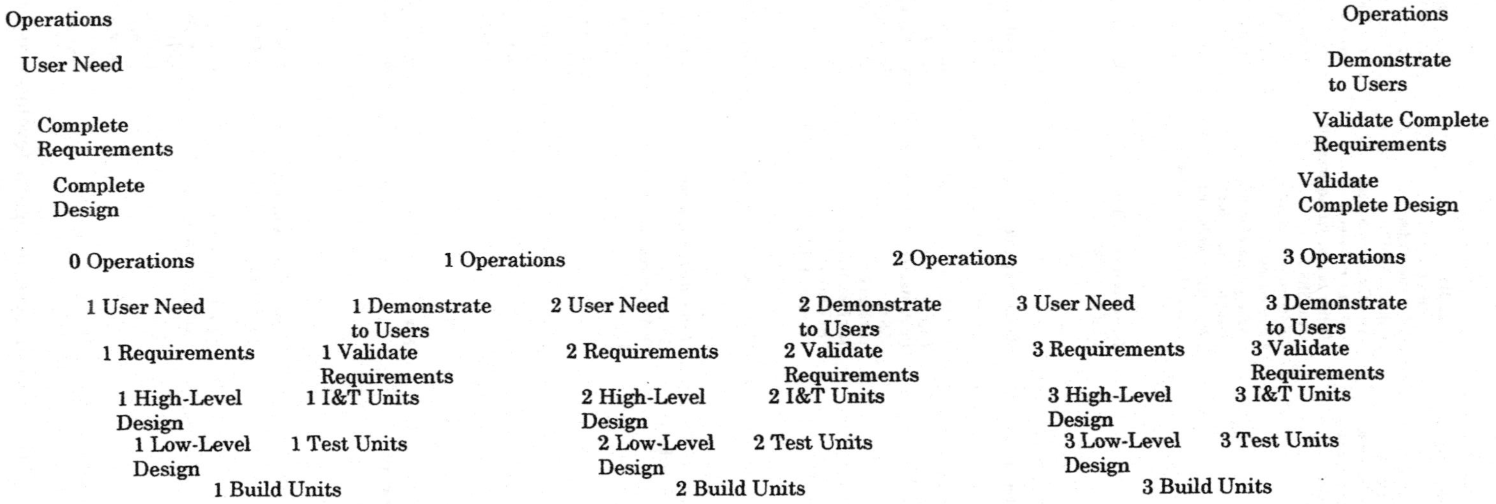

Operations

User Need

Complete
Requirements

Complete
Design

0 Operations

1 User Need

1 Requirements

1 High-Level
Design
1 Low-Level
Design
1 Build Units

1 Demonstrate
to Users
1 Validate
Requirements
1 I&T Units

1 Test Units

1 Operations

2 User Need

2 Requirements

2 High-Level
Design
2 Low-Level
Design
2 Build Units

2 Demonstrate
to Users
2 Validate
Requirements
2 I&T Units

2 Test Units

2 Operations

3 User Need

3 Requirements

3 High-Level
Design
3 Low-Level
Design
3 Build Units

3 Demonstrate
to Users
3 Validate
Requirements
3 I&T Units

3 Test Units

3 Operations

Operations

Demonstrate
to Users

Validate Complete
Requirements

Validate
Complete Design

Figure 11.3 Diagram for the system upgrade (evolutionary) project.

Phase	User Need	Complete Requirements	Complete Design
Activities	. Users and management see a need for a new HW SW system . Exec sponsor agrees and signs memo starting the project . PM writes context document . PM, lead customer, and exec sponsor write CM plan . PM builds MIC . Think about 3Ps	. Think 3Ps . Choose a process . RM Pre top ten list . Write Pre SPMP 0 . Write Conops with users . Write User's Manual . Gather and analyze requirements . Write SRS 0 . Write test plan 0.0 per User's manual . Write test procedure 0.0 . Write test plan 0.1 per SRS . Write test procedure 0.1 . Capture Functional baseline 0	. Do pre design for complete system . Cards on the wall planning session for complete project . RM top ten list . Write SPMP 0 for complete project . Create a hi-level design for complete system . Write SDD 0 . Write Test Plan 0.2 per SDD 0 . Write test procedure 0.2 . Capture Allocated baseline 0 . Manage day by day
Control Gate Question	N/A	Do we know who will build what for whom?	Does everyone understand the problem?
Question	Who is who and what does everyone need?	What is the problem?	How will we solve the problem (at a high level)?
Products	User statement of need Exec sponsor memo Context Document CM Plan MIC	Pre SPMP 0 Conops User's Manual SRS 0 Test Plan 0.0 Test Procedure 0.0 Test Plan 0.1 Functional Baseline 0	SPMP 0 SDD 0 Test Plan 0.2 Test Procedure 0.2 Allocated Baseline 0
Phase	0 Operations	1 User Need	1 Requirements
Activities	This evolution aims to add the new functions to the existing system.	. Gather the user needs for this evolution. . PM writes context document for this evolution	. Write Conops with users . Write User's Manual 1 . Gather and analyze requirements . Write SRS 1 . Write test plan 1.0 per User's manual 1 . Write test procedure 1.0 . Write test plan 1.1 per SRS 1 . Write test procedure 1.1 . capture Functional baseline 1
Control Gate Question	Have we expressed the high-level solution as best we can?	N/A	Do we know who will build what for whom for this evolution?
Question	N/A	Who is who and what does everyone need?	What is the problem to be solved in this evolution?
Products	None	User statement of need Context Document	Conops User's Manual 1 SRS 1 Test Plan 1.0 Test Procedure 1.0 Test Plan 1.1 Test Procedure 1.1 Functional baseline 1

Figure 11.4 Details for the system upgrade (evolutionary) project.

Phase	1 High-Level Design	1 Low-Level Design	1 Build Units
Activities	. Do pre design for this evolution . Cards on the wall planning session for this evolution . RM top ten list . write SPMP 1 for this evolution . Create a hi-level design for this evolution . Write SDD 1 . Write Test Plan 1.2 per SDD 1 . Write test procedure 1.2 . Capture Allocated baseline 1 . Manage day by day	Create low-level design Write SDD 1.1 Write test plan 1.3 per SDD 1.1 Write test procedure 1.3 Capture design baseline 1 Manage day by day	. Write software units . Inspect code as necessary . Manage day by day
Control Gate Question	Does everyone understand the problem for this evolution?	Have we expressed the high-level solution as best we can?	Do we know everything we need to know to write the software units?
Question	How will we solve the problem faced in this evolution?	How will we fill in the details of the solution for this evolution?	How do we write the code?
Products	RM top ten list SPMP 1 for this evolution SDD 1 Test Plan 1.2 Test Procedure 1.2 Allocated Baseline 1	SDD 1.1 Test Plan 1.3 Test Procedure 1.3 Design Baseline 1	Software units Unit development folders
Phase	1 Test Units	1 I&T Units	1 Validate Requirements
Activities	. Perform test procedure 1.3 (outsiders) . Test software units . Write test 1.3 report . Control resulting units . Manage day by day	. Integrate tested software units . Perform test procedure 1.2 . Write test 1.2 reports . Control resulting integrated units . Manage day by day	. Perform test procedure 1.0 . Perform test procedure 1.1 . Write test report 1.0 . Write test report 1.1 . Control resulting software . Capture development baseline 1 . Manage day by day
Control Gate Question	Are the software units ready to be tested by outsiders?	Are the integrated software units ready to be tested by outsiders?	Is the software ready to test against the requirements?
Question	Do the software units perform per the low-level software design?	Do the integrated software units perform per the high-level design?	Does the software meet the requirements?
Products	Correctly functioning Software Units Test 1.3 report	Correctly functioning integrated units Test 1.2 reports	Test report 1.0 Test report 1.1

Figure 11.4   (continued; also see next page).

Phase	1 Demonstrate to Users	1 Operations	2 User Need
Activities	. Train the users . Let the users use the software safely . Executive sponsor writes memo of acceptance . Capture product baseline 1 . Manage day by day	. Do nothing	. Gather the user needs for this evolution. . PM writes context document for this evolution
Control Gate Question	Are the products ready for the users to use?	Are the products ready to work at work?	Should we continue on to the next evolution or stop here?
Question	Did the developers meet the user's needs?	N/A	Who is who and what does everyone need?
Products	User accepted software Executive sponsor memo of acceptance Product baseline 1	None	User statement of need Context Document

Phase	2 Requirements	2 High-Level Design	2 Low-Level Design
Activities	. Write Conops with users . Write User's Manual 2 . Gather and analyze requirements . Write SRS 2 . Write test plan 2.0 per User's manual 2 . Write test procedure 2.0 . Write test plan 2.1 per SRS 2 . Write test procedure 2.1 . capture Functional baseline 2	. Do pre design for this evolution . Cards on the wall planning session for this evolution . RM top ten list . write SPMP 2 for this evolution . Create a hi-level design for this evolution . Write SDD 2 . Write Test Plan 2.2 per SDD 2 . Write test procedure 2.2 . Capture Allocated baseline 2 . Manage day by day	Create low-level design Write SDD 2.1 Write test plan 2.3 per SDD 2.1 Write test procedure 2.3 Capture design baseline 2 Manage day by day
Control Gate Question	Do we know who will build what for whom for this evolution?	Does everyone understand the problem for this evolution?	Have we expressed the high-level solution as best we can?
Question	What is the problem to be solved in this evolution?	How will we solve the problem faced in this evolution?	How will we fill in the details of the solution for this evolution?
Products	Conops User's Manual 2 SRS 2 Test Plan 2.0 Test Procedure 2.0 Test Plan 2.1 Test Procedure 2.1 Functional baseline 2	RM top ten list SPMP 2 for this evolution SDD 2 Test Plan 2.2 Test Procedure 2.2 Allocated Baseline 2	SDD 2.1 Test Plan 2.3 Test Procedure 2.3 Design Baseline 2

Figure 11.4   (continued).

Phase	2 Build Units	2 Test Units	2 I&T Units
Activities	. Write software units . Inspect code as necessary . Manage day by day	. Perform test procedure 2.3 (outsiders) . Test software units . Write test 2.3 report . Control resulting units . Manage day by day	. Integrate tested software units . Perform test procedure 2.2 . Write test 2.2 reports . Control resulting integrated units . Manage day by day
Control Gate Question	Do we know everything we need to know to write the software units?	Are the software units ready to be tested by outsiders?	Are the integrated software units ready to be tested by outsiders?
Question	How do we write the code?	Do the software units perform per the low-level software design?	Do the integrated software units perform per the high-level design?
Products	Software units Unit development folders	Correctly functioning Software Units Test 2.3 report	Correctly functioning integrated units Test 2.2 reports
Phase	2 Validate Requirements	2 Demonstrate to Users	2 Operations
Activities	. Perform test procedure 2.0 . Perform test procedure 2.1 . Write test report 2.0 . Write test report 2.1 . Control resulting software . Capture development baseline 2 . Manage day by day	. Train the users . Let the users use the software safely . Executive sponsor writes memo of acceptance . Capture product baseline 2 . Manage day by day	. Do nothing
Control Gate Question	Is the software ready to test against the requirements?	Are the products ready for the users to use?	Are the products ready to work at work?
Question	Does the software meet the requirements?	Did the developers meet the user's needs?	N/A
Products	Test report 2.0 Test report 2.1	User accepted software Executive sponsor memo of acceptance Product baseline 2	None

Figure 11.4   (continued; also see next page).

Phase	3 User Need	3 Requirements	3 High-Level Design
Activities	. Gather the user needs for this evolution. . PM writes context document for this evolution	. Write Conops with users . Write User's Manual 3 . Gather and analyze requirements . Write SRS 3 . Write test plan 3.0 per User's manual 3 . Write test procedure 3.0 . Write test plan 3.1 per SRS 3 . Write test procedure 3.1 . capture Functional baseline 3	. Do pre design for this evolution . Cards on the wall planning session for this evolution . RM top ten list . write SPMP 3 for this evolution . Create a hi-level design for this evolution . Write SDD 3 . Write Test Plan 3.2 per SDD 3 . Write test procedure 3.2 . Capture Allocated baseline 3 . Manage day by day
Control Gate Question	Should we continue on to the next evolution or stop here?	Do we know who will build what for whom for this evolution?	Does everyone understand the problem for this evolution?
Question	Who is who and what does everyone need?	What is the problem to be solved in this evolution?	How will we solve the problem faced in this evolution?
Products	User statement of need Context Document	Conops User's Manual 3 SRS 3 Test Plan 3.0 Test Procedure 3.0 Test Plan 3.1 Test Procedure 3.1 Functional baseline 3	RM top ten list SPMP 3 for this evolution SDD 3 Test Plan 3.2 Test Procedure 3.2 Allocated Baseline 3

Phase	3 Low-Level Design	3 Build Units	3 Test Units
Activities	Create low-level design Write SDD 3.1 Write test plan 3.3 per SDD 3.1 Write test procedure 3.3 Capture design baseline 3 Manage day by day	. Write software units . Inspect code as necessary . Manage day by day	. Perform test procedure 3.3 (outsiders) . Test software units . Write test 3.3 report . Control resulting units . Manage day by day
Control Gate Question	Have we expressed the high-level solution as best we can?	Do we know everything we need to know to write the software units?	Are the software units ready to be tested by outsiders?
Question	How will we fill in the details of the solution for this evolution?	How do we write the code?	Do the software units perform per the low-level software design?
Products	SDD 3.1 Test Plan 3.3 Test Procedure 3.3 Design Baseline 3	Software units Unit development folders	Correctly functioning Software Units Test 3.3 report

Figure 11.4   (continued).

	3 I&T Units	3 Validate Requirements	3 Demonstrate to Users
Phase			
Activities	. Integrate tested software units . Perform test procedure 3.2 . Write test 3.2 reports . Control resulting integrated units . Manage day by day	. Perform test procedure 3.0 . Perform test procedure 3.1 . Write test report 3.0 . Write test report 3.1 . Control resulting software . Capture development baseline 3 . Manage day by day	. Train the users . Let the users use the software safely . Executive sponsor writes memo of acceptance . Capture product baseline 3 . Manage day by day
Control Gate Question	Are the integrated software units ready to be tested by outsiders?	Is the software ready to test against the requirements?	Are the products ready for the users to use?
Question	Do the integrated software units perform per the high-level design?	Does the software meet the requirements?	Did the developers meet the user's needs?
Products	Correctly functioning integrated units Test 3.2 reports	Test report 3.0 Test report 3.1	User accepted software Executive sponsor memo of acceptance Product baseline 3

	3 Operations	Validate Complete Design	Validate Complete Requirements
Phase			
Activities	. Do nothing	. Integrate complete software . Perform test procedure 0.2 . Integrate complete manual chapters into books . Review manual books . Write test 0.2 reports . Control resulting software . Manage day by day	. Perform test procedure 0.0 . Perform test procedure 0.1 . Write test procedure 0.0 . Write test procedure 0.1 . Capture development baseline 0 . Manage day by day
Control Gate Question	Are the products ready to work at work?	Is the complete software package ready to be tested against the complete design (outsiders)?	Is the complete software package ready to be tested against the complete requirements (outsiders)?
Question	Are we ready to move up to the right side of the big V?	Does the complete software perform per the complete design?	Does the complete software perform per the complete requirements?
Products	None	Complete software Manuals for complete software Test report 0.2	Test report 0.0 Test report 0.1 Development baseline 0

Figure 11.4   (continued; also see next page).

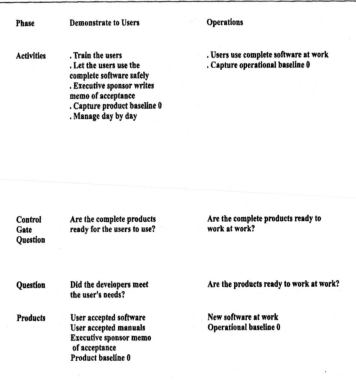

Phase	Demonstrate to Users	Operations
Activities	. Train the users . Let the users use the complete software safely . Executive sponsor writes memo of acceptance . Capture product baseline 0 . Manage day by day	. Users use complete software at work . Capture operational baseline 0
Control Gate Question	Are the complete products ready for the users to use?	Are the complete products ready to work at work?
Question	Did the developers meet the user's needs?	Are the products ready to work at work?
Products	User accepted software User accepted manuals Executive sponsor memo of acceptance Product baseline 0	New software at work Operational baseline 0

Figure 11.4   (continued).

ware system that has a full set of CM baselines. The new project will work with these baselines.

User Need. As in the previous project, people began talking about replacing the existing system. It is growing old. The hardware is not made anymore and maintenance will be unavailable in a few years. New equipment will be cheaper, faster, smaller, and will free floor space that can be used for the main part of Acme's business—flower arranging. Also, a faster system means the customers will not wait as long on the telephone.

The president of Acme decides to replace the existing system. He becomes the executive sponsor and signs a memorandum tasking you with the project.

You discuss the project with the executive sponsor and the lead customer and write a context document. The CM staff writes a CM plan, and you, the executive sponsor, and the lead customer sign it. You create an MIC and place the memorandum, context document, and CM plan in it.

Start talking with the users. Build a relationship of trust with them as you will need them often in this project.

In thinking about the people and product, you realize that this product may be difficult to develop. Acme employees have no experience with the new operating system or with GUIs. Acme could solve this problem by firing the current employees and hiring new ones, but although that is a viable business alternative, it is one Acme has never taken. The president of Acme (the executive sponsor) is adamant about keeping his current employees. This means that Acme cannot solve this problem in one V-chart without taking a major risk. As before, you form the core team from members of the IS department. Everyone in the IS department will help on the project at one time or another. The core group will work on the project full-time. Designate these people and place their names in a prominent location in the MIC. Reassure the people whom you do not select to be core team members. They are important and you and Acme need them.

The user need phase ends with a control gate. Meet with the executive sponsor and lead customer to discuss who will build what for whom. Agreeing on these points is critical. Without full agreement, people will waste time gathering the wrong information.

Complete Requirements. This is where the evolutionary process begins to diverge from the waterfall process in the previous project. The goal of this phase is understand the requirements for the *complete* project—both the user and developer views. The first task in this phase is to think in more depth about the people and product. Sketch out the larger parts of the V-chart in Figure 11.3 and leave the middle—the number of evolutions—blank.

It is also time to begin the SPMP. The first few sections again concern company policies, goals, and structure and the basic process model—things you already know. Paste them into the SPMP. Start risk management tasks and put all this information into the preliminary SPMP (SPMP 0).

The project team gathers information and writes the ConOps and user manual. The users help in these tasks, so concentrate on the new functions and new GUI. The new operating system means nothing to the users because they will not see it.

The project team then gathers the requirements. They begin with the functional baseline of the existing system, which contains the functions the new system must retain. The users help them add the new functions. The resulting SRS does not have all the details; the evolutions will add these. However, take care to ensure that delays do not cause people to become lax. This is a common pitfall in an evolutionary project.

The project team records the requirements in SRS 0. Have the team keep in touch with the lead customer while writing SRS 0. The lead customer must approve this before you can proceed. Do not surprise him with it during a control gate. They also write the test plan and procedure 0.0 per the user manual; they write test plan and procedure 0.1 per SRS 0.

The CM staff captures functional baseline 0. It contains the ConOps, user manual, SRS 0, and test plans and procedures 0.0 and 0.1. (The numbers of the documents may be a little confusing. I use X.Y with X designating the evolution and the Y the document. If using words instead of numbers makes more sense in your organization, do it that way.) The baseline documents are put in a safe place and a copy is displayed in the MIC. The Configuration Control Board for this baseline is made up of you, the executive sponsor, and the lead customer.

The phase ends with a control gate. Meet with the lead customer and project team to discuss the user manual and SRS 0. These must express the needs of the lead customer. The designers state their understanding of these products to ensure that everyone agrees on the problem—no solutions until you understand the problem.

Complete Design. During this phase, the project team designs a solution at a high level and plans the project in detail. The work is similar to that in the high-level design phase of the waterfall project. The project team will design an overall system. Once they know the major parts, they can plan the project. Let the eventual programmers see the design as it takes shape. Start to have them own the design so that they will work toward its success.

The first step is a preliminary design. The designers spend several days designing the subsystems. The preliminary design shows that the product will

- Contain new functions
- Operate with a new operating system
- Use a new GUI

Thus, a logical approach is to break the project into three evolutions or subprojects that deliver these new items.

The project team uses basic planning techniques—a WBS for each product, cards on the wall, and a network of tasks for the entire project. Have the team members participate so that they can own the plan; do not dictate it to them. You can then fill in the middle of Figure 11.3 (left blank in the previous phase) with the three evolutions or small V-charts. Create time boxes for each phase in that figure to get a first estimate for the entire project.

The remainder of this phase consists of the tasks in the high-level design phase of the waterfall project. The project team analyzes risks and writes SPMP 0—a high-level plan for the entire project. They finish the preliminary design and put these high-level concepts in SDD 0. They write test plan 0.2 and test procedure 0.2 on the basis of SDD 0. The CM staff captures allocated baseline 0, which contains SPMP 0, SDD 0, and test plan and procedure 0.2. You and the designers are the Configuration Control Board for this baseline.

The phase ends with a control gate. Meet with the executive sponsor and lead customer to discuss the design and project plan. The lead customer must accept that you will be delivering the system in three pieces. Customers want everything now, and are not always receptive to pieces over time. The executive sponsor must understand that the product is difficult for your people.

Trying to deliver everything at once would be a major risk and using the proposed approach reduces that risk. The project continues only after everyone agrees.

Evolutions. Each small V-chart in Figure 11.3, is a project in itself. The only difference between them and a large project is that they do not run to a final conclusion, where the users use the product at work. Instead, they end when the product is ready to be installed and used at work. When one evolution completes, you, the executive sponsor, and the lead customer must make a business decision. You can skip the remaining evolutions and install this small product at work or you can continue with the remaining evolutions. If a succeeding evolution fails, you can always back up and use the small product from the preceding evolution. This reduces risk because after the first evolution, you can quit any time and the users will have more than when the project began.

Because each evolution is a small project, I do not describe every phase in detail for every evolution. All the phases are similar to those in the waterfall project. Figure 11.4 lists the details—activities, questions, control gate questions, and products—of all the phases.

Give your team a short break between evolutions. You should always celebrate and have a short break between projects. The evolutions are short projects and deserve the normal celebration and break. If you skip these time-honored traditions, your team will see evolutionary projects as a way to work harder with fewer celebrations. They will hate them and work to see them fail.

First Evolution. The first evolution will add new functions to the existing (text-based) software using the existing terminals and operating system. The new functions are the product for this evolution. If you succeed only in this evolution and no other, Acme still has software that is better than when the project began.

The requirements will list the new functions. The design will show how to insert them into the existing software. The programmers will code the new functions and make the necessary changes to the old ones. The tests will verify that the project team performed these tasks correctly.

In Figure 11.3, the first evolution is a complete V-chart, but the effort in each phase is smaller than in the corresponding phases of the waterfall project example. This is because the product (new functions) is smaller and requires less effort. All the phases require less time and all the documents are shorter.

This is basically an adaptive software maintenance project (see Chapter 10). All projects that begin with existing software are software maintenance projects. Most people will disagree with this because most people disdain software maintenance in favor of development. However, the project team is adapting existing software to a new situation, not creating new software, as they did in the OPT project.

At the 1 Operations phase in Figure 11.3, the software with new functions works. It has passed all its tests and been accepted by the clerks in a setting that closely resembles the workplace. The hardest part here is the acceptance of the clerks. If you have worked with them day by day and kept them in the project, they will accept the product. If not, you have a hard sell ahead of you.

There is a major control gate between the first two evolutions (between 1 Operations and 2 User Need). As I described earlier, you, the executive sponsor, and the lead customer must decide whether or not to go to the second evolution. Is the software from the first evolution good enough? It might be best to stop here. Will the benefit of the next evolution justify its cost? This is a business decision for the executive sponsor. Do not assume that it is best to continue.

Second Evolution. The second evolution will move the software with new functions to a new operating system. Many issues are involved because the requirements and design involve the inner workings of the software. However, there are no user interface items involved, so user involvement will be low.

The software on the new operating system is the product for this evolution. The requirements will detail the move, the design will show how to modify the software so that it will function with the new operating system, the programmers will make the necessary changes to the code, and the tests will verify that the project team performed these tasks correctly.

It is possible and probable that the programmers will change code that they just wrote during the first evolution. They are throwing away work that may be only a month old. This is a waste and it happens in evolutionary projects. The next section (Time out!) discusses other wasteful inefficiencies of the evolutionary process and why we endure them.

The second evolution is also a complete V-chart of another adaptive software maintenance project. Acme is reusing large parts of their software and saving tremendous amounts of money. This is an indication of the quality of the prior software system. Acme would have to discard the prior system and start fresh if the system had been poorly designed and documented.

At the 2 Operations phase in Figure 11.3, the software with new functions runs on the new operating system but still has a simple, text-based user interface. The project has not delivered everything required in the complete requirements phase.

There is another major control gate between the second and third evolutions (between 2 Operations and 3 User Need in Figure 11.3). Should the project go on to the third evolution or stop now? Will the benefit of the third evolution justify its cost? Again, this is a business decision for the executive sponsor.

Time Out! Aren't We Repeating Ourselves? By now some readers may be asking, "Isn't this redundant? Aren't you doing the same phases over and over? How many requirements and design documents do they have to write on this project?"

I admit that the evolutionary project is inefficient compared with the waterfall project. However, the inefficiency is because the people are learning. They did not know the product well enough to build it with a straightforward approach. They divided it into smaller, simpler products and built them one at a time, which means they necessarily repeat the basic process.

This repetition (inefficiency) also reduces the risk. People can attempt to build a difficult product in one leap, but the product is likely to collapse when the team is confronted with multiple problems. In this example, conflicting operating systems and GUI problems could trap the project team. Solving one problem would exacerbate the other and cause a downward spiral of test–fix–test–fix. All the money spent on the project would be wasted. The evolutions are small projects. Small projects cost less; if they fail, the loss is small.

Explain these facets of evolutionary projects to your team. Explain them well enough so that everyone understands and accepts them. Your team is doing tasks over and over and feeling the boredom. Your team will blame the users ("if they knew what they wanted we wouldn't have to do it three times") and blame management ("if they knew what they were doing we wouldn't have to do this three times"). Keep the environment good. Take breaks and celebrate between evolutions. Emphasize the learning opportunities the evolutionary process affords.

Third Evolution. The third evolution will add a GUI to the software that has new functions and runs on the new operating system. Building a user interface involves the user. It is a low-tech, high-emotion endeavor. The project team *must* involve the users. If the users do not own the resulting GUI, they will not use it.

The GUI is the product for this evolution. The requirements will show the GUI in pictures, screen displays, or videotapes. Much of this will come from the user manual and SRS 0, which were completed before the evolutions began. The design will show how to modify the software to incorporate the GUI. The programmers will make the necessary changes to the code, and the tests will verify that the project team performed these tasks correctly.

At the 3 Operations phase in Figure 11.3, the software has met the basic requirements of the entire project. The software has new functions, works on the new operating system, and has a GUI. What remains is to validate the design and requirements created before the evolutions began.

The control gate between the 3 Operations and validate complete design phases is simple. All the difficult work is finished, and the project should proceed up the right side of the main V-chart to completion. Nevertheless, do not skip this control gate. There may be a reason to stop work either temporarily or permanently. Acme may be in a peak business season and cannot afford the slowdown installation and training will cause. Let the executive sponsor make and document a decision.

After the Evolutions. The remainder of Figure 11.3 is the right side of the main V-chart. These phases are almost the same as those in the waterfall project V-chart in Figure 11.1. The difference is the final operations phase. Here, the new software system replaces an old one instead of being introduced into a workplace where no software previously existed.

The project team must remove the existing system and then install the new one. This changeover is never easy. Many organizations have replaced existing systems with new ones on a weekend only to have the business collapse on Monday. People overlook items that occur all the time at work. These items kill new systems.

The safest strategy is to have both the old and new systems on-line at the same time. Have two clerks sit side by side and take telephone orders. One clerk uses the old system, while the other uses the new system. This will halve the number of clerks taking orders, but it will test the new system at work. If the new system functions properly for several weeks, it is safe to remove the old one. If Acme cannot afford to have two clerks take every order, have a member of the project team act as the clerk using the new system. After a few days, have the real clerk use the new system and the project team member use the old one.

Whatever the strategy, be careful during the transition. Use redundant systems whenever possible.

Hold a big celebration for your team. They have worked through a long, hard project and have repeated their work three and four times. They are tired and need a rest.

11.4   CTran: A SPIRAL PROJECT

This project uses a spiral process, which is good for projects that have many unknowns and are thus high risk. Again, in describing the project, I will borrow details from the previous two projects.

11.4.1   Context

Your name is Emily Cass. You head the 20-person software development group of Emca, Inc.—a 100-person company that performs digital signal processing (DSP) for the U.S. Department of Defense. Emca uses custom hardware and runs software written in a language that resembles assembly code. Your group writes and maintains the specialized software.

Emca's hardware and software are expensive to maintain. Modifying the software requires weeks of careful study and work because it is easy to break the existing software. Because the hardware is custom-made, expensive design engineers are needed to maintain it.

The software situation limits flexibility. Emca's programmers are some of the best DSP people in the country, but Emca cannot use this expertise in the commercial arena because none of the software will run on commercially available computers. The defense industry is making cuts, and Emca can see cuts coming in the next couple of years. The company must use their expertise in other markets.

The president of Emca wants to move to commercial, off-the-shelf (COTS) hardware using standard programming languages like Fortran and C. He has asked you to manage this transition in the Ctran project (for COTS *Tran*sition).

11.4.2 Risks

There are many risks in this project. Emca had custom hardware and software in the first place because the required number-crunching performance is at or beyond state of the art. You can't simply call a computer company and order a few machines. In fact, at first glance, the problem seems hopeless. You decide to reduce the problem repeatedly until you can solve it.

Approaching from another angle, Emca could write its DSP programs in a standard language and host them on a COTS computer. However, this also would be a major risk. All of Emca's software is in a special language. Even though Emca's people know DSP, they would be starting with a blank screen. They would need to code every line of software—no possibility of reusing any old code. This effort would be long and costly and would take programmers away from their current tasks of supporting Emca's defense contract. In the end, all the expense could be wasted because the COTS computer might not perform fast enough.

You need answers to a lot of questions before you even begin the project: Do workstations or supercomputers have the required performance? Do they have it now? If not, when will they have it? Can we write standard language programs for them? Do math libraries exist for them? Are the libraries portable? Can we have the source code for them?

This project has too much uncertainty for an evolutionary process. Emca could possibly resolve all the risks in a series of evolutions (small V-chart projects), but this type of project has never been done. The evolutionary process worked in the last project because there was precedence: moving from a text-based minicomputer system to a windows-based one has been done many times. Acme's people had never done it before, but they had a high degree of certainty that they could because there were similar projects out there. In contrast, no one at Emca or anywhere that you know of has used a COTS system to obtain the required performance.

This project carries a big people risk. Emca has lived on complex, custom hardware and software that requires expertise to maintain and operate. You are moving toward commercial computers and products that do not require this expertise. Some of your best people will grumble about being replaced by trained seals. Emca has experts and wants to have the experts use simple hardware and software. Some people may work to see this project fail so that they can maintain their status as elite experts. Watch out for this situation. You may need to fire these people. Some elitists don't mind maintaining their status as an expert even if the company fails and others lose their jobs.

11.4.3 Project Details

Figures 11.5 and 11.6 illustrate this project. Figure 11.5 is a simple diagram that shows how the project starts as the left side of a V-chart and then moves into a spiral with four cycles. Figure 11.6 contains the details of the phases (as in Figures 11.2 and 11.4). This project, even though it is a spiral, has phases with control gates between them and baselines.

Operations. The operations phase is the current state of Emca as described above. You will need to use the requirements (functional baseline) for the current software because the requirements will not change with the new system.

User Need. The user need evolved as I described earlier. The president of Emca becomes the executive sponsor and signs a memorandum tasking you with the project. After discussing the project with the executive sponsor and the lead customer, you write a context document. The CM staff writes a CM plan, and you, the executive sponsor, and the lead customer sign it. You then build a MIC and have the CM staff place a copy of the memorandum, context document, and CM plan in it.

The users on this project are Emca employees who use Emca's DSP hardware and software. The lead customer manages these Emca employees. Emca wants to sell the product of Ctran commercially. They have a marketing person surveying the market and relaying the findings to the Ctran project. The marketing representative has surveyed the marketplace and presents his ideas as a user.

As always, work with the users every day. You will need their help if this project is to succeed. Watch out for possible experts who want this project to fail.

The executive sponsor plays a larger role in this project because his interest is greater than anyone else's. If this project fails, Emca will go out of business in five years. The users and a lead customer have critical input, but the executive sponsor will make more of the decisions at the control gates. Later in the project, if it continues, the users will decide the user features.

You start to think about the 3Ps at this time. There is little doubt about the

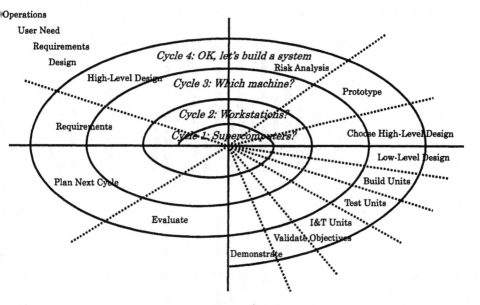

Figure 11.5 Diagram of the CTran (spiral) project.

process. As I described earlier, no one has ever used COTS computers on this problem with these performance requirements. This is a risky endeavor and will need a creative process. The spiral process model seems to offer the best chance for success.

The CM staff will play a bigger role in this project. Spiral projects have baselines, and these baselines will change more times than with simpler processes. Up to this point, you have only used one CM person to help with the Ctran CM plan. You will soon add several more and will probably use 50% more CM people than on the other projects.

The user need phase ends with a control gate. You meet with the executive sponsor and the lead customer to determine who will attempt to build what for whom. Agreement on these points is vital in such a high-risk project.

Notice how this project begins. Even though the project's originators know it will be unusual, the project starts with the basic steps of user need, requirements, and design. All projects, regardless of the risk, begin by admitting there is a need, trying to understand the problem, and creating a basic solution.

Requirements. The goal of this phase is to understand the requirements for this project. It begins with you deciding on the people and product. A waterfall process is eliminated immediately, as a type of iterative process is necessary. You choose four people in the software development group who will be

Phase	User Need	Requirements	Design
Activities	. Users and management see a need for a new HW SW system . Executive sponsor agrees and signs memo starting the project . PM writes context document . PM, lead customer, and Executive sponsor write CM plan . PM builds MIC . Think about 3Ps	. Think 3Ps . Gather and analyze requirements . Write SRS 0 (functions and performance requirements, no constraints) . Write test plan 0 per SRS . Write test procedure 0 . Capture Functional baseline 0	. RM top ten list . TOO MUCH RISK! . Preliminary plan of the spiral (time box each spiral) . Write SPMP . Create a design concept . Write SDD 0 . Plan (cards on the wall) the first cycle . Write SPMP for first cycle
Control Gate Question	N/A	Do we know who will build what for whom?	Does everyone understand the problem?
Question	Who is who and what does everyone need?	What is the problem?	What is the solution?
Products	User statement of need Executive sponsor memo Context Document CM Plan MIC	SRS 0 Test Plan 0 Test Procedure 0 Functional Baseline 0	Top ten risk list SPMP (entire spiral) SDD 0 SPMP for first cycle

Phase	Cycle N Quadrant 1	Quadrant 2	Quadrant 3	Quadrant 4
Activities	. Gather and analyze requirements . Write SRS N . Write Test Plan N.0 per SRS N . Write Test Procedure N.0 . Capture Functional Baseline N . Create several high-level designs . Write SDD N.0 with multiple sections	. Examine each high-level design in SDD N.0 . Perform risk management for each high-level design . Prototype as needed to explore the risks of each high-level design . Choose a high-level design . Write SDD N.1 . Write Test Plan N.1 per SDD N.1 . Write Test Procedure N.1 . Capture Allocated Baseline N	. Perform low-level design . Write SDD N.2 . Write Test Plan N.2 per SDD N.2 . Write Test Procedure N.2 . Capture Design Baseline N . Build units . Test units with Test Procedure N.2 . I&T units with Test Procedure N.1 . Capture Development Baseline N . Validate requirements with Test Procedure N.0 . Capture Product Baseline N . Write test reports for each test . Write a final report on this cycle	. Evaluate product of quadrant 3:quit now? . Plan (cards on the wall) the next cycle . Write SPMP N+1 for the next cycle . Control gate on the next cycle (go/no go) . Executive sponsor writes a go/no go memo . Either quit the project or go on to next cycle
Control Gate Question	Do we understand what we want to accomplish in this cycle and have a plan to accomplish it?	Do we fully understand our objectives, constraints, and alternatives?	Do we understand the alternative chosen?	Have we met the objectives of this cycle?
Question	What are our objectives, constraints, and	Which high-level design will we build?	How well does our product meet the objectives of this cycle?	Should we continue to the next cycle?

Figure 11.6 Details of the CTran (spiral) project.

the core of the project team. Spiral processes are different, so you select four competent and flexible people. These need to be well-respected members of the software development group. Remember that this project may be quite unpopular with many of your developers. You will need people who are respected, or this unpopularity can defeat the project.

The project team gathers the requirements. The functional baseline of the existing system lists the DSP functions and the system's performance requirements. The project team uses a facilitated session to capture these and to augment them with the requirements of COTS hardware and standard software. Make sure the lead customer participates in the entire session. You will need his support at the upcoming control gate. The team records the requirements in SRS 0. They then write test plan 0 and test procedure 0 per SRS 0.

The CM staff captures the functional baseline (SRS 0, test plan 0, and test procedure 0). These all go into safe storage and into the MIC. You, the executive sponsor, and the lead customer make up the Configuration Control Board for this baseline.

The phase ends with a control gate. Meet with the lead customer and project team to discuss SRS 0. SRS 0 must express what Emca needs. The designers state their understanding of SRS 0. Make sure everyone agrees about the problem, particularly the risks involved.

Design. This phase attempts to create a solution to the problem and plan the project. The development team is certain that the spiral process is right for this project. You will need to convince the executive sponsor to agree; that will not easy. The spiral process is rare and unfamiliar, and managers do not like either of these qualities in a development process. The first task is to work the risk management activities. The result of risk analysis must show that the risks are too high to use anything but a spiral process. This analysis is not easy, but it is necessary.

The next step is to sketch the spiral in Figure 11.5 and place a time box on each cycle. Even this early in the project, you know the general phases. The first cycle will explore how well supercomputers execute Emca's DSP problem using a standard programming language. The next cycle does the same using workstations or a network of workstations. The third cycle, if it occurs, concentrates on one type of machine and chooses a particular manufacturer's model. The product of the first three cycles is knowledge. These cycles tell you which computer meets the performance requirement with which standard programming language. The last cycle, if it occurs, builds a system using the machine and standard programming language the first three cycles selected.

Much of this project deals with hardware. The hardware issues are related to buying computers, not designing their details. Key issues are the availability of optimizing compilers and libraries of number-crunching routines. These computer issues are related to software.

It is time to write an SPMP for the entire project that contains the general company information, risk management results, and a description of the spiral with the content and time boxes for each cycle. This SPMP is not detailed because you do not know many details at this point.

You should also create a design concept and place this in SDD 0. This concept describes a system built from COTS hardware and general-purpose software. The concept lacks detail, but makes the basic idea of the project visible. One difference in this project is the team. It has only four people, all of whom will work on everything all the time, including programming their own designs.

Together with the project team, make a detailed plan for the first cycle of the spiral. The team knows the cycle's product and its phases so they perform a cards-on-the-wall exercise and create a network of tasks. Put this information into the SPMP for the first cycle (SPMP 1).

The design phase ends with a control gate. You and the team must convince the executive sponsor that a spiral process is necessary and that you are ready to proceed into the first cycle of the spiral. Communicate that the product will be a report on supercomputer capabilities relative to Emca's DSP work. Show how your plan for the first cycle will produce this report. You and the executive sponsor meet to discuss these issues.

11.4.4 Quadrants of the Spiral

As Figure 11.5 shows, every cycle in the spiral has four quadrants and, as Figure 11.6 shows, the activities in each quadrant are the same. This is not exactly how Barry Boehm defined the spiral process (Boehm, 1988), but project management is about using what works, even if that means creatively adapting an existing process definition.

Each cycle is similar to a project plus a phase to plan the next cycle. The risk management activities receive special attention in the second quadrant. Use prototyping, iterations, and everything else that helps understand risk. The basic elements of the waterfall are also present.

First Quadrant. The first quadrant (upper left) determines objectives, constraints, and alternatives. Objectives describe what we want or are required to accomplish during the cycle. Constraints limit the possible solution or require the solution to fit in a particular solution space. Because objectives and constraints can be considered requirements, the first phase of the first quadrant is the *basic requirements* phase. Its activities and products are the same as the requirements phases in other processes. The project team gathers, analyzes, and documents the problem for this cycle. The functional baseline for the cycle contains the requirements (and, yes, spiral projects have basic baselines, too).

The alternatives are different products that will meet the objectives of the cycle within the constraints. They are alternative solutions, or high-level designs. The second phase of the first quadrant is the *basic high-level design* phase. The difference in the spiral process is that one high-level design is insufficient. The project team has the responsibility and the freedom to create several.

Second Quadrant. The second quadrant (upper right) *identifies and resolves the risks* in the different alternatives (high-level designs). The project team performs a detailed risk analysis on each high-level design. If warranted, they build *prototypes* to help understand and reduce the risk. In the other processes, the project team has one high-level design and they manage the risks in it. In spiral projects, the project team spends extra time and effort to explore several alternatives. This is more formal and rigorous. It is also more expensive, but not as expensive as attempting to build a product in the presence of much uncertainty and failure.

The increased work and expense is to identify risk. Each high-level design has plenty of risk. The goal is to find the high-level design that offers the most benefit with the lowest risk.

The final phase of the second quadrant *chooses one high-level design*. This is the best of the alternatives proposed in the first quadrant, and it becomes the allocated baseline for the cycle.

Third Quadrant. In the third quadrant (bottom right), the project team builds the product of that cycle (I describe cycles later). As shown in Figure 11.5, the phases of this quadrant are the remaining elements of the V-chart. The project team takes the high-level design chosen in the second quadrant and adds detail to it in a *low-level design* (the design baseline for the cycle). The programmers then *build the units*. The next phases are the right side of the V-chart. Testers *test the units* using procedures written for the low-level design. The programmers *integrate the units and test the subsystems* using tests written with the high-level design. The CM staff captures this as the development baseline for that cycle. The next test *validates the requirements or objectives* of the cycle using tests written for them back in the first quadrant. The project team *demonstrates* this to the executive sponsor and lead customer. The result is the product baseline for that cycle.

Fourth Quadrant. The fourth quadrant (bottom left) evaluates the product of the third quadrant and plans the next cycle. The project team writes a report summarizing the cycle. This report details the lessons learned and how these lessons reduced the project's risk. The *evaluate* phase brings in the executive sponsor to decide if the project should end or continue. The project ends if this cycle has discovered something that will prevent the entire project from succeeding (current COTS hardware is two orders of magnitude too slow).

If the evaluation decides to continue, the project team *plans the next cycle*. They use the results of the current cycle and follow the general SPMP created before the first cycle. They employ cards on the wall and other planning techniques and write an SPMP for the next cycle.

11.4.5 Cycles of the Spiral

As Figure 11.5 shows, the spiral for this project has four cycles. The number of cycles depends on the number of major questions you have at the start of the project. A rule of thumb is there will be one cycle per major question plus one more cycle to build the final product. I will not describe each phase in detail. The project team will perform all the activities; produce all the requirements, designs, plans, and tests; capture all the baselines; and hold all the control gate meetings in the manner described for the waterfall project and in other chapters in this book.

Celebrate and take a short break between cycles. The cycles can have the same effect on your team as evolutions in the System Upgrade project. If you don't celebrate each cycle like a finished project, people will hate cycles. Consider the celebration part of maintaining a good work environment.

First Cycle. The first cycle explores how well supercomputers execute Emca's DSP problem using a standard programming language. Supercomputers are expensive, but they offer the best performance from a single machine. If current supercomputers do not give the performance required, neither will any other COTS machine, and the project will end.

The final product of this cycle is a report stating how well a system based on a supercomputer and standard languages will perform Emca's DSP problems. The objectives are speed, ease of programming, portability, potential market for Emca's product, cost of hardware, and cost of programming. The constraints are that the four project team members and you will have six months to complete the first three quadrants of the cycle. Your expenses should be low. Supercomputer makers are generally anxious to demonstrate their products and are likely to give you free time on their machines.

Your team selects supercomputer vendors A, B, and C. Each differs in languages, math libraries, operating systems, programmer support, and so on. The team begins the cycle and the first quadrant by writing a design concept for each vendor. Each concept calls for writing software that will execute a problem similar to the DSP problems Emca performs. The software attempts 25% of the Emca DSP suite.

The second quadrant begins with risk analysis. The project team probably cannot write 25% of the software for three different computers given the constraints of this cycle. Attempting that would be too risky. It is also too risky to choose one of the three machines given only sales presentations. The project team runs prototypes to reduce these risks. They execute basic DSP programs on each of the three machines in the respective vendor facilities. With the results of these prototypes, the project team selects supercomputer B for the third quadrant.

The third quadrant builds 25% of the Emca DSP suite on supercomputer B. The team creates a low-level design and writes the software for a machine at the vendor's facility. The remainder of the quadrant tests the software units, integrates and tests, tests the complete system, and demonstrates the results to the executive sponsor.

The fourth quadrant begins with an evaluation of supercomputers. The project team found that current supercomputers can satisfy Emca's DSP performance requirements. This is not a final conclusion, however, because the team did not base the evaluation on the same problems that Emca runs at work. It is a best guess based on similar problems executed. The results are satisfactory, so the project team plans the next cycle.

Second Cycle. The second cycle will explore how well workstations execute Emca's DSP problem using a standard programming language. The performance of engineering workstations has leaped forward in the last five years and their cost has fallen. Their performance per price ratio is excellent, but is their performance good enough for Emca's problems?

The final product of this cycle is a report stating how well a system based on a workstation and standard languages will perform Emca's DSP problems. The objectives are speed, ease of programming, portability, potential market for Emca's product, cost of hardware, and cost of programming. The constraints are that the four project team members and you will have six months to complete the first three quadrants and a budget to purchase three different workstations in the third quadrant. Workstations are much more affordable than supercomputers, so workstation makers tend not to offer the free demonstration time you had from the supercomputer vendors.

The alternatives are workstations made by companies D, E, and F. As with the supercomputers, each vendor offers different trade-offs. The project team again writes a design concept for each vendor after executing a problem similar to the DSP problems Emca performs. The software attempts 25% of the Emca DSP suite. The project team has done this once in a standard language. They will reuse as much of the first quadrant's software as possible. This will allow them to extend the software and remain in the cycle's constraints.

The second quadrant begins with risk analysis. Once again, the project team does not have the time to write 25% of the software for three different workstations. It is also too risky to choose one workstation given only the sales presentations, so the project team runs prototypes to reduce these risks. They execute basic DSP programs on each of the three machines either in the vendor's facility or on machines they purchased. On the basis of the results of these evaluations, the project team selects workstation D for the third quadrant.

The third quadrant builds 25% of the Emca DSP suite on workstation D. The project team creates a low-level design and writes the software using a machine they purchased. The remainder of the quadrant tests the software units, integrates and tests, tests the complete system, and demonstrates the results to the executive sponsor.

The fourth quadrant begins with an evaluation of workstations. The team worked with a workstation from vendor D for most of this cycle, but they are not ready to eliminate anyone because vendors often leapfrog one another in performance and features. The project team found that current workstations are about 30% short of meeting Emca's DSP performance requirements. However, this is not a big shortcoming, since workstation performance doubles every 18 to 24 months. The project team believes that top-of-the-line workstations will meet the performance requirements in one year. This is a best guess based on the software executed.

The project team briefs the executive sponsor on the results of the first two cycles. They believe that workstations are the answer to Emca's problems. Workstations should have the power needed in a year—soon enough for Emca. The team wants one more cycle to explore workstations. The executive sponsor, after careful thought, agrees. The project team plans the next cycle.

Take an extra break after this cycle. Your team has just built a crippled system twice in a row (25% functionality). They met the goals of the cycles, but they have yet to build a complete system. Building crippled systems can cripple morale. Your people can also be receiving grief from other members of the software development group. "You guys have been working for a year and haven't built anything yet." Take a little extra time and let everyone return refreshed and ready to work.

Third Cycle. The third cycle chooses one vendor's workstation and builds a system that runs 40% of Emca's DSP suite. As mentioned earlier, the team is not ready to eliminate any vendor from consideration. Emca will look at business issues during this cycle; in previous cycles, they have considered only technical issues. The team believes that workstations in general will meet the technical needs in a year. Will vendors D, E, and F be in business in one year? In five years?

The final product of this cycle is a report recommending one vendor's workstation for Emca. The objectives again are speed, ease of programming, portability, potential market for Emca's product, cost of hardware, cost of programming, and business viability. The constraints are that the project team will have three months and enough money to buy three different workstations.

The alternatives are once again workstations made by companies D, E, and F. The project team again writes a design concept for each vendor for a system that will execute 40% of the Emca DSP suite. This system will give Emca a better, less risky indication of each workstation's performance (because 40% vs. 25% of the suite was tested). The project team has already written a 25% system. They will reuse much of that and should be able to complete the rest in the shorter time given for the cycle.

The second quadrant begins with risk analysis. The project team does not have the time to write 40% software for three different workstations. They already have 25% of the software and can have it running on the three candidate machines quickly. The project team executes this software on each machine purchased. On the basis of these results, the team selects workstation D for the third quadrant.

The third quadrant builds 40% of the Emca DSP suite on workstation D. The project team creates a low-level design and writes the software using a machine they purchased. The remainder of the quadrant tests the software units, integrates and tests, tests the complete system, and demonstrates the results to the executive sponsor.

The fourth quadrant begins with an evaluation of workstations built by vendor D. The additional testing (40% vs. 25%) confirmed the earlier thoughts that, although the workstation does not meet performance requirements, it will do so in less than a year. The project team now bases this on nine months of experience with the workstation.

The project team presents their conclusions to the executive sponsor. They believe the workstations will work and attempt to present their information to the executive sponsor in a convincing manner. The executive sponsor must place the interests of Emca first. He cannot allow the enthusiasm of the project team to convince him. He must have sound engineering data. If he commits to a fourth cycle, Emca will spend considerable resources to build a full DSP system. The project team convinces the executive sponsor to move forward and they plan the fourth cycle in detail.

Fourth Cycle. The fourth cycle builds a complete Emca DSP system using vendor D's workstation and a standard programming language. Emca's current DSP users will use this system. In addition, Emca hopes to sell copies of the system to the commercial market (engineering firms, colleges, and so on). The objectives are the full Emca DSP suite (functional baseline 0), meeting all performance requirements, and a user interface that will compete on the commercial market. The project team must work with Emca's users in a manner similar to the way Acme worked with its users in the waterfall and evolutionary projects. They should also use occasional consultants to help learn what the commercial market wants in DSP systems. The project team has nine months to build this system and the money to buy the needed workstations.

The alternatives are three high-level designs. The project team has learned much about the performance of workstations using a standard language and operating system. The knowledge gained in risk-reducing cycles gives them several alternative ideas, but they are not quite expert enough to be positive that one design will work better than the others.

The risk analysis of the second quadrant lets the team build prototypes to answer questions about the high-level designs and increase the team's level of certainty. As a result, the team selects a high-level design with confidence.

The third quadrant builds the Emca DSP system. It follows the classic V-chart to completion. There is no fourth quadrant, since there is nothing left to plan.

11.5 OTHER SOFTWARE PROJECTS

The following sections discuss some other software projects and how to apply the principles discussed in this book to these projects. These "other" projects are becoming more prevalent at work, but because of their nature, people pay little attention to them. One or two people write some software and use it, and no one else seems to care. The key phrase in that last sentence is "seems to care." Many of these "little software projects" are important to the health and well being of organizations. Although they don't make an organization, they can break one. Therefore, the principles of this text—the three Ps, visibility, configuration management, and IEEE standards can apply to them.

11.5.1 My Little Spreadsheet

People create spreadsheets and use them in their jobs. Few people consider this to be a software project because making a spreadsheet isn't considered to be programming. Business majors and accountants create and use spreadsheets and those people are not programmers. What most of us often overlook is that people use spreadsheets to make important decisions for the organization (Panko, 1998; this paper is an excellent source on the importance of and common practices in creating spreadsheets). Major business errors costing millions of dollars have come from errors in spreadsheets. We need to accept that typing formulas into spreadsheet cells is a type of programming.

People, Process, and Product. Let's consider a little spreadsheet that I will create for myself. The product is the spreadsheet that only I will use at work. It appears that since I am the only user, I can create it any way I wish and everything will be fine. This is rarely true. If I am using it at work, I am using it to make decisions that affect the entire organization. I may look at the spreadsheet and recommend decisions to managers. I may use it to gather and present status to managers who will use that status to make business decisions. When considered in this light, the little spreadsheet takes on growing importance.

The "people" involved in the spreadsheet includes just me. I am the requirements analyst, designer, programmer, and tester. I know something about creating and using spreadsheets, but I probably don't know enough about all these phases of a project to perform them well. Hence, this little project is in big trouble right at the start.

The process for spreadsheets is usually haphazard. I type formulas into a few cells, enter my numbers, and look to see if the results are reasonable. If they are, I am ready to use the spreadsheet to influence managers in their decisions.

The preceding paragraphs paint a bleak picture for the little spreadsheet that may have a big influence on the organization. The first step in correcting this situation is to realize the importance of the spreadsheet. If I will use its results to influence anyone in the organization, I need to create and use it well. If I won't use it to influence anyone at work, I shouldn't be creating and using it at work.

Once I understand the importance of the spreadsheet, I need to use a process that works. I recommend starting with the basic waterfall model. The first step is the requirements: What information must the spreadsheet provide? Who will use the results of the spreadsheet? How important is this to the organization? And so on. I can document the requirements by typing them into cells of the spreadsheet on a sheet in the spreadsheet workbook. The next step is the high-level design. I have a problem at work and I will use a spreadsheet to solve it. This is the high-level design: use a spreadsheet on the operating system on the computer on my desktop at work.

The next step is the detailed or low-level design. This is where most spreadsheets fall apart at work. We don't design them—we simply type numbers and formulas because we "know" how everything will look in the end. I should take the time to lay out the spreadsheet on a blank piece of paper. I recorded the requirements for the spreadsheet (calculate X, Y, and Z), so I can trace the required answers to cells that provide them. I can also check the formulas and data needed to produce these answers. I type this information into the same sheet that I used to record the requirements. In this way, I am building a small requirements verification traceability matrix (RVTM).

The next step is the implementation. I know the requirements and the layout of the spreadsheet. I know the data and formulas I need, so now I type these into the spreadsheet. I record which cells produce which answers on the RVTM sheet. This will help me in testing and also in maintenance.

The next step is testing. I need to do more than "enter some numbers and see if the answers look right." The IDEA concept of testing provides several ways for me to ensure that the spreadsheet will provide reliable information. Inspection is an excellent method of testing spreadsheets. I should have colleagues read through my spreadsheet to ensure that I typed the formulas correctly. I can also enter numbers from a proven example and demonstrate that the spreadsheet yields the correct answer.

The preceding process may seem a bit much for a little spreadsheet. That is the nature of spreadsheets. Just a few hours of work produces a tool that provides valuable information for an enterprise. The large value of the information divided by the small number of hours needed to produce it is a very large ratio. If the spreadsheet is error-free, that ratio is a big benefit to the organization. If, however, there are a couple of errors in the spreadsheet, this means big trouble for the organization. Please note that error-prone people like me type spreadsheets, so there probably are a couple of errors in the spreadsheet.

Visibility. Building a useful spreadsheet may only take one person a few tens of hours. Given this, there is little reason to create a management information center and post progress on the walls. What is important and deserving of visibility is the existence of the spreadsheet. It is part of my work and provides information that influences business decisions. The spreadsheet itself should be visible so people can examine and improve it. A simple way to do this is to put it in a directory on the office LAN where people can see and use it, but not modify it.

Configuration Management. CM plays an important role in the life of the little spreadsheet. The process described above includes all six of the basic baselines from Chapter 2 and Appendix C. The Functional baseline holds the requirements; the Allocated baseline holds the high-level design; the Design baseline holds the low-level design; the development holds the spreadsheet that I am creating; the Product holds the spreadsheet under test, and the Operational baseline is the spreadsheet I use. These baselines exist even though the phases of the development process may only consume a few hours.

The key part of CM in the life of the spreadsheet comes when I change the spreadsheet. As mentioned in Chapter 10, if the spreadsheet is useful and used often, I will probably modify it to meet new requirements. That short phrase means I will be changing all six baselines—Functional through Operational. I will be the sole member of all Configuration Control Boards (CCBs); I will control the changes, and I will need to save copies of the spreadsheet before making changes. This requires self-discipline, as changing the spreadsheet may only take a few minutes. All that extra CM work might take longer than the "real work." All that CM work, however, can save me from ruining a useful spreadsheet. I should save the existing spreadsheet with a new file name, one that holds the version number of the spreadsheet. I should type the date and version number in the upper left corner cell of the spreadsheet. The printouts resulting from the spreadsheet should also include this date and version number.

IEEE Standards. The IEEE software standards have little if any influence on the spreadsheet project. Knowledge of the concepts from these standards (baselines, CM, requirements, design, etc.) is helpful.

11.5.2 Let's Make a Web Page

It seems that everyone has a Web page these days either on the public Internet or on an organization's private intranet. People create Web pages either by using a Web publishing tool or typing raw HTML. Regardless of the method, making a Web page is a software project involving programming (the "L" in HTML does mean language, as in programming language). Some Web page projects support major on-line businesses and require dozens of people and millions of dollars. Most Web page projects, however, are like the spreadsheets discussed earlier. One or two people work for a couple of days and create a Web page. They modify the Web page weekly as part of their jobs. It doesn't seem that the principles presented in this text would have much influence on such projects. Nevertheless, these little Web pages provide information that people use to make business decisions. Therefore, they qualify as software projects at work and deserve some attention.

The remainder of this section discusses creating a Web page for a project. This is like a management information center on-line. I create on of these pages for each project I work at work. The Web site groups all the information related to a project. It usually contains descriptions of the project and links to documents, spreadsheets, and briefings. The Web page enables people to find information on the project in a manner that is easier than searching through the directories of a network of servers. The following discussion of principles does not go into as much detail as the previous section on spreadsheet projects. This is because much of the material is the same.

People, Process, and Product. As with the spreadsheet, I am the only person involved with creating my Web page for a project. I must perform all the steps in all the phases. This requires reviewing the basics of process and paying attention to what I am doing. I make typing mistakes, and these break links in Web pages. Therefore, I must be careful and ask for assistance in reviewing and testing the pages.

I use a basic waterfall process to create the initial version of the Web page. Modifications follow a similar process of maintenance. The key step is analysis of requirements. Web pages are so prevalent in business and personal computing that people assume that everyone knows why a Web page exists. The failure of many Web-based businesses, however, shows that many people have faulty views of Web pages. Robin Miller has written an excellent discourse of the proper use of Web pages and why people require them (Miller, 2002).

The project Web page has two main requirements: (1) explain the project in a few sentences and (2) provide links to key documents, spreadsheets, and briefings related to the project. These are short requirements, and I type them into comment lines in the HTML file of the Web page.

The high-level design comprises the statement, "Provide project information via a Web page on the office intranet." The low-level design is a little more involved. I want the Web page to appear quickly on a workstation, so I don't put large graphics files on the home page. I don't want people to scroll through lots of text, so I put a concise introduction to the project at the top of the Web page. I group the links to documents and such by topic and place large print headings on these groups. I find it helpful to sketch the appearance of the Web page on a piece of paper before attempting to type the HTML statements.

Implementation involves typing the HTML statements. It is easy to have errors in the document links. Hence, I save the HTML file and test each link right after typing it. After typing and testing each link, I have a colleague open the Web page and test each link. This completes the development of the Web page.

Visibility. As with the spreadsheet, building a project's Web page only takes a few hours so there is no reason to create a management information center. Once the initial version is complete, the Web page needs visibility. If people don't know that it exists and where it is, they will not use it and it will be a failure. Part of the visibility is to have my name and e-mail address at the bottom of each page on the Web site. This allows people to provide comments and suggestions.

Configuration Management. As with the spreadsheet, the simple Web page involves all the basic baselines from Functional through Operational. I will keep copies of each HTML file as I update the Web page through its lifetime. I should be able to revert back to every prior version of the Web page. Also, I include the date of update on the Web page. This allows users to know that they are viewing a Web page that is being updated and managed.

IEEE Standards. The IEEE software standards have little if any influence on the Web page project. Knowledge of the concepts from these standards (baselines, CM, requirements, design, etc.) is helpful.

11.5.3 An Agile Methods Project

Many organizations are moving to the use of agile methods (refer back to Chapter 6). There are many reasons behind this movement. Some people are trying agile methods because what they are doing now is not working well and they want to try something else.

People, Process, and Product. I will emphasize this section of the discussion. This is because the movement to agile methods concentrates on how people build products for other people (people, process, and product). I urge organizations to consider the issues I discuss in this section as they are at the core of attempting to develop software with agile methods or nonagile methods.

First and foremost, consider the people working in your organization. It is most likely that your organization is using a form of the waterfall process. The people working for you were hired to work in such a process. They have worked in such a process and are accustomed to it. Moving to agile methods is a change. Many of your people may not want to or be able to make this change. Agile methods require more interaction and collaboration among programmers and users. Some of your programmers may welcome and excel at interacting with other people. Many, however, may fear such interactions.

A usual step in adopting agile methods is to run a small pilot project to test how the methods will work in your organization. Most pilot projects succeed. This is because the product is smaller and less complex than normal (you need to do a small product so your pilot will end soon). The other factor is that pilot projects are usually led and staffed by people who want to try the agile methods. They like the ideas in the methods and they work hard to see that these methods lead to a successful project.

The problem with successful pilot projects is that they lead managers to believe that the agile methods (or whatever we try in a pilot project) will be successful in all projects all across the organization. Pilot projects are pilot projects, not real projects. As mentioned above, we build simpler products in these projects and, most importantly, we use people who are anxious to see the new thing work well. When an organization moves to real projects with workers who more accurately represent the "average" person in the organization, the agile methods don't work so well.

From the preceding discussion, I advise against a pilot project. It is accepted that the agile methods can work. People have used them, built high-quality products, and documented their results. The question is not "do agile methods work?" but instead "will agile methods (a process) work with our people on our products?" I think they can work in most organizations with most products. Agile methods may not be the most efficient process for your people and product. Nevertheless, given the high rate of failure in software projects (mentioned earlier in this text) it is worthwhile to find a method that works at all instead of searching for an optimum method.

I advise inserting agile methods into your organization using what Jerry Weinberg calls "incremental consensus" (Weinberg, 2003). This begins with one person who wants to use agile methods on an upcoming project. That person finds another person who also wants to use agile methods. The consensus is that they will both work on the project and use agile methods. The project team grows one person at a time. When a member of the team finds another person who would like to join the team and use agile methods, the current team members must all agree that they would like that other person to join the team. Therefore, no one enters the team without the consensus of the team. This team will probably succeed because they want to work together and succeed. This idea may seem too obvious, but I have worked on teams where some people really didn't want to work with some of the other people and project success was not high on their list of goals. I don't think that I am alone in that experience.

The successful incremental consensus will demonstrate that agile methods can work with your people to build a product. Allow that team to stay together and work on another project. Resist the temptation to break up that team and put its members into other teams to "spread the techniques." Allow other teams to grow themselves using incremental consensus, too.

This is the end of the last section of the last chapter of this book. In it I am urging people to do what I urged in the first chapter of this book. Stay with the people on the project. If they are enthusiastic about agile methods, these methods will work. If they don't like the ideas in agile methods, the projects will fail from lack of commitment. It may sound as if I am belittling agile methods and saying that they will only work if people try. Please remember that your organization is starting with people who were hired and retained because they worked well with traditional process models. Making them change to agile methods will probably be filled with problems.

Visibility. An important tenet of agile methods is to increase the visibility on projects. Extreme programming teams sit in one room with information covering the walls and they program in pairs so they can see how colleagues write code. Teams using SCRUM hold daily SCRUM meetings so they know what everyone is doing. Use the visibility techniques that the creators of the various agile methods encourage. Don't try extreme programming without having a room large enough to house the entire team. Don't try SCRUM if the team is scattered among different buildings. Those methods will fail.

Configuration Management. The agile methods are specific renditions of iterative and evolutionary projects. As such, configuration management (CM) plays a critical role in agile methods. The requirements change often in projects using agile methods, and these changes ripple through the remaining baselines. A proper use of CM can handle these frequent changes. "Formal" CCB meetings are not necessary to approve and track the changes. The CCBs can comprise three people who gather after a daily SCRUM meeting to ensure that the RVTM and the baselines are updated properly. Perform the four basic activities of CM and use the baselines to keep track of everything. Remember that CM should help the project rather than hinder it. If CM is a nuisance, adjust the practices to fit the situation. CM is about the integrity of the product, and that is important on projects using agile methods and any other process.

IEEE Standards. Knowledge of the concepts from these standards (baselines, CM, requirements, design, etc.) is helpful on agile methods projects. You will probably not write an SRS or SDD per the IEEE standards. Nevertheless, you should document the requirements, design, and so on. during the project. The standards will help you remember the type of information to document. Use them as checklists and guides instead of rulebooks.

11.6   KEY THOUGHTS IN THIS CHAPTER

This chapter presented three sample projects using the concepts described in previous chapters. The examples illustrated the waterfall, evolutionary, and spiral process models. The V-chart and its principles were the foundation of these projects.

These project descriptions illustrate two points. First, the software management and engineering principles described in this book have a place in real projects. They are not just theories to discuss in a class and forget at work. The system storyboarding technique, cards-on-the-wall sessions, management information centers, earned value tracking, and so on, are practical tools you can use to solve real problems.

Second, there is a trade-off between efficiency and risk with the three process models. The waterfall is an efficient process. Requirements, design, and coding occur once. The evolutionary and spiral processes repeat these in various ways. In the waterfall process, the user sees the product at the end of development. This is a scenario with the greatest potential for disaster. If the developer misunderstood and built the wrong product, the project and all its effort have been wasted. The evolutionary process presents the product to the user several times during development. The user and developer have several opportunities to resolve misunderstandings. The spiral process also gives the user and developer frequent opportunities to look at evolving software. The spiral process has better risk management capabilities. It also brings more inefficiency. It is the only process to use if the project you are attempting has never been done before.

The sample projects also underline the need to pay attention to people every day. Try to place yourself in their position. How would you feel if you were chosen to do a job? If you were not chosen to do a job? What would your peers be telling you about your part of the project? Who might take offense at the entire project and work to see it fail? Why would they do that? People are different (recall the eight causes of failure in Chapter 4) and react differently. Stay in touch with everyone and do what you can to encourage those who want to help and dissuade those who want to hinder.

Above all, think about the people, process, and product. Some people have worked on projects that were wildly successful and did not use such detailed processes. A closer look at the project reveals that the people knew the product exceptionally well. Do not expect to get away with shortcuts on every project. Learn to combine the people, process, and product factors to fit the situation.

REFERENCES

B. Boehm, "A Spiral Model for Software Development and Enhancement," *Computer*, May 1988, pp. 61–71.

R. Miller, *The Online Rules of Successful Companies: The Fool-Proof Guide to Building Profits*, Pearson Education, Upper Saddle River, NJ, 2002.

R. Panko, "What We Know About Spreadsheet Errors," *Journal of End User Computing*, Spring 1998, pp. 15–21.

G. Weinberg, a private discussion in June 2003, www.geraldmweinberg.com.

E. Weiss, *How to Write A Usable User Manual*, ISI Press, Philadelphia, 1985.

Documents for the OPT Project

This appendix contains seven documents related to the OPT project described in Chapter 11: the executive sponsor memorandum, the project context document, the configuration management plan, the concept of operations, the *Software Requirements Specification*, the software project management plan, and the *Software Design Description*. Although the text is specific to the OPT project, the format of these documents is suitable for any project.

A.1 OPT EXECUTIVE SPONSOR MEMORANDUM

This is the memorandum for the record from Acme Inc.'s president. It initiates the OPT project.

Memorandum for the Record
From: John Wayne, President Acme, Inc.
1 January 1999

It is apparent to the Acme family that we need to be more efficient in how we process orders from our customers. We have succeeded and grown beyond our ability to process orders end-to-end with pencil and paper. We are doing so well we must change to keep up with our customers' needs.

Therefore, I have asked Rachel Widmark, head of the IS department, to create a computer system that will help our clerks process orders. After the clerks type the order, the system will record orders in the Order department and pass the appropriate information to the Arranging, Shipping, and Accounting departments. The project will be called the Order, Processing, and Tracking (OPT) project.

The goal is to better serve our customers by processing and tracking orders more quickly and accurately. No more putting people on hold for fifteen minutes while we run around trying to find an arrangement.

The Software Project Manager's Handbook. By Dwayne Phillips.
ISBN 0-471-67420-6 © 2004 IEEE Computer Society

The system will not replace any people. In fact, it will allow us to process more orders, so we may be able to hire more people.

I expect everyone to help Ms. Widmark and her people. I have faith in them. Let's all work together so that this project and the Acme family can continue to succeed.

John Wayne
President, Acme, Inc.

A.2   OPT PROJECT CONTEXT DOCUMENT

This document is written by the project manager, who is head of the IS department, to the OPT project team members.

To: OPT project team members of the IS department
From: Rachel Widmark, OPT project manager

John Wayne, president of Acme Inc., has asked us to build an order-processing and tracking system (see executive memorandum). Mr. Wayne is taking a personal interest in this project, which means we will have all the support we need to succeed.

Figure 1 shows the context for this project. We in the IS department are to build the system to serve the Order, Arranging, Accounting, and Shipping departments. This will be a challenge because it is the first time we have tied all our departments together with one system.

We will have the assistance of several consultants during the project. The consultants will help us with some new technologies, but we will master these technologies in time.

Mr. Wayne's *customer marketplace objectives* are in the top middle of the figure. We are replacing our proven pencil-and-paper methods with computers. We all know how that often brings resentment and turnover from some employees. Mr. Wayne wants us to retain our current employees (they are good at the flower business) and improve their skills. Therefore, we must ease fears and tensions. Each of us will spend time with each user to ensure that all users are comfortable with the new system. Mr. Wayne wants 100% accuracy in tracing orders. Acme has lost a few customers recently because we have too many orders to trace accurately with pencil and paper. The system must trace an order's status in two minutes. Mr. Wayne hates it when he waits on the phone for status from someone and knows our customers hate it too.

At the top far right of Figure 1 are the *external requirements* for this project. The new system must be compatible with our existing LAN of PCs. The new PCs must fit in the existing work spaces. This could be tricky in the Arranging department because the arrangers sling water about. We will investigate waterproof keyboards, mouse devices, monitors, and processors. The Shipping department is also a rugged environment. Only the head of the Shipping department and his secretary will need PCs, so we may escape some hazards there. The new system must meet the up-time requirements of our current systems.

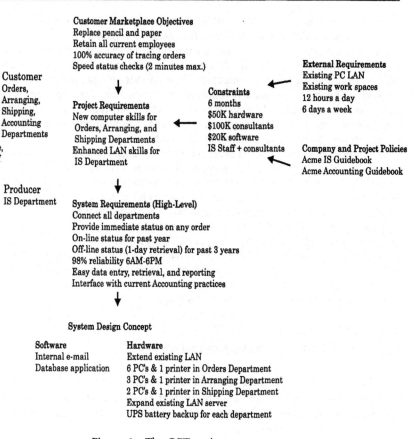

Customer Marketplace Objectives
Replace pencil and paper
Retain all current employees
100% accuracy of tracing orders
Speed status checks (2 minutes max.)

External Requirements
Existing PC LAN
Existing work spaces
12 hours a day
6 days a week

Customer
Orders,
Arranging,
Shipping,
Accounting
Departments

John Wayne,
President of
Acme Inc.

Constraints
6 months
$50K hardware
$100K consultants
$20K software
IS Staff + consultants

Project Requirements
New computer skills for
Orders, Arranging, and
Shipping Departments
Enhanced LAN skills for
IS Department

Company and Project Policies
Acme IS Guidebook
Acme Accounting Guidebook

Producer
IS Department

System Requirements (High-Level)
Connect all departments
Provide immediate status on any order
On-line status for past year
Off-line status (1-day retrieval) for past 3 years
98% reliability 6AM-6PM
Easy data entry, retrieval, and reporting
Interface with current Accounting practices

System Design Concept

Software
Internal e-mail
Database application

Hardware
Extend existing LAN
6 PC's & 1 printer in Orders Department
3 PC's & 1 printer in Arranging Department
2 PC's & 1 printer in Shipping Department
Expand existing LAN server
UPS battery backup for each department

Figure 1 The OPT project context.

The *company and project policies* (middle far right) are the same as always. We must meet our internal standards for everything. The Accounting department has their usual standards, but we've worked well with them in the past.

Toward the top middle of Figure 1 are the *constraints* of the project. This is going to be a tight schedule—six months. Mr. Wayne wants this system ready for the Christmas season. That is the key constraint. We may be able to stretch the others to meet this one. The $50K for hardware should buy the new PCs, printers, LAN hardware, and software. The $100K for consultants should suffice.

To the left of constraints are the *project requirements*. This project must produce new computer skills in the Order, Arranging, and Shipping departments. Maintaining and growing our business depends on happier customers, and that means giving them the information they want right now. Acme's employees in those departments know the customers by name, can make arrangements they love, and know where to deliver those arrangements without looking at a map. They do not, however, know how to use a computer to retrieve the information our customers want. This project must also enhance the LAN skills of our department.

We know we can handle a LAN of 10 PCs. Can we double that? Can we add database queries across the LAN? We, too, need to improve.

Beneath the project requirements are the *system (high-level) requirements*. The new system must do the things listed there. We must learn how much storage is required to process orders. We must also learn about on-line and off-line storage systems, including high-reliability redundant disk systems. The consultants can help us with those topics. The system need not be user-friendly, but once the users are trained, it must be easy for them to use. The arrangers wear those funny gloves, so we cannot require them to type much.

The bottom of Figure 1 is the *system design concept*. This is (probably) not the design we will build, but it gives everyone an idea of the basic concept. The software will be a commercial product that stores and retrieves data and allows a person to send that to another person. Many products perform these basic functions, so we'll sort through them and choose what's best for us. On the hardware side, we'll buy PCs for each department and extend our LAN to them. We'll need to increase the capacity of our UPS systems.

Let me remind everyone that this document is for our team members only. We are not trying to hide anything, but it is easy for people to see this and assume all sorts of things. Nothing in this document is written in stone. It can change easily. This is just to keep everyone on the same page.

A.3   OPT CONFIGURATION MANAGEMENT PLAN

This CM plan is probably too brief to work in a real project, but the goal is to illustrate the plan's contents, not to write another book. IEEE-Std-1042, discussed in Chapter 2 and Appendix B, contains adequate information and examples to write a complete CM plan for any project.

1   Introduction

This is the configuration management (CM) plan for the Order-Processing and Tracking (OPT) project for Acme Inc. The OPT system records and tracks flower arrangement orders through all departments of Acme.

1.1   Purpose

This plan describes the activities, procedures, and requirements that implement configuration management on the OPT project. It establishes how Acme will perform identification, control, status accounting, and audits.

1.2   Scope

This plan applies to all software, hardware, documents, and training in the OPT project. Figure 1 shows the organizations involved in this project. Rachel Widmark, head of the IS department, will be the project manager.

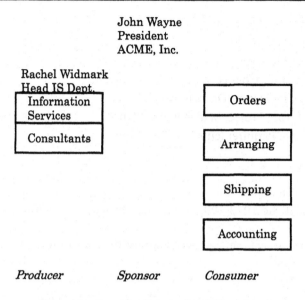

Figure 1   Organizations in the OPT project.

One member of the IS department will be the CM person for this project. As head of the IS department, Ms. Widmark will identify that person during the first week of the project. This person will use the existing resources of the IS department.

The configuration items (CIs) controlled by this plan include

- Client software
- Server software
- LAN
- Training materials
- Operations manual
- PC platform

This plan will cover the development and the operations and maintenance phases of the OPT system. The development phase is expected to last six months. The system should serve Acme for at least three years.

1.3   Acronyms and Their Definitions

CCB—Configuration Control Board
CI—Configuration Item
CM—Configuration Management
ConOps—Concept of Operations

LAN—Local Area Network
PC—Personal Computer
PM—Project Manager
RFC—Request for Change
SDD—Software Design Description
SPMP—Software Project Management Plan
SRS—Software Requirements Specification

1.4 References

[1] *Acme IS Guidebook*

[2] ANSI/IEEE Std 1042-1993, *IEEE Guide to Software Configuration Management*

[3] Software Project Management Plan for the OPT Project

2 Management

This section describes how Acme Inc. will manage the CM activities for the OPT project.

2.1 Organization

Figure 2 lists the CM-related activities and who plays what role in each activity.
     The PM is responsible for the project. The president of Acme will assign members to the various CCBs during the first week of the project. See Section 2.3 for further discussion of the CCBs.

2.2 CM Responsibilities

The CM person will assist the PM in all CM areas. The CM person will perform the CM activities including identification, control, status accounting, and audits.
     The CM person will identify each CI in the OPT project and give it a

Activity	PM	IS Dept.	CM Person	CCB(s)
Identification		approve	originate	assist
Control	assist		assist	approve
Status Accounting	approve		originate	
Audits	approve		originate	
Store Items	approve	assist	originate	
Approve Baselines	assist	assist	assist	approve
Release Products		approve	assist	
Records Collection & Retention	approve		originate	

Figure 2   Organization of CM-related activities.

unique label. Reference [1] contains Acme's standard labeling scheme.

Once labeled, each CI will be carefully controlled. Anyone on the project can request a change to a CI or a baseline via an RFC. Attachment A contains the standard Acme RFC form. Figure 3 shows the flow of a change request.

The CM person will conduct status accountings weekly and produce status reports. The status accountings will comprise inspections of the IS department's working directories on the disk system. This will provide needed status without interrupting work. Copies of the weekly status reports will go to the president of Acme and the PM.

The CM person will audit software and hardware being sent to Acme from outside vendors. The CM will also audit all CIs before they are submitted to a CCB for approval.

2.3 Interface Control

This section describes how Acme's departments will work together on the OPT project. The fundamental objects in CM are the baselines. Controlling the baselines are the CCBs. Figure 4 shows each baseline, its content, and who controls it.

The PM and CM person will coordinate the different CCBs. If an issue arises that concerns several CCBs, the PM will call a meeting of them.

The PM will initiate all contact between members of the IS department and all other Acme departments. The PM will first contact the head of the involved department, and the two department heads will start conversations among their department's employees. After that introduction, the working-level employees will work together on the project. This will reduce unnecessary work stoppages.

The PM will initiate all contact between the consultants on this project and all other Acme employees. The consultants are not to approach Acme employees without this introduction.

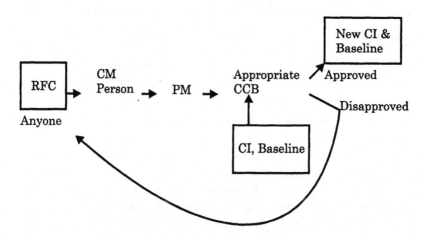

Figure 3 The flow of a requested change.

Functional	What the system must do Includes: Exec Sponsor Memo CM Plan CONOPS User's Manual Test Plan 0 Test Procedure 0 SRS Test Plan 1 Test Procedure 1	ACME President PM User Represetatives from all departments IS Department
Allocated	High-level design of system Includes: SPMP Test Plan 2 Test Procedure 2	ACME President PM User Represetatives from all departments IS Department
Design	Low-level design of system Includes: SDD 1 Test Plan 3 Test Procedure 3	PM IS Department
Development	A system that satisfies the developers Includes: Unit Development Folders Integrated, functioning units Test Reports 1, 2, and 3	PM IS Department
Product	An off-line system that satisfies the users Includes: User accepted software Test Report 0	ACME President PM User Represetatives from all departments IS Department
Operational	System in use at ACME	ACME President PM User Represetatives from all departments IS Department

Figure 4   Baselines and the CCBs.

The PM will initiate all contact between Acme and outside software and hardware vendors. Once the PM introduces an IS department employee to an outside vendor and assigns that person as the Acme contact, she can remove herself from the proceedings. This will reduce confusion in vendor contacts.

2.4 *CM Plan Implementation*

The CM plan will take effect when the president of Acme signs it. It will become part of the functional baseline. Each baseline takes effect when the members of its CCB sign a memorandum stating such. These events happen at the end of project phases, as shown in Figure 5.

The functional baseline CCB considers its baseline at the end of the *developer requirements* phase. The PM will arrange a meeting of the CCB and present evidence why she believes the parts of the functional baseline are ready. The CCB members must challenge the PM to ensure the quality of the baseline.

The same activities will occur to establish each succeeding baseline. The allocated baseline CCB meets at the end of the *high-level design* phase. The design baseline CCB meets at the end of the *low-level design* phase. The development baseline CCB meets at the end of the *validate developer requirements* phase. The product baseline CCB meets at the end of the *demonstrate to users* phase. The operational baseline CCB meets at the end of the *operations* phase (upper right in Figure 5).

2.5 *Applicable Policies, Directives, and Procedures*

All policies, directives, and procedures for CM for this project are described in reference [1] and the following section.

3 CM Activities

This section describes how the CM person will perform the CM activities.

3.1 *Identification*

The CM person identifies the CIs. The CCBs assist in this, and the IS department has final review and approval.

Reference [1] describes specific naming and labeling schemes for CIs. This includes where and how to name and date each item. It also includes the scheme for unique CM codes. Each code includes the baseline name, CI name, date, and version number.

The baselines will be identified and controlled as described in Section 2.4 and will contain the items listed in Section 2.3.

Operations	Operations
User Need	Demonstrate to Users
User Requirements	Validate User Requirements
Developer Requirements	Validate Developer Requirements
High-Level Design	Integrate and Test
Low-Level Design	Test Units
Build Units	

Figure 5 The OPT project phases.

3.2 Control

The CM person will coordinate all control activities. The CM person will keep a safe copy of each CI and approved baseline. All RFCs are given to the CM person. He will record and process the RFC per Section 2.2. The CM person and PM will coordinate the appropriate CCBs to consider RFCs. If changes are approved, the CM person will handle the details (new documents, labels, storage, and so on).

3.3 Status Accounting

The CM person will perform all status accounting activities. Each week, the CM person will inspect the work in progress per the current project phase (defined in the SPMP [3]). The CM person will write a report on his findings and submit copies to the president of Acme and the PM. The report is due at noon on Monday and covers the activities of the previous week.

3.4 Audits

The CM person will audit all products in the OPT project. Functional audits comprise inspecting all test reports. The goal is to ensure that all functions the users require are present and working properly. The inspections will compare the test results to the test plans and procedures. The inspections will also consider the documents (requirements and designs) that led to the test plans and procedures.

The CM person will physically audit products coming into Acme from outside vendors. These audits will ensure that incoming products arrive as ordered.

Audit reports will go to the president of Acme, the PM, and the appropriate CCBs.

3.5 Release Process

The CM person will assist the IS department in releasing products. The IS department will create the products in the OPT project. When they are ready to elevate a product to the product or operational baseline, the IS department must write a product description memorandum. That memorandum will describe the media on which the product resides, the functions performed by the product, any special user considerations, a list of source and executable items in the product, and installation procedures.

4 Tools, Techniques, and Methodologies

All tools for CM run on Acme's existing LAN of PCs. Acme uses the D-Suite of office and programming products. Figure 6 shows the CM functions and what products will be used for them.

Function	**Product**
Project Planning	D-Planner V3.0
Documentation	D-Word V3.2
Drawing	D-Raw V2.9
Programming	D C/C++ Compiler V4.5
Database	D-Ata Base V3.4
Source Code Management	D Revision Controller V3.3
Problem & RFC Tracking	D-Tracker V2.2

Figure 6   The CM functions and corresponding products.

Copies of approved project CIs and baselines will be kept in the CM library room. Only Acme's president, the PM, and the CM person will have keys to that room. A level 5 PC with tape drives will be in the CM library room for the exclusive use of the CM person. This will provide the CM person with the computing resources, privacy, and security needed.

The CM person will work with the IS Department's programmers in using the D-revision controller. They will capture the latest working version of development software each Friday morning. A copy of that will be stored in the CM library room.

5   Supplier Control

The CM person and the PM will be the gate through which vendor products enter the OPT project. No vendor-supplied products will be used by the IS Department until (1) audited and approved by the CM person and (2) a written report passing the product is given to the president of Acme and the PM. The audits will ensure conformance to specifications as described in Section 3.4.

6   Records Collection and Retention

The CM person will keep one copy of all records in the CM library room and another copy in the Management Information Center. All versions of all CIs and baselines will be kept until the OPT system becomes operational. Once operational, only the latest copy of each CI and baseline will be kept.

A.4   OPT CONCEPT OF OPERATIONS

This is one possible concept of operations. Regardless of the form you choose, the ConOps should be informal and written in language the users understand.

1 Introduction

This is the Concept of Operations (ConOps) for the Order-Processing and Tracking (OPT) system for Acme Inc. The OPT system records and tracks flower arrangement orders through all departments of Acme.

This is the user's view of the system. It has sections for each department that will use the OPT system. In each section, department members tell what they expect. The development team recorded these expectations verbatim from interviews conducted during the user requirements phase of the project.

2 Overall System View

Figure 1 shows a sketch of the four departments that will use the OPT system. This document will refer to Figure 1 throughout. Each department will have PCs connected to a single LAN. The piece of paper with a bar code and the odd-looking pen indicate that the system will print orders on paper with a bar code in the corner of the paper. Any user who reads the bar code with the bar-code reading pen will see all the order information on his or her PC screen.

Figure 1   Overall view of the OPT system.

3   System View from the Orders Department

The Orders department will use the OPT system in two ways. The first is taking orders over the phone. The second is checking on an order for a customer.

3.1   *Taking Orders*

Interviewee 1—Well, this is what we do now. The phone rings and I talk to the customer. The new system will mean I have to type instead of write.

Interviewee 2—I expect something simple to type. I also expect a phone I don't have to hold with my hand or neck. Writing takes one hand, but typing takes two.

Interviewee 1—The computer should remember everything about our usual customers. We have all that on cards, so when Motel 9 calls, they don't waste time telling me their address. They haven't moved and no one wants to waste time telling me something that never changes.

Interviewee 3—Some computers aren't very flexible, and that could be a problem here. The customers usually want something special, so I need a place to describe what they have in mind. I also need a place to type in the special price we agree to. That's what our customers like, special deals.

Interviewee 2—When we're finished, I want to push one big special button to send the order to the Arranging department.

3.2   *Checking Orders*

Interviewee 2—This should be easy and it should help my aching feet. I am tired of running around the factory trying to find an order. The customer tells me she wants to know where her flowers are. She gives me her name, I type it, and the computer tells me all about her last dozen orders. I want it to tell me if her last order made it to shipping or what.

4   System View from the Arranging Department

The Arranging department will use the OPT system in two ways. The first is to be told to make an arrangement. The second is to inform the system that the arrangement is finished.

Interviewee 4—When the Orders people have an order they want us to make, the computer should beep-beep-beep and the order should come out of the printer. That piece of paper should have everything on it we need. Then I just do my job.

Interviewee 5—When I'm done with the arrangement, I'll run that pen across the bar code just like in the grocery store. The computer will beep and show me the order, and I push one button to tell it I'm done with the arrangement. Then I carry it over to shipping just like usual, except I attach that piece of paper to the arrangement.

5   System View from the Shipping Department

The Shipping department will use the OPT system in one mode—to track the progress of a flower arrangement from receipt in the shipping department to the customer.

Interviewee 6—When one of the arrangers hands me an arrangement, I read the bar code. The computer should show me the order, and I push one button to tell the computer that the order made it to our department.

Interviewee 7—I deliver the flowers just like always. There are a couple of differences. When the crew loads the flowers on the truck, they read that bar code and push a button to tell the computer the flowers left the factory. When the customer receives the flowers, he or she signs the piece of paper, and I bring it back to the shipping department.

Interviewee 6—The delivery man will come back from his run with signed pieces of paper. I'll read the bar code on each one and push a button on the computer. Then the computer will know that the customers got their flowers.

6   System View from the Accounting Department

The Accounting department will use the OPT system in one mode—to enter and track payment information.

Interviewee 8—The new system will not affect me to any great extent. I use a computer accounting system now and expect to use the same system in the future.

Interviewee 8—The only difference will concern billing orders. At this time, the Orders department carries a small box of orders to us each afternoon. Our clerk enters this information into the computer, pushes a button, and all the invoices and mailing labels are printed. We expect the new system to print the invoices and mailing labels when the Orders department enters an order—no more boxes of messy notes and no more entering the orders into the computer. The Orders department will enter orders into the billing system for us without even knowing it. We'll mail out invoices as usual, collect payments through the mail as usual, and our clerk will learn to be an accountant like he always wanted to.

A.5   OPT SOFTWARE REQUIREMENTS SPECIFICATION

This SRS is probably too brief to work on a real project (in fact, I note several deliberate omissions), but the purpose is to illustrate the form of an SRS, not to write a book. IEEE Std 830 (see the annotated bibliography in Appendix D) contains adequate information to write a complete SRS for any project. This SRS uses diagrams generated using the structured analysis method described in Appendix C.

1 Introduction

This is the Software Requirements Specification (SRS) for the Order-Processing and Tracking (OPT) system for Acme Inc. The OPT system records and tracks flower arrangement orders through all departments of Acme.

1.1 Purpose

This SRS describes the requirements for the software in the OPT project. Figure 1 shows the organization of Acme Inc. The Concept of Operations (ConOps) document [6] describes the requirements as seen by the customers. This SRS describes the requirements as seen by the producers. The producers will be the primary users of the SRS.

1.2 Scope

This SRS describes the requirements for the software in the OPT project. Figure 2 shows how the OPT system will serve Acme, Inc.

The software will allow the Orders department to enter customer orders and check their status. The software will notify the Arranging department of orders and instruct the Shipping department where to ship finished flower arrangements. The software will also interface with the software the Accounting department currently uses.

The software will exist in one product. That product will probably run on an extension of the PC LAN Acme already uses. The server will store all

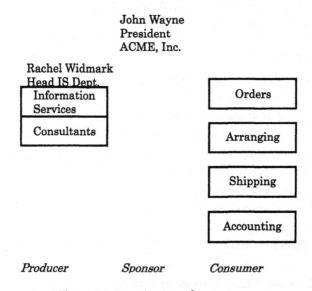

Figure 1 Organization of Acme Inc.

Arranging Department

Orders Department

Shipping Department

Accounting Department

Figure 2 How the OPT system will serve Acme Inc.

records as it does now. The additional PCs will allow the Orders, Arranging, and Shipping departments to access the data.

1.3 Acronyms and Definitions

CCB—Configuration Control Board

CI—Configuration Item

CM—Configuration Management

ConOps—Concept of Operations Document

DFD—Dataflow Diagram

ERD—Entity Relationship Diagram

LAN—Local Area Network

PC—Personal Computer

PM—Project Manager

RFC—Request for Change

SDD—Software Design Description

SPMP—Software Project Management Plan

SRS—Software Requirements Specification

1.4 References

[1] *Acme IS Guidebook*

[2] *Acme Accounting Guidebook*

[3] Software Project Management Plan for the OPT project

[4] ANSI/IEEE Std 830-1993, *IEEE Recommended Practice for Software Requirements Specifications*

[5] Executive Sponsor Memorandum for the OPT project

[6] Concept of Operations for the OPT project

[7] Configuration Management Plan for the OPT project

[8] E. Yourdon, *Modern Structured Analysis*

[9] Super-LAN Operating System Specification

[10] Super-PC Operating System Specification

1.5 Overview

The rest of this document describes what the OPT software must do for Acme Inc. Section 2 describes the situation in which the OPT system will operate. That section is intended for managers and others wanting an overview of the requirements. It makes the OPT requirements easier to understand.

Section 3 lists the requirements in detail. It presents the results of a structured analysis [8] of the OPT situation. Section 3 gives the requirements as functional requirements, emphasizing the input–processing–output form. The designers of the OPT software will use Section 3.

2 General Description

This section provides a management overview of the requirements for the OPT system.

2.1 Product Perspective

The OPT system will operate within the Acme facility. It will be the first automated system that serves every department in Acme. Figure 3 shows the level-0 dataflow diagram (DFD) for the OPT system. The Accounting department already uses a computer system to assist in sending invoices to and collecting payments from customers. The OPT system will work with that system.

2.2 Product Functions

The following lists what the OPT system will do for each department and for Acme as a whole.

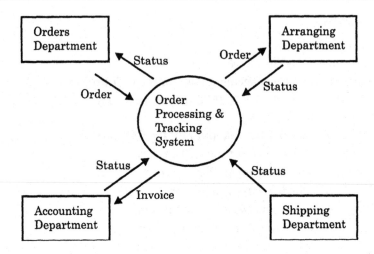

Figure 3   Level-0 DFD for the OPT system.

Orders department
[1] Enter customer orders
[2] Retrieve the status of a customer order
[3] Notify the Arranging department of a new order

Arranging, Shipping, and Accounting departments
[4] Change the status of an order

Arranging and Shipping departments
[5] Read the printed bar code
Accounting department
[6] Print invoices to be mailed

All departments
[7] Store order information
[8] Retrieve order information
[9] Store customer information
[10] Retrieve customer information
[11] Put customer information into orders

2.3   User Characteristics

As shown above, the Orders, Arranging, Shipping, and Accounting departments will use the OPT system. The people in each department and the conditions in which they work influence the requirements and constrain the eventual design of the OPT system. The Concept of Operations (ConOps) [6] discusses the users and their desires.

The Orders department will interact with the OPT system more than any other. Orders department employees can type. That is the extent of their experience with office equipment. They have always recorded orders on 5" × 7" cards. They want, yet fear, an automated system. Therefore, the OPT system must be easy to use. The system and the training for it must enable these users to do their jobs more easily than they do with the cards.

The employees in the Arranging and Shipping departments have no experience with computers or any other office equipment. The use of PCs must be simple. The OPT system cannot require these employees to type. One-step input (read a bar code, push one button) is required.

2.4 General Constraints

Several characteristics of Acme will constrain the OPT system design. The Arranging and Shipping departments have environments that are hard on PCs. The Arranging department is full of wet, dirty flowers. The employees' hands are also wet and dirty. The Shipping department handles the finished, still-wet flower arrangements. Therefore, the PCs in these departments require protection.

The OPT system will run on Acme's existing LAN of PCs, which serves the Accounting and IS departments. This LAN uses the Super-LAN operating system [9] and each PC uses the Super-PC operating system [10] and windowing system. The OPT system will use the facilities of these operating systems and will run under them.

The OPT system must be built in six months. It must exist with approximately $50K of new hardware, $20K of new, purchased software, and $100K in consultant services.

2.5 Assumptions and Dependencies

The designers can assume that the OPT system is for Acme only. It will not be used in any other facilities. The OPT system will depend on the state of Acme. This includes the user characteristics and general constraints discussed above.

3 Specific Requirements

This section details the software requirements for the OPT system. It is intended for the designers who will create the *Software Design Description* (SDD).

Figure 4 shows the DFD from a structured analysis of the OPT environment. Figure 5 shows the entity relationship diagram (ERD) for the OPT system. Figure 6 shows the data dictionary describing the lowest level data elements of Figure 5.

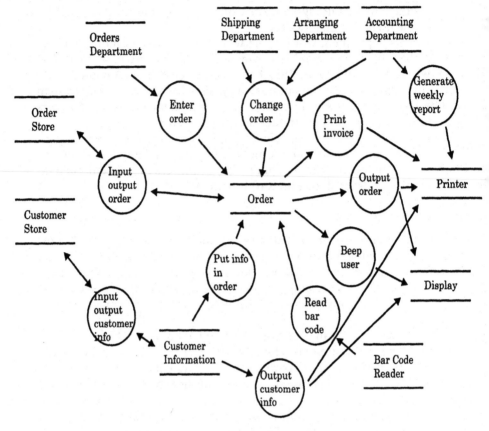

Figure 4   Dataflow diagram for the OPT system.

3.1 Functional requirements

The following describe the functions that each bubble in Figure 4 must perform.

Functional Requirement 1—Enter Order
Introduction: This functional requirement is that the OPT system must permit the Orders department to enter orders from customers.

Input: The input to this is the order information typed by the user. The ERD and data dictionary provide the details of the order.

Processing: This performs error checking. The input order must comply with the data dictionary specification. If it does not, the function must report an error condition to the system and the user.

Output: The output of this is the order information in an internal format. The ERD and data dictionary give the details of the order.

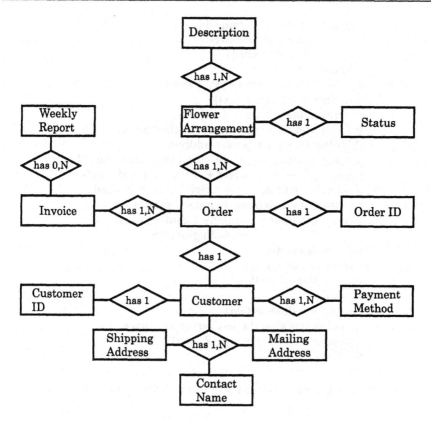

Figure 5 Entity relationship diagram for the OPT system.

Functional Requirement 2—Change Order
Introduction: This functional requirement is that the OPT system must permit the Arranging, Shipping, and Accounting departments to change the status of an order.

Input: The inputs to this are an order and the new status of the order. The possible states of the status are listed in the data dictionary.

Processing: This changes the status of the order to the input status.

Output: The output of this is the order with the changed status.

Functional Requirement 3—Output Order
Introduction: This functional requirement is that the OPT system must print and display an order.

Input: The input to this is the order information. The ERD and data dictionary give the details of the order.

Processing: This performs error checking. The input order must comply with the data dictionary specification. If it does not, the function must report an error condition to the system and the user.

```
. status = [ordered | arranged |
        shipped | received |
        billed | payed]
. customer-ID = #
. order-ID = mm + dd + yyyy + ####
. description = {line-of-text}
. contact-name = {line-of-text}
. mailing-address = [p-o-box | street-address]
. shipping-address = {street-address}
. payment-method = [credit-card | internal-account]
. street-address = # + street + city + state + zip-code
. p-o-box = "P O Box" + # + city + state + zip-code
. credit-card = company + contact-name + #
. internal-account = company + contact-name +
                     # + mailing-address
. street = {line-of-text}
. city = {line-of-text}
. state = {line-of-text}
. zip-code = #
. company = {line-of-text}
. line-of-text = alphabetic-character + space
. alphabetic-character = [A-Z | a-z]
. # = [0-9]
```

Figure 6   Data dictionary for the OPT system.

Output: The output of this is a printed page and screen display. The follow-ing figures show samples of these outputs. [*I have omitted these figures.*]

.

.

.

[*The remaining functional requirements would detail each bubble in the DFD in the same format as the functional requirements given.*]

3.2   External Interface Requirements

The user interface for the OPT system will follow the guidelines established in the *Acme IS Guidebook* [1]. The user characteristics and general constraints in this SRS will supersede those guidelines if necessary.

The OPT system will run on the hardware and software specified in Section 2.4. It must operate under the specifications in [9] and [10]. In particular, it must interface with a bar-code reader using the bar-code interface specifica-tion in [10].

The OPT system will not communicate with any other software systems. Therefore, there are no communications interfaces to which it must adhere.

3.3 Performance Requirements

The OPT system must meet the performance requirements listed in Figure 7.

3.4 Design Constraints

The design resulting from this SRS must fit within the constraints listed in Section 2.4. The largest constraints come from the LAN and PC systems that will host it (see [9] and [10]). The OPT system must abide by the guidelines of Acme in [1] and [2].

A.6 OPT SOFTWARE PROJECT MANAGEMENT PLAN

This SPMP is probably too brief to work on a real project, but its purpose is to illustrate the form of an SPMP, not to write a book. In places, I note deliberate omissions I made to save space. IEEE Std 1058.1-1987 contains adequate information to write a complete SPMP for any project.

Attribute		Worst Case	Expected	Best Case
[PR1]	. # of PC's on LAN	12	18	30
[PR2]	. # of Simultaneous Users	12	18	30
[PR3]	. # of Records Added per Day	150	180	240
[PR4]	. Reaction Time for Status	30 secs	10 secs	5 secs
[PR5]	. Records in On-Line Storage	3 days	5 days	10 days
[PR6]	. Records in Off-Line Storage	270 days	365 days	700 days
[PR7]	. Reaction Time to Add Record	10 secs	5 secs	1 secs
[PR8]	. Time to Print a Record	60 secs	30 secs	15 secs
[PR9]	. Daily Availability	10 hr/day	12 hr/day	15 hr/day
[PR10]	. Weekly Availibility	6 day/wk	6 day/wk	7 day/wk

Figure 7   Performance requirements for the OPT system.

1 Introduction

This is the Software Project Management Plan (SPMP) for the Order-Processing and Tracking (OPT) project for Acme Inc. The OPT system records and tracks flower arrangement orders through all departments of Acme. This plan describes the OPT project and how the IS department will execute it. Members of the development team will use this plan to guide their daily activities. The management of Acme Inc. will use this plan to monitor the progress of the project.

1.1 Project Overview

The OPT system will enable Acme employees to record and track orders from customers. Figure 1 shows how the system will serve Acme.

The objective of the OPT system is to help Acme serve its customers better by processing and tracking orders more quickly and accurately [5]. Acme's goal is that the system will not replace any people. Acme wants to be able to process more orders and possibly hire more people.

The product of this project will be an extension of the existing Acme LAN of PCs plus new software. The SRS [3] describes the software requirements for the OPT system.

Figure 1 How the OPT system will serve Acme Inc.

This project will follow a basic waterfall represented by the V-chart in Figure 2. Rachel Widmark, head of the IS department is the project manager. Five IS department employees—Chris Hall, Evan Anderson, Christine Hill, Truong Nguyen, and Genesis Tyler—will participate in the project. Three consultants will assist the IS department. There will be major reviews at the end of each phase (see Figure 2).

The project plan, described later, extends 75 working days. The project personnel will use the existing IS department computing resources. Consultants will cost the project approximately $100K. The project will purchase up to $50K of new hardware and up to $20K of new software.

1.2 Project Deliverables

The OPT project will deliver

[1] A LAN extended to the Orders, Arranging, and Shipping departments

[2] PCs for employees in the Orders, Arranging, and Shipping departments

[3] Software that fulfills the requirements in [3]

[4] Software documents as listed in Section 4.2

1.3 Evolution of the SPMP

This SPMP is part of the allocated baseline (see the configuration management plan [7]). As such, the allocated baseline Configuration Control Board controls its contents. Changes to this document will follow the procedures in [7].

1.4 Reference Materials

[1] *ACME IS Guidebook*

[2] *ACME Accounting Guidebook*

[3] The Software Requirements Specification for the OPT project

[4] ANSI/IEEE Std 1058-1993, *IEEE Standard for Software Project Management Plans*

[5] Executive Sponsor Memorandum for the OPT project

[6] The Concept of Operations for the OPT project

[7] The Configuration Management Plan for the OPT project

[8] E. Yourdon, *Modern Structured Analysis*

[9] Super-LAN Operating System Specification

[10] Super-PC Operating System Specification

[11] Super-Builders Programmer Suite Specification

1.5 Acronyms and Definitions

CCB—Configuration Control Board

CI—Configuration Item

CM—Configuration Management
ConOps—Concept of Operations Document
LAN—Local Area Network
PC—Personal Computer
PERT—Program Evaluation, Review, and Tracking
PM—Project Manager
RFC—Request for Change
SDD—Software Design Description
SPMP—Software Project Management Plan
SRS—Software Requirements Specification

2   Project Organization

2.1   Process Model

This project will use a basic waterfall process model. Figure 2 shows this as a V-chart.

2.2   Organization Structure

Figure 3 shows the organization of the OPT project team. The project manager, Rachel Widmark, will lead the five IS department employees listed in Section 1.1. Chris Hall will serve throughout the project as the CM person. Evan Anderson will write all test plans and procedures and will help conduct all tests. Christine Hill will help write the software. Troung Nguyen and Genesis Tyler will install the LAN extension and new PCs.

Acme will employ three consultants during the project: Pat Day, Joe Knight, and Kathy Miller. Pat Day will serve as the system engineer. Joe Knight will help with requirements analysis and programming. Kathy Miller will help with design and programming.

2.3   Organizational Boundaries and Interfaces

Figure 4 shows the organization of Acme Inc. The producer comprises the PM, project team in the IS department, and consultants. The producer will

Operations   Operations
  User Need   Demonstrate to Users
    User Requirements   Validate User Requirements
      Developer Requirements   Validate Developer Requirements
        High-Level Design   Integrate and Test
          Low-Level Design   Test Units
                        Build Units

Figure 2   Process model for the OPT project.

Project Manager
Rachel Widmark

Chris Hall
CM Person

Pat Day
(Consultant)
Evan Anderson   System Engineer
Tester   Joe Knight
                              (Consultant)
Christine Hill   Requirements
Programmer   & Programmer

Troung Nguyen   Kathy Miller
Genesis Tyler   (Consultant)
Network   Designer
Administration   & Programmer

Figure 3   Organization of the OPT project team.

work with the customer departments throughout the project. The PM will report progress weekly to the president of Acme.

2.4   Project Responsibilities

Figure 5 shows who is responsible for what during the OPT project. The IS department employees will perform duties familiar to them from their normal

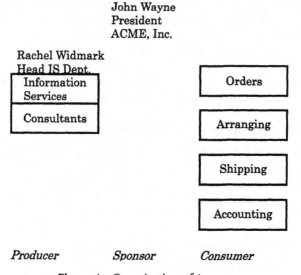

Producer   *Sponsor*   *Consumer*

Figure 4   Organization of Acme.

Person \ Task	Rachel Widmark	Chris Hall	Evan Anderson	Christine Hill	Troung Nguyen Genesis Tyler	Pat Day	Joe Knight	Kathy Miller
Management	X							
CM		X						
Planning	X	X	X			X	X	X
Requirements						X		
Design								X
Programming				X		X	X	X
Testing			X			X		X
Training						X		
Installation					X			

Figure 5 Project responsibilities in the OPT project.

jobs. The three consultants will concentrate on the nonrecurring engineering for the project. Once the project ends, Acme Inc. will no longer need the consultants. The IS department employees will participate in this project enough to be able to operate and maintain the system. The project manager is responsible for all management tasks. This includes selecting and managing the IS department employees and the consultants.

3 Managerial Process

3.1 Management Objectives and Priorities

The management and employees of Acme Inc. state their objectives for the OPT system in [5] and [6]. The first objective is to better serve the customers of Acme. This will allow Acme to prosper and grow.

The highest priority of the OPT project is to have the OPT system in operation for the Christmas season. The next priority is to have a system that the current employees of Acme can operate easily. The president of Acme is adamant about retaining all current employees.

3.2 Assumptions, Dependencies, and Constraints

The OPT project is based on the history of success of Acme. Acme is a home-grown company that exists because its employees have built close personal and professional relationships with their customers and one another. The job skills of the employees can be replaced. The relationships cannot.

The OPT project depends on three things:

1. Commercial hardware and software products
2. One-time consultant expertise
3. The skill of the IS department employees

The OPT system will use commercial products to reduce cost. The IS department employees do not have the experience needed to expand the existing computer system. Consultants will perform the necessary engineering. The IS department employees will learn from the consultants. At the conclusion of the project, the IS department employees will have the skills needed to operate and maintain the system.

The constraints of the project are time and people. As stated earlier, the OPT project must finish before the Christmas season. The President of Acme will retain all current employees. The OPT system must fit the people, not vice versa.

3.3 Risk Management

The OPT project team will manage risks in a disciplined manner. Figure 6 shows the top-10 risks for the project. Each risk identified has a risk referent,

Risks

Risk	Probability (0.0-1.0)	Consequence (1-10)	Product	Cause
R1. OPT system not ready in time	0.6	8	4.8	Not enough people to do the work
R2. Message passing not working	0.2	9	1.8	Insufficient knowledge of client/server systems
R3. User interface too complicated	0.2	5	1.0	Lack of user interface design experience

...

Risk Referent for R1
Project Objective - Have new system in place for the Christmas season
Referent = 2.5

Aversion Strategies for Risk R1	New Probability	Cost
R2.AS1 - Hire temporary programmers	0.4	$20K
R2.AS2 - Hire additional consultant	0.3	$50K
R2.AS3 - Out-source all test preparation and testing	015	$45K

Risk Leveraging
RA.AS1 (0.6 - 0.4)/$20K = 0.2/0.2 = 1.0
RA.AS2 (0.6 - 0.3)/$50K = 0.3/0.5 = 0.6
RA.AS3 (0.6 - 0.15)/$45K = 0.45/0.45 = 1.0

Figure 6 Top-risks in the OPT project.

risk aversion strategies, and risk leveraging calculations. [*I list only three risks and the aversion strategies for only one of these.*]

The PM will meet weekly with all project personnel listed in Figure 3 to discuss the project in light of the top-10 risks. This group will change the list as needed. The PM will report changes to the list to the president of Acme Inc. during their weekly meetings (see Section 3.4).

3.4 Monitoring and Controlling Mechanisms

The PM will manage the OPT project, monitor its progress, and report to the president of Acme Inc. The CM person will assist the PM in these duties through the status accounting and audits described in the CM plan [7]. The PM will monitor work down to the level of tasks and work packages in Section 5.

The PM will report to the president of Acme in a weekly meeting. The PM will discuss project issues with the project team each week. They will adjust the project plan (Section 5) as necessary.

3.5 Staffing Plan

Figure 7 shows the staffing plan for the OPT project. The network of tasks (Figure 9) was the source of the staffing plan.

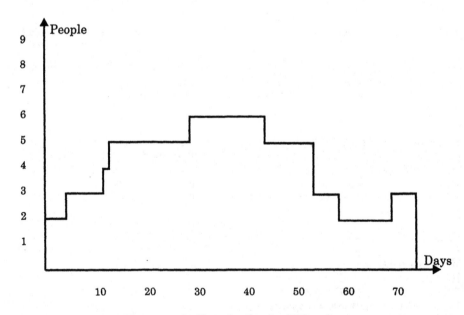

Figure 7 Staffing plan for the OPT project.

4   Technical Process

4.1   Methods, Tools, and Techniques

The OPT project will use the methods, tools, and techniques common to Acme IS projects [1]. The basic method is the waterfall as defined in Section 2.1. The project will use the structured approach [8] to requirements and design. The programming will also follow the structured method.

The OPT system will run on an extended version of the LAN of PCs in Acme. The tools used to build the OPT system must run under the LAN and PC operating systems [9], [10]. The OPT project will use the Super-Builder Programmer Suite described in [11].

4.2   Software Documentation

Figure 8 shows the software documents to be produced in each phase of the OPT project. Each document will be part of the baseline for its part of the project. The OPT CM plan [7] specifies those baselines. The *ACME IS Guidebook* [1] describes the standards for writing software documents.

Operations
  User Need
    Executive Sponsor Memo
    CM Plan

    User Requirements
      Concept of Operations
      Test Plan 0
      Test Procedure 0

      Developer Requirements
        SRS
        Test Plan 1
        Test Procedure 1

        High-Level Design
          SPMP
          SDD 0
          Test Plan 2
          Test Procedure 2

          Low-Level Design
            SDD 1
            Test Plan 3
            Test Procedure 3

Operations
  Demonstrate to Users
    Memo of Acceptance

    Validate User Requirements
      Test Report 0

      Validate Developer Requirements
        Test Report 1

        Integrate and Test
          Test Report 2

        Test Units
          Test Report 3

Build Units

Figure 8   Software documents to be produced during the OPT project.

4.3   Project Support Functions

The IS department and consultants will provide the project support functions. Chris Hall will perform the CM functions—the project's major support functions. The CM plan [7] describes this support. Evan Anderson will write all test plans and procedures and assist in all testing. These activities will be the verification and validation function. Quality assurance support is part of the standard software practice at Acme [1].

The three consultants on the project (Pat Day, Joe Knight, and Kathy Miller) will provide technical support in areas where the IS department lacks expertise. These include the analysis and design of company-wide LANs and writing requirements and design documents. The consultants will also provide support in training users.

5   Work Packages, Schedule, and Budget

5.1   Dependencies

Figure 9 shows the PERT chart for the OPT project. This diagram shows all tasks in the project and how they depend on one another. Each task contains the initials of the person(s) assigned and the number of days allowed for the

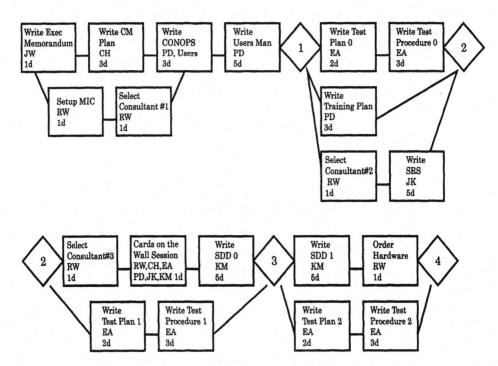

Figure 9   The PERT chart for the OPT project.

task. Each diamond represents a major review at the end of a project phase. The next section contains details of each task.

5.2 Work Packages

There is a work package for each task in Figure 9. Each work package has an input, task, output, resources, and time allowed. The task describes what the resources must do with the input to produce the output in the time allowed. The following figures give the work packages. [*Only the work package for the task "Write ConOps" is shown.*]

5.3 Resource Requirements

Figure 7, the staffing profile for the OPT project, shows the people resources required. The IS department will use its existing PCs in this project. The three consultants will use their own computing resources (laptop PCs). Acme will provide temporary offices for the consultants. This project will not require any travel or special support resources.

5.4 Budget and Resource Allocation

Figure 11 shows the earned value plan for the OPT project. The PERT chart in Figure 9 was the source for the earned value plan. There are 204 person-days planned in this project. Figure 12 shows how these resources are allocated to the major development activities.

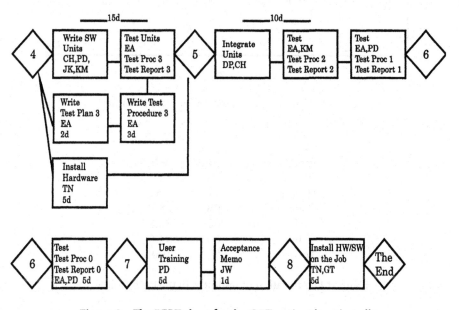

Figure 9 The PERT chart for the OPT project (continued).

Work Package x
Task Title: Write CONOPS .
Input: none
Task: Interview the users and write a CONOPS
   that expresses their view of the OPT system.
Output: A CONOPS document.
Resources: Rachel Widmark, Pat Day, users
Time Allowed: 3 days

Figure 10   OPT project work package "write ConOps."

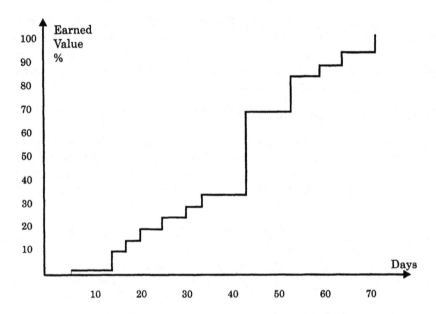

Figure 11   The earned value plan for the OPT project.

Function	Value	% Value
Requirements	18	8.8
Design	11	5.4
Code	58	28.4
Int&Testing	67	32.8
Other	50	24.6
Total:	204	100

Figure 12   Allocation of resources in the OPT project.

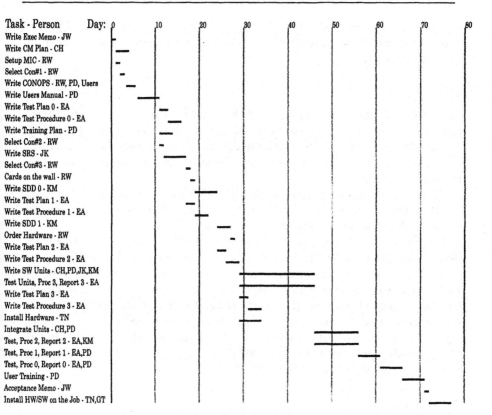

Figure 13 The Gantt chart.

5.5 Schedule

Figure 13 shows the Gantt chart for the OPT project. This illustrates the tasks of Figure 9 on a calendar.

A.7 OPT SOFTWARE DESIGN DESCRIPTION

This SDD is probably too brief to work on a real project, but its purpose is to illustrate the form of an SDD, not to write a book. In places, I note deliberate omissions to save space. IEEE-Std-1016 contains adequate information to write a complete SDD for any project.

1 Introduction

This is the Software Design Description (SDD) for the Order Processing and Tracking (OPT) project for Acme Inc. The OPT system records and tracks flower arrangement orders through all departments of Acme.

The SDD contains both the high-level and low-level designs. The high-level design is the architecture. The low-level design contains the details that let programmers start coding.

1.1 Purpose

This SDD describes the design of the OPT system. This design meets the requirements expressed in the Software Requirements Specification (SRS) [3]. The OPT team produced the requirements via the structured analysis method [8]. The team used these products and the structured design method [8] to produce the design.

Sections 3 through 5 present the high-level design of the OPT system. This information lets people review the design at an architectural level to ensure that the design meets the requirements.

Section 6 presents the low-level design of the OPT system. This low-level design adds the final details that enable programmers to begin coding.

This SDD describes the design using four design views, which are presented in [4]. Section 3 gives the decomposition description. This divides the design into design entities and lists five attributes for each entity. Section 4 gives the dependency description, which describes the relationships among the design entities. Section 5 gives the interface description, which is the external view of each entity. Section 6 gives the detail description, which is the internal view or detailed design of each entity.

1.2 Scope

This SDD contains the design for the software in the OPT system. The software products will allow the Orders department to enter customer orders and check the status of these orders. The software will also notify the Arranging department of orders and instruct the Shipping department where to ship finished flower arrangements. The software will also interface with the software currently used by the Accounting department.

The software will exist in one product that will run on an extension of the LAN of PCs Acme is already using. The server will store all records as it does now. The additional PCs will allow the Orders, Arranging, and Shipping departments to access the data.

1.3 Acronyms and Definitions

CCB—Configuration Control Board
CI—Configuration Item
CM—Configuration Management
ConOps—Concept of Operations Document
LAN—Local Area Network
PC—Personal Computer

PERT—Program Evaluation, Review, and Tracking

PM—Project Manager

RFC—Request for Change

SDD—Software Design Description

SPMP—Software Project Management Plan

SRS—Software Requirements Specification

2 References

[1] *ACME IS Guidebook*

[2] *ACME Accounting Guidebook*

[3] The Software Requirements Specification for the OPT project

[4] ANSI/IEEE Std 1016-1993, *IEEE Recommended Practice for Software Design Descriptions*

[5] Executive Sponsor Memorandum for the OPT project

[6] The Concept of Operations for the OPT project

[7] The Configuration Management Plan for the OPT project

[8] E. Yourdon, *Modern Structured Analysis*

[9] Super-LAN Operating System Specification

[10] Super-PC Operating System Specification

[11] Super-Builders Programmer Suite Specification

3 Decomposition Description

This section describes the structure of the OPT system. The structure comprises design entities. These are shown as products of structured design and flow from the structured analysis [8] presented in the SRS [3].

Figure 1 shows the processor model for the design. Each bubble in the figure is a design entity. This figure comes from the dataflow diagram (DFD) in the SRS [3]. The heavy lines divide the bubbles into groups per processor. The three bubbles in the lower left will run on the server, whereas the other bubbles will run on the desktop client PC's.

The design entities are further specified in the task model in Figure 2. This figure shows how the design entities fit into tasks on the different processors. The top part of Figure 2 shows the tasks in the server; the bottom part shows the tasks in the client PCs.

In the server, the order store and customer store are in a disk drive task. The other tasks communicate with the disk drive task via the operating system. A similar situation exists in the client PCs.

Figure 3 shows the structure chart of the server tasks, in which each box is a design entity. The figure shows how the design entities communicate. [The structure chart for the client tasks is omitted.]

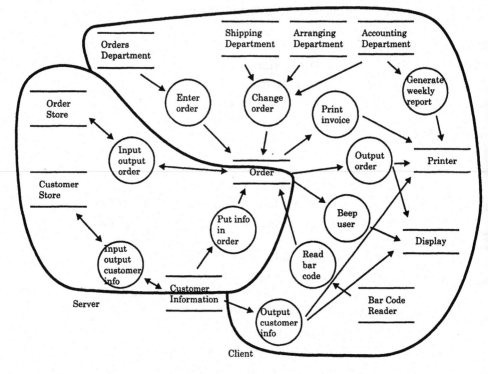

Figure 1   Processor model for the OPT project.

Server

Operating System		
Order store	Input-output order	
Customer store	Input-output customer info	
	Put info in order	

Order
Customer Info

Client

Operating System		
Printer	Enter order	Generate weekly report
Display	Change order	Print invoice
Bar code reader	Beep user	Output order
	Read bar code	Output customer info

Order
Customer Info

Figure 2   Task model for the OPT project.

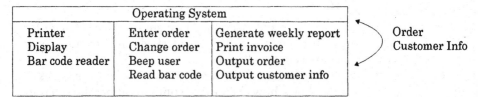

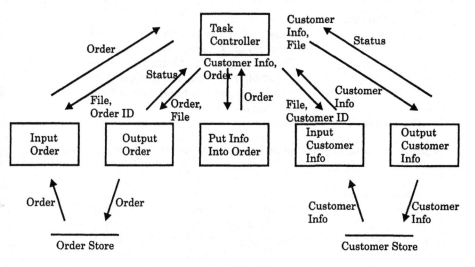

Figure 3   Structure chart for the OPT project.

The decomposition description concludes with the attributes that describe each design entity. Figure 4 shows the attributes for each entity. [The figure shows attributes only for the input order entity.]

4   Dependency Description

This section describes the relationships among design entities. Key to the relationships are the structure charts shown in Section 3. Figure 5 shows the design entities and their attributes relating to relationships. [*The figure shows attributes only for the input order entity.*]

5   Interface Description

This section presents the external view of each design entity. Figure 6 shows the design entities and their attributes relating to interfaces. The details of the

Identification:	input_order
Type:	Subroutine
Purpose:	Satisfies the requirement that the OPT system must retrieve order information.
Function:	This subroutine reads order information from the disk.
Subordinates:	None

Figure 4   Decomposition description of the input order entity for the OPT system.

Identification:	input_order
Purpose:	Satisfies the requirement that the OPT system must retrieve order information.
Dependencies:	This entity is called by the server task controller. It calls the operating system resources to retrieve information stored on disk.
Resources:	None

Figure 5   Dependency description of the input order entity for the OPT system.

Identification:	input_order
Function:	Satisfies the requirement that the OPT system must retrieve order information.
Interfaces:	Inputs: file name of the order store file, order_id
	Output: order

Figure 6   Interface description of the input order entity for the OPT system.

Identification:	Input_order
Processing:	check file_name
	handle errors if necessary
	check order_ID
	handle errors if necessary
	open order_store file
	handle errors if necessary
	read order from order_store
	handle errors if necessary
	close order_store
	end
Data:	file_name
	order_ID
	order

Figure 7   Detailed description of the input order entity for the OPT system.

data are shown in the entity relationship diagram and data dictionary in the SRS [3]. [The figure shows attributes only for the input order entity.]

6   Detailed Description

This section describes the details of each design entity. The low-level design document contains this section; the high-level design document does not.

Requirement	Design Element
FR1	input_order, put_info_into_order
FR2	input_order, put_info_into_order
FR3	output_customer_info
...	...
PR1	operating system
PR2	operating system
PR3	order data store
PR4	ouput_customer_info, order data store
PR5	order data store

Figure 8 The requirements traceability matrix.

Figure 7 shows the design entities with their detailed attributes. [*The figure shows attributes only for the input order entity.*]

7 Traceability

This section shows how the design elements trace back to individual requirements. The requirements traceability matrix in Figure 8 lists the requirements and the design elements that will satisfy them.

Configuration Management

This appendix is a tutorial on configuration management. I'm not introducing a lot of new material here. Much of it appears in other places in the book, and a careful reader could piece it together. However, I wanted to make it as easy as possible to learn about and use CM. If you have read as far as the preface in this book, you know that I believe CM is one of the critical elements in a successful software project.

Most people do not think of CM in such charitable terms. At best, they view it as well-meaning bureaucratic nonsense; at worst, they see it as a way to slow down and abuse others. In all my years of software development, I have not seen many people cheer when the project manager announced that everyone will use CM throughout the project.

What I hope to show concisely in this appendix is that proper CM helps the development team hold software projects together and improve the quality and timeliness of their products. Software projects comprise countless details and often slow to a crawl as key people chase details instead of doing their intended jobs. CM helps organize people into efficient and effective groups. These groups contain only the necessary people and those people work on only their part of the project. CM bundles details into packages that are manageable, freeing developers to do the exciting parts of their job.

The most benefit goes to the project manager. Good use of CM and a good CM staff empower the project manager to concentrate on what is important—talking with people and working on technical challenges.

B.1 WILL THE REAL CM PLEASE STAND UP?

CM is the single most misunderstood aspect of software development and maintenance projects (Phillips, 1996a, b). Ignorance and fear have driven

The Software Project Manager's Handbook. By Dwayne Phillips.
ISBN 0-471-67420-6 © 2004 IEEE Computer Society

people away from CM, or at least what they called CM. People, including myself, are not taught CM in college or in the workplace. I had three degrees and 15 years on the job before I learned what CM was and how it could help me.

Most organizations that have discarded CM have tried to keep some form of CM practice, calling it data management document boards. Unfortunately this has given rise to a false CM, a distortion that companies continue to use with a peculiar blend of superciliousness, inefficiency, and malevolence.

This is not the CM I describe here. The real CM makes everything visible. It does not surprise you with performance details someone has collected behind your back in a misguided attempt to motivate you. It does not make you do paperwork without a reason. It does not tie your hands and keep you away from your "real" work. Most of all, it does not show up near the project's end to say, "But I thought you understood we needed X."

What it *does* do is free you from running down the hall after Joe to see what's in the test plan or chasing users away from programmers because they will discuss and implement one more neat idea on the fly. The real CM says you can go to one spot and see exactly where everyone is on the project and exactly what state the product is in.

That is the character of the real CM. It doesn't operate behind the scenes to create mountains of detail that bury the project manager, kill off every creative urge in the designers, and cause everyone to rethink their career decisions. It packages details so that you attend meetings only when you absolutely must, always work on the correct version of the software, and look forward to being part of similar projects.

B.2   THE MAIN INGREDIENTS

Let us assume that your attitude toward CM is changing. You would like to know more. You are still suspicious, but willing to go a level deeper. Where do you begin?

CM has four main elements:

1. *Products.* The products are the *baselines*, each of which corresponds to a stage of the waterfall process, although these baselines are equally valid across process models. Note that there is more than one baseline per project. Understanding this lets you avoid saying things like "we need to baseline the system," which does not mean anything. People who say this, and some are quite intelligent, mean that they want turn the system into a baseline so that they can control it. As you will see, this approach convolutes the real CM practice.

2. *Activities.* The four primary CM activities are identification, control, auditing, and status accounting. Most people think change control is the only CM activity. People cannot, however, control changes to something that has not been identified. They also cannot be sure the intend-

ed changes were made without auditing, and they cannot know the status of everything without an accounting.

3. *People.* The people are the Configuration Control Boards, the CM staff, and the project manager. Each baseline has its own CCB. If the project is small, the project manager may be on all the CCBs.

4. *CM plan.* The CM plan is the roadmap that links the people to the CM activities. Every project needs its own CM plan. Projects can share parts of the plan, but each project has its own mix of people, process, and product, which the CM plan must reflect.

Introduce CM into your organization via a CM sketch (see Section B.6), which shows the four main elements in a single, understandable picture.

B.3 BASELINES

A baseline in one development stage forms the foundation for subsequent stages. Establishing and maintaining them are fundamental CM tasks. Baselines exist whether you acknowledge them or not. I can walk into any project and pick out the baselines. They lie around just waiting to be used. They are the problem, the solution, the code—the fundamentals.

The major benefit of baselines is visibility and this comes only by formally identifying them. A formally established baseline is visible. Anyone can put their hands on it and use it. There is no more "I thought the I/O subsystem would use sockets." Everyone can see what the I/O subsystem uses.

B.3.1 Basics

Figure B.1 shows the basic, generic baselines. The sample projects in Chapter 11 used these baselines in various ways.

The *functional* baseline contains the requirements for a system. This is usually in the form of a document or database. The requirements are the foundation for the remainder of the baselines and the project. The software being developed must satisfy the requirements.

Functional
Allocated
Design
Development
Product
Operational

Figure B.1 Basic baselines.

The *allocated* baseline is a high-level design that will satisfy the requirements. This will be a document or set of documents that shows how the requirements will be allocated to or satisfied by large subsystems. Most people seem to "know" the high-level design before the project starts. The trouble is, unless captured as the allocated baseline, everyone knows something different.

The *design* baseline is a detailed design. The design baseline shows the low levels of software design. A set of documents usually comprise this baseline. People often try to skip this baseline. They rely on the programmers to fill in the details. Capturing the design details in a baseline ensures that everyone's details agree.

The *development* baseline is what the programmers are working on or developing—the source code. This is the most fluid baseline. It is born when coding begins and ends when testing begins. Because of its nature, this baseline is hard to control. This is where basic control tools such as RCS (revision control system) and its many commercial counterparts function. Programmers love to live in this baseline as this is their element—programming. They hate it when code moves on to the next baseline because they cannot tweak it anymore.

The *product* baseline contains tested and approved components and systems. When a programmer is writing a set of subroutines, he is in the development baseline. When the subroutines have been tested and approved by someone, they become part of the product baseline. The product baseline is not used by users; it is used in the development environment only.

The *operational* baseline is what the users use in their daily operations. It is a finished product that the developers believe is good enough for the customers.

A project's progress is summarized as the creation, maturation, completion, and change to baselines. The baselines are the work completed in a project. When seen in this correct manner, it is easy to understand how CM and baselines are an integral part of a well-organized project.

B.3.2 Applying Baselines in a Waterfall Project

A sample project can help explain baselines. Suppose Acme Software is to build and maintain a word processor called "D-Word." Figure B.2 shows the baselines for this project. Acme decides what features and compatibilities they want in D-Word. This list of desires, the *functional* baseline V1.0, is put in a document and displayed in an easily accessible place.

Now Acme is ready to design D-Word. The high-level design breaks D-Word into basic subsystems. Three senior designers do the high-level design, which becomes *allocated* baseline V1.0. The high-level design must satisfy every item in the requirements baseline and nothing more. A document contains allocated baseline V1.0.

Baseline	Contents
Functional	Features and capabilities of D-Word
Allocated	Subsystems of D-Word
Design	Details of subsystems
Development	Code being written
Product	Finished and tested code
Operational	D-Word being used on the job

Figure B.2 Baselines for the D-Word project.

Different groups of programmers take their subsystem assignments and perform the detailed design. Their detailed designs must meet the specifications given in the allocated baseline. The detailed designs go into a document and become the *design* baseline V1.0. Everything in the design baseline flows from the allocated baseline; there are no omissions and no additions.

The programmers start programming. The source code under development is the *development* baseline V1.0. This is a messy, constantly changing baseline. When a group of programmers finishes a subsystem and it passes all tests, that subsystem moves on and becomes part of the *product* baseline V1.0. The product baseline is an executable program and its documentation.

When the product baseline is complete and accepted, Acme releases D-Word V1.0 to the users, and this release is the *operational* baseline V1.0. This is the end of the development phase and the beginning of the maintenance phase.

The users begin to grumble about the spell checker in D-Word V1.0. It does not run as fast as they required (as fast as functional baseline V1.0 requires). The developers knew about this problem, but decided to release D-Word anyway. The programmers who designed and developed the spell checker start again. They change the detailed design of the spell checker to make it faster. These changes become part of the *design* baseline V1.1. They rewrite the code for the spell checker in the *development* baseline V1.1. The revised spell checker is integrated into D-Word in *product* baseline V1.1. After sufficient use and testing, Acme releases this as *operational* baseline V1.1 and releases D-Word V1.1. Notice that the functional and allocated baselines did not change because the requirements and high-level design stayed the same.

Now suppose Acme wants a dozen new features in D-Word. These new features warrant the release of D-Word V2.0. The new features are added to the requirements and this becomes the *functional* baseline V2.0. The new high-level design becomes the *allocated* baseline V2.0. This process continues through the baselines until Acme releases D-Word V2.0.

B.3.3   Applying Baselines in a Nonwaterfall Project

The discussion thus far has used the simple waterfall model, in which development flowed from one phase to the next without any iterations or evolutions. Now, what about the real-world scramble we all know? As Figure B.3 shows, baselines can exist in a project using fluid techniques. In this example, the users are not sure what they need and the programmers have little experience in the business area. Now, this sounds familiar. At the top center of the figure, users work with a facilitator who is an expert with a GUI builder (screen generator). They discuss their jobs and thoughts for the future while the facilitator generates screens for them. They then videotape users working through the screens as they would in their jobs. These videos document the work flow requirements of the users. The videos of the users and the screens become the *functional* baseline.

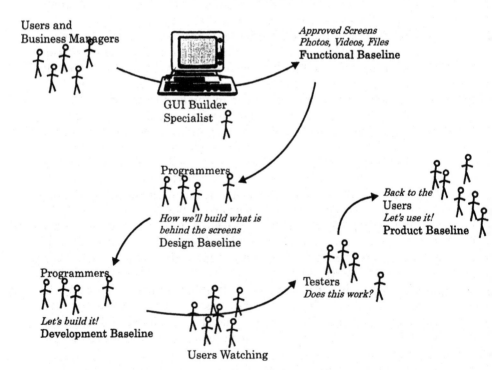

Figure B.3   Baselines in a fluid project.

Programmers (center of the figure) work from the functional baseline to design software that will use the screens and implement the work shown in the video. This is the *design* baseline. These programmers and others write code to implement the design. This is the *development* baseline and includes code from the GUI builder. The next activity is testing. Testers (members of the development team) run the code from the development baseline and compare it to the videos. When satisfied, the testers place the software into the *product* baseline.

When the product baseline satisfies the users, it passes on to the workplace and the final users. There, it becomes the *operational* baseline.

The preceding description is admittedly oversimplified. In most cases, the users observe the programmers and testers and go back to the facilitator and videotape. The users revise the functional baseline many times, which causes the programmers to revise their design and development baselines many times. At first, new functional baselines appear every week. The pace of change slows as the users learn exactly what they need and the developers learn how to build it. Functional baselines change every two weeks, then once a month, then stop changing. As the project progresses, the programmers cause the users to think more about their changes. The changes cost more time and money as the system grows, so a growing sense of discipline is needed.

CM works to prevent the iterations from degrading into chaos. The baselines are something solid to design, program, test, and use. Without them, programmers code features no one wants anymore and testers test against how they think the business operates. Rapid prototyping, videotaped requirements, iterations, evolutions, and frequent changes can exist with CM.

Notice how CM did not stifle creativity or prevent needed change. In fact, it worked to permit rapid change without confusion.

For more on how baselines work on nonwaterfall projects, read Chapter 11, which describes the use of baselines in an evolutionary and a spiral project.

B.3.4   Documenting Baselines

Document a baseline in the most visible manner possible (paper document, executable code, videotape, etc.). Everyone should be able to see it, think about it, discuss it, and improve it. Put copies in the management information center (see Chapter 4) and on-line. Keep everything open and above board.

B.3.5   Baseline Contents

Each baseline contains one or more *configuration items* (CIs)—information created during a software project. Each CI is self-contained and has clear, well-defined interfaces to the other CIs. A CI in a software project can be an SCI (software configuration item) or a CSCI (computer software configuration item).

The size of each CI varies according to the situation and the level of detail the executive sponsor and project manager want to control. If an operational baseline is a software system with six independent subsystems, each subsystem can be a CI. CIs divide a problem into parts that are easier to work with and manage.

Consider a satellite-tracking software system. The system can be divided into a user interface and a set of routines that perform orbit calculations. The functional baseline could have two CIs: a concept of operations and a *Software Requirements Specification*. These CIs would trace through the baselines to the operation baseline, which could have a user interface CI and a orbit calculation CI. The orbit calculation CI in turn may be divided into several other CIs.

CIs comprise smaller elements called components, or *computer software components* (CSCs). CSCs comprise smaller elements called units or *computer software units* (CSUs). Baselines, CIs, CSCs, and CSUs are the accepted (but not the only) names for the levels of abstraction in software. Using abstraction and formally identifying the pieces in the level of abstraction helps projects succeed. People refer to things by their name rather than "that code that Joe and Jane are writing." Joe and Jane are probably writing six CSUs, so calling the specific CSU by name reduces confusion and expensive errors.

CIs, CSCs, and CSUs let people see the different levels of abstraction. No one wonders why a unit is in the design. They can se it is there as part of a CI that meets specific requirements.

Typically, the larger the software system, the fewer the CIs. Systems of a half-million lines of code will have three or four CIs. In large systems, management has more than enough headaches. They happily welcome ways to reduce the number of CIs.

Small groups of people are responsible for each CI and can change the inside of it any way they wish. Changes to the outside, however, require meeting with other groups to discuss the implications of the change.

B.3.6   Interface Control Documents

Interface control documents define the interfaces between pairs of CIs and between a CI and the outside world. In the satellite-tracking software system just described, the user interface CI and orbit calculation CI must pass information back and forth. If this communication is direct, a user interface to the orbit calculation ICD would define the communication protocol. If the two CIs communicate through operation system facilities, there would be two ICDs, one to define a user interface to the operating system and one to define an orbit calculation interface to the operating system.

ICDs begin life in the *allocated* baseline (high-level design). At this point, the designers show the system in large blocks. Each block could become a CI and interface with either one or more other blocks or the outside world. The designers can capture these interfaces in ICDs. The ICD helps designers at the next level of detail because it specifies the format of the input and output for each CI.

ICDs are difficult to create, but pay for themselves. This is especially true if different CIs are to be built by different groups of people in different cities. The different groups use the ICDs as the input/output specifications. I do not advocate writing specifications and mailing them to people across a continent. However, when this situation is forced on your project, the use of ICDs should be mandatory.

On large projects, you may need to expand the interface documentation. An ICD describes an interface, so it may be the third in a series of documents (see the CM control activity description). The first is the *Interface Requirements Specification*, which lists the requirements of the interface (the interface is required to pass orbital parameters, is required to pass them in one second, and so on). The second is the *Interface Design Description* (IDD), which describes the interface design ("The interface will pass data via the operating system"). The *Interface Control Document* describes how the different CIs implement the interface.

ICDs are written by Interface Control Working Groups (ICWGs). Here are a few more nagging acronyms, but stay with me because ICWGs bring knowledgeable people face to face instead of chasing shadows and rumors through the halls. Figure B.4 illustrates this situation. Suppose team A builds CI A, team B builds CI B, and CI A and B must interface. Members of teams A and B form the A-to-B ICWG. The people on the ICWG understand their own product and what they need from the other product. They resolve what they need and what the other team can give them. The ICWG is Joe and Jane working with Carol and Bill, not detached committees mailing memos across the country.

ICDs add visibility to the critical interfaces in the software. When someone needs to know what goes on between major pieces of software, they

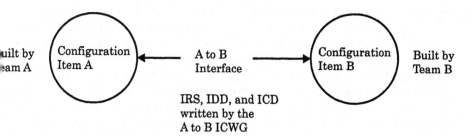

Figure B.4 How interface control working groups generate interface control documents.

pick up the ICD. There is no confusion, no assumptions, and no misunderstandings.

B.4   CM ACTIVITIES

B.4.1   *Identification*

Identification, the first of the four main CM activities, takes an idea or concept, separates it from everything else, and gives it a name. That idea becomes a concrete, specific, visible item. Identification establishes visibility and brings all its benefits.

Establishing baselines with CIs, CSCs, and CSUs is the goal of identification. People don't tap strangers on the shoulder in the coffee room and ask, "What's that code you are writing that does some kind of compression?" People know what others have done. This is the foundation of the other CM activities.

The identification activity includes how to name and label items. If a person picks up a piece of paper labeled "FB V07 CI27 of 1-2-95," he knows it is configuration item 27 of the seventh version of the functional baseline approved on January 2, 1995.

Identification schemes given to everyone on day one of the project save time and energy. People don't have to invent their own individual schemes and work with others to blend them into a common scheme six weeks later. They are free to use their creative energy to develop software.

The final identification artifact is the *Version Description Document*. The VDD describes a version or release of a software product. It lists the versions of everything related to the software including versions of the SRS and SDD that lead to it. It describes the differences between this version of the software and the prior version (new features, corrections to errors, and so on). The VDD shows people what the product is.

B.4.2   *Control*

Control is the most often recognized CM activity. When a baseline exists, people must control it. Seeing items in baselines is important, but it means nothing if those items are changing without control. A document has no value if it can be changed during a conversation in the hallway.

The first aspect of control is safeguarding. Misplacing a baseline is catastrophic, but it happens. Store copies of each version of each baseline in a secure place, Consider keeping extra copies of baselines in another city. Fires, floods, tornadoes, and earthquakes happen, and although insurance will pay you to rebuild your facility, it will not pay you to rebuild your baselines.

The major work of control is with controlling change. Change happens in software projects; control deals with it responsibly.

Many people discard CM because they become disillusioned when CM does not prevent change. This is one of those CM misconceptions I mentioned earlier. *Change control is not change prevention.* Change control is thinking and making informed decisions.

A change begins when someone requests it formally (according to the procedures given in the CM plan). A common name for this request is the *request for change,* or RFC. The IEEE's term discussed in Chapter 10 is *modification request* or MR. The RFC or MR is a one-page statement of requirements. IEEE-Std-1042 (IEEE, 1993) gives several examples. The request is written, not "Hey, I've got a neat idea."

If the change is contained in one baseline, the CCB (more on CCBs later) for that baseline meets to consider the change. If the change affects more than one baseline, several CCBs will meet.

Change requests trigger tracing and impact analysis. *Tracing* looks back at previous baselines for possible effects. Suppose someone wants to replace inches in the software being coded with centimeters. Tracing backward finds that the both the allocated and design baselines called for inches because the functional baseline specified it. Changing from inches to centimeters would cause the users (those paying the bills) to protest. If there is an excellent reason for this change, the requesters must meet with the people controlling the functional and design baselines. These meetings will give them an opportunity to describe why they requested the change. If everyone agrees, the change is made.

Impact analysis looks forward to succeeding baselines. Suppose late in the project (coding is in progress), a user requests changing inches to centimeters. This request first appears at the functional baseline. Impact analysis looks forward to the design and development baselines. The inches requirement shows up in those baselines. Changing the functional baseline will require reworking these baselines. Once again, the requesters will meet with the people controlling the design and development baselines. These meetings will give them an opportunity to describe why they requested the change. If everyone agrees, the change is made.

The project manager and the CM staff perform the tracing and impact analysis and present the results to different groups. When tracing and impact analysis occur, people make informed decisions openly and visibly—not on Sunday afternoon when no one else is around.

The *requirements verification traceability matrix* aids in tracing and impact analysis. Figure B.5 shows a sample RVTM. The RVTM clearly shows how a requirement leads to a design element, which leads to a code unit, which leads to tests. If someone wants to change requirement FR1, the team must first look at the command interpreter to see the possible impact. In the same manner, if someone wants to change the design of the text formatter, the team must trace back to see if the new design will still satisfy requirement FR3 and look forward to see how it will cause `format_text_line` to change.

The RVTM is a simple yet powerful tool. It shows how everything in the system connects to the wants of the user and the method of verifying that the

Requirement	Design Element	Code Unit	Code Unit Test #	System Test Element	Test Method
FR1	Command interpreter	get_options()	CU1	ST2	I
FR2	text reader	read_text_line()	CU3	ST4	E
FR3	text formatter	format_text_line()	CU6	ST1	D
...	...	...	...	...	...
PR1	Operating system	DOS	CU7	ST6	E
PR2	text data store	N/A	CU9	ST4	D
PR3	windows package	Fred's windows	...	ST8	A

Figure B.5   A requirements verification traceability matrix.

system will satisfy the user. Of all the visibility techniques discussed in this text, the RVTM is probably the most necessary. If you only use one type of visibility tool on a project, use an RVTM. I once worked on a $20M project where we decided not to use an RVTM. The final cost of the project was $33M. The absence of an RVTM attributed to the 50-plus percent cost overrun. The toll on the people in the project was even higher.

B.4.3   Auditing

Auditing checks to see if reality agrees with intentions. An audit examines a delivered product to see if it does what it should and is what it should be. The "does" portion is a *functional* audit. The "is" portion is a *physical* audit.

Functional audits determine if the required functions are in a product. For example, the auditors will ensure that the software calculates the interest on a 30-year mortgage. A separate test group will verify that the interest calculation is correct.

Physical audits document the state of a product. For example, when a new PC arrives, the auditors will compare the contents with the order form. The audit ensures that the PC has the right amount of RAM, the right disk drive, the right BIOS version, the right processor speed, and so on.

Physical audits are crucial in software development. This may be hard to believe unless you, like me, have had the misfortune of spending weeks trying to find an error in development code only to discover that the problem was an outdated version of a compiler library. Physical audits check the dates and versions of software delivered to your development team. Physical audits are needed more now than ever before because compiler versions arrive every three months on CD-ROM or every week over the Internet. Do not make assumptions about the tools your programmers are using. Audit them when they arrive.

The benefits of audits far outweigh their costs. The CM staff performs the audits according to the CM plan and reports the results to the project manager, who is then saved from running around trying to make sure that all the details of all the products are correct. Audits also save time for the programmers and others, who no longer need to check the products that come to them to see if the versions are correct. Instead, they can just start using them.

Most people don't like audits because they delay the use of the new tool. Setting up an auditing office in a building away from the development team can help. When the product leaves that building, the developers know it is ready to use.

B.4.4 *Status Accounting*

Status accounting tells everyone what is where this week. It typically looks at the work areas. For example, source code development takes place in known disk areas. Checking the disks weekly tells what routines are under development, are being tested, or have been accepted. Similar accounting reveals the status of baselines, documents, revisions, and so on.

This is not big brother spying on people to see if they are on working. This is visibility, communication, and coordination. Everyone knows how the code is advancing without interrupting the programmers every 10 minutes to ask.

Take care that status accounting is done in a way that does not cause people to fear for their jobs, which can paralyze the project. The purpose of status is to allow the project manager to make decisions that help the project and its people succeed. Status accounting used to place blame is destructive.

B.5 CM PEOPLE

B.5.1 *Configuration Control Boards*

The CCB for a particular baseline knows more about that baseline than anyone else—they control it; it is their part of the project. They are not, as another popular CM misconception would have you believe, a group of gray-beards who know nothing about the project and love to say no. The people on a CCB are immersed in the project, intimate with its details, and striving to see it succeed.

A particular CCB comprises only the people who need to discuss the issues relevant to that baseline—no more and no fewer. The *functional* baseline CCB comprises customers, users, or marketing—those who know best what they need in the software. The *allocated* baseline is a system or high-level design, so the members of its CCB should be the senior or best designers. Senior programmers will make up the *design* baseline (low-level design) CCB. The *development* baseline CCB comprises the programmers. Programmers and testers will be on the *product* baseline CCB, and the users will return to be on the *operational* baseline CCB.

The CCB considers requests for changes to its baseline. If the requested change is internal to a single baseline, the CCB decides on the request by itself and reports the result to the CM staff. If the request will change the external interface of the baseline, several CCBs are involved. A CCB meets only when its baseline is involved in a change request. CCB meetings are substantive and efficient—people make decisions that shape the project.

CCBs are empowered to control their own baselines. They never say "We cannot make that decision, but we'll get back to you on that." For that empowerment to work, however, CCBs require visibility. They must see what they are discussing. CCB meetings without displays, sketches, posters, and documents are at best a waste of time and at worst dangerous. CCBs also enhance visibility by adding the weight of their decisions to the contents of baselines. When something is in a baseline, it is there because a CCB has examined and authorized it.

B.5.2   CM Staff

While CM is holding the project together, the CM staff is holding CM together. CM staffers take care of the CM details so that others can concentrate on their jobs. This gives the project the benefits of CM without turning it into a hated bureaucracy for everyone.

The CM staff is involved in all the CM activities. They write the CM plan, capture the baselines, keep safe copies of baselines, perform baseline tracing and impact analysis, report the results of that analysis, audit products, report results of audits, perform status accounting, and submit status reports. The CM staff attends meetings daily. Face to face, they listen, talk, understand, record, and report what people need. They make visible the invisible thoughts of others.

The size of the CM staff depends on the size of the project. If the project has a project manager and four other people, the project manager will be the CM staff. If 100 people are on the project, four or five should be devoted to the CM staff.

The CM staff works with details and works behind the scenes. They need to be disciplined, meticulous people who take their job seriously but have the maturity and humility to cater to the egos of others without developing a poor self-image.

B.5.3   Project Manager

The project manager is the person responsible for the project. The project manager has many responsibilities, but here I focus only on only those related to CM.

The most important CM task for the project manager is establishing CM. This means having the project's executive sponsor endorse and enforce CM and the CM plan. If this is not done, the project manager's job is much more difficult. People will still change project details in the halls and the project manager will chase the details all day.

Once CM is established, the project manager can ride the wave. The CCBs will take care of the baselines, and the CM staff will record the details. The project manager can spend time and energy on the important tasks: working with people and working on technical problems.

The project manager coordinates the CCBs. When a change request affects more than one baseline, the project manager brings together the different CCBs to debate it. During these meetings, he presents the results of tracing and impact analysis and leads the ensuing discussion. He closes the discussion with a well-documented and understood decision.

Last but not least, the project manager must nurture the CM staff. Give them credit for what they do, recognize their contribution publicly, and reward them in a way they want—even if it means moving them off the CM staff on the next project.

B.6 CM PLAN

The CM plan—the roadmap for implementing CM—must have the executive sponsor's weight. The executive sponsor is a person who is high up in the organization, above everyone working on the project, and who takes a personal, visible interest in the project's success. Many experts agree that an executive sponsor is a key to success. The executive sponsor's endorsement tells everyone that the CM plan is not just part of a mandatory checklist. The CM plan will be a fundamental day-in and day-out resource for the project.

IEEE-Std-1042 offers a format that will fit almost any project (IEEE, 1993). The standard is tough going, but the content is worth the trouble. After the usual introductory material, the standard has three parts: a description of CM, how to write a CM plan, and four sample CM plans as appendices. The four appendices are what moves this from a good standard to a great one.

The description of CM runs through much of the material presented in here, discussing baselines, CCBs, and the CM activities.

The how-to section presents the table of contents for a CM plan, shown in Figure B.6. The *introduction* is fairly typical of IEEE-based documentation. The *management* section discusses the organization of the people on the project and the baselines. Required in this section are figures showing who is who and their associated baselines. These figures make visible what is sometimes obvious, but unless they are stated obviously, the team can become confused and waste time. The *CM activities* section describes how the organization will

1. Introduction
   1.1 Purpose
   1.2 Scope
   1.3 Definitions
   1.4 References

2. Management
   2.1 Organization
   2.2 CM Responsibilities
   2.3 Interface Control
   2.4 CM Plan Implementation
   2.5 Applicable Polices, Directives, & Procedures

3. CM Activities
   3.1 Configuration Identification
   3.2 Configuration Control
   3.3 Configuration Status Accounting
   3.4 Audits and Review
   3.5 Release Process

4. Tools, Techniques, & Methodologies

5. Supplier Control
   5.1 Subcontractor Software
   5.2 Vendor Software

6. Records Collection and Retention

Figure B.6   Table of contents for a CM plan.

perform the CM activities described. The remaining sections discuss technical details of implementing CM for a project.

This standard contains plenty of practical and helpful tips. Each section has a block titled "Issues to consider in planning the section." The blocks contain practical questions that help in writing a complete plan.

The sample CM plans in the appendices show how CM works in four types of software projects. They also show that good CM plans need not be 50 pages long. Writing a CM plan is not easy, but it is within reach of every software organization—even ones with only a few dozen employees.

B.7   A CM SKETCH

A complete written CM plan may not be possible for every organization right away. Cultural change, no matter how beneficial, requires time. When in the middle of a hectic project, writing a first CM plan is out of the question. The customers and management will not stop work for a couple of weeks while the project team learns how to do this.

A CM sketch such as that in Figure B.7 is a good alternative. It shows who is who in a project and their areas of responsibility. It brings to a project much of the organization and benefit of a CM plan.

The top of Figure B.7 shows the organization chart (who is who) for the fictitious company. Below the organization chart is a table showing what is what and who is responsible for what. The table establishes the baselines, describes their content, and states who is on the corresponding CCB.

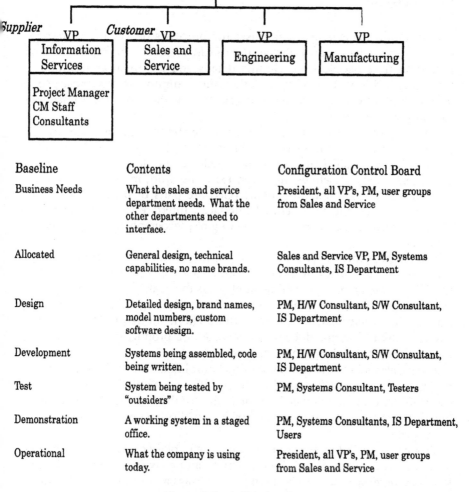

Baseline	Contents	Configuration Control Board
Business Needs	What the sales and service department needs. What the other departments need to interface.	President, all VP's, PM, user groups from Sales and Service
Allocated	General design, technical capabilities, no name brands.	Sales and Service VP, PM, Systems Consultants, IS Department
Design	Detailed design, brand names, model numbers, custom software design.	PM, H/W Consultant, S/W Consultant, IS Department
Development	Systems being assembled, code being written.	PM, H/W Consultant, S/W Consultant, IS Department
Test	System being tested by "outsiders"	PM, Systems Consultant, Testers
Demonstration	A working system in a staged office.	PM, Systems Consultants, IS Department, Users
Operational	What the company is using today.	President, all VP's, PM, user groups from Sales and Service

Figure B.7   A CM sketch.

The CM staff and project manager should sketch this CM chart on a large piece of paper and discuss it with the project participants. The sketch should show how each group of people will control the part of the project they know best. It should show the lines of communication. Finally, it should show how the project manager will coordinate the different groups so that the people who know the issues best can discuss and solve substantive problems.

The CM sketch is a good way to let people experience the benefits of CM without making a big formal step. The CM staff should put the CM sketch in a public place so that the project manager can discuss questions using the sketch as a visual aid. As the team gets used to CM, they may be ready in the next project for a full CM plan.

B.8 SUMMARY

Configuration management comprises the processes people use to preserve the integrity of the product. Proper use of CM imposes a management discipline that frees people from chasing details and lets them concentrate on their intended jobs. CM is coordination and communications. Most people do not think of CM in these terms because CM is the single most misunderstood topic in software.

CM has four main elements. *Baselines* are the work completed and accepted and form the foundation of future work. The basic baselines follow the familiar waterfall (functional, allocated, design, development, product, and operational). Baselines, however, exist and work in projects using any process model. Configuration items (CIs) are parts of baselines that have clear boundaries and well-defined interfaces. Interface Control Documents (ICDs) defines these interfaces and help group geographically separated developers.

CM *activities* include (1) identification, (2) control, (3) auditing, and (4) status accounting. Identification gives an idea a name to make it a concrete, specific, visible item. Establishing baselines is the goal of identification. Control manages change to established baselines. Auditing confirms that reality agrees with intentions. Functional audits check for required capabilities, whereas physical audits document the state of a product. Status accounting reveals the status of the product this week.

CM *people* include the Configuration Control Boards, the CM staff, and the project manager. A CCB comprises the people responsible for a baseline. The CM staff performs the detailed CM activities for the PM. The PM is responsible for the project. His primary CM task is establishing CM as an integral part of the project.

Proper use of CM requires a CM *plan* to be in place on day one of the project. The plan should follow IEEE-Std-1042 and carry the weight of the project's executive sponsor. A CM plan is not always an option. In such cases, a CM sketch is a good alternative.

REFERENCES

R. Berlack, *Software Configuration Management*, Wiley, New York, 1992.

IEEE, ANSI/IEEE Std 1042, *IEEE Guide to Software Configuration Management*, IEEE CS Press, Los Alamitos, CA, 1993.

D. Phillips, "Project Management: Filling in the Gaps," *IEEE Software*, July 1996a, pp. 17–18.

D. Phillips, "Configuration Management: Understanding the Big Picture," *Software Development*, Dec. 1996b, pp. 47–53.

D. Whitgift, *Methods and Tools for Software Configuration Management*, Wiley, New York, 1991.

Structured Analysis and Design

Structured methods have influenced software developers for the last 15 years. This appendix contains a brief description of the structured analysis and design method developed by Ed Yourdon (Yourdon, 1989), which you may know better as SA/SD. This is a basic, proven method of analyzing requirements, documenting them via diagrams, continuing the analysis through to design, and documenting the design via diagrams.

SA/SD is one of many proven methods you can use to systematically manage software development. Others can be found in the object-oriented world, for example (Coad & Yourdon, 1990, 1991; Rumbaugh et al., 1991). I include this appendix because I have seen too many projects managed and executed by people who do not know or use any proven method. This may seem unbelievable, but I have three degrees and, after my first 10 years on the job, I still did not know of or use a method. One day I backed up, read several books on methods, and started to learn how to use them. This is a sad commentary on our industry.

If your organization is not using a proven method, start with this one. It is not the best method for every project, but it will work in most cases. Realtime and embedded systems do not fit the method as Yourdon describes it, but the extension by Paul Ward and Stephen Mellor works for these systems (Ward & Mellor, 1986,1987, 1989). The object-oriented methods are best for new systems, those without legacy code. Yourdon himself says this in the two object-oriented texts he wrote with Peter Coad. Coad and Yourdon, two strong object-oriented proponents, also stated that people should not attempt the object-oriented paradigm unless they are at SEI CMM level 3. I agree. Whether or not you follow the CMM, you should master basics before attempting the more complex methods.

The Software Project Manager's Handbook. By Dwayne Phillips.
ISBN 0-471-67420-6 © 2004 IEEE Computer Society

C1 STRUCTURED ANALYSIS

Structured analysis is a specific method of analyzing requirements by building a series of system models. These models—environmental, preliminary behavioral, and final behavioral—make up the *essential model* of the system being analyzed.

To illustrate structured analysis and design concepts, I use the example of DP, a document publishing system. The example begins by analyzing the complete DP system, including software, hardware, and people. SA/SD starts at this system level. As you progress through analysis, you draw lines between manual and automated tasks and finally allocate functions to the software.

The first step is to understand the boundary between the system being built and the environment. Draw an environment diagram like that in Figure C.1. It shows who and what are and are not involved. This puts boundaries on the system and the project to focus attention. These boundaries are important, especially in the early part of a project. Developers do not waste time attempting to pull requirements from those not obviously part of the environment. A writer's accountant, for example, would not be concerned with the system, so there is no point in trying to have the system accommodate an accountant's needs.

C.1.1 *Environmental Model*

The next step creates the first of the three models that comprise the essential model. The environmental model has three elements:

Figure C.1   Environment diagram for DP.

1. *Statement of purpose.* The statement should briefly (one paragraph maximum) tell why the system should exist. DP's statement of purpose is simply "The purpose of DP is to take handwritten notes and typed drafts from writers and turn them into books that are marketed by stores."

2. *Context diagram.* Figure C.2 shows the context diagram (see Chapter 5 for more on context diagrams) for DP. Writers send their notes into DP. Management directs the systems and receives status from it. Stores send requests into DP for certain books. The DP system sends finished books out to distributors.

3. *Event list.* The event list consists of statements of actions the system will take on data. There are three basic types of events. *Flow-oriented* events describe the flow of data like "User types command." *Temporal* events are triggered by the arrival of a point in time. *Control* events are external events at some point in time such as "DP formatter hits end of input file." Figure C.3 lists part of the DP event list. This figure, and several others to follow, only shows one part of the system analysis results. This example is a large system and space does not permit showing all the details.

The next task is to write the data dictionary (see Chapter 4 for more on data dictionaries) for the system. Figure C.4 shows part of the data dictionary for the DP program.

C.2 Preliminary Behavioral Model

The next actions create a first version of the behavioral model—a model of how the system must behave to operate in its environment. This model is an

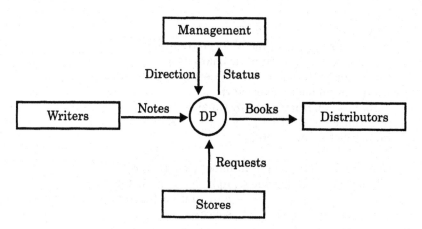

Figure C.2   Context diagram for DP.

. Writer sends notes to DP
. Type notes into ASCII file
. Add formatting commands
. Create figures
. Format document
. Add figures to document

...

. Build books
. Distribute books

Figure C.3   Partial event list for DP.

initial dataflow diagram (see Chapter 5 for more on DFDs). It is an initial diagram because the full DFD is too complicated to create in one step.

Build the initial DFD in four steps. First, draw a bubble or circle for each item in the event list. Second, name each bubble by describing the system's response to that event. For example, if an event is "customer makes payment," the response and bubble name could be "update customer's account." When you have bubbles for each action, draw the necessary inputs and outputs for each bubble and place each bubble in a data store box. Do not let bubbles communicate directly, only through the data store boxes. Finally, check the DFD against the context diagram drawn earlier for consistency and correctness.

Figure C.5 shows one version of the initial DFD for DP. Many other dataflows are possible. You can see how notes from writers enter at the upper left and finished books leave at the lower right. Notice also that this is a system dataflow diagram. Many of the items in the diagram are not software.

. input-paragraph = {line-of-text}
. output-paragraph = {line-of-formatted-text}
. line-of-text = {alphanumeric-character}
. line-of-formatted-text = word + space + (punctuation)
. word = {alphabetic-character}
. alphabetic-character = [A-Z | a-z]
. punctuation = [! | : | ; | " | ' | , | . | ?]
. numeric-character = [0-9]
. delimiter = \
. command = delimiter + alphabetic-character
. alphanumeric-character = [alphabetic-character |
                              punctuation | numeric-character |
                              space]

Figure C.4   Part of a data dictionary for DP.

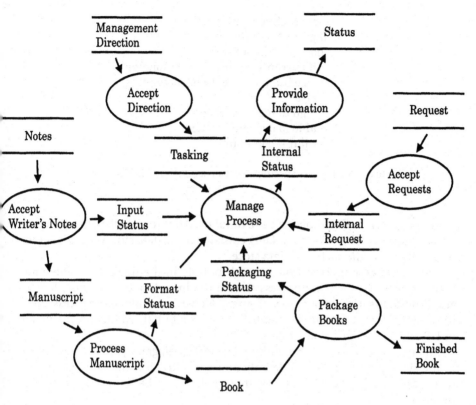

Figure C.5   A possible dataflow diagram for DP.

C.13   Final Behavioral Model

Finishing the behavioral model requires completing the DFD and the data dictionary and adding three other diagrams. The DFD is finished after it has been leveled up and down. In leveling up, you group several bubbles into one. Group closely related bubbles (processes) because they usually deal with related data. Try to group bubbles to hide or bury stored data. If several bubbles work with a data store exclusively (no other bubbles use it), group those. Keep the detail just combined in a lower-level diagram. Try to group bubbles so that each DFD has seven bubbles (plus or minus two).

Leveling down splits a bubble into several bubbles and data stores. This adds needed detail and creates lower-level diagrams. Keep leveling down until DFDs document all the necessary detail. Do not assume someone else will know about the details hidden in a bubble. Figure C.5 contains seven process bubbles; the final detailed diagrams could contain as many as 70 bubbles. Later, I show the result of leveling down the "Accept Writer's Notes" bubble.

Process Spec for Scan Text
input = line-of-text
loop over line-of-text
    if current-character == delimeter
        command = next-character
    else
        go to next-character
    end loop over line-of-text
output = command

Figure C.6   Process specification in pseudocode for "scan text".

The next step in finishing the behavioral model is to complete the data dictionary started earlier. The final DFD contains more data stores. The data dictionary must define each new data store.

Write a process specification for each bubble in the final DFD. There are many ways to state what a process should do, including pseudocode, tables, and flow charts. Use what works. Figure C.6 gives a pseudocode process specification for a process called "scan text." This is a bubble hidden in the detail of DP and not shown in any figure.

The next step is to draw an entity-relationship diagram (ERD) for the data in the system (the DFDs and data dictionary). ERDs illustrate the important relations among data elements. Figure C.7 shows an ERD for part of the DP program.

The last task in finalizing the behavioral model is to do a state transition diagram (see Chapter 5 for more on these). Systems have important states and transitions, and this diagram makes them clear to everyone. Figure C.8 shows the state transition diagram for the "Manage Process" bubble of Figure C.5. Each bubble in the context diagram should have its own state transition diagram.

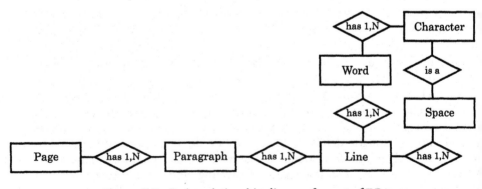

Figure C.7   Entity-relationship diagram for part of DP.

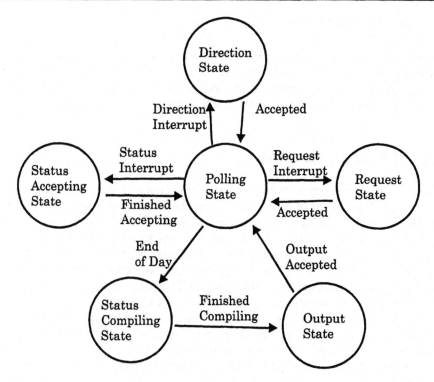

Figure C.8   State transition diagram for the "Manage Process" bubble in Figure C.5.

C1.4   Finished Essential Model

The finished essential model contains everything the system must do to meet the users' requirements. Figure C.9 lists the contents of the essential model. These statements, lists, and figures are invaluable to those who must design a solution. Place them in the *Software Requirements Specification*.

. Context Diagram
. Event List
. Statement of Purpose
. Data Flow Diagrams (leveled)
. Entity Relationship Diagrams
. State Transition Diagrams
. Data Dictionary
. Process Specifications

Figure C.9   Contents of the finished essential model file for DP.

C2   STRUCTURED DESIGN

Structured design uses parts of the essential model to create a design. As in structured analysis, structured design has a series of models: user implementation, systems implementation, and program implementation. I will continue with the DP example described in the structured analysis section.

C2.1   User Implementation Model

The user implementation model is halfway between requirements analysis and design. It is similar to constraints being placed on requirements. Much of the work put into software today falls in this area.

The first task determines the automation boundary—where the user wants the automated system to stop and the user to start. Next is the human interface, which includes the I/O devices (mouse and keyboard), I/O codes, and GUI. The GUI is what users emphasize today. Use Joint Application Development and other visibility techniques described in Chapter 5.

The next task specifies operational constraints. This deals with the volume of data; response times; and political, environmental, and reliability constraints. These limit the size of the design solution space.

Figure C.10 shows the detail of leveling down the "Accept Writer's Notes" bubble in Figure C.5. I refer to this diagram to explain the implementation model issues. The first task is to label the automation boundary. The "Enter Notes" bubble shows a process that takes handwritten or typewritten pages from writers and enters them into an ASCII file on a computer. A page could be rekeyed and entered by a typist or read by an optical character reader. The same is true of the "Draw Figure" bubble (an artist can redraw it or scan the original). The system analyst, users, and management must work through the dataflow diagrams and make these decisions.

Once you know what to automate, it is time to look at user interface issues. If you plan to have a typist rekey the written or typed material, you must specify the user interface for typing. This usually means a word processor, but it may mean a database program. If you are building an all-in-one system, you can create your own text-entering and -editing program. Again, the system analyst must work with users and management to make these decisions.

The final decisions concern operational constraints. How many manuscripts a month must DP handle? What type of people will perform the manual tasks? What type of people will interface with the software? How often will status be required? How often can stores submit requests? How quickly must DP respond to management direction? The questions seem endless, but they must be answered.

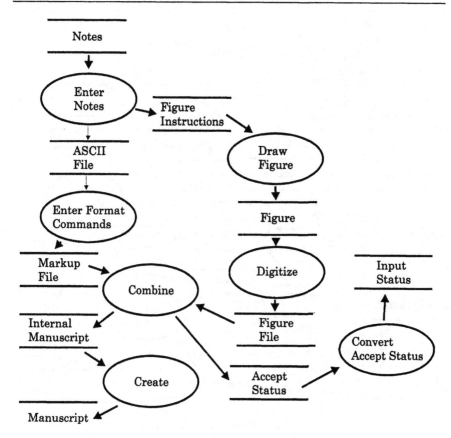

Figure C.10   Detail of "Accept Writer's Notes" bubble from Figure C.5.

C.2.2   Systems Implementation Model

The systems implementation model begins the true design process. It comprises the task and processor models. The *processor* model assigns processes and data stores to processors. Software systems often use several processors (which was true long before client-server and Internet systems). Draw lines to separate processors on the highest level dataflow diagram from the essential model (structured requirements). Figure C.11 shows the processor model for the DP program. Processes in different processors communicate via data stores.

The DP processor model shows four processors. Three of the processors deal largely with input and output at the edges of the system. The "Accept Writer's Notes" bubble or process could be done at a field office. The "Package Books" bubble can sit in a warehouse or shipping building. The "Accept Requests" bubble occurs in bookstores where people request books. This

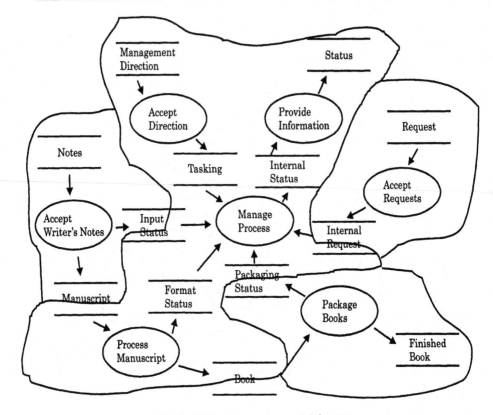

Figure C.11   Processor model for DP.

could occur at hundreds of different bookstores, so this processor will probably be duplicated many times. The "Accept Direction," "Provide Information," "Process Manuscript," and "Manage Process" group will probably occur
in a central computer, where the DP system is based.

The *task* model assigns processes and data stores to individual tasks in each
processor. Different operating systems have different concepts of tasks. Unix
has long allowed a user to have several distinct tasks running at the same time
(database, spell checker, document formatter, and so on). The PC world finally gained this capability in the mid-1990s. If the software system being designed has enough processes and can benefit from multiple tasks, create a task
model.

Figure C.12 shows the task model for the central processor of the DP system. The central processor is the four-bubble group in the center of Figure
C.11. Figure C.12 shows that the "Manage Process" and "Process Manuscript"
bubbles will run as one task and communicate with one another through the
"Format Status" data store. The "Provide Information" bubble will run as a
second task and communicate with the first task via operating system facili-

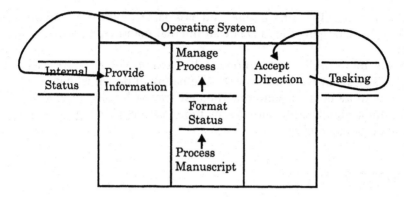

Figure C.12   Task model for the central processor of the DP system.

ties and the "Internal Status" data store. The "Accept Direction" bubble will run as a third task and communicate with the first task in a similar manner.

C23   Program Implementation Model

The program implementation model is a set of structure charts (see Chapter 5), one for each task in each processor in the processor model in Figure C.11. Use the bubbles in the DFD to create the program units (subroutines). Pass the data items listed in data stores as parameters. The structure charts should include all the bubbles and data stores in all the DFD levels.

Figure C.13 shows a structure chart for the dataflow diagram in Figure C.10. This shows the inside of the "Accept Writer's Notes" task. It shows how

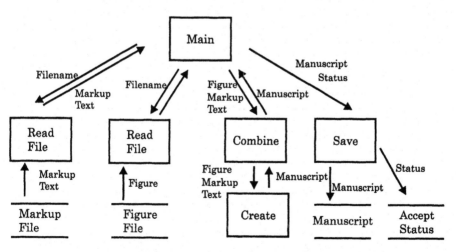

Figure C.13   A structure chart for the dataflow diagram in Figure C.10.

the routines would call one another and pass data to automate combining the markup file and figure file to create an internal manuscript and final manuscript. This is not the only way to automate the "Accept Writer's Notes" task. Other approaches may work just as well. The nature of design is that there is always one more possible solution. The best approach is to create several designs, think about each, and design more before selecting a design and beginning programming.

REFERENCES

P. Coad and E. Yourdon, *Object-Oriented Analysis*, Yourdon Press, Englewood Cliffs, NJ, 1990.

P. Coad and E. Yourdon, *Object-Oriented Design*, Yourdon Press, Englewood Cliffs, NJ, 1991.

J. Rumbaugh et al., *Object-Oriented Modeling and Design*, Prentice-Hall, Englewood Cliffs, NJ, 1991.

P. Ward and S. Mellor, *Structured Development for Real-Time Systems: Vol. 2, Essential Modeling Techniques*, Prentice-Hall, Englewood Cliffs, NJ, 1987.

P. Ward and S. Mellor, *Structured Development for Real-Time Systems*, Vol. 2, Prentice-Hall, Englewood Cliffs, NJ, 1987.

P. Ward and S. Mellor, *Structured Development for Real-Time Systems: Vol. 3, Implementation Modeling Techniques*, Prentice-Hall, Englewood Cliffs, NJ, 1987.

E. Yourdon, *Modern Structured Analysis*, Yourdon Press, Englewood Cliffs, NJ, 1989.

Annotated Bibliography

The following resources are some I have found especially helpful in managing software projects at work.

D.1 PROCESS

Encyclopedia of Software Engineering, John J. Marciniak, ed., Wiley, New York, 1994, http://www.wiley.com. If there is one resource to have in your office, this is it. It contains more knowledge about the technical aspects of software per inch of bookshelf than anything I have come across. If a question arises, look it up here first. I find a complete answer eight out of 10 times. The other two times I find a quick answer and references to other sources that suffice.

Humphrey, Watts, *A Discipline for Software Engineering*, Addison-Wesley, Reading, MA, http://www.awl.com/cseng/. 1995. Watts Humphrey (http://www.sei.cmu.edu) has written an essential book for the professional and student software engineer. His text teaches how to write more software in less time with fewer errors; in short, how to be a better software engineer. There's no magic here, just basic, disciplined, often unpleasant hard work. Learn and apply his lessons to individual and group projects.

IEEE Computer Society, 10662 Los Vaqueros Cir., Los Alamitos, CA 90720; http://computer.org. The IEEE Computer Society is one of the largest organizations of computer professionals in the world. It is *the* source of periodicals, books, and software-related standards. The list below contains the publications I have found most helpful. The standards are difficult to read, but if you put the effort into them, the return on investment is extremely high.

The Software Project Manager's Handbook. By Dwayne Phillips.
ISBN 0-471-67420-6 © 2004 IEEE Computer Society

- IEEE Standards Collection, *Software Engineering,* 1999, IEEE Press, Piscataway, NJ. This is a all the IEEE's software engineering standards bound together. Difficult to read, but worth it.
- IEEE Standard 1042-1993, *IEEE Guide to Software Configuration Management,* IEEE Press, Piscataway, NJ. This configuration management standard is significant enough to list by itself. Configuration management is widely and wildly misunderstood. This standard is a major step towards removing these misunderstandings.
- *Computer,* a monthly magazine for practitioners that covers all aspects of computer technology.
- *IEEE Software,* a bimonthly magazine devoted to software-development issues.

McConnell, Steve, Code Complete, 1993, and Rapid Development, 1996, Microsoft Press, Redmond, WA, 1993, http://mspress.microsoft.com/. Steve McConnell is a rising star in the software community (www.construx.com/stevemcc). *Code Complete* tells you everything you ever wanted to know about writing good programs. It also tells you what to look for in programs written by people you supervise. I mention this text because coding is one topic I do not cover in my book, but it is one that bears learning. *Rapid Development* covers managing software projects. Steve defines rapid development as development that is faster than what you are doing today— something that is everyone's goal.

Paulk, Mark C., et al., *Key Practices of the Capability Maturity Model, Version 1.1,* Software Engineering Institute, Pittsburgh, Penn., 1993, http://www.sei.cmu. edu.— The SEI's Capability Maturity Model has had perhaps the single greatest influence on the software community in the last 20 years. The SEI offers a number of other products and seminars that cover all aspects of software.

D.2   VISIBILITY

Buzan, Tony, *Use Both Sides of Your Brain,* 3rd ed., Penguin Books, New York, 1991, http://www.penguinputnam.com. Tony Buzan (http://www.buzan. co.uk) is a lecturer and original thinker who teaches people how to do everything better by improving their basic capabilities. This book describes mind maps, a great visibility technique, and many other fundamental, personal improvement activities like reading faster with more comprehension and remembering things better.

Gilb, Tom, *Principles of Software Engineering Management,* 1988, and Tom Gilb and Dorothy Graham, *Software Inspection,* 1993, both from Addison-Wesley, Reading, MA, http://www2.awl.com/cseng/. These two classic works should be on every software practitioner's bookshelf. *Principles of Software Engineering Management* teaches how to run evolutionary projects and quantify qualitative information. *Software Inspection* teaches how to do the single most effective practice in a software project.

Putnam, Lawrence, and Ware Myers, *Measures for Excellence —- Reliable Software On Time, Within Budget*, Yourdon Press, Englewood Cliffs, NJ, 1992 (available through Prentice-Hall, http://www.prenhall.com). Lawrence Putnam and Ware Myers write about their experience with the Rayleigh model, a model that characterizes key aspects of the software process. Putnam's company, Quantitative Software Management (http://www.qsm.com), uses the Rayleigh model in the SLIM tool, a tool to estimate, plan, and track software projects. Both this text and SLIM are excellent resources for the software project manager. They can tell you if someone has bid on a project (including your own) is attainable or folly.

Zahniser, Richard. Mr. Zahniser is the most underrated thinker in the software community. He has created several outstanding low-tech techniques that help people produce software quickly. The following articles written by him are just a sample.

- "Design By Walking Around," *Communications of the ACM*, Oct. 1993, pp. 114–123.
- "SST: System Storyboarding Techniques," *American Programmer*, Sept. 1993.
- "Time Boxing," *Software Development*, Mar. 1995, pp. 34–38.

D.3 PEOPLE

DeMarco, Tom, and Timothy Lister, *Peopleware*, 2nd ed., Dorset House Publishing, New York, 2000, http://www.dorsethouse.com. The authors wrote the first version in 1987, but it still applies. Every software project manager should read this and try to apply it daily. People issues are extremely important. A big part of a manager's job is to enjoy solving difficult problems with all types of people. If you are having people problems, I highly recommend this book.

Weinberg, Gerald, *Quality Software Management: Vols. 1–4*, (1994) Dorset House Publishing, New York (see Web site above). Gerald Weinberg (www.geraldmweinberg.com) has been working in software longer than anybody, at least it seems that way. He always talks about people. If you want to learn how to work with people better, read everything Gerald Weinberg ever wrote. This four volume set is just one of a string of classics. Mr. Weinberg teaches seminars and moderates an online discussion about software as a human activity. The four volumes on Quality Software Management describe

- *Quality Software Management: Vol. 1, Systems Thinking,* 1992—understanding complex situations to help plan projects and keep them progressing
- *Quality Software Management: Vol. 2, First-Order Measurement,* 1993—observing what is happening with people during a project
- *Quality Software Management: Vol. 3, Congruent Action,* 1994—acting appropriately in difficult people situations
- *Quality Software Management: Vol. 4, Anticipating Change,* 1994—creating an environment that supports software engineering and the changes needed to have a good environment

Gerald Weinberg now moderates the SHAPE forum (Software as a Human Activity Performed Effectively) on his web site (*www.geraldmweinberg.com*). An excellent discussion forum for many topics related to the people aspect of software (and everything else).

O'Bryan, Roy, and Dwayne Phillips, *It Sounded Good When We Started,* 2003, IEEE Press/Wiley. A colleague and I wrote this book after we finished working on a project together. It discusses many aspects of working with people on projects. It got its title because when we started the project everything was in place, so the project sounded good. We were wrong; the project had many large problems, and we learned much about working with people as a result.

D.4   JOURNALS

The Cutter IT Journal   (formerly *American Programmer*), http://www.cutter. com. Ed Yourdon is one of the top engineers, writers, and lecturers in the software world. He started this journal and has since turned it over to Cutter. This is still an excellent journal. The cost is high (over $500 a year), but worth it.

Software Development, Miller-Freeman, http://www.sdmagazine.com. This monthly offers practical advice from people who work in software every day. The focus is at a lower level than *American Programmer* as *Software Development* talks to programmers, team leaders, and managers of small-to-medium-size projects.

STQE (formerly *Software Testing and Quality Engineering*), *http://www.stqe magazine.com* This bimonthly focuses on testing and quality issues. It also covers the management, people, and other facets of software development and maintenance. An excellent journal.

Index

About the Author

Dwayne Phillips has worked as a software and systems engineer with the U.S. government since 1980. He has a PhD from Louisiana State University in Electrical and Computer Engineering. His interests include software engineering and how people work together in all endeavors. He is the author of *Image Processing in C*, published by R&D Publications (now CMP, *www.cmp.com*), and has a second edition of that book available on CD-ROM. He and Roy O'Bryan wrote *It Sounded Good When We Started*, published by the IEEE Computer Society and Wiley (wiley.com/ieeecs). He has also written several dozen magazine articles for computer magazines.

The Software Project Manager's Handbook. By Dwayne Phillips.
ISBN 0-471-67420-6 © 2004 IEEE Computer Society